T0329849

'This extensive and comprehensive text draws on the author's extended experience of working in the insurance sector in a variety of roles and levels over many years, whilst drawing on his unique insight gained in working in other spheres and disciplines, to provide a highly insightful and relevant account of the application and future application of analytics in insurance in the context of the emergence of Big Data. The text covers an extensive and impressive range of contemporary applications within insurance, including financial risk, finance, underwriting, claims, marketing, property insurance and flood risk, liability insurance, life and pensions, people and talent management. The text goes further in boldly providing a practical account and guidance on the approaches to the implementation of analytics.*

Tony Boobier adopts a pragmatic and confident account that is useful to practitioners involved in insurance, and more widely in the use and application of Big Data. The text is also useful and accessible to those studying in the areas of finance, investment and analytics in providing an exhaustive account of the profession from the lens of a highly experienced and proven practitioner. I have no hesitation in recommending this text to practitioners and students of insurance and Big Data alike and I am sure it will become a highly valuable contribution to the "art of insurance".'

—David Proverbs, Professor, Birmingham City University

'This publication covers a huge amount of ground. "Big Data, analytics and new methodologies are not simply a set of tools, but rather a whole new way of thinking" seems to sum up the approach and value of this book, which offers fascinating insights into developments in our industry over recent years and raises important questions regarding how we approach the future. I found the Claims section full of illuminating information about the roles and approaches of all the parties involved in the process – insurers, supply chains and experts' roles and attitudes that makes for a fascinating read – it is technical, insightful, challenging and full of vision to take the insurance industry into the future. The section on leadership and talent should resonate with all of us working in insurance.'

—Candy Holland, Managing Director, Echelon Claims Consultants;
Former President, Chartered Institute of Loss Adjusters

'I feel it comprehensively brings the insurance business and analytics together in an easy-to-read/ understand and professional, researched way. This book certainly indicates the width and depth of Tony's insurance and analytics knowledge. I also feel that it could be an effective overview and reference for existing and incoming insurance management, through to IT suppliers, other professions involved in the insurance markets, and also for students.

As someone who has been beavering away for thirty-five years at trying to narrow the divide between insurance and IT at strategic level, much of the content is music to my ears, and underlines that the author and I are, as always, singing from the same hymn sheet – analytics in its broadest sense is indeed an ideal catalyst to achieve this objective.'

– Doug Shillito, Editor, *Insurance Newslink/Only Strategic*

'Analytics programs that are business driven have proven they deliver substantial benefits within the general insurance industry over a number of years. One of the key analytics challenges facing the market is to establish similar routes to value in more specialist sectors such as the London Markets. This book provides valuable food for thought for those keen to take on this challenge and gain a competitive advantage.'

—Glen Browse, MI, Data and Analytics Specialist
(with over 20 years' experience across the banking and insurance industries)

Analytics for Insurance

The Wiley Finance series contains books written specifically for finance and investment professionals as well as sophisticated individual investors and their financial advisors. Book topics range from portfolio management to e-commerce, risk management, financial engineering, valuation and financial instrument analysis, as well as much more. For a list of available titles, visit our Web site at www.WileyFinance.com.

Founded in 1807, John Wiley & Sons is the oldest independent publishing company in the United States. With offices in North America, Europe, Australia and Asia, Wiley is globally committed to developing and marketing print and electronic products and services for our customers' professional and personal knowledge and understanding.

Analytics for Insurance

The Real Business of Big Data

TONY BOOBIER

WILEY

This edition first published 2016
© 2016 Wiley

Registered office
John Wiley & Sons Ltd, The Atrium, Southern Gate, Chichester, West Sussex, PO19 8SQ, United Kingdom

For details of our global editorial offices, for customer services and for information about how to apply for permission to reuse the copyright material in this book please see our website at www.wiley.com.

Wiley publishes in a variety of print and electronic formats and by print-on-demand. Some material included with standard print versions of this book may not be included in e-books or in print-on-demand. If this book refers to media such as a CD or DVD that is not included in the version you purchased, you may download this material at http://booksupport.wiley.com. For more information about Wiley products, visit www.wiley.com.

Designations used by companies to distinguish their products are often claimed as trademarks. All brand names and product names used in this book are trade names, service marks, trademarks or registered trademarks of their respective owners. The publisher is not associated with any product or vendor mentioned in this book.

Limit of Liability/Disclaimer of Warranty: While the publisher and author have used their best efforts in preparing this book, they make no representations or warranties with respect to the accuracy or completeness of the contents of this book and specifically disclaim any implied warranties of merchantability or fitness for a particular purpose. It is sold on the understanding that the publisher is not engaged in rendering professional services and neither the publisher nor the author shall be liable for damages arising herefrom. If professional advice or other expert assistance is required, the services of a competent professional should be sought.

Library of Congress Cataloging-in-Publication Data is available

A catalogue record for this book is available from the British Library.

ISBN 978-1-119-14107-5 (hbk)   ISBN 978-1-119-14109-9 (ebk)
ISBN 978-1-119-14108-2 (ebk)   ISBN 978-1-119-31624-4 (ebk)

Cover Design: Wiley Background image: © polygraphus/Shutterstock; Lightning image: © Ase/Shutterstock; Road image: © Alexlky/Shutterstock; Chart image: © adempercem/Shutterstock

Set in 10/12pt TimesLTStd-Roman by Thomson Digital, Noida, India
Printed in Great Britain by TJ International Ltd, Padstow, Cornwall, UK

Contents

Preface	xiii
Acknowledgements	xv
About the Author	xvii

CHAPTER 1

Introduction – The New 'Real Business' — **1**

1.1	On the Point of Transformation	2
	1.1.1 Big Data Defined by Its Characteristics	3
	1.1.2 The Hierarchy of Analytics, and How Value is Obtained from Data	6
	1.1.3 Next Generation Analytics	7
	1.1.4 Between the Data and the Analytics	9
1.2	Big Data and Analytics for All Insurers	10
	1.2.1 Three Key Imperatives	10
	1.2.2 The Role of Intermediaries	13
	1.2.3 Geographical Perspectives	14
	1.2.4 Analytics and the Internet of Things	15
	1.2.5 Scale Benefit – or Size Disadvantage?	15
1.3	How Do Analytics Actually Work?	17
	1.3.1 Business Intelligence	18
	1.3.2 Predictive Analytics	20
	1.3.3 Prescriptive Analytics	22
	1.3.4 Cognitive Computing	23
	Notes	24

CHAPTER 2

Analytics and the Office of Finance — **25**

2.1	The Challenges of Finance	26
2.2	Performance Management and Integrated Decision-Making	27
2.3	Finance and Insurance	27
2.4	Reporting and Regulatory Disclosure	29
2.5	GAAP and IFRS	29
2.6	Mergers, Acquisitions, and Divestments	30
2.7	Transparency, Misrepresentation, the Securities Act and 'SOX'	31

2.8   Social Media and Financial Analytics   32
2.9   Sales Management and Distribution Channels   33
       2.9.1   Agents and Producers   34
       2.9.2   Distribution Management   35
       Notes   36

CHAPTER 3
Managing Financial Risk Across the Insurance Enterprise   **37**
3.1   Solvency II   37
3.2   Solvency II, Cloud Computing and Shared Services   40
3.3   'Sweating the Assets'   40
3.4   Solvency II and IFRS   41
3.5   The Changing Role of the CRO   42
3.6   CRO as Customer Advocate   45
3.7   Analytics and the Challenge of Unpredictability   45
3.8   The Importance of Reinsurance   46
3.9   Risk Adjusted Decision-Making   46
       Notes   49

CHAPTER 4
Underwriting   **51**
4.1   Underwriting and Big Data   52
4.2   Underwriting for Specialist Lines   54
4.3   Telematics and User-Based Insurance as an Underwriting Tool   55
4.4   Underwriting for Fraud Avoidance   56
4.5   Analytics and Building Information Management (BIM)   57
       Notes   58

CHAPTER 5
Claims and the 'Moment of Truth'   **61**
5.1   'Indemnity' and the Contractual Entitlement   61
5.2   Claims Fraud   62
       5.2.1   Opportunistic Fraud   63
       5.2.2   Organized Fraud   64
5.3   Property Repairs and Supply Chain Management   66
5.4   Auto Repairs   71
5.5   Transforming the Handling of Complex Domestic Claims   73
       5.5.1   The Digital Investigator   73
       5.5.2   Potential Changes in the Claims Process   75
       5.5.3   Reinvention of the Supplier Ecosystem   76
5.6   Levels of Inspection   77
       5.6.1   Reserving   78
       5.6.2   Business Interruption   79
       5.6.3   Subrogation   80
5.7   Motor Assessing and Loss Adjusting   81
       5.7.1   Motor Assessing   82
       5.7.2   Loss Adjusting   83

5.7.3 Property Claims Networks   84
5.7.4 Adjustment of Cybersecurity Claims   87
5.7.5 The Demographic Time Bomb in Adjusting   87
Notes   88

CHAPTER 6
Analytics and Marketing   **91**
6.1   Customer Acquisition and Retention   93
6.2   Social Media Analytics   96
6.3   Demography and How Population Matters   97
6.4   Segmentation   98
6.5   Promotion Strategy   100
6.6   Branding and Pricing   100
6.7   Pricing Optimization   101
6.8   The Impact of Service Delivery on Marketing Success   102
6.9   Agile Development of New Products   103
6.10 The Challenge of 'Agility'   104
6.11 Agile vs Greater Risk?   105
6.12 The Digital Customer, Multi- and Omni-Channel   105
6.13 The Importance of the Claims Service in Marketing   106
Notes   107

CHAPTER 7
Property Insurance   **109**
7.1   Flood   109
      7.1.1 Predicting the Cost and Likelihood of Flood Damage 110
      7.1.2 Analytics and the Drying Process   111
7.2   Fire   112
      7.2.1 Predicting Fraud in Fire Claims   113
7.3   Subsidence   115
      7.3.1 Prediction of Subsidence   116
7.4   Hail   119
      7.4.1 Prediction of Hail Storms   120
7.5   Hurricane   121
      7.5.1 Prediction of Hurricane Damage   121
7.6   Terrorism   122
      7.6.1 Predicting Terrorism Damage   123
7.7   Claims Process and the 'Digital Customer'   124
Notes   125

CHAPTER 8
Liability Insurance and Analytics   **127**
8.1   Employers' Liability and Workers' Compensation   127
      8.1.1 Fraud in Workers' Compensation Claims   128
      8.1.2 Employers' Liability Cover   130
      8.1.3 Effective Triaging of EL Claims   130

8.2   Public Liability   131
8.3   Product Liability   132
8.4   Directors and Officers Liability   133
        Notes   134

CHAPTER 9
Life and Pensions   135
9.1   How Life Insurance Differs from General Insurance   136
9.2   Basis of Life Insurance   137
9.3   Issues of Mortality   138
9.4   The Role of Big Data in Mortality Rates   139
9.5   Purchasing Life Insurance in a Volatile Economy   140
9.6   How Life Insurers Can Engage with the Young   141
9.7   Life and Pensions for the Older Demographic   142
9.8   Life and Pension Benefits in the Digital Era   143
9.9   Life Insurance and Bancassurers   145
        Notes   147

CHAPTER 10
The Importance of Location   149
10.1   Location Analytics   149
        10.1.1   The New Role of the Geo-Location Expert   149
        10.1.2   Sharing Location Information   150
        10.1.3   Geocoding   150
        10.1.4   Location Analytics in Fraud Investigation   151
        10.1.5   Location Analytics in Terrorism Risk   152
        10.1.6   Location Analytics and Flooding   152
        10.1.7   Location Analytics, Cargo and Theft   154
10.2   Telematics and User-Based Insurance ('UBI')   155
        10.2.1   History of Telematics   155
        10.2.2   Telematics in Fraud Detection   157
        10.2.3   What is the Impact on Motor Insurers?   157
        10.2.4   Telematics and Vehicle Dashboard Design   158
        10.2.5   Telematics and Regulation   159
        10.2.6   Telematics – More Than Technology   160
        10.2.7   User-Based Insurance in Other Areas   161
        10.2.8   Telematics in Commercial Insurances   162
        Notes   164

CHAPTER 11
Analytics and Insurance People   167
11.1   Talent Management   167
        11.1.1   The Need for New Competences   168
        11.1.2   Essential Qualities and Capabilities   169
11.2   Talent, Employment and the Future of Insurance   173
        11.2.1   Talent Analytics and the Challenge for Human Resources   173

11.3	Learning and Knowledge Transfer	174
	11.3.1 Reading Materials	175
	11.3.2 Formal Qualifications and Structured Learning	175
	11.3.3 Face-to-Face Training	176
	11.3.4 Social Media and Technology	177
11.4	Leadership and Insurance Analytics	178
	11.4.1 Knowledge and Power	179
	11.4.2 Leadership and Influence	179
	11.4.3 Analytics and the Impact on Employees	181
	11.4.4 Understanding Employee Resistance	182
	Notes	184

CHAPTER 12
Implementation **185**

12.1	Culture and Organization	188
	12.1.1 Communication and Evangelism	192
	12.1.2 Stakeholders' Vision of the Future	193
12.2	Creating a Strategy	193
	12.2.1 Program Sponsorship	194
	12.2.2 Building a Project Program	195
	12.2.3 Stakeholder Management	197
	12.2.4 Recognizing Analytics as a Tool of Empowerment	198
	12.2.5 Creation of Open and Trusting Relationships	199
	12.2.6 Developing a Roadmap	200
	12.2.7 Implementation Flowcharts	202
12.3	Managing the Data	202
	12.3.1 Master Data Management	203
	12.3.2 Data Governance	203
	12.3.3 Data Quality	204
	12.3.4 Data Standardization	204
	12.3.5 Storing and Managing Data	205
	12.3.6 Security	207
12.4	Tooling and Skillsets	207
	12.4.1 Certification and Qualifications	208
	12.4.2 Competences	208
	Notes	209

CHAPTER 13
Visions of the Future? **211**

13.1	Auto 2025	211
13.2	The Digital Home in 2025 – 'Property Telematics'	214
13.3	Commercial Insurance – Analytically Transformed	218
13.4	Specialist Risks and Deeper Insight	220
13.5	2025: Transformation of the Life and Pensions Industry	221
13.6	Outsourcing and the Move Away from Non-Core Activities	223
13.7	The Rise of the Super Supplier	224
	Notes	225

CHAPTER 14
Conclusions and Reflections   **227**
14.1   The Breadth of the Challenge   229
14.2   Final Thoughts   230
       Notes   231

APPENDIX A
Recommended Reading   **233**

APPENDIX B
Data Summary of Expectancy of Reaching 100   **235**

APPENDIX C
Implementation Flowcharts   **239**

APPENDIX D
Suggested Insurance Websites   **265**

APPENDIX E
Professional Insurance Organizations   **267**

Index   **269**

Preface

I never intended to work in insurance, technology or analytics, but rather those three things found me. Like so many others, my journey to insurance and analytics started elsewhere and for me it was on the engineering draughtsman's table. There I used mathematics to design new structures but my heart was not so much in the creation of new structures, but rather in the understanding of why structures fail – and then who might be responsible for such failure.

In the failure of structures, all roads lead to the insurance industry. Structures fail because of defective design, workmanship or materials, and there is insurance cover for all of these. With the passage of time I was to learn that in some cases it might be possible to anticipate the cause of failure even before a physical investigation by using data. It seemed an important thing to step away from my engineering background and qualifications to learn a new trade, that of insurance, and in time I became qualified in that industry. Along the way I also discovered the professions of marketing and supply chain management and added these as strings to my bow.

Each time I stepped outside one profession to learn another, it felt like stepping off the top diving board at the diving pool. Looking down, I could see the water but had no real sense of how deep or even how warm it was. I discovered the main barriers between professions were not just of capability but of language, with each profession having its own terminology. Beyond this, as an outsider I couldn't help but see the interdependency between all these professions within the insurance community.

Ten years ago, the lure of technology became overwhelming for me, and there was something in the North American market that I found compelling. At that time they were some years ahead of the UK market although since then the gap has narrowed significantly. They seemed to have recognized technology as the great enabler and not as a threat. Not only did I want to understand why, but also how.

I stepped off the top of the proverbial diving board yet again from the relative safety of the insurance community into the dark waters of technology but this time it was more difficult. The fast moving world of that newer environment made the transition harder. I came to realize that the future of insurance is not just about technology nor about insurance but rests somewhere in between. In a short time, insurance and technology will be irretrievably intertwined and because of this, the insurance industry will have become transformed. New professions will inevitably emerge which sit in that 'no-man's land' between insurance and technology and those who reside there will probably hold the key to the future of the insurance profession.

So my challenge is, who is best placed to sit in that 'no-man's land'? Is it the technologist who has to understand insurance to appreciate the subtleties and nuances of the insurance contract, and without which any attempt to apply the opportunities of data and analytics will fail? Or is it the insurer who has to reconcile the principles of insurance with the new problems of data and gaining deeper insight? Or will new professions emerge, occupying not that place called 'no-man's land' but rather some 'higher ground'? Won't this allow them to see in both directions, both towards the line of business and also towards the technology department (if in the future it still exists, as we currently know it)?

How will those individuals cope with stepping off the high diving board? What capabilities and characteristics will they have? How will they be supported by professional institutions which appear, at least for the moment, to be behind the times? How will those individuals learn?

This book aims to be some sort of guide for those looking to occupy either no-man's land or the higher ground, however they see it. It doesn't set out to be either a compendium of insurance, nor of technology. I have resisted commenting on any particular insurer or vendor. Others with a more independent viewpoint can do this elsewhere, and provide 'real time' assessment. For those readers who, like myself, are 'longer in the tooth' there is also a different, perhaps harder challenge, which is that of learning to forget old approaches in a new dynamic world.

Finally, I have attempted to offer some thoughts about implementation. Many insurers have a notion that they want to become 'analytical' but their challenge seems to be implementation. They think about the 'what' but struggle with the 'how.' At a time when many if not all insurers will want to jump on the data and analytics bandwagon, what are the issues around putting this into practice, and how might they be overcome? At a time when 'agile' is the trend, how might this be accommodated into our rather conservative industry?

So in conclusion, this book reflects what I have personally learned on my own journey. Emotional ups and downs; floods and droughts; risks and realities; integrity and fraud; suppliers and supplied to; inspectors and inspected; and the rest. It's really been quite a trip.

Tony Boobier
February 2016

Acknowledgements

Many of the ideas that appear in this book have been amassed whilst working in the insurance and technology industries for over 30 years. My thanks are therefore to all those who contributed directly and indirectly, and sometimes unknowingly, to all my experiences and learning over that time, leading to this book being created.

In particular, I want to thank Terry Clark and Stuart Hodgson at Robins who gave me the foundations of insurance, Garry Stone and Stuart Murray who both started me on the analytic path and Francesca Breeze who gave me the confidence to write.

In addition, I would like to thank all those who helped me on my journey in the technology sector, provided essential comradeship and shared their insights into industry trends. These especially include Craig Bedell, Owen Kimber and Vivian Braun at IBM, but there are many more there who have played an important part and to whom I owe a debt of gratitude.

Throughout my career I have depended on professional institutions to provide me with a window into their industries and professions. To that extent I would like to thank the Institute of Civil Engineers, the Chartered Institute of Marketing, the Chartered Institute of Loss Adjusters (these three institutes awarded me with Fellowship status), the Chartered Institute of Supply and Procurement, and last but not least, the Chartered Insurance Institute.

Many thanks to all those at Wiley who provided comments, suggestions and guidance, especially Thomas Hykiel. I first met Thomas at a conference in Amsterdam and I am extremely grateful to him for helping turn an idea into reality.

Last but not least I have my family in the UK, Chile and China to remember. Michelle for her support, patience and belief in my ability to finish this task. Chris for his unflagging support and for introducing me to new markets and cultures. Tim for his constructive suggestions when I started to run out of steam. And Ginette for always being in touch and keeping my feet on the ground.

About the Author

Tony Boobier BEng CEng FICE FCILA FCIM MCIPS has almost 30 years of broad-based experience in the insurance sector. After over 20 years of working for insurers and intermediaries in customer-facing operational roles, he crossed over to the world of technology in 2006, recognizing it as one of the great enablers of change in an increasingly complex world.

Based in Kent, UK, he is an award-winning insurance professional holding Fellowship qualifications in engineering, insurance and marketing 'with other stuff picked up along the way.' A frequent writer and international public speaker, he has had many articles published over three decades on a wide range of insurance topics ranging from claims management to analytical insight, including the co-creation of industry-wide best practice documents.

His insurance focus is both broad and deep, covering general insurance, life and pension, healthcare and reinsurance. He is particularly interested in the cross-fertilization of ideas across industries and geographies, and the 'Big Data' agenda which he believes will transform the insurance industry. 'I lie awake at night thinking about the convergence between insurance and technology,' he says.

CHAPTER 1

Introduction – The New 'Real Business'

'The real business of insurance is the mitigation of countless misfortunes.'
—Joseph George Robins (1856–1927)

T he purpose of this book is not to create a textbook on either insurance or technology, so those who are looking for great depth of information on either are likely to be disappointed. Others who need to know the ins and outs of legal case law such as *Rylands v Fletcher*, or the detailed working of a Hadoop network are also likely to be disappointed, and will need to look elsewhere. Indeed, there are many books which already do good service to that cause. Perhaps helpfully, a list of recommended other reading is shown in Appendix A. This book is somewhat different as it seeks to exist in one of the exciting interfaces between insurance and technology which we have come to know as the topic of Big Data and Analytics.

Readers are most likely to come from one of two camps. For those whose origins are as insurance practitioners, they are likely to either have taken technology for granted, perhaps turned a blind eye or simply become disaffected because of the jargon used. After all, isn't technology something which happens 'over there' and is done by 'other people'?

The technologist might see matters in a different way. Their way is about the challenges of data management, governance, cleansing, tooling, and developing appropriate organizational and individual capabilities. The language of 'apps' and 'widgets' is as foreign to the insurance practitioner as are terms like 'indemnity' and 'non-disclosure' to the technologist.

The practice of insurance, and the implementation of technology should not – and cannot – become mutually exclusive. Technology has become the great enabler of change of the insurance industry, and will continue to be so especially in the area of Big Data and Analytics which is one of the hottest topics in the financial services sector.

So there is the crunch: 21st-century technology and how it impacts on a 300-year-old insurance industry. To understand the future it is necessary to think for a short while about the past, to allow current thinking to be placed in context.

1.1   ON THE POINT OF TRANSFORMATION

The starting point of this journey is over 350 years ago, in 1666, when Sir Christopher Wren allowed in his plans for rebuilding London for an 'Insurance Office' to safeguard the interests of the leading men of the city whose lives had been ruined by the destruction of homes, businesses and livelihoods. Some might even argue that a form of insurance existed much earlier, in China, Babylon or Rome. Before the end of the 17th century several insurance societies were already operating to provide cover in respect of damage to property and marine, and the insurance of 'life' emerged in the early 18th century. It might be argued that mutuals and co-operatives existed much earlier, but that debate can be put aside for the moment.

The principles of insurance are founded on case law with the foundations of insurable interest, utmost good faith and indemnity being enshrined in the early 18th century, and remain substantially unchanged. Even some of the largest global insurance companies themselves have their feet in the past albeit with some name changes. Royal Sun Alliance can trace their history to 1710 and Axa to about 1720. Those walking the streets of London will be familiar with names and places on which are founded the heritage of the insurance industry as it is known today.

It is against that background of tradition that the insurance industry now finds itself in a period of transition, perhaps transformation, maybe even radicalization. Traditional approaches for sale and distribution of insurance products are being cast aside in favor of direct and less expensive channels. The industry is on the cusp of automated claims processes with minimal or perhaps no human intervention. Fraudsters have always existed in the insurance space, but are now more prevalent and behaving with a degree of professionalism seldom seen before. Insurers are increasingly able to develop products suited to an audience of one, not of many. Quite simply, the old rules of engagement are being reinvented.

Coupled with this is the challenge of different levels of analytical maturity by market sector, by company, by location, even by department. Figure 1.1 starts to give some indication of the way the insurance industry is structured.

But this is not just a book about an industry, or an insurance company, or department. It is as much a book about how individuals within the profession itself need to become transformed.

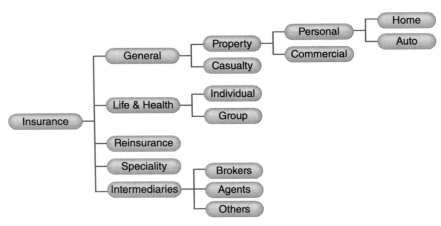

FIGURE 1.1   The insurance industry

Traditional skills will increasingly be replaced by new technologically driven solutions. New job descriptions will emerge. Old campaigners who cannot learn the new tools of the industry may find it difficult to cope. Professional institutes will increasingly need to reflect this new working environment in their training and examinations. The insurance industry as a whole also comprises multiple relationships (Figure 1.2), some of which are complex in nature.

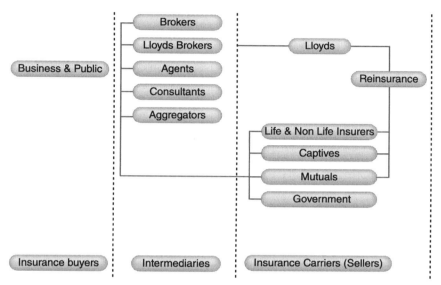

FIGURE 1.2   Relationships between parties

Even within single insurance organizations there are many functions and departments. Some operate as relative silos with little or no interference from their internal peers. Others such as Head Office functions like HR sit across the entirety of the business (Figure 1.3). All of these functions have the propensity for change, and at the heart of all these changes rests the topic of Big Data and Analytics.

FIGURE 1.3   Insurance functions

1.1.1   Big Data Defined by Its Characteristics

Big Data may be 'big news' but it is not entirely 'new news'. The rapid growth of information has been recognized for over 50 years although according to Gil Press who wrote about the history of Big Data in Forbes[1] the expression was first used in a white paper published in 2008.

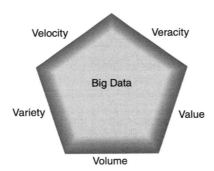

FIGURE 1.4   Big Data defined by its characteristics

With multiple definitions available, Big Data is best described by five key characteristics (Figure 1.4) which are:

- **Volume** – the sheer amount of structured and unstructured data that is available. There are differing opinions as to how much data is being created on a daily basis, usually measured in petabytes or gigabytes, one suggestion being that 2.5 billion gigabytes of information is created daily.[2] (A 'byte' is the smallest component of computer memory which represents a single letter or number. A petabyte is 10^{15} bytes. A 'gigabyte' is one-thousand million bytes or 10^{20} bytes.) But what does this mean? In 2010 the outgoing CEO of Google, Eric Schmidt, said that the same amount of information – 5 gigabytes – is created in 48 hours as had existed from 'the birth of the world to 2003.' For many it is easier to think in terms of numbers of filing cabinets and whether they might reach the moon or beyond but such comparisons are superfluous. Others suggest that it is the equivalent of the entire contents of the British Library being created *every day*.

    It is also tempting to try and put this into an insurance context. In 2012 the UK insurance industry created almost 90 million policies, which conservatively equates to somewhere around 900 million pages of policy documentation. The 14m books (at say 300 pages apiece) in the British Library equate to about 4.2 billion pages or equivalent to around five years of annual UK policy documentation. In other words, it would take insurers five years to fill the equivalent of the British Library with policy documents (assuming they wanted to). But let's not play games – it is sufficient to acknowledge that the amount of data and information now available to us is at an unprecedented level.

    Perhaps because of the enormity of scale, we seek to define Big Data not just by its size but by its characteristics.
- **Velocity** – the speed at which the data comes to us, especially in terms of live streamed data. We also describe this as 'data in motion' as opposed to stable, structured data which might sit in a data warehouse (which is not, as some might think, a physical building, but rather a repository of information that is designed for query and analysis rather than for transaction processing).

    'Streamed data' presents a good example of data in motion in that it comes to us through the internet by way of movies and TV. The speed is not one which is measured in linear terms but rather in bytes per second. It is governed not only by the ability of the source of the data to transmit the information but the ability of the receiver to 'absorb' it. Increasingly the technical challenge is not so much that of creating appropriate bandwidth to support high speed transmittal but rather the ability of the system to manage the security of the information.

In an insurance context, perhaps the most obvious example is the whole issue of telematics information, which flows from mobile devices not only at the speed of technology but also at the speed of the vehicle (and driver) involved.

■ **Variety** – Big data comes to the user from many sources and therefore in many forms – a combination of structured, semi-structured and unstructured. Semi-structured data presents problems as it is seldom consistent. Unstructured data (for example plain text or voice) has no structure whatsoever.

In recent years an increasing amount of data is unstructured, perhaps as much as 80%. It is suggested that the winners of the future will be those organizations which can obtain insight and therefore extract value from the unstructured information.

In an insurance context this might comprise data which is based on weather, location, sensors, and also structured data from within the insurer itself – all 'mashed' together to provide new and compelling insights. One of the clearer examples of this is in the case of catastrophe modeling where insurers have the potential capability to combine policy data, policyholder input (from social media), weather, voice analysis from contact centers, and perhaps other key data sources which all contribute to the equation.

■ **Veracity** – This is normally taken to mean the reliability of the data. Not all data is equally reliable as it comes from different sources. One measure of veracity is the 'signal to noise' ratio which is an expression for the usefulness of information compared to false or irrelevant data. (The expression has its origin in the quality of a radio signal compared to the background noise.)

In an insurance context this may relate to the amount of 'spam' or off-topic posts on a social media site where an insurer is looking for insight into the customers' reaction to a new media campaign.

As organizations become obsessed with data governance and integrity there is a risk that any data which is less than perfect is not reliable. This is not necessarily true. One major UK bank for example gives a weighting to the veracity, or 'truthfulness' of the data. It allows them to use imperfect information in their decisions. The reality is that even in daily life, decisions are made on the best information available to us even if not perfect and our subsequent actions are influenced accordingly.

■ **Value** – the final characteristic and one not widely commented on is that of the value of the data. This can be measured in different ways: value to the user of the data in terms of giving deeper insight to a certain issue; or perhaps the cost of acquiring key data to give that information, for example the creditworthiness of a customer.

There is a risk in thinking that all essential information is out there 'in the ether' and it is simply a matter of finding it and creating a mechanism for absorption. It may well be that certain types of data are critical to particular insights, and there is a cost benefit case for actively seeking it.

In an insurance context, one example might be where remote aerial information obtained from either a satellite or unmanned aerial device (i.e., a drone) would help in determining the scale of a major loss and assist insurers in more accurately setting a financial reserve. Drones were used in the New Zealand earthquake of 2011 and currently US insurers are already investigating the use of this technology.

Beyond these five 'V's of data, it is likely that other forms of data and information will inevitably emerge. Perhaps future data analysis might even consider the use of 'graphology' – the study of people's handwriting to establish character – as a useful source of information. Those who are perhaps slightly skeptical of this as a form of insight might reflect on the words of Confucius who about 500 BC warned 'Beware of a man whose handwriting sways like a reed in the wind.'

Such thinking about graphology has become a recognized subject in many European countries and even today is used in some recruitment processes. Perhaps one day, the use of analytics will demonstrate a clearer correlation between handwriting, personality, speech and behavior. In an insurance context where on-line applications prevail, the use of handwriting is increasingly likely to be the exception and not the norm. Because of this the need for such correlation between handwriting and behavioral insight is probably unlikely to be very helpful to insurers in the short term.

1.1.2 The Hierarchy of Analytics, and How Value is Obtained from Data

Analytics, or the analysis of data, is generally recognized as the key by which data insights are obtained. Put another way, analytics unlocks the 'value' of the data.

There is a hierarchy of analytics (Figure 1.5).

- Analytics which serves simply to report on what has happened or what is happening which is generally known as descriptive analytics. In insurance, this might relate to the reporting of claims for a given date, for example.
- Analytics which seeks to predict on the balance of probabilities – what is likely to happen next, which we call 'predictive analytics.' An example of this is the projection of insurance sales and premium revenue, and in doing so allowing insurers to take a view as to what corrective campaign action might be needed.
- Analytics which not only anticipates what will happen next but what should be done about it. This is called 'prescriptive analytics' on the basis that it 'prescribes' (or suggests) a course of action. One example of this might be the activities happening within a contact center. Commonly also known as 'next best action,' perhaps this would be better

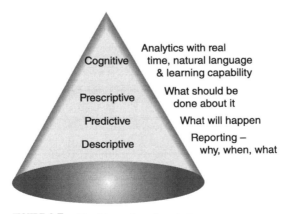

FIGURE 1.5   The hierarchy of analytics

expressed as 'best next action,' as it provides the contact center agent with insight to help them position the best next proposed offering to make to the customer to close the deal.

It need not unduly concern us that predictive and prescriptive are probabilistic in nature. The insurance industry is based on probability, not certainty, so to that extent insurers should feel entirely comfortable with that approach. One argument is that prediction is a statistical approach responding only to large numbers. This might suggest that these methods are more relevant to retail insurance (where larger numbers prevail) rather than specialty or commercial insurances which are more niche in nature. Increasingly the amount of data available to provide insight in niche areas is helping reassure sceptics who might previously have been uncertain.

In all these cases there is an increasing quality of visualization either in the form of dashboards, advanced graphics or some type of graphical mapping. Such visualizations are increasingly important as a tool to help users understand the data, but judgments based on the appearance of a dashboard are no substitute for the power of an analytical solution 'below' the dashboard. One analogy is that of an iceberg, with 80% of the volume of the iceberg being below the waterline. It is much the same with analytics: 80% or more of the true value of analytics is out of the sight of the user.

The same may be said of geospatial analytics – the analytics of place – which incorporates geocoding into the analytical data to give a sense of location in any decision. Increasingly geospatial analytics (the technical convergence of bi-directional GIS and analytics) has allowed geocoding of data to evolve from being an isolated set of technical tools or capabilities into becoming a serious contributor to the analysis and management of multiple industries and parts of society.

Overall it is important to emphasize that analytics is not the destination, but rather what is done with the analytics. Analysis provides a means to an end, contributing to a journey from the data to the provision of customer delight for example (Figure 1.6). The ultimate destination might equally be operational efficiency or better risk management. Insight provided should feed in to best practices, manual and automatic decisioning, and strategic and operational judgments. To that extent, the analytical process should not sit in isolation to the wider business but rather be an integral part of the organization, which we might call the 'analytical enterprise.'

1.1.3   Next Generation Analytics

Next generation analytics is likely to be 'cognitive' in nature, not only providing probabilistic insight based on some degree of machine learning but also with a more natural human interface (as opposed to requiring machine coding). Cognitive analytics is not 'artificial intelligence' or 'AI' out of the mold of HAL in Kubrick's '2001 – A Space Odyssey' but rather represents a different relationship between the computer and the user. We are already on that journey as evidenced by Siri, Cortana and Watson. Speculators are already beginning to describe 'cognitive' analytics as 'soft AI.' This is a trend which is likely to continue as a panacea to the enormous volumes of data which appears to be growing exponentially and the need for enhanced computer assistance to help sort it. Cognitive analytics may also have a part to play in the insurance challenges of skill shortages and the so-called demographic explosion.

Forms of cognitive computing are already being used in healthcare and asset management and it is only a matter of time before it finds its way into mainstream insurance activities.

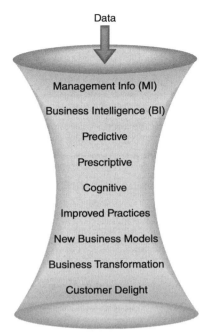

FIGURE 1.6   From 'data' to 'customer delight'

Coupled with this is the likely emergence of contextual analytics. Insurance organizations will become increasingly good at knowing and optimizing their own performance. Unless consideration is given to what is happening outside their own organization, for example amongst their competitors, then these viewpoints are being made in a vacuum. The American scientist Alan Kay expressed it succinctly in these words: 'Context is worth 80 IQ points.'

In the cold light of day, there are two key objectives which need to be adopted by insurers: Firstly, to outperform direct competitors, and secondly, to achieve strategic objectives. To do one and not the other is a job only partly completed. Often but not always the two key objectives go hand in hand.

Outperformance of competitors by insurers may be measured in varying forms:

- Finance performance – profit, revenue, profitable growth.
- Customers – retention, sentiment, propensity to buy more products.
- Service – both direct and through third parties such as loss adjusters who are considered, by extension, as part of the insurer themselves.
- Staff – retention, sentiment.

These issues need to be considered in the context of the wider environment, for example the macro-economy or the risk environment. In a time of austerity or where there is rapid growth in the cost of living, individual families may choose to spend more on food than on insurance products. At a time when the agenda of insurers has been dominated by risks associated with capital and solvency, perhaps their eyes have been temporarily taken off the ball in terms of other risks such as underwriting risk, reputational risk and political risk but that position is relatively easily and quickly remedied.

1.1.4   Between the Data and the Analytics

Big Data in either its structured or unstructured forms does not naturally flow into analytic outcomes, which usually takes the form of reports, predictions or recommended actions, but relies on intermediate processes which exist 'between the data and the analytics.'

How this is done in practice is a matter for the technical experts but in simple terms the raw data needs to be captured, then brought into the system where it is filtered, cleansed and usually stored. Massive volumes of data lend themselves to complex sorting systems or 'landing zones,' most of which have their own language and jargon. Often a datamart or staging layer is created to ensure that an analytical outcome can be created relatively quickly. The process by which data is moved through the system is referred to as ETL, or 'extract, transfer, load.'

There are other alternatives, such as 'data warehouse appliances' which provide a parallel processing approach and create a modular, scalable, easy-to-manage database system. These high speed solutions allow very rapid computing power by providing an alternative to traditional linear processing, and often come with pre-bundled analytical and geospatial capabilities. In effect this is a 'plug and play' approach to Big Data and Analytics. These serve as a reminder that, as was experienced with the internet in the early days, both organizations and individuals will increasingly press for computing power in the form of analytics to be provided 'at speed.' It doesn't seem that long ago that, in a domestic environment, connecting to the internet was accompanied by some form of whistling and other strange noises down the telephone line. Now instant 4G connectivity is expected anytime, anyplace, anywhere – within reason. Perhaps in that light, if one level of differentiation between technology vendors is that of the breadth and depth of analytical capability, the other differentiating factor may well be speed of delivery of the analytical insight. The need for speed potentially opens the door for interesting alliances of what might previously have been competing organizations.

'Cloud' computing also needs to be considered here. One good and simple description of cloud computing, often just referred to as simply 'the cloud,' is the delivery of on-demand computing resources. This includes everything from applications to data centers – on a pay-for-use basis, often accessible through wireless. For the record (and just in case anyone is thinking it) this is not a process in the sky or somewhere in the ether, but rather is an expression to reflect a capability. Users should not be misled by the fact that there are usually no cables or physical connectivity involved. As with the other processes described above, the technology is too complex to be considered in detail, and in fact cloud computing as a topic is worthy of its own book (and there have been many of them). But cloud computing also provides another example of how a paradigm shift in the thinking of the insurance industry needs to take place. The entire concept opens the door to new thinking, and those who do not have an open mind will be disadvantaged. In their 2014 document 'Predicts 2015: Cloud Computing Goes Beyond IT into Digital Business' Gartner indicate that business leaders will need to 'constantly adapt their strategies to leverage increasing cloud capabilities.'

It is increasingly critical that business users need to have some understanding not only of current IT capabilities but what are likely to be the IT capabilities of the future, in order to effectively manage their business and create new and compelling strategies.

It is easy to get bogged down in terminology. Readers should try not to become either distracted or confused by many expressions which are not familiar to them. It may be sufficient for individuals simply to become aware of what they do *not* know, and as a result have an open mind about technology and change. Some may view this as a catalyst, a personal challenge or perhaps a call to action in order to find out about new elements of their own industry and other associated industries. Managers may wish to encourage their direct reports to become more familiar with technology as part of their annual personal development planning.

1.2   BIG DATA AND ANALYTICS FOR ALL INSURERS

At face value, Big Data and Analytics are for big insurers who have the economy of scale to supplement data external to their organization with a firm foundation of internal information. Many of the industry proof points, for example fraud analysis and telematics, are firmly aimed at the property and casualty market, and especially at the B2C sector. But insurance is a broad church, and there are many parts of the industry, perhaps all of them, that can benefit from an analytical approach.

1.2.1   Three Key Imperatives

At the highest level, all insurers are interested in three key elements

- Operational efficiency – delivered through cost reduction, claims management and productivity strategies.
- Profitable growth – delivered through profitable customer acquisition and retention, cross selling and upselling.
- Risk management – delivered through capital efficiency and operational risk management.

Underpinning these three elements is what might be described as a 'pure play,' that of financial performance management. It is called 'pure' because the analytical approaches used in the Office of Finance are generally transferable from industry to industry. All CFOs are interested in the financial performance of their organization and need to report to stockholders using standardized techniques. In the case of insurance CFOs, there is often less certainty in the figures which invariably make projections for 'IBNR' (Incurred But Not Reported), a situation where insurers need to take into account the amount owed by them to customers who are covered for a claim but have not yet reported it, such as in the case of a major weather event. The effect of long tail claims, i.e., claims of lengthy duration, is also an important part of the consideration of the insurance CFO and their team.

Increasingly insurers are gaining greater insight into the convergence of the risk, compliance and financial performance management process. This approach, where data is reused and where reporting software for instance is repurposed, allows insurers to gain added value from the compliance process. It also creates a soft benefit in that it starts to break down the silos of risk and finance that exist in many organizations and increasingly embeds a risk culture into operational decisions.

It is tempting to suggest what are the typical trends for any given segment of the insurance sector, but different trends occur within the industry, in different sectors at different times and in different places. A typical example of this might be the Solvency II initiative in Europe, replicated to some degree in many other locations such as South Africa and parts of Latin America. While Solvency II has been a burning (and non-negotiable) platform, insurers had no real option but to pour in money and resource albeit to the detriment of other programs. For some insurers this represented 80% of their IT development budget. To that extent, risk and regulation have been at the top of the league table in terms of prioritization, although risk and compliance in Europe are increasingly assuming a 'business as usual' status. Although some fine tuning is likely to occur especially around risk reporting, the topic seems less critical at the moment. Even so, there is a school of thought which indicates that now that insurers have crossed the Solvency II compliance 'deadline' of January 2016, the topic of risk and compliance will be revisited as insurers drive for improved operational efficiency and cost reduction.

Standard techniques such as PEST and SWOT analysis remain available to insurers to allow them to identify key issues. Such a methodology remains valid although increasingly there is concern that some traditional management school thinking may be slowly becoming out of date due to the nature, impact and speed of change. In such formal techniques, topics such as disruptive technology may be both an opportunity *and* a threat. Beyond this, the influence of disruptive technology and 'agile' change is forcing organizations to re-evaluate their view towards risk management.

Notwithstanding, it is still possible to identify the key business drivers of each industry sector albeit that the prioritization of each business driver may differ at a local level, and these have been tabulated below.

Life and pensions insurance comprises the largest sector representing 60% globally and usually also at a local level (although there are some exceptions due to local economic considerations and market maturity). Life and pension companies have similar key drivers (Table 1.1).

TABLE 1.1   Key drivers of life and pension insurers

Business driver	External influences	Analytical response
Profitable growth	Market conditions and volatility	Asset and liability management
Risk management	Political, technological and economic uncertainty	Operational risk management
Customer behavior	Competitive environment, personal and corporate uncertainty, disposition to withdraw funds	Predictive behavioral analysis

Healthcare takes on different flavors geographically. Many insurers offer healthcare insurance cover, as well as travel accident insurance. That part of the insurance industry generally comprises two elements with similar business drivers (Table 1.2):
- Healthcare (wellness)
- Travel and Accident.

Property and casualty – often known as General Insurance – comprise 40% of the market, although this is also broken up into subsets such as retail (or personal lines), commercial lines, and specialty lines such as terrorism, marine, fine art and the like.

TABLE 1.2 Key drivers of healthcare insurers

Business driver	External influences	Analytical response
Rising cost of healthcare provision	Lifestyle and behavior, effectiveness and availability of state provision.	Effective underwriting
Increased claims cost	Rising cost of treatment	Effective triage, claims management, fraud analytics
Regulatory changes	Shift from public to private purse	Customer analytics, risk and operational management

Key business drivers (Table 1.3) are consistent to some degree although invariably differ dependent on the type of insurance business in operation:

- Retail
- Commercial Lines
- Specialty.

TABLE 1.3 Key drivers of general insurers

Business driver	External influences	Analytical response
Cost containment	Claims experience through weather volatility; too many frictional process costs	Effective claims management; effective customer onboarding; effective supply chain management
Fraud management	Economic environment, consumer behavior	Fraud management at point of claim and underwriting
Customer retention and growth	Overcapacity of local insurance marketplaces; retail insurance as a commodity; low consumer trust/loyalty	Customer analytics to understand and avert propensity to churn.
Regulatory compliance	Solvency and other local regimes	Capital and risk management

Reinsurers and Captives: Beyond these, there are reinsurance companies who underwrite the primary carriers or cedants, and captive insurers who act only for their commercial owners. Their key business drivers (Table 1.4) are less orientated towards issues

TABLE 1.4 Key drivers of reinsurers and captives

Business driver	External influences	Analytical response
Effective understanding of major incidents	Climate change, political volatility	Predictive modeling; what if modeling; understanding of risk accumulation through spatial analytics
Financial risk management	Economic and political volatility, risk accumulation	Capital and risk management

concerning the customer and more towards the management of financial performance and risk.

- Reinsurance
- Captives.

1.2.2 The Role of Intermediaries

Insurers do not operate in a vacuum but rather depend on third parties to help them discharge their obligations, or optimize their operations. If insurers have an interest in Big Data and Analytics, then so too must their intermediaries. Such 'intermediaries' include:

- **Tied Agents** – A company sales person who promotes the products of their employer only. Under section 39 of the Financial Services Markets Act 2000 (FSMA) they must make their status clear to the applicant/purchaser at the earliest opportunity.
- **Independent Agents** – Also known as an insurance sales agent or 'producer,' the independent agent usually sells a variety of insurance products and is paid a commission or remuneration. Usually the independent agent is an independent contractor, often with an individual business. National Alliance Research indicates that on average an independent (US) agent concurrently works with 13 property and casualty insurers, and six life insurers on a regular basis.
- **Loss Adjusters** – Independent or tied claims specialists whose duty is to administer a submitted claim within the terms and conditions of the policy. The expression 'adjuster' leads many to believe that the role of the professional involved is one of adjusting, or 'reducing' the claim as presented. Whilst that may the case in some instances, the profession can trace its roots back to the late 17th century and since that time they have been variously known as 'valuers,' 'surveyors,' 'assessors' and more recently 'adjusters' – a term which seems to have become more commonplace in the mid-1950s.
- **Repairers, Body Shops and Restoration Contractors** – A broad group who are variously appointed either directly or indirectly by the insurer, or the policyholder in the event of a claim occurring. Their responsibility is to undertake the repair of either a property or vehicle to a prescribed required standard. This must be to the standard of the local building or construction regulation, or the required standards of the motor manufacturer. In the case of a restoration contractor, this function is usually initially to 'stabilize' the building following fire or flood prior to permanent works taking place. In some cases, the restoration contractor is able to undertake the permanent repairs.

These independent parties directly involved in the repair/fulfillment process came to the fore as a result of the desire of insurers to gain greater control over the repair process, usually in the light of claims costs increasing and also the impact of policyholder fraud. Historically the policyholder was invited to provide three estimates for a repair, and from time to time these were found to be provided by the same repairer albeit using different letterheads. (Astute claims handlers were usually able to identify spelling errors which were consistently made in each of the three estimates.)

In more recent times, as well as exercising better control over the process of repair, insurers have been able to secure cost discounts with these intermediaries based on volume and term agreements, e.g., two-year contracts or longer. In addition, this has also been presented to the policyholder customer as an 'added value' attribute, removing the burden of concern away from their customer at the moment of distress.

As with all parts of insurance, the specific business drivers for intermediaries (Table 1.5) are complex and will depend heavily on the nature of the intermediary involved.

TABLE 1.5 Key drivers of intermediaries

Business driver	External influences	Analytical response by insurers
Customer retention	Customer behavior, reduced loyalty	Better insight into channel effectiveness
Continued profitability	Pressure on commissions	Agent optimization and management
Claims management	Customer pressure to obtain the 'best deal'	Agent control, management and audit regime

1.2.3 Geographical Perspectives

Not all insurance markets are moving at the same speed nor have the same level of maturity. Insurance penetration and market maturity tend to go hand in hand. This can potentially be analyzed by type of insurance and by geography, and micro segmentation helps allow analysis by demographic group.

It generally follows that insurance penetration directly correlates to the level of maturity in the banking sector. For example, with the exception of South Africa, the level of insurance penetration in the African nations is very low. Notwithstanding, the emergence of micro-insurance (insurance products whose purpose is to be both affordable and provide protection for low income people – those living on $1–$4 per day) has the potential to 'buck the trend.' Also this is a historical perspective – the rate of growth in the telecom industry in Africa may open the door to new thinking driven by the convergence of mobile technology and financial services. One other model which is beginning to emerge is the convergence of insurance with other industries, e.g., retail, which may lead to an acceleration of insurance market penetration and growth.

For the purpose of this publication, only a limited number of territories have been considered:

- North America and Canada
- Western Europe
- China
- Latin America.

These four groups of countries represent approximately 90% of the insurance market as we currently know it. It is possible to identify some correlations between these territories, for example by contrasting growth markets with mature markets, but even these generalizations can be misleading as they can fail adequately to reflect the cultural and economic differences which prevail across vast regions.

1.2.4 Analytics and the Internet of Things

By 2020, everybody will have 5.1 connected devices, according to one management analyst and Gartner indicate that there will be 15 billion networked devices, many of which will be able to communicate with each other.

The concept of 'Smart Devices' isn't new, in fact starting off 20 years ago. High tech manufacturers such as LG and Samsung already offer 'internet-enabled refrigeration.' It is already possible to control the central heating remotely, and turn the lights off and on (or even just dim them) using an android phone. The increased popularity of mobile devices such as 'Fitbit' and 'Jawbone,' amongst others, is leading fashion companies and watchmakers to consider embedding devices in attractive jewelry and timepieces. We are rapidly entering the period of the Internet of Things ('IoT') with significant future impact on the insurance industry.

What are the consequences for insurance and insurers? Can we see over the horizon something which we might call the 'Insurance of Things' and if so, what is this and what will be the consequences? There is no doubt that Big Data and Analytics will play a part in this new environment. Enormous amounts of data will be created, analyzed and interpreted.

The use of connected devices is not entirely new in the insurance industry. The initial focus seems to have been on personal lines but will the next big wave of innovation find itself in the commercial sector? Whilst much of the focus has been on personal vehicle telematics, this is readily extended to vehicle fleet insurances. Some insurers have already obtained indirect benefit from a broad range of technologies from RFID ('Radio Frequency Identification') tagging of container shipments to monitoring of supply chain conditions to ensure fresh produce.

The Internet of Things in an insurance capacity will be considered later but starts to open up interesting new areas. Naturally there will be issues of security, standardization and privacy all to contend with, but these are topics which go beyond insurance and rather affect the 'new' modern world as we (currently) know it. If insurance in the future will be increasingly dependent on data and devices, where will the burden of maintaining and future-proofing those devices rest? Will insurance start to consider the introduction of new conditions and warrantees which are directly influenced by the new Big Data environment?

1.2.5 Scale Benefit – or Size Disadvantage?

Insurers are increasingly recognizing the value in their data but are often faced with the challenge of working out how to get started, how to find and gain access to the data they need, then to convert this into a useable form. Even before they start any analysis, they have major issues in setting up the organization, systems and software to be used. Part of the complexity is in respect of the skill sets needed to undertake this journey, ranging from systems management, data management, analytical capability and the ability to translate the data and eventual insight into a solution which is 'consumable' by the end user.

The increased change in mood towards more 'agile' organizations which undertake change through a series of 'sprints' rather than a consequential 'waterfall approach' may result in larger insurers having the same dynamic approach to change as that of the smaller company. On the other hand, perhaps smaller companies will want to adopt a more 'risk-averse' approach until such time as technologies are proven. Smaller insurers with more to lose might perhaps approach change with a 'second mover advantage' view of the world, adopting safe and incremental change which provides them with greater certainty

The effective implementation and adoption of data and analytics by insurers and inter-mediaries will almost certainly and eventually lead to transformation of the entire industry. The first question is not 'if,' but 'how quickly.' The second question is 'how'. Where will the change start?

The immediate thought is that change will occur initially within the larger organizations which have the funds and ambition to change. But larger firms are complex by their nature, have legacy issues to contend with, and may not have the nimbleness to change quickly albeit they may have the desire to do so.

On the other hand, smaller more agile firms with shorter chains of command may feel that the case for change is less clear, may be reluctant to incur expenditure, and simply may not know where to start their journey. These relatively smaller insurers, including specialist insurers, may also struggle to see the value of change. However, there are signs that even smaller insurers which embrace an analytical approach can grow rapidly. Specialty insurers can obtain greater insight into their existing book of business and become both more profit-able and less vulnerable to volatile market conditions.

European insurance carriers will have already started their analytical journey, forced to take the first steps by regulators who have demanded that insurers improve the management of solvency. Effective management of the Solvency II program or local equivalent has resulted in insurers needing to address a large proportion of the structured data within their control, especially financial data. The timetable for Solvency II implementation may have slipped but larger 'Tier 1' insurers have got an early start in managing their wider data program. As a result, they may also have the time, skills and perhaps also the confidence to start looking at other data areas with greater purpose.

Another interesting conundrum emerges in that the effective management and analysis of data may start to have an equalizing effect, reducing the perceived differences between Tier 1 and other insurers. Larger insurers may become more 'agile' and mimic the smaller company. Smaller insurers may become cautious and keen only to adopt proven technologies which with time may have become less expensive in any event. Analytics in the virtual enterprise may also allow both larger and smaller insurers to become more confident in their outsourcing arrangements.

At its most basic, an insurance company simply comprises three elements:

1. Manufacturing of the insurance product – that is to say, underwriting, capital allocation and regulatory reporting
2. Distribution – the way that a product is brought to market, which may be directly or through a third party
3. Servicing – for example claims management and collection of premiums.

Two of these three elements need not sit within the insurer, but rather can be discharged through third parties and partnerships, leaving only the 'manufacturing' of the product to be undertaken. As insurers increasingly identify the value of integrating their own data with that of their supply chain, outsourced and third-party activities will have the opportunity to be-come more fully integrated. We will have entered the era of the virtual insurance enterprise.

Because of this new 'virtual enterprise,' fully supported by adequate data security and privacy, it is entirely feasible that Tier 2 and other insurers will be able to compete with and perhaps even outperform their larger competitors, not only as a result of more effective use of data and analytics but by virtue of their greater flexibility and nimbleness.

Intermediaries will also have a part to play in this story. They will also need to develop data and analytical capabilities just to stay in the game. Supply chain experts will demand these capabilities from their supply chain simply to allow them to stay in the procurement process. Through this change which is likely to be driven by the procurement process itself, the insurance industry is increasingly likely to see the emergence of the 'super supplier.'

It follows that as procurement experts will be involved in the setting of the data and analytics requirements of their vendors, then the procurement professional will also need to have knowledge and insight into available analytical technologies. The supply management professional seems already to have many of the characteristics of an analytical professional especially in that part of the industry known as 'category management.' These particular experts use data and analytics in either spreadsheet or proprietary forms to understand vendor capacity, process and response times, costs and pricing and contingency management. These seem to be valuable analytical capabilities which may be of wider benefit to the insurance industry downstream as the analytical maturity of organizations increases. With an anticipated skill shortage of analysts predicted not just in insurance but across the wider business world, might supply chain professionals have a future part to play?

Taking all this into consideration, the insurance picture begins to transform. Existing business models start to be stretched into areas which a decade ago were probably inconceivable. The traditional value chain starts to break down, replaced by other perhaps loosely coupled contractual arrangements and now enabled by the new data and analytical technologies.

Future underwriting is also likely to be transformed. Both personal lines and commercial underwriters will have significantly more data and information on which to make more accurate decisions and more representative pricing. Better statistical models are also likely to emerge. Furthermore, there will be improved integration between analytics, GIS (location) and the use of more sensors. The development of the 'semantic web' – an expression coined by Tim Berners Lee, the father of the World Wide Web, to provide a way for it to operate in a more standardized way through common data formats and protocols – will provide the insurance industry with a common framework whereby data can be shared and reused across 'applications.' In doing so this is likely to increasingly break down enterprise and community boundaries. The consequence of all this will inevitably lead to the role of the insurance underwriter being transformed, as well as their working environment, skill set and almost certainly their career path.

1.3   HOW DO ANALYTICS ACTUALLY WORK?

It is in the nature of insurance people to want to know how things are done. They want to understand how business intelligence happens from a technological point of view, how predictive and prescriptive intelligence works and what really sits beneath the covers in cognitive analytics. That is not to say that they want to be able to do it themselves, but rather in understanding the basic mechanics they are able to recognize the key issues and also the limitations of the technology. It will also help them in terms of the implementation conversation.

Let us start by saying that this is not a simple matter nor was the concept of Big Data and Analytics invented overnight. Rather that the insurance industry finds itself in today's analytical environment as a result of evolution, sometimes also an element of the step change and also from time to time, as a result of different thinking. In insurance which already has a legacy of analytical thinking as a necessary result of actuarial processes, new ideas increasingly find their way into the industry from other sectors such as retail or telecom. The use of 'Smart Meters' and predictive maintenance of machinery is already present – but how can this thinking be adapted and extended to the insurance sector? What comprises innovation for the insurance sector may be relatively 'old hat' for other industries. For insurance practitioners, it is critical that they maintain a 360-degree view of all that is happening in the wider world of analytics to be able to take full advantage of the opportunities before them, and then to be able to take that thinking and apply it to their own industry.

1.3.1   Business Intelligence

The starting point of any discussion regarding business intelligence arguably goes back to the concept of measurement and control. Without measurement there can be no control, and without control there can be no improvement. Such straightforward thinking found its way into the challenges of industrial productivity of the automotive and other manufacturing lines of the 1920s and later, and was subject to continuous refinement both in process and methodology. As organizations drove for increased profitability, the management of activity and its translation into activity-based costing (which identifies activities within a process and assigns cost to each activity) started to dominate, and up to the present day still heavily influence our thinking. Cynics reasonably argue that cost rather than value is being measured, and that the measurement process drives a quantitative rather than qualitative agenda.

But regardless, the essence is that measurement of operational activity in the form of performance metrics became prevalent and to a great degree remains so. What organizations have come to realize is that the metrics which drive performance improvement also drive changes in behavior, and that these changes are not always beneficial. Individuals measured against performance metrics often seek ways of manipulating data to show themselves in the most positive possible light, for example, in the case of sales progression. The psychological linkage between performance management and individual behavior cannot and should not be underestimated. To counter this, some organizations are also building behavioral traits into the assessment process, although like 'soft benefits' these behavioral traits may struggle to avoid a degree of subjectivity.

The topic of 'conduct risk,' that is, how we manage the performance and behavior of our sales people for example, becomes increasingly important especially in the shadow of Dodd-Frank and other consumer-orientated legislation. Analytical capability can sit behind the sales process not only in terms of sales performance management but also in the way that sales are conducted. If performance metrics drive behaviors (as might remuneration packages of sales staff) then analytics can be used as part of the solution in ensuring sensible behavior.

In essence, information collected can be assembled and structured to create management information. Historically this has been through tabulation but increasingly has been managed through spreadsheets. Information from outside the immediate organization, for example from the supply chain, can be obtained by 'enforcing' the supplier to provide information in a prescribed format as part of the supplier contract, so that information from many suppliers can be merged and consolidated to give a view of the broader environment. In other words, the procurement process can form one of the tools whereby suppliers provide information in a consistent way allowing the insurer to gain greater insight into multiple factors, such as cost, value and customer satisfaction drivers.

By collating this information from many suppliers as part of an RFI ('Request for Information') or ongoing process, insurers and others may find themselves with a clearer view of particular parts of the industry than some of the so-called expert vendors themselves. The challenge for such insurers is to recognize that knowledge in such circumstances *is* power, especially in a vendor negotiation process. Procurement professionals have recognized this for some time and use it ruthlessly in the negotiation process.

For many insurers, a spreadsheet approach to management information remains a critical capability but even spreadsheets have evolved. Those who were once experts by being adept at creating a pivot table now find themselves needing to be conversant with the advanced capabilities of spreadsheets with better visualizations and analytical capability. Spreadsheets, like the whole topic of analytics, continue to evolve and allow the user to have greater insight and improved visualization. The challenge for users of spreadsheets is most probably not only that of data capacity but also the increasing complexity of the business operation and its interdependencies. If it is argued that the insurance business is too complex to be managed either by intuition or experience (or both), then we are increasingly reaching the tipping point (if we have not reached it already) that it is also too complex to be managed by spreadsheet especially in the larger organizations.

Business intelligence is more than a form of enhanced management information. Rather it is a fundamental tool which allows insurers to understand if they are on track to meet their strategic objectives and where appropriate provide early warning signals that corrective action needs to be taken. If the sole purpose of executives is to ensure that the strategy of the organization is achieved, then it is critical that they have access to information which tells them, in indisputable ways, that the organizational ambition is on track or whether corrective action is needed. It follows that the metrics of business intelligence should align themselves to the strategic objectives of the insurance organization. There is no point in measuring things which are irrelevant to the strategy of the insurer.

The mood is increasingly for relevant information to be placed in the hands of the decision-maker, from a common source, so that, regardless of personal interpretation, there can be no doubt as to the source of the information and its veracity. This is often described as a 'single version of the truth.' To do this requires an information infrastructure which places data at the heart of the organization, centrally stored and accessible but with access appropriate to need and clearances. Many if not all business intelligence systems provide such capability which has become in effect a hygiene factor in creating a BI or 'Business Intelligence' solution.

The concept of a 'single version of the truth' lends itself to a data warehouse where information is held for the common benefit and is accessible accordingly. Such warehouses are usually in the form of an OLAP 'cube' of inter-related or 'relational' data and in most cases form the foundation of a business intelligence strategy for the insurance organization. ('OLAP' is an acronym for 'Online Analytical Processing.') Think of this as data held in a form of 'Rubik's Cube' rather than held in a flat form, and allowing the user (with appropriate access) to cut and slice the data according to their needs. In some cases, the data may be so large as to require the need for an intermediate data warehouse, or 'datamart,' so that the most important data allows more rapid interrogation.

Such an approach also demands a change in the function of the IT department who are also transforming from being the gatekeepers of the organization to the facilitators of information. They have a role in terms of the integration of systems and capabilities but as the demand for information increases it is critical that the IT department are seen as the 'key enablers' rather than any form of bottleneck. The days of waiting for reports from the IT department are rapidly disappearing. The most insightful organizations are transforming the function of the IT department into a role which fully supports the business – perhaps something they themselves have always aspired to be. The change is as much around culture and capability as it is around attitude.

Such an approach requires the IT department to be much more aligned with the business issues of the organization as with the technological requirements. It requires technology experts to sit with line of business decision-makers to understand their issues and to consider how technology can help an insurer reduce cost, improve profitability and reduce risk. It is a conversation about business issues converged with technology rather than forcing new technologies into business scenarios. Technologists increasingly need to understand that in the future (perhaps current) world of insurance, business and technology need to work absolutely hand in hand.

At its core are issues of leadership as well as technical capability, although it has to be said that analytics is advancing so quickly that no-one can afford to be complacent. Effective IT leadership demands organizational empathy and not isolation. Both business and technology leaders must understand and essentially be able to communicate the changes happening in the commercial environment, what has to be done to react to them and to anticipate likely changes. To do so specifically requires technology leaders to use language familiar to the line of business and not to hide behind IT jargon. Equally technology leaders need to be familiar with the terms of business users and understand the key business drivers that sit behind these terms. Maybe IT within the insurance organizations is finally coming of age.

How professional organizations also react is a matter of considerable interest. Insurance institutes often still see IT as a different profession, and IT institutes see insurance as simply an application of some of their technology. This attitude will not suffice in the new era of digital insurance. Convergence of professions will inevitably occur, most likely through subgroups within established professional organizations. Will individuals personally choose to join the technology subgroup of the insurance institute, or the insurance subgroup of a computer institute? Aren't both trying to achieve the same aims, and aren't they two sides of the same coin?

Business Intelligence is often seen and described as being one step beyond 'management information' or 'MI,' at least in aspiration and delivery (usually through mobile devices rather than paper driven). It is more than this, it is an essential tool related to strategic delivery as opposed to just sitting in isolation as some form of output from a set of performance metrics. But what next? The rather more complex issue of prediction is the next area that needs to be addressed and considered.

1.3.2   Predictive Analytics

If the future could be predicted with certainty, then some of us would definitely be richer men and women. Realistically it needs to be accepted that prediction and hence predictive analytics is not a precise science. Insurers need to be comfortable with that notion and realistic about what can be achieved. Insurance has never been about certainty but rather probability. The insurance industry has always used probability in the form of statistics to help understand the propensity of an individual to live to a particular age, a driver to have an accident in their car, or a property to flood, burn to the ground or to subside.

However, as predictive analysis is considered in the context of insurance, it is helpful to have an appreciation of the tools of the trade. These help practitioners also gain insight into whether a customer will leave or stay, buy more, or have a propensity to be fraudulent at the point of claim.

Although many seek to explain predictive analytics in terms of data and algorithms, perhaps a different (and more helpful) place to commence is in the realms of personal intuition. Individuals carry out personal predictions thousands of times every day without the aid of technology. This is variously described as intuition or judgment, but in reality they both have the same source in that decisions are made based on what is known, what has been past experience and what is likely to happen. In the days before technology, the claims manager or adjuster might 'smell a rat' in that the story given by the policyholder by way of explanation might not fit with the physical circumstances. Or perhaps a bodyshop inspector has heard anecdotally about a particular repairer and there are inconsistencies with invoices as submitted from that supplier. Individuals usually place certain weighting against particular facts, and some are more important than others. From time to time, it is discovered, often with the benefit of hindsight, that certain factors proved to be more important than had initially been thought to be the case, and this modifies the consideration given to a similar situation next time. The starting point is one of experience and from there greater insight into the future can be obtained.

With predictive analytics, the starting point is much the same, except that 'experience' is replaced by information normally in the form of data. 'Intuition' is replaced by algorithms or mathematical formulae based on interpretation of factual information. To make predictions about which customers are likely to be fraudulent at point of claim needs good data about fraud behaviors in the past. This may extend to the typical types of claims most likely to give rise to fraud. What types of customers are most likely to be fraudulent by nature, where do they live, what is their profession? What is the time interval between the inception of the policy or its cancellation, and the date of the claim occurring? These data points and others help to provide a picture of the likelihood of a fraud having being committed but there is no absolute certainty of fraud (unless of course there is physical evidence such as a fraudulent invoice or a witness statement, perhaps).

A similar situation may arise in respect of customer loyalty. Having information or 'data' which helps an insurer gain insight into buying behaviors, which may be a factor of age, gender, location, or channel will also give an insight into the likelihood of policy renewal. This data may not solely exist within the insurer but could potentially be found from other sources such as the individual's behavior in other industries such as telecom or utilities.

The opportunity to integrate fraud insight and customer insight becomes increasingly compelling when the data points are combined, potentially giving an insurer a 360-degree viewpoint of their customer. It not only helps insurers to understand their potential customer's propensity for particular behavior but also allows the insurer to decide whether a customer is commercially desirable (i.e., profitable or influential), or not.

Looking more specifically to the statistical element of predictive analytics, the analyst, often in tandem with the experienced line of business executive, is able to identify that particular factors are associated with a particular outcome. A tool called 'regression analysis' is used to gain better understanding as to the importance of this association. 'Regression analysis' is the primary tool used by analysts in this research. It is a statistical tool showing the correlation between the input and the outcome. This is not a new concept, in fact the first regression analysis in the form of a linear analysis (or a best fit line between the data points) goes back to 1805 and sought to explain the movement of planets around the Sun.

Not all relationships are as simple as a straight line. More complex scenarios require the data to be fitted against a curve rather than a straight line. Not surprisingly this regression analysis is known as 'curve fitting.' There are different approaches to the use of 'curve fitting' – it can either be an exact curve aligned to the data points, or a smoothed curve. A process called 'statistical inference' allows users to understand the degree of inaccuracy in the curve which helps provide the level of confidence in the predicted output. Ultimately this leads to the creation of a regress equation, regression coefficients, and ultimately a score predicting the likelihood of any particular event or behavior occurring.

The scoring element may have the tendency to change with time due to economic conditions, market changes and even for example in the case of a major weather incident. It becomes important therefore to consider the predictive 'models' as live entities, continually being refreshed and with actual outcome measured against predicted outcome.

Many statisticians find their way into the world of analytics and naturally will bring with them their numerate skills and experience. They also have a personal challenge in so far as they need to understand or at least be aware of the advanced technical analytics which increasingly support their numerical acumen. More importantly they also have to understand the business issues which their statistical insights ultimately need to directly and indirectly support.

1.3.3 Prescriptive Analytics

As a concept, prescriptive analytics comes in for some slight criticism in that it is viewed at best as an intermediary between predictive analytics and cognitive analytics. It is understood as an extension of predictive analytics which incorporates a degree of machine learning. In many ways it is the precursor to 'cognitive analytics' discussed later.

Prescriptive analytics is a concept introduced by IBM around 2003, and extended and copyrighted by Ayata who are a US-based software consultancy who describe themselves as having 'invented prescriptive analytics.' As an idea prescriptive analytics talks not only to the idea of anticipating what will happen – prediction – but more importantly what should be done to benefit from the predictions. Ayata describe 'prescriptive' as 'a series of time dependent actions to improve future outcomes.' It considers for example what might be the buying propensity of a prospective policyholder and what offer is most likely to be accepted, and in the event of rejection, what is the fall-back offer to be made. By its nature, prescriptive analytics is dynamic, subject to continuous learning and helps organizations optimize the predicted future.

Prescriptive analytics is similar to any other form of analytics in so far as it does not represent the destination but rather is a means to an end. The dominant purpose of all analytics is to change process, inform best practice and (in the most commercial of applications) improve sales or operational performance. The fact that there is no precise separation in the definition between prescriptive and predictive analytics should not be the source of any angst. It is merely a reflection of the growing maturity of the analytical journey. Innovation often occurs incrementally rather than in step changes – although step changes can occur in terms of new sources of information and interpretation such as in the case of the IBM and Twitter partnership in 2014.

Prescriptive analytics by its nature incorporates both new and associated technologies into the analytical recipe such as:

- Machine learning
- Natural language processing
- Applied statistics

- Signal processing
- Image processing
- Metaheuristics.

Insurance experts considering analytics need not necessarily consider the detail of any or all of these capabilities. Perhaps in time the most important of all these may be thought to be 'machine learning.' This has a slightly threatening implication – but insurers need to consider that technology, through the use of precise technical capabilities, as an enabler rather than a threat. However, the concept of 'machine learning' will sound slightly ominous to some.

These are discussions and conversations for a future generation of insurance professionals. What we can be sure of is that as technology develops, then so will the financial services sector and insurance specifically. Analytics has been previously considered in the context of insurance. Perhaps a better (or at least different) question to consider is the future of insurance in the context of analytics. Instead of viewing analytics as a tool to meet traditional insurance needs, perhaps insurance will be transformed by the advances of data and analytics. Actually, there is no question here – insurance will be transformed and perhaps the main issue is to what degree.

1.3.4   Cognitive Computing

For some professionals, the expression 'cognitive computing' has the potential to create nervousness and concern. But technology organizations are keen to downplay the concept that this is a form of artificial intelligence, but rather the next phase of analytics which improves the integration of technology and business (and all) decisions. The reader should not be shocked by this development. Most cars for example tell the driver when a service is needed based on mileage or duration. It is not beyond the scope of current technology even today for the 'car' not only to identify that there is a need for an oil change, but conceptually (in newer models) to even make the garage appointment, ratifying the date with the driver and entering it automatically into their diary.

Cognitive computing is complex. It is dependent not on one technology but rather on many. Multiple APIs or 'Application Programming Interfaces' form part of the overall solution. At the most basic of definitions, these comprise a series of technical processes, protocols and tools which allow and create capabilities such as speech recognition. APIs are a form of 'software to software' capability allowing different parts of the 'system' to talk to each other without human intervention. If that sounds rather scary, many of these technologies are already in place and you already use them when booking a cinema ticket on-line. As a user, you only see one element – the ticket portal – but so much is happening behind the scenes. And this is the case with cognitive analytics. The user may ask a question 'in natural language' but the answer is generated in a complex and technologically driven way. When we book the cinema ticket, technology is taken for granted. What might be the equivalent in the insurance profession?

One of the great challenges of cognitive computing is that for individuals it is viewed with a legacy perspective. There are plenty of examples of our viewing the world through our own personal legacy lens. In fact, in many cases there is no option but to do so. One of the big challenges for the insurance industry (and maybe all industries) is that there is no precedent to follow or to base our opinions or decisions on. Imagine the conversation about the potential of electricity in a world of steam.

The insurance industry needs to be realistic about this. In many parts of business, indeed in many parts of life, decisioning has already been subsumed to the machine or system. As we mentioned earlier, your car may already tell you when it needs a service. The information on the auto dashboard nowadays tells us the level of oil in the engine when, a decade ago, the driver would rely on the dipstick. At what point will the car itself refuse to move in order to 'protect itself'? Are the days of turning the radio louder in a company car when there is a strange noise from the engine completely gone? In the transitional period there are enough individuals with experience to ask appropriate questions if there are doubts regarding the insights provided by the analysis, but as this particular demographic passes into retirement, how much legacy knowledge and experience will be lost to the insurance industry? Perhaps one option is that retirement will not occur overnight, but rather some insurance experts will remain in semi-retirement to guide the industry. The danger is of course whether those offering advice from retirement will be like the legacy generals of the First World War in Europe, suggesting that mounted cavalry in the face of machine guns is still a good thing provided that the cavalry charge is implemented properly.

Perhaps the industry adoption of cognitive analytics, taking all the current tools and invariably future tools and data sets as well, is not so much a technology issue but rather a cultural issue. It is about how the insurance professional relates and interacts with technology, and perhaps even exploits it rather than becoming a victim of it. It might even be necessary to think of technology in a different way. As technology pervades every part of our life and increasingly affects our business decisions, it starts to become 'the way things happen around here' rather than some form of additional electronic or technical capability reinforcing old methods.

In conclusion, the essence of this particular sector is to understand 'how it happens,' or 'how it works.' In summary, perhaps analytics works through a combination of three elements, recognizing that:

- Increasingly advancing technology is irresistible.
- Changing culture is inevitable, including our personal and corporate relationship with the computer.
- Leadership is critical, which includes having a vision for the future in terms of using these capabilities to transform industries and organizations.

These are not unexpected attributes – but continue to remind us of the complexity of this particular change. Analytical transformation is not solely a technology issue for insurers but in addition there are other important cultural and personal aspects to bear in mind.

NOTES

1. Press, Gil. 'A Very Short History of Big Data.' Forbes Magazine, 2013. http://www.forbes.com/sites/gilpress/2013/05/09/a-very-short-history-of-big-data/ (accessed May 17, 2016).
2. International Business Machines 'Annual Report 2013.' Published IBM, 2013. http://www.ibm.com/annualreport/2013/ (accessed May 17, 2016).

CHAPTER 2

Analytics and the Office of Finance

Some readers may be tempted to think that analytics in the office of finance need not be industry-specific or indeed insurance-specific, believing that all finance officers and accountants are more or less the same and undertake the same functions. To some degree they are right in that accounting practices by necessity have a degree of standardization to enable organizations to be benchmarked against each other. Often they also believe that financial analytics are too complex to be understood and managed by other than professionally trained accountants – an attitude which is arguably unhelpful to stockholders and non-executive directors.

Many industries necessarily have distinct characteristics. Insurance falls within that grouping especially by virtue of the fact that insurers need to allow in their books for payments not yet made and where perhaps there is a degree of uncertainty in the payments required. This particularly shows itself in complex or lengthy ('long-tail') claims which may take many years to settle. Similarly, in the life and pensions sector, expert accountants and actuaries constantly need to consider events, i.e., usually death, which may not happen for 20 or 30 years and allow for this in their calculations.

It is also important that the office of finance in insurance companies consider the breadth and depth of their organization. They need to consider multiple and often diverse products and offerings, multiple routes to market and channels, and in more complex organizations to reflect multiple geographies. Put simply, except perhaps in the case of monoline or specialist insurers, the financial environment is becoming too complex for management by spreadsheets. A future, more 'agile' insurance industry with shorter product development lifecycles, new distribution models and perhaps also a tendency to more regularly sunset products or continually add value will require all insurers to be much more proactive.

Increasingly the mood is one of the Office of Finance being a dynamic, interactive part of the organization rather than simply a 'bean counter.' Finance professionals need to be interlocked with the wider business, engaged with strategic (and sometimes even tactical) considerations, supporting and acting as a trusted adviser and not just a custodian of finances. In many cases, especially in smaller insurers, responsibility for risk management and regulatory compliance also falls to the Office of Finance when arguably some are under-prepared to undertake such a role.

The relationship between the CEO and the CFO is critical in understanding the relationship between finance and the wider business. If the CEO is the 'pilot' of the organization, then the CFO is the co-pilot. Co-operatively they must work as a fully integrated team for the benefit of the business. Such statements are not of course insurance-specific but rather represent the changing nature of many professions as a result of the digital and Big Data revolution. Cedric Read's book *eCFO – Sustaining Value in the New Corporation*[1] recognizes that many organizational functions undertaken will need to be transformed including the finance function. If the reader is to be left with one enduring thought, it must be that the world of insurance is being transformed by the era of Big Data and Analytics and nothing will quite be the same again.

2.1   THE CHALLENGES OF FINANCE

In 2009 Mossiman, Dussalt[2] and others identified the issues attaching to the Office of Finance. These were:

- A lack of information to regulate what has happened and what will happen.
- The relevance, visibility and credibility of financial information.
- The need for balance between short and long term, detailed focus and the big picture.
- Finding a path between top down vision and bottom up circumstances.

They recognized the challenge of coping with multiple decision-makers within the organization, each often holding budgets and more importantly carrying accountability for delivery; the balance between cash flow and working capital; decisions regarding *capex* vs *opex*; and the management of the treasury. In only five years, much of that world has moved on.

In the same way that the IT department has needed to change and perhaps in some ways has been slightly marginalized in favor of the line of business decision-maker, the role of the Office of Finance has also needed to change. Decisions are increasingly in the hands of the line of business. Big Data has brought with it 'big empowerment' and also 'big accountability.' The Office of Finance inevitably need to justify their decision to withhold funding or restrict budgets more than ever before.

The rules of engagement have also changed as well especially around the use of analytic capabilities. Line of business executives and staff are increasingly able to identify tools which meet their particular operational needs. Technology vendors are making their tools free of charge ('freemium') in an effort to get engagement.

Self-service identification of analytic tooling is dangerously becoming the norm. The expression 'dangerous' is not used lightly in that multiple tactical purchases potentially lead to a disjointed outcome. The insurance organization is broad and complex, and to some degree requires standardization to ensure alignment. Independent decision-making and choice of technology inevitably leads to tooling for specific needs rather than for the greater good of the organization. Fragmented purchasing cuts across everything that procurement hopes to achieve – standardization, price leverage, management of upgrades and integration of tooling. Strategic procurement remains the optimum approach rather than a series of individual tactical relationships that may be more difficult to manage and maintain.

2.2 PERFORMANCE MANAGEMENT AND INTEGRATED DECISION-MAKING

One of the key tenets of analytics is that there is a single version of the truth. What this means in technology terms is that all information is derived from the same data. Gone are the days, in theory at least, of disagreement around the numbers albeit that there may still be scope for a degree of interpretation. It is in these grey 'interpretative' areas that disputes might occur, but nevertheless it is a step forward to think in terms of all information being reliable because it comes from the same accepted source.

It's also helpful to bear in mind that different industries are at different levels of maturity, with banking for example having a greater level of maturity than insurance. It follows therefore that a banker entering the world of insurance might have a higher expectation of the level of analytics available than might be found to be the case. Movement of individuals across industries is likely to have a levelling effect. Some industries are likely to be more advanced than others and there will be some degree of knowledge and capability transfer, which overall is a desirable outcome.

For example, retailers have their finger on the pulse in terms of what is selling and what is not, and what level of discount needs to be offered to encourage the customer. Behavior management is as much a financial issue as it is a marketing and psychological issue. This requires absolute and indisputable agreement about issues such as revenue, profitability and growth, and how they are linked to product, channel and reputation.

Insurers would be well advised to look outside their peer groups to find a benchmark of progress. It is clear that in terms of customer analytics, retailer and telecom companies are far ahead of insurers in terms of their analysis of buying behaviors but the gap is rapidly closing. A room full of bankers and insurers listened avidly to a retailer describing how, through loyalty cards, they understood the customer's buying behavior with absolute granularity and could not only pitch an attractive offer, but anticipate where and when that offer should be made. What, in one question, is the insurance equivalent to loyalty cards?

2.3 FINANCE AND INSURANCE

Insurance is heavily affected by a combination of social and economic factors, regulation, intensifying competition and customer behaviors. Different levels of insurance penetration arise by product, location and channel. In order to improve penetration levels, it is critical that insurers optimize their financial performance and improve their service flexibility, as well as increasing insurance awareness amongst their customers in order to indirectly improve on the financial security of their policyholders.

In its broadest context, effective financial management comprises:

- **Actuarial management**: The Society of Actuaries (SOA, 2010)[3] describe an actuary as 'a business professional who analyzes the financial consequence of risk. . . . They evaluate the likelihood of (those) events and design creative ways to reduce the likelihood and decrease the impact of adverse events that actually do occur.' According to the Institute of Actuaries of Australia (IA Aust, 2010)[4] they do this by:
  - measuring and managing risk and uncertainty
  - designing financial contracts

- advising on investments
- measuring demographic influences on financial arrangements
- advising on a wide range of financial and statistical problems.

Actuaries operate through a process called the Actuarial Control Cycle which typically comprises a three-step approach – 'Define the problem, Design the solution, and Monitor the results.' Whilst this is a fairly generic approach to most problem solving, actuaries often (but not always) also need to consider future uncertain cash flows.

- **Asset and Liability Management**: Also known as ALM, this is the process which manages the risk undertaken by an insurer (or other financial institution) as a result of a mismatch between assets and liabilities, either as a result of an institution not being able to meet its liabilities or as a result of a change in interest rates. Beyond this, it is also used as a technique to coordinate the management of assets and liabilities so that an adequate return may be earned. It is also known as 'surplus management.'
- **Capital management**: The accounting process by which an insurer maintains sufficient levels of working capital (the 'short-term' operating resource of a company) to help them meet their expense obligations, typically arising in the claims process as well as maintaining sufficient cash flow.
- **Calculation of embedded value**: This is a calculation of the value of a block of business. Differing from short-term financial management, the process of embedded value allows calculation of the long-term profitability. The embedded value of an insurer is a valuation of its current business rather than its ability to win new business, and is often used as the 'minimum value' of the business. Making an allowance for future business is known as 'appraisal value.'
- **Hedging**: This is often considered as an advance investment strategy, where the insurers make an investment in the event of losses occurring in a 'companion investment.' For an insurer, it is a form of insurance against investment losses.
- **Reinsurance strategy**: Reinsurance is insurance that is purchased by an insurance company either directly or through a broker as a form of risk management. This can assist in risk transfer, income smoothing or 'surplus relief' which allows them to take new business when they have reached their solvency margin. In some cases, the reinsurer can underwrite business at a lower cost than the insurer due to special expertise or scale efficiency. The insurer is known as the 'ceding' or 'cedant' company.
- **Reserving**: Also known as 'loss reserving' or 'claims reserving,' this is the calculation of the future cash flows of an insurer taking into account the likelihood of future claims expenditure. The total liability of an insurer is the aggregate of the claims reserves of individual policies. Insurers are obliged to release assets to meet their claims obligations and it is for this reason that accuracy of claims reserving is critical, especially in a major loss scenario. The process of 'reserve releasing' occurs when insurers believe they have over-reserved, and this has the effect of increasing insurer profitability. Regulators have expressed concern that by releasing reserves in order to boost profits, insurers endanger their ability to meet claims.[5]

It is probably sensible at this point to recap the key financial drivers of the insurance industry (Table 2.1).

TABLE 2.1   Key drivers of the insurance industry overall

Strategic	Mergers and Acquisitions
	New Processes and Models
	New Products
Revenue Growth	Upsell and Cross-Sell
	Better Customer Insight
Cost Reduction	Operational Efficiency
	Avoidance of Fines and Penalties

2.4   REPORTING AND REGULATORY DISCLOSURE

The reporting process for insurers is complex, can be expensive, usually requires assumptions and is often influenced by local reporting requirements. With many insurers, although not all, being associated with external financial stakeholders, unambiguous disclosure is a critical part of the financial 'mix.' Institutional stakeholders make large decisions which impact on investments and pensions. Smaller investors increasingly seek clarity of performance. Both are intolerant of wrongful description, in terms of numbers or words.

Coupled with this are the demands of regulatory disclosure, which provide the means to compare one organization with another. Effective and accurate disclosure beyond being a legal obligation also evidences an organization's ability to meet its obligations to its financial stakeholders. At an operational level, for insurers it also reassures their customers at the point of claim that money will be available in settlement (even if there might be some discussion regarding the actual amount agreed as quantum). All insurers have an obligation to demonstrate solvency, and their obligation is to ensure that their key stakeholders are adequately protected.

Solvency II has been one principal area of focus in terms of regulatory compliance and this is covered in more detail elsewhere.

2.5   GAAP AND IFRS

'GAAP' or 'Generally Accepted Accounting Principles' are best described as the standard framework of guidelines financial accounting used in any given jurisdiction. In effect these are the local accounting standards or practices, and embrace the standards, conventions and rules that need to be followed by the accounting profession in the preparation of financial reports and statements. GAAP is a process which appears mainly to focus on profit and can be seen as a short-term viewpoint, which is unhelpful for investors especially as the profits of many insurance products emerge late in the product's life. There are also issues of consistency across geographies. Often companies use a combination of metrics – GAAP, Regulatory Reporting and Embedded Value.

By comparison, IFRS (International Financial Reporting Standards) are intended as a common global approach to financial reporting so that a company's accounts are understandable and comparable internationally. They arise as a result of increased international shareholding and trade and are especially important for companies that deal in multiple countries. The argument put forward is that it makes it easier for public companies to compete abroad, raise capital and provide financial details. Although progress is arguably slow, IFRS is gradually replacing the many various standards of accounting by region.

Much of the work done by insurers in preparing for Solvency II and other solvency requirements can be put to good use. Ernst and Young effectively make this point in their 2012 report 'Facing the Challenge – Business Implications of IFRS 4, 9 and Solvency II for insurance.' There they recognized that 'Insurers face a huge challenge in synchronizing the implementation of IFRS 4 Phase II with IFRS 9 in the coming years. Managing the timelines and interdependences between these two frameworks, alongside other new IFRS standards, Solvency II and other finance transformations . . . will place many companies in a conflicting position.' They emphasize the need to 'assess overlapping requirements' and to understand mutually beneficial options. Solvency II is now largely behind us but insurers will almost certainly want to revisit the topic in 2017/18 when the pains of initial expenditure have been largely forgotten, and with the intention of improving efficiency and reporting performance at reduced cost. They would do well to reflect on EY's viewpoint on this topic, to 'inform their timing and approach.'[6]

Whilst these reports are quantitative in nature, the issue of 'qualitative' reporting should not be overlooked. 'Qualitative Reporting' reflects the sentiment and wording of non-financial statements which often accompany the quantitative elements. In other words, they are the non-financial expressions of performance that are seen in annual reports. For example, this includes commentary in an annual report to individual and institutional investors which gives an indication of the strategic intent of an insurance (or any other) organization. Non-financial expressions are critical expressions of the proposed direction of a business or provide an explanation of the financial results.

As a result, it is also important to ensure absolute alignment between sentiment, quantitative reporting and narrative embedded in formal reports. The methodology for this is 'eXtensible Business Reporting Language' or more commonly known as 'XBRL.' Developed by XBRL International, a not-for-profit company comprising 600 public and private organizations, 'xbrl' is a process by which data including text is 'tagged.' It is the 'tag' which is embedded into the report rather than a number or commentary. The effect of this tagging is that if any change to the content of the tag occurs, then the change is replicated in all associated documents. It also allows information to be exchanged beyond the boundaries of organizations.

There are two elements of this tagging: first, the creation of the content, and secondly, the consumption of the content. 'Creation' of the content is critical for insurers especially in regulatory reporting. 'Consumption' is critical for the regulators who will increasingly look to use advanced analytics to interrogate the information and obtain 'actionable insight.' There may be a natural tendency to aggregate information and manage by outlier but it is important that regulators resist this approach in favor of having a clear understanding of each insurer and their mix of business.

2.6 MERGERS, ACQUISITIONS AND DIVESTMENTS

As data and analytics produced in an environment of the Internet of Things start to disrupt existing business models it is likely that this will lead not only to new partnership arrangements but also probably to more mergers and acquisitions. These mergers and acquisitions may not simply be between insurance carriers but may also include brokers, agents, other financial institutions, possibly also with technology companies and other differentiators. Also, as insurers potentially gain more confidence with their outsourcing arrangements because of better controls and the likely emergence of 'super suppliers,' then it is equally likely that insurers will divest some competences in a drive to reduce cost and improve profitability.

As markets consolidate and then in return refocus, it also becomes critical that decision-makers are able to understand the potential impact in advance of the transaction taking place. These issues affect not only profit and performance, but also how acquisition costs are reflected in statutory reports. Under GAAP reporting mentioned previously, acquisition costs are typically deferred so investors may perhaps be uncertain of the true impact. It becomes essential that insurers have a clear idea of value creation through M & A activity especially where there is cross-industry consolidation.

Much academic work has been done on the topic of mergers and acquisitions. Referring specifically to the insurance industry, Boston Consulting Group[7] said that of insurance mergers which took place between 1998 and 2008, over half did not create shareholder value. In the 1,100 mergers examined, they identified four key business rationales for merger:

1. Increased volume
2. To complement existing business
3. Expansion internationally
4. To take advantage of distressed markets.

Their report specifically reflected on M & A activity in difficult economic times and emphasized the point of good due diligence and effective modelling. In their words: 'In normal times M & A provides exceptional opportunity for growth but it almost invariably poses significant challenges. The stakes are even higher now.' There also appeared to be clear differences between the outcomes of mergers/acquisitions involving large businesses as opposed to smaller ones. Their advice is to 'prioritize smaller, more strategic deals' which they describe as being 'looked upon more favourably by investors.' At the heart of any merger or acquisition must be a business plan which sets out the rationale of the decision. This goes beyond simply the question of whether this is a good fit but rather needs to consider what the expectation is in terms of additional revenue, expenses and how the acquisition is to be funded. Inevitably there will also be cultural issues to address including leadership, location and processes.

The advance in analytical capabilities in the Office of Finance suggests that a much more comprehensive viewpoint can be created in terms of predicting the likely effects of acquisition, merger and divestment. Analytical modeling in the Office of Finance, including scenario testing, can play a vital part in that exercise, allowing sandbox testing to be done in a safe environment. (A 'sandbox' is a form of testing environment that allows the isolated execution of programs or systems in a way that does not affect the working environment.) Beyond this, social media analytics may also help to address employee concerns.

2.7 TRANSPARENCY, MISREPRESENTATION, THE SECURITIES ACT AND 'SOX'

Effective and accurate reporting is a critical business function in the Office of Finance, and legislation also exists to reinforce this criticality. US companies generally operate in a more litigious environment and shareholders are especially keen to ensure that Securities law is complied with. This is not solely a US company matter with foreign companies representing about 14% of all US-listed companies.[8]

The US stock market crash of 1929 was the driving force behind securities legislation which was enshrined in the Securities Act of 1933, requiring companies to make full disclosure of all material facts. The Securities Act of 1934 set out the requirement that companies make ongoing disclosures on a periodic basis to ensure that all shareholders are informed of important business matters, and the financial state of the company.

The Sarbanes-Oxley Act of 2002 also known as the 'Public Company Accounting Reform and Investor Protection Act' or 'Corporate and Auditing Accountability and Responsibility Act' – generally better known as 'SOX' – further increased the level of corporate governance. It arose following a series of major scandals including (amongst others) Enron, a Texas-based energy company that was discovered to be undertaking systematic, creative and corruptive fraud by recording assets and profits which were non-existent.

The major elements of SOX were to create a framework of key components:

1. Public Company Accounting Oversight Board (PCAOB) – a central independent group responsible for agreeing and implementing specific tasks and processes.
2. Auditor Independence – to avoid conflict of interest.
3. Corporate Responsibility – forcing executives to have personal accountability.
4. Enhanced Financial Disclosures – including enhanced reporting requirement.
5. Analyst Conflicts of Interest – requiring disclosure of conflict of interest.
6. Commission Resources and Author – relating to investor confidence in securities analysts.
7. Studies and Reports – relating to wider investigations relative to the activities of others such as investment banks.
8. Corporate and Criminal Fraud Accountability – defining specific penalties and protections for 'whistle-blowers.'
9. White Collar Crime Penalty Enhancement – including the failure to certify financial reports as a criminal act.
10. Corporate Tax Returns – and the obligation on the CEO to sign the corporate tax return.
11. Corporate Fraud Accountability – linking corporate fraud to criminal offences and specific penalties.

Sarbanes-Oxley places much greater emphasis on accountability and 'up the ladder' reporting. One of the critical parts of 'SOX' is Section 404 which lays out the requirement of a US company to report on the internal controls. The cost of compliance was estimated for a UK-based company to be in the order of £10m–£20m, and can take up to 20 years of FTE.[9] In the UK, corporate governance is already moving towards a SOX-type regime with the Company Law Reform white paper recommending tougher penalties for accounting offences.

2.8   SOCIAL MEDIA AND FINANCIAL ANALYTICS

At face value, there is no obvious interlock between analytics in the form of financial performance management and the use of social media. However arguably that is not strictly the case, as highlighted by three examples.

Firstly, and as has been commented on elsewhere, it is important that information – either qualitative or quantitative – is taken in context. Poor results remain poor but if no worse than competitors then this may be a softening blow. One impact of the Big Data environment is that it is easier to understand the market context of financial outcomes. Some might say that this capability has to some degree always existed but the current climate of greater information and more transparency makes this easier.

The second example is that of the value of a company's reputation. In their 2015 report[10] and other associated papers[11] Reputation Dividend, who are a specialist firm in reputational insight, sought to assess how the market capitalization of a company is derived from its reputation and how this has increased or decreased in the past 12 months relative to reputational impact. They were able to identify that 1% improvement in a company's reputation would be expected to increase its market value by 1.4%, notwithstanding that there was considerable variation between industries. In cash terms they identified that on average in FTSE 100 firms, a 1% improvement of reputation has the potential to deliver £266 million of additional value.

This insight is particularly interesting in that there have been challenges in correlating reputation with value. Social media management is a very effective way of gaining insight into reputational issues and to some degree managing the reputation of a company. For insurers whose main currency is trustworthiness, the improvement of their reputation may have wider benefits beyond simply how they are seen in the eyes of the policyholder.

The third example comes from research by Colt Technology Services[12] who, based on a survey of 360 UK finance professionals, suggested that share price volatility is affected by public opinion on social media sites such as Twitter and Facebook. Colt's research found that 63% of respondents which included brokers and heads of trading desks believed that the valuation of individual stocks can be directly linked to social media sentiment. Drilling more deeply into the research, 7% of respondents viewed social media sentiment as a leading indicator, which is a measure used to anticipate change. On the other hand, 45% of respondents regard it as a trailing indicator, which confirms trends. Whilst there is some residual uncertainty, it remains the case that social media is important in terms of reputation management, and seems to have some bearing on company value.

2.9   SALES MANAGEMENT AND DISTRIBUTION CHANNELS

Today insurers use multiple routes to market as part of the sales process to engage with their prospective customers. Traditionally sales have been through brokers and agents who are either company-employed or acting independently. Increasingly other direct and indirect channels such as the contact center, internet, banks, aggregators and third-party retailers are part of the mix. There is also considerable variation across geographies in terms of the usage of intermediaries for insurance sales, often based on a combination of culture and local market tradition. In Asia and parts of the US, for example, agents still hold the greatest market share. The use of brokers and agents is more expensive for insurers than the direct approach. Consequently, it is critical that accurate cost allocation is made to have a clear understanding of the respective profitability of individual channels.

This also extends to claims cost management, especially where a broker or agent has the permission, sometimes known as 'delegated authority,' to settle claims for insurers on their behalf. In a declining sales channel heavily affected by the use of new technologies by the consumer, agents are under pressure not only to offer a good service but perhaps also to protect 'their' client's (i.e., the policyholder's) interests by being more generous in the claims settlement. Alternatively, they may not take full advantage of repair and replacement services put in place by the insurer, affecting bulk purchasing discounts which might otherwise be available to the insurer. As a result, insurers often see different and usually higher 'loss ratios' emerging from the broker channel for the same type of claim, in the same location, at the same time.

2.9.1   Agents and Producers

Analytical processes can also be used as an important part of the management of both tied and independent insurance agents, validation of agents' credentials to trade, and their authorization to service a policy. In the US, agents are generally known as 'producers,' with the typical regulatory bodies being NIPR, National Insurance Producer Registry, FINRA (the Financial Regulatory Authority) and DTCC (Depository Trust and Clearing Corporation).

In the US 'producers' are required to be licensed. NIPR are a public/ private partnership that supports the work of the individual states and the National Association of Insurance Commissioners (NAIC) to create a 'producer portal' or 'gateway,' enabling NAIC to support their State Producer Licensing database. The National Association of Insurance Commissioners (NAIC) is the US standard-setting and regulatory support organization which supports state insurance regulators to establish standards and best practices, conduct peer review and coordinate their regulatory oversight.[13] Beyond this, it also prevents those who are not qualified from trading. By ensuring competence, it seeks to protect the general public from mis-selling.

To qualify for a license, the state regulator has certain individual requirements. In the case of Washington State for example, 20 hours of Pre-License Education for each major line of authority are expected, i.e., life or commercial. Subsequently there is an exam process with a minimum pass mark. Licenses are generally for a two-year period and then the agent must renew.

This compares to the UK situation whereby the expression 'insurance broker' became a regulated term as per the Insurance Brokers Registration Act 1977 although that Act is now repealed. Currently all organizations that 'sell' insurance products must be approved by the Financial Conduct Authority (known as the 'FCA'). All firms approved by the FCA can sell insurance. Rules came into effect in 2012 for independent financial advisers (known as 'IFAs') following the Retail Distribution Review ('RDR') and all independent financial advisors must now give unbiased advice and offer a range of products. This UK program is intended to ensure financial education and a level of literacy comparable to the US and other OECD countries.

Increasingly insurers are viewing their agent network as part of their 'virtual enterprise' and using them as an extension of their own business through which they can collect performance data, allowing:

- Improved remuneration reporting
- Commission management including commission reporting
- Better agent/broker performance evaluation
- Communication strategy and broker recognition for good performance
- Cost savings in training, audit and commission management.

2.9.2   Distribution Management

Distribution Management, sometimes known as 'Sales Performance Management' (or SPM) is the process by which distribution channels are financially managed in terms of commissions, quotas and incentives. It is often considered as an extension to financial performance management in that it focuses on alignment of the behavior of the sales organization with the strategic goals of the business. Additionally, it increases sales productivity, improves organizational agility and helps support sale compliance issues.

Based on research[14] sales compensation is managed in multiple ways as shown in Figure 2.1.

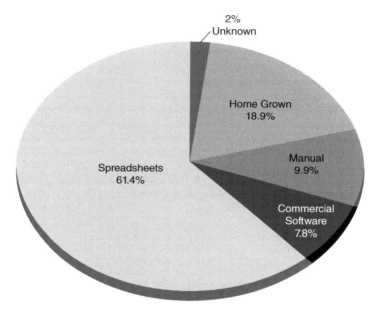

Ref: CSO Insights
2012 Sales Compensation Key Trends Analysis

FIGURE 2.1   Management of sales compensation

Companies adopt sales and distribution performance management solutions to:

- Reduce errors in the calculation of achievement.
- Improve territory management, allowing them to find the right number of agents and representatives and manage their productivity more effectively.
- Improve the planning of quotas and create more appropriate and meaningful targets.
- Manage and rationalize compensation plans.
- Meet compliance issues such as Dodd-Frank in the US, and equivalent compliance issues in other territories which in part relates to issues of seller conduct.
- Reduce processing time in the calculation of compensation and other key metrics.
- Reduce staffing, primarily in the process of calculation of sales results – but it may also assist in creating and maintaining the seller network.

NOTES

1. Read, Cedric et al. *eCFO Sustaining Value in the New Corporation*. London: John Wiley & Co., 2001.
2. Mosimann, Roland, Mosimann, Patrick, Connelly, Richard et al. *The Performance Manager for Insurance*. Ottawa: Cognos Press, 2008.
3. Also Institute and Faculty of Actuaries. 'Why Become an Actuary'. http://www.actuaries.org.uk/become-actuary/why-become-actuary (accessed May 16, 2016).
4. Bellis, Clare, Shepherd, John and Lyon, Richard. 'Understanding Actuarial Management. The Actuarial Control Cycle,' Section 1.2, pp. 1–3. Published by the Institute of Actuaries of Australia, 2010.
5. Gray, Alastair. 'Regulators to probe insurers over drawing down reserves.' FT.com, November 14, 2014 (accessed November 25, 2015).
6. Ernst and Young. 'Facing the Challenge: Business Implications of IFRS 4, 9 and Solvency II for Insurers.' Published by EYGM Ltd, 2012.
7. Freese, Christopher, Imholz, Michael et al. 'Value Creation in Insurance.' Published by Boston Consulting Group, 2009.
8. National Insurance Producer Register. Annual Report 2014. http://www.nipr.com/docs/annual-reports/nipr_annual_report_2014_nipr_profile.htm (accessed March 3, 2016).
9. Continuity Central. Published online May 6, 2005. http://www.continuitycentral.com/feature0203.htm (accessed November 26, 2015).
10. Reputation Dividend. 'The 2015 UK Reputation Dividend Report.' www.reputationdividend.com (accessed March 11, 2016).
11. Cole, Simon, Brown, Michael and Stur, Brian. 'Applying Reputation Data to Enhance Investment Performance.' (December 2010) *World Economics* 15(4).
12. Colt Technology Services. 'Stock prices influenced by Twitter and Facebook, according to UK finance professionals.' Published by Colt Technology Services. February 12, 2013. http://www.colt.net/news/stock-prices-influenced-by-twitter-and-facebook-according-to-uk-finance-professionals/ (accessed November 26, 2015).
13. National Association of Insurance Commissioners. 'About the NAIC.' http://naic.org/ (accessed March 11, 2016).
14. Chief Sales Officer Insights. '2012 Sales Compensation and Performance Management, Key Trends,' White Paper. Published by CSO Insights, 2012. http://www.synygy.com/private/Casestudies/2012%20Sales%20Compensation%20and%20Performance%20Management%20Report%20-%20Synygy.pdf (accessed March 11, 2016).

CHAPTER 3

Managing Financial Risk Across the Insurance Enterprise

It should perhaps be a matter of concern that one of the biggest issues in the insurance industry of recent years is something which is of relevance not to the masses, but to the specialists. Solvency II affects all parts of the insurance value chain to differing degrees as well as the customer who, some will argue, has had to ultimately bear the cost.

Risk in the insurance world is, for many, confusing. Many general practitioners take the term to mean underwriting risk. That topic will be addressed elsewhere. In this context we seek to address the issue of the risks associated with the management of capital to ensure that the insurance company remains solvent, and also the regulatory framework within which it is enclosed.

3.1   SOLVENCY II

Overall this is a complex subject and it is not the intention to cover in a few paragraphs what can readily comprise the content of one book (or more) but simply to provide an overview for those who might be new to the subject. An authoritative book on this topic is *Value and Capital Management* by Tom Wilson[1] which includes the impact of effective risk management on claims and marketing staff for instance. In effect Solvency II is the European regulation that governs the amount of capital that an EU insurance company needs to remain solvent. The principle has also been expanded to many other countries who have created their own regulatory models. In addition, the process of 'equivalence' allows insurers headquartered in other non-European countries to operate in Europe.

Capital is either sourced by insurers externally, is gained from earnings, or freed from existing businesses, and may be held by an insurer in multiple ways such as assets and bonds. It is used by insurers to fund current initiatives, strategic initiatives, assist with financing or to return to shareholders.

Solvency II is meant to be a principle-based approach but has evolved into 2000 pages of Directives – many would argue that it has become over complicated. The regulator in their defense might argue that the amount of documentation has arisen due to the need for guidance and direction, rather than insurers using their initiative but this is a moot point.

The regulator in Europe is the Insurance and Occupational Pensions Authority commonly known as 'EIOPA.' It replaced the Committee of European Insurance and Occupational Pensions Supervisors (CEIOPS) in 2011. EIOPA is in effect a sort of industry watchdog whose duties are to support the stability of the financial system, and ensure transparency of markets and financial products. Also, critically, their mandate is to provide protection to insurance policyholders and members of pension schemes by ensuring that there are adequate funds available and that the insurer does not become 'insolvent.'

The intention primarily is to protect the policyholder in the event that the insurance company is unable to pay claims, and in doing so restore trust in the insurance sector. Regulation does this by providing the regulator with an early warning system. The model adopted is not unlike that used in the banking sectors under a process called 'Basel II' on which many of the Solvency II solutions are modeled. Experts would argue that this is not an exact comparison but for the sake of simplicity it is one that is easiest to understand. In fact, both the banking and insurance regulators are based in the same building, the so-called 'Tower of Basel' which potentially opens the door to a unified regulatory framework downstream, but this is unlikely to happen overnight, if ever at all.

Solvency II comprises three elements, usually described as the 'three pillars.'

Pillar 1: This sets out the qualitative and quantitative provisions for capital that an insurer needs to remain 'solvent,' and able to meet its obligations (normally through claims payments) with a probability of 99.5%. This is simply a statistical measure, much in the same way that insurance underwriters cannot be certain of a 100-year flood occurring only once in one hundred years but it is a reflection of their degree of confidence in that occurring. This capital provision is called the Solvency Capital Requirement or 'SCR.' In addition a lower level of capital requirement is calculated called the Minimum Capital Requirement (called 'MCR') below which the regulator will step in. If that happens, the regulator has a number of options including winding up the insurer.

There are two ways of calculating this capital requirement – a 'Standard Model' which is a calculation method provided by the regulator, or alternatively an 'Internal Model' which is a more precise assessment of the capital needed by an insurer themselves. This latter approach is considered to be more relevant to insurers with specialty lines, where the nature of underwriting risks taken is more specialized in character. The internal model calculation needs to be pre-approved by the regulator.

Pillar 2: This sets out requirements for the risk management of the insurer and how it protects itself against weaknesses such as breaches in IT security, operational processes and internal fraud. This is called the ORSA, or 'Own Risk Solvency Assessment.' Insurers are obliged to put capital aside to safeguard themselves against such risks, called 'capital drawdown.' It follows that it is in an insurer's interest to have effective operational risk management processes in place to mitigate any potential losses. In doing so, the amount put aside as part of the solvency requirement can be reduced. This is a good example of the Solvency II process being a catalyst in raising awareness of the effect of risk across the entire enterprise, and being a stimulant for insurers taking appropriate mitigating action.

Pillar 3: This is the reporting element of the Solvency II Regulation, where insurers are forced to lay out in both quantitative and qualitative terms a statement of their capital position. There is also a requirement for the data to be electronically tagged, which is done using a process called 'eXtensible Business Reporting Language,' more commonly known as 'XBRL.'

XBRL is a standards-based method of sharing information between different business systems using tagging of the data, or 'metadata.' In effect it means that if there is a change in any of the data, then by virtue of the tagging any changes are automatically driven through any associated and linked document. In the UK, HM Customs and Excise already require companies to file their annual reports in an XBRL format when making their Corporate Tax returns.

In the US, a similar model exists for Solvency II, acronymed RMORSA 'Risk Management and Own Risk and Solvency Assessment.' It has much in common with the Solvency II regime which aims to demonstrate that the insurer has a comprehensive approach to risk management and sufficient capital to meet any contingencies which may arise. The way in which contingencies are measured is what is called 'stress testing,' where multiple scenarios are run through analytical systems to gain a better understanding of the amount of capital needed to remain solvent in extreme situations. The role of the US Insurance Commissioners is crucial in this process and whilst there is some degree of consistency across the piece, nevertheless one challenge for pan-US insurers is the relatively fragmented State regulatory environment. It has been suggested that any insurer providing services across the whole of the United States has the daunting challenge of satisfying not one, but 50 'regulatory authorities.'

The new Solvency II regulation which came into effect in January 2016 has come in for some criticism. Firstly, the cost of compliance has been much higher than the regulator expected, with some major insurers incurring tens of millions of euros. According to Insurance Europe, a Brussels-based industry lobby group, Solvency II will have cost insurers between 2 billion euros ($2.7 billion) and 3 billion euros initially and 500 million euros a year once the rules are in place. One argument for the very high initial expenditure is that perhaps this work needed to have been done regardless of the regulation, and it was in effect nothing other than insurers needing to put their house in order. Some suggest that many housekeeping costs were conveniently placed under a Solvency II program for expediency. An unfortunate side effect was that monies which might otherwise have been used to bolster consumer trust through improved service were otherwise diverted, and there is anecdotal evidence that other customer-facing activities were put on hold due to lack of funding.

The other main criticism has been in the calculation of the capital amounts required to demonstrate solvency, with one London-based insurer saying that the 'internal model' should be scrapped in favor of a Europe-wide 'standard model' – an idea that has been very firmly pushed back on the basis that it will be impossible to create a 'one-size-fits-all' calculation model.[2]

By January 2016, Solvency II will have come into operation, the culmination of a lengthy stop–start journey which has caused executive and practitioner fatigue. Inevitably there will have been a last-minute flurry of activity for those organizations seeking 'second mover advantage' and putting implementation off until the last minute in the hope of there being a magic bullet to achieve success. However, even then the Solvency II process will not have come to an end. There is even discreet talk about 'Solvency III.' Notwithstanding, insurers are already thinking about revisiting the topic and understanding how best to improve efficiency and reduce cost, without compromising quality.

3.2 SOLVENCY II, CLOUD COMPUTING AND SHARED SERVICES

One approach which is emerging is that of cloud computing, on the basis that Solvency II reporting requires heavy computing power relatively infrequently and for short durations. This clearly lends itself to a cloud approach but some insurers and regulators appear concerned about sensitive data leaving the premises, the country or both. In an attempt to manage those fears, insurers are increasingly thinking about hybrid solutions which are a combination of on-premise and external analytics. A 2014 survey of 60 European insurers[2] indicated that 60% of them had considered or were considering the use of cloud for Solvency II, but the biggest barrier to change was stakeholder resistance rather than any technical or financial reason. There is no reason to think that this position will not soften with the passage of time, and it is a matter of when the insurance community reach the tipping point at which most if not all deployments will be cloud-based (at least in part).

Beyond this there are also specific challenges for smaller insurers in complying with Solvency II. Their business models and data sets are simpler and they have certain relaxations (known as 'proportionality') but the cost of compliance is still likely to remain disproportionately expensive. In some territories there may be local requirements (within the broader Framework) which may lend themselves to some form of customized approach.

Additionally, the overall skills needed for compliance in a smaller insurer may well be beyond those of a CFO who may not wish to fund the ongoing existence of a Solvency II project team. It is likely therefore that the concept of a shared service will eventually emerge, with one of the main provisos being that of ensuring appropriate firewalls between data from competing organizations. Again this may be a perception issue rather than a problem of reality. Cloud providers such as Amazon and others already provide services to competing retailers without any conflict arising, so it is a matter of time before this replicates itself in the insurance model in much the same way that insurers are following retailers in terms of customer management techniques.

Shared services, or Solvency II 'utilities,' are therefore increasingly likely to emerge. These may be from organizations which have all the capabilities 'in house' and can therefore provide a one-stop-shop. Alternatively, utilities will come from partnerships which combine specialist analytical awareness with others who have technology capability. Some larger insurers might even consider creating some form of service for other insurers which generates revenue and offsets their own cost of compliance. Specific local requirements of regulators may result in multiple local organizations springing up and providing a localized and customized service at a lower cost than the insurers can deliver themselves.

3.3 'SWEATING THE ASSETS'

The expression 'sweating the assets' is a business term that came out of the manufacturing industry and is generally thought of in terms of full utilization of buildings, equipment and people. In an insurance context, and more particularly Solvency II, it relates to the full utilization of software, processes and data.

The story of Solvency II compliance is one of a long haul, since 2008 (although some would argue as far back as 1973 and Solvency I) when Northern European insurers started to get their act together, but with a program punctuated by a number of false deadlines which were from time to time extended. The impact of the deadline being allowed to slip was to create an element of uncertainty amongst insurers that the January 2016 date was in fact the final destination. There was even a sense amongst some insurers that it was better to wait than to act so as not to incur untimely expenditure. However, the regulations were to make it clear in no uncertain terms that January 2016 was the target. Maybe the regulators too had lost patience.

For insurers who had conscientiously started early on the basis perhaps of recognizing the scale of the task ahead of them, there must have been a sense of annoyance and frustration that cost had been incurred without the benefit of compliance at that time. It quickly became apparent that at least some of the work they had undertaken could be reused in other parts of the finance function. In fact, some even went so far as to suggest that the benefits of reuse of assets were such that the cost of compliance was capable of being turned into a return on investment.

Typical areas where Solvency II assets could be reused were:

- Calculation of internal capital requirements
- Risk aware decisions
- Financial performance management
- Regulatory disclosure.

In effect what was beginning to emerge was a convergence of risk and finance, reusing tooling and assets to provide a more holistic view and in effect transforming the office of finance. Whether this was in EIOPA's contemplation at the outset is doubtful but if the eventual outcome is one of providing insurers with a more complete and holistic view of their business then this will be a good outcome.

3.4 SOLVENCY II AND IFRS

IFRS, the International Financial Reporting Standards, are a European mechanism which has forced insurers and many other industries to review the financial processes, especially at the close of accounts. The latest iterations, IFRS 4 (Insurance Contracts) and IFRS 9 (Financial Instruments) are now unlikely to be implemented before 2019 but in many ways replicate the challenges of Solvency II for insurers in that IFRS requires review of data, process and reporting.

In their 2011 white paper 'Facing the challenge: Business implications of IFRS 4, 9 and Solvency II for Insurers,'[4] Ernst and Young identified the interdependencies between IFRS 4, IFRS 9 and Solvency II. Their paper discusses the concept of transformation of the office of finance, transformation founded on common data. They imply that financial and risk management, and risk and financial reporting, are in effect four sides of the same square. Their suggestion was that all four elements should be considered as an integrated program of work due to the level of interdependency and overall dependence on common financial data. Although the concept is already quite old, there is some evidence that insurers have started to take this thinking on board. Whether this is deliberate or a natural convergence of processes is unclear, but this approach is likely to become more common amongst insurers everywhere, especially as insurers start to rethink the Solvency II process in terms of improved efficiency and reduced cost.

In considering this approach, it is fair to say that there must almost certainly be economies of process and scale, avoidance of rework, probably more effective use of resources and ultimately a more integrated solution. As with Solvency II in the early days, an imbalance of supply and demand of expert resources might also emerge, pushing up implementation costs. A converged approach between IFRS and Solvency II might provide a useful remedy to that particular problem.

It is probable but not certain that with time full integration between all these programs will take place. A great deal appears to depend on the uncertainties of the timelines. Such uncertainty means that even if there was a desire for insurers to undertake such a coordinated approach, the timing of such an inclusive program might make this impossible. On reflection it is a pity that the authorities did not cooperate more but perhaps if they had, then the overall demand upon insurers would simply have been too much, even if the overall cost would have turned out to be cheaper. There might also have been questions about the resources available to carry through such change, with a resource imbalance resulting in implementation costs being pushed up again. At the end of the day, perhaps fate played a part and helped moderate the progress of transformation of the insurance sector in the office of finance.

3.5   THE CHANGING ROLE OF THE CRO

As with C-level board members, the new analytics era will bring with it a series of personal challenges. None more so than that of the Chief Risk Officer ('CRO') whose role will be projected into the spotlight by virtue of the increased and sustained focus on risk within the insurance organization.

Looking specifically at the topic of enterprise risk management, this generally falls into two key categories:

- Financial or capital risk: This is in effect the risk attaching to the financial security of the insurance organization.
- Operational risk: This relates to the risk of loss arising from inadequate or failed processes, people or systems, or from external events.

Focusing on operational risk, this can arise in four key areas (Table 3.1).

One increasing area of risk is the impact of new so-called 'disruptive technologies' and also the ongoing impact of the 'mega trends' within insurance such as the trend in mobile technology. Insurers not only need to be able to recognize the continued impact of mobile technology in the customer relationship, but also anticipate the next wave of mobile innovation. This 'next wave' may not originate in insurance or even in financial services but perhaps in the retail or consumer goods sector. As insurers start to mobilize for these changes, they need to consider the inherent risks that might also arise in the future and even allow for the 'unknown unknowns.'

Similarly, in the areas of FinTech ('Financial Technology') and 'InsureTech,' insurers need to understand the impact of disruptive ideas within the overall matrix. Whilst FinTech is generally seen as new technology for the financial services sector, it is characterized by smaller start-ups with a disruptive frame of mind. Much of FinTech seems to sit in the Back Office, for example in optimizing payment processes, and usually relies on relatively classical

TABLE 3.1 The four key areas of operational risk

Type of Risk	Type of Failure
Risk from people	These risks emerge from internal or external fraud, loss of key staff, training failures, poor supervision or reputational damage.
Risk from failed process	These risks emerge from failed payment processes, poor procurement of the supply chain, weak project management, poor pricing or underwriting models, incorrect reporting and the like.
Systemic risk	Risks that emerge from failures of the system or implementation of new systems, and inadequate resources to maintain existing systems.
Risk as a result of external events	Risks emerging from major weather events, political risk, regulatory change or competitor behavior.

technologies – data and record administration. There is increasing evidence of a desire on the part of FinTech companies to move into the Front Office and play more of a part in customer-facing activities. Risk managers not only need to think about how payment processes might change, but also how new capabilities such as Blockchain and Sidechain will start to transform the role of insurers and other insurance distributors.

Blockchain is an underlying technology which supports the concept of Bitcoin, and allows parties to trade with each other without any 'trusted environment.' It is described as a potential gamechanger as dramatic as the World Wide Web. According to Brookings Education:[5]

> *The elegance of the Blockchain is that it obviates the need for a central authority to verify trust and the transfer of value. It transfers power and control from large entities to the many, enabling safe, fast, cheaper transactions...*

What this means in the simplest terms is that Blockchain potentially provides a methodology to transform the payment and transaction process within the insurance industry, reducing cost, changing relationships and creating new distribution models. For those who might be somewhat skeptical, Sidechain is an associated methodology which allows insurers to try the process in a safe 'sandbox' environment without risk to their ongoing operations.

Whilst it is inevitably tempting for insurers to consider these step change ideas in the drive for innovation, at the same time they also bring risk perhaps of a type and level which insurers or other organizations have not experienced previously. The CRO needs not only to have an understanding of how to ensure there are adequate controls within the organization, but must also have an awareness of new risk categories emerging. That is to say, the CRO needs to be more 'outwards looking' than ever before, or the organization runs the risk of being caught on the hop. This potentially places the risk officer in a difficult position. On the one hand, the main duty of the CRO is to the organization and all its stakeholders to provide appropriate 'lines of defence.' On the other hand, the CRO will not want to be seen as the person who constantly puts the brake on progress especially where innovation is concerned.

It is potentially a fine line and much may depend on the corporate culture of the organization. A report prepared by the UK Parliamentary Commission on Banking Standards in 2003[6] makes reference to the very real issues faced by risk executives when expressing concern regarding internal processes they consider to be flawed.

It may be helpful however to understand how risk officers manage operational risk. Traditionally insurers manage operational risk through what are known as the three lines of defense:

1. Risk management at the operational level, i.e., the point of delivery. This is called the 'first line' of defense.
2. The risk and control function, in effect a series of controls and compliance processes. This is known as the 'second line' of defense.
3. The internal audit function, known as the 'third line.'

The defence analogy is mildly unfortunate as it has military and therefore combative connotations, and perhaps does not accurately reflect the changing role of the CRO in the new climate. Increasingly, as internal and external stakeholders such as the Board of Directors, analysts and investors are keen to better understand risk, the CRO needs to acquire new skills beyond those historically associated with the job. Not only do they need to have better knowledge of the new analytical technologies available but must also acquire the skills of influencing, communication and media management. Perhaps they should also have a strong imagination (due to the nature of 'new' risks which are likely to occur in the new Big Data environment).

This role extension from the historical position is not entirely different to the transformation of the Chief Marketing Officer whose world is also being changed by the 'digital customer,' and as a result needs to learn (or develop on the team) new analytical marketing and campaign management skills.

It is inevitable that greater, more powerful and quicker analytics will emerge in the risk area almost certainly fueled by Big Data and provided via a cloud, or hybrid cloud. Furthermore, insurers will increasingly recognize the relevance and criticality of advanced analytics, providing them with deeper and quicker insight especially around the most volatile parts of their portfolio. The question again needs to be asked of the professional institutions – what are they doing, if anything, to address the emerging impact of technology on their members? Elsewhere we have asked whether it is easier for a 'line of business' expert to learn technology, or for a technologist to learn about the line of business. In the case of risk, although there are some IT-driven controls that can be adopted, the nature and complexity of financial risk are such that this is likely to firmly remain in the domain of risk experts especially where it relates to compliance and capital adequacy.

In the same way that cognitive analytics has depended on the interaction of man and machine in respect of healthcare and cancer treatment, it is likely the onus will be on the risk professional to use developing technology as an enabling tool as opposed to being threatened by it. Perhaps new technology will allow the risk officer to adversely comment on controversial issues with more confidence. Risk professionals will increasingly view analytical skill as an essential part of the toolbox, not least because there will be a greater level of expectation by internal and external stakeholders (including regulators) to use appropriate levels of analytical support in this most critical of all areas, with improved access and ease of use.

3.6   CRO AS CUSTOMER ADVOCATE

As insurers increasingly consider the issue of Big Data and practitioners reflect on the ethical impact and whether more granular underwriting (and possibly even refusal to offer cover) is in the public interest, it is likely that regulation in one of its many forms will step in primarily in the guise of customer-orientated legislation. Typically, this might embrace issues such as distribution, transparency of products, TCF ('Treating the Customer Fairly') and more local issues such as the future of annuities in the UK pension industry.

What is clear is that, regardless of how people think about the benefits or challenges of Big Data in the insurance context, it will be impossible to put the genie back in the bottle. It is unlikely that the regulator or legislators will be the sole savior and custodian of customer data even if they choose to impose stringent and punitive fines for breaches. In cases where commercial interests prevail, it is often the case that businesses will try to find a lawful way around legislation. It would be nice to think that insurers would take the ethical high road, and continue to recognize their 300-year-old heritage as an overall contributor to social good over the centuries.

It is to be hoped that the CRO will, in a desire to ensure compliance in the customer space, also become the consumer's friend in the insurance process at least in spirit if not explicitly. This is not to say that there will be any commercial imprudence, but rather that where insurance products are either unprofitable or capital-heavy, the CRO using all the intellect and tools at their disposal will be able to recommend and perhaps even help create new and better customer-facing propositions which tick all the appropriate boxes.

3.7   ANALYTICS AND THE CHALLENGE OF UNPREDICTABILITY

Insurers operate in a volatile environment yet are obliged to anticipate what may happen going forward and make appropriate capital provision. This is extremely challenging in the case of long-tail insurances such as life and pension, where insurers try to anticipate events 50 years hence. It is as much an art as a science and much has been written on the topic discussing such ethereal issues as 'black swans.' (A 'black swan' is an expression coined by Nassim Taleb to describe 'an event, positive or negative, that is deemed improbable yet causes massive consequences.') Perhaps these descriptions are an attempt to bring excitement into what might otherwise be considered a relatively dull world – at least compared to the claims department of the insurance company which seems to be where most of the action is. There is clearly a pecking order within this risk-specific discipline. Are economists really just frustrated mathematicians, as is sometimes suggested?

Some experts would seek to argue that 'crises' are just the 'norm' and that any attempt to rationalize the prediction process is bound to be fraught with grief. The interconnectivity and interdependency of events results in developments which are anything but linear. If dashboards as a means of analytical visualization provide CFOs and CROs with the ability to see what has happened or what is happening, it is difficult to predict with absolute certainty what will happen. At best, analytics can help the CFO and CRO 'sandbox' the possible outcome of scenarios – the actuarial equivalent of war gaming. This approach is also increasingly likely to find some comfort in the process of storyboarding, which is one method of exploring different hypotheses, allowing better organization of thoughts, and making it easier to present findings. The concept of storyboarding comes from the film production industry where storyboarding techniques allow directors to pre-visualize the shot and work out potential problems.

Perhaps the biggest imminent crisis is partly one of the industry's own making. Low interest rates are beyond the control of insurers as is political instability in some regions, but these, when coupled with a solvency regime which seems to amplify everything, might appear to be the equivalent of two trains facing each other on the same track.

3.8   THE IMPORTANCE OF REINSURANCE

It is well recognized that insurers use reinsurance as a method of limiting their exposure but, from a capital modeling point of view, reinsurers have a wider role to play.

Reinsurers are used to:

- Preserve the value of the insurance brand and protect it from volatility.
- Protect the insurer from peak exposures by reducing underwriting risk.
- Provide alternative capitalization where local regulatory constraints are too onerous or disproportionate.

About half of reinsurance is placed through 'reinsurance brokers' who will then deal directly with reinsurance companies. The other half are direct reinsurance companies who have their own sales staff. Reinsurers are often specialists in particular risks and whilst they already have a great deal of expertise, the availability of greater insight from data and analytics can only enhance that capability. Reinsurers typically will be interested in advanced catastrophe modeling and the integration between analytics and location – so-called 'spatial analytics.' Increasingly there is a need for speed of calculation and this is not only driving reinsurers down an analytical route, but also forcing them to think about the platform capabilities they require.

For risk managers, reinsurance is not a silver bullet but rather a critical element in the mix. As a result of the impact of more data and better analytics, new risk transfer techniques are likely to emerge as reinsurers and risk managers gain a deeper understanding of industries and the implication of major events. Speaking at the 2011 FERMA (Federation of European Risk Management Associations) Risk Summit, the President for that year, Peter den Dekker, called on reinsurers to work more closely with their clients and emphasized the need for better lines of communication and understanding between reinsurers and risk managers.

3.9   RISK ADJUSTED DECISION-MAKING

Increasingly the trend is to move towards an environment of risk adjusted decision-making whereby every decision by the executive, senior management, product management, or asset managers is made taking into account the risk appetite of the insurance organization. By 'risk appetite' we mean the propensity of an organization to make certain decisions which carry a degree of risk or uncertainty.

The level of risk of an organization may differ from function to function, and from department to department, and is often influenced by the leader or manager of that department. Risk appetites are generally categorized as:

- Averse – avoidance of risk and uncertainty is an organizational imperative.
- Minimal – where the organization takes an ultra-safe approach to risk and recognizes that this will limit their rewards.
- Cautious – preference for safe options with limited risk and limited reward.
- Open – a willingness to be open-minded and balance risk against reward opportunity.
- Hungry – eagerness to innovate despite risks, in the knowledge that greater rewards may follow.

Some organizations pride themselves on their attitude to risk by constantly encouraging innovative processes and procedures. One reflection of this is the mood of 'agility' or 'agile working' which seems to positively encourage innovation to take place in a controlled-risk environment. Innovation is by its nature risky as it encourages behaviors which seek to create revolutionary products or services, and often aims to create new markets rather than simply imitate others in existing markets.

Risk appetite does not confine itself to the insurance and financial services sector. The largest retailer in the world, the Chinese company Alibaba, has increased its gross market value by 10,000% since its start-up in 1999. It constantly encourages its employees to be innovative in thinking which inherently must carry some element of risk. Li & Fung, another Chinese example, ensure that each business unit of this consumer goods company is run by an entrepreneur.

Having an effective risk-informed decision process will almost certainly emerge as a by-product of effective integration between the risk and finance functions. Such integration might happen more quickly in smaller organizations where there is a lower level of complexity, for example monoline insurers, and where there are shorter management chains of command. In larger organizations, the risk department often still see themselves as a separate function with a degree of independence. They are often vexed by the issue of needing to be both poacher and gamekeeper simultaneously as they seek ways to support and advise on business decisions. In fact, this 'paranoia' can often extend to the way that the risk function talks, often describing the remainder of the organization as 'the business,' as if the risk department is not part of that same business.

The challenge for the risk department is that they need to ask themselves 'are we helping things happen, or are we stopping things happening?' In reality, whilst this might almost promote a 'Dr Jekyll and Mr Hyde' syndrome, these are not necessarily mutually exclusive. Ultimately the role of the CFO is to turn available capital into an enhanced combined ratio and into profitable advantage. This can be done not only by offering insight into complex matters but also by ensuring that risk is embedded into business decisions.

Whilst banking appears to be ahead of the insurance industry in such matters, the relative immaturity of the insurance sector means that it is often left to individuals to assess how best to develop that capability. Perhaps the leading lights in this area come from insurers who are more aligned to the banking sector, such as bancassurers whose business is often more related to the life business than property and casualty insurance (also known as 'P & C'). Insurers with banking insight especially recognize the need to focus on governance and structure coupled with the need for increased transparency. They recognize the necessity of bringing different views to the table in a non-confrontational way. Much of the transformation of risk in banking came from the 'tailwind' of the banking crisis in 2008. Insurers have not so far had to face such a crisis as a call to action.

Much also seems to depend on the quality of the management team, the interlock or 'chemistry' between participants and also the capabilities of the individuals involved. It is sometimes suggested that that the role of the CRO is one of the more difficult positions on the board because of the need to satisfy all the stakeholders, both internal and external, to simultaneously play offense and defense and to constantly 'add realism' to the discussion.

The effectiveness of the CRO is often governed by the approach they take. Do they take the 'left path', that of the controller or compliance function, and the person who is there to ensure that the rules are complied with? Or do they take the 'right path,' as an internal business partner providing insight into risk appetite, and the creation/maintenance of a risk framework? Is the role of the CRO at a cross-road? Not really, as both these issues are in effect two sides of the same coin, but what is clear is that the expectations of the new CRO are increasingly more than just a tick-box approach. The role is complementary to the rest of the team. What is interesting is that very few CROs reach the CEO role. There are exceptions – Amer Ahmed, the Chief Risk Officer of Allianz Re, the reinsurer, was appointed Chief Executive of his company in 2011 – but it is as if the CRO prefers to play in defense rather than attack. In reality, and in American football imagery, the CRO increasingly has the opportunity to become the quarterback or 'playmaker.'

Many CROs originate from the actuarial function. It is interesting to discuss whether the professional actuary best sits in the risk department or the finance department. Certainly their skills are equally important to both, and maybe it is as much an issue of individual behavioral characteristics as of mathematical proficiency. There are also some relatively 'domestic' issues, for example, did Solvency II aim also to change the role of the CRO? There is a sense that amongst the 20,000 words of explanation, perhaps there could have been greater guidance regarding roles and responsibilities. Regulators on the other hand appear to have no desire to interfere in the organization of insurers or the responsibilities of their officers. Where does the role of the CFO stop and the CRO start? In smaller organizations, the two roles are conjoined, with the specific risk function sometimes being undertaken by a project or program manager.

In terms of the need for analytics in this most complex of areas, one question to be asked of CROs is whether they consider they are adequately supported by technology. It is important that they have adequate controls in place to help them support (and in some cases run) the business, and to stress test any potential major decisions before they are made. The Board increasingly needs this information quickly, sometimes in minutes or less rather than hours or days. (Is this increased urgency a function of the evolving role, or just a greater impatience for better insight as a by-product of the pressures of the modern world?)

The CRO does not want to be spoon fed by analytics but rather wants to use analysis as part of a toolkit to answer difficult, mission-critical insurance problems. Arguably, many technology vendors are not close enough to the problems of this function to come up with all the answers. It is for CROs to recognize the capability of technology, and for the technologists to work in partnership with professionals to create enterprise-wide, agile risk management solutions. Risk solutions in the insurance organization will inevitably need to be 'owned' by the CRO rather than the IT department. This requires CROs to better understand technology as well as being better communicators, media managers and collaborators, as we have indicated earlier. Because of the new data and analytics environment, the role of risk professionals will inevitably change. The major question is how quickly will this occur, and are both the individual and the industry ready?

NOTES

1. Wilson, Thomas C. *Value and Capital Management*. London: John Wiley and Sons, 2015.
2. Crowley, Kevin. 'Europe Should Scrap Solvency II's Internal Models, Hiscox Says.' Published by Bloomberg Business. February 12, 2013. http://www.bloomberg.com/news/articles/2013-02-12/europe-should-scrap-solvency-ii-s-internal-models-hiscox-says (accessed November 26, 2015).
3. International Business Machines (IBM) 'Cloud Computing and Solvency II.' Published by IBM. March 26, 2015. http://www.risklibrary.net/abstract/cloud-computing-solvency-ii-24325 (accessed July 1, 2015).
4. Ernst and Young. 'Facing the Challenge: Business Implications of IFRS 4, 9 and Solvency II for Insurers.' Published by EYGM Ltd, 2012.
5. Kaushal, Mohit and Tyle, Sheel. 'The Blockchain: What It Is and Why It Matters.' Published online by Brookings, 2015. http://www.brookings.edu/blogs/techtank/posts/2015/01/13-blockchain-innovation-kaushal (accessed March 11, 2016).
6. House of Lords. House of Commons. Parliamentary Commission on Banking Standards. 'An Accident Waiting to Happen, The Failure of HBOS.' HL Paper 144 HC 705. Published by the House of Commons. London: The Stationery Office Limited, 2013. http://www.publications.parliament.uk/pa/jt201213/jtselect/jtpcbs/144/144.pdf

CHAPTER **4**

Underwriting

The process of underwriting is at the heart of the insurance contract. The role of insurance underwriters is to consider the nature and frequency of risks which might attach to a particular prospective customer, and then calculate terms which will form the basis of the insurance cover. The dominant purpose of the underwriting process is to ensure that an insurer carries a book of business which is both profitable and commensurate with the insurer's own risk appetite.

An insurance underwriter is a highly skilled individual working closely with other members of the team such as risk managers and actuaries. Most underwriters focus on one of five areas of business:

- General insurance which covers household, pet, motor, travel.
- Life insurance/assurance which covers illness, injury, death.
- Commercial insurance which covers businesses and companies.
- Reinsurance where part of the risk is placed with another insurer.
- Specialist lines, such as aviation, terrorism and marine.

Results for establishing the right premium come from a combination of actuarial analytics, experience and judgment. It might reasonably be argued that underwriting is one of the most analytical functions within an insurance organization and that this department needs to be at the cutting edge of the Big Data discussion.

For an insurer to properly and consistently assess the risk, insurance companies usually develop underwriting guidelines. For example, in a proposal for life cover, certain specific information is required dependent on the applicant's age. An individual in the US aged 30 applying for $500,000 of cover would generally need to provide an application form, some form of paramedical examination and a blood profile to include the following tests – glucose, SGPT, GGTP, SGOT, urinalysis, HIV and others. To properly interpret this information and results, the underwriter needs some form of basic knowledge of the medical field and to understand the significance of abnormal test results. Additionally, or alternatively, the underwriter may also have access to skilled medical help to assist in interpreting the information and gaining greater insight into issues of mortality.

In the insurance of property, underwriters also have access to other suitably qualified professionals in the different relevant fields such as engineers and architects in the commercial insurance business, reports from third parties like mapping agencies, and other appropriate specialists plus the results of physical and other on-site experts. All these combine to determine an accurate risk assessment in accordance with the guidelines of the insurer themselves.[1]

4.1   UNDERWRITING AND BIG DATA

The essence of the use of Big Data and analytics within the insurance underwriting function is to provide the underwriter with greater visibility of the potential risks on which to base their assessment of exposure and price. It does not automatically follow that an underwriter will be able to make better decisions with more information – the information has to be relevant, reasonably accurate and appropriate. One fundamental aspect of insurance is that it is an industry which is not based on certainty but rather on probability. By this we mean the probability of an event which may or may not happen, the probability of certain costs or consequences arising and the vulnerability of a property or person to the effect of that event. Insurers limit their exposure through the wording of the insurance contact but also by forcing the policyholder to take certain mitigating actions. For example in a commercial environment underwriters will want to ensure that the factory has a fully maintained water sprinkler system, or in a domestic situation that an intruder alarm is fitted.

Having access to all available information may not be the absolute key to prediction. Taleb's theory of 'black swans'[2] recognizes that major unforeseen events can happen which, with hindsight, might have been predictable. Major catastrophic loss can always occur but it is the intention of the underwriter to ensure that if the worst does happen, then appropriate protections are in place such as reinsurance arrangements. Even then, there may be legal issues to consider in the interpretation of the insurance contract in place. For example, in the case of the World Trade Center, for the purposes of insurance cover the courts needed to decide whether the 9/11 disaster was only one attack or two.

The dominant effect of the data and analytics era is to make the information more relevant so that insurers are underwriting to a more granular or personalized level. What this means is that professions, locations, age and gender will continue to serve as indicators, but more information will become available about the individual, and that this more detailed information will become the dominant decision driver. There are interesting moral issues to consider. In their paper 'Social Justice and the Future of Flood Insurance'[3] the Joseph Rowntree Trust comment on the fact that there are two contrasting types of insurance emerging:

- *Individualist, risk-sensitive* insurance provided through a market in which individuals' payments are proportional to their level of risk.
- *Solidaristic, risk-insensitive* insurance in which those at lower risk contribute to the support of those at higher risk.

It is Rowntree's view that the UK for example is moving towards the former where insurance is being rated at an individual level whereas other countries are moving towards the latter. This is probably a generalization and arguably one which is incorrect as the spread of 'user-based-insurance' (UBI) becomes more dominant in North America and Western Europe. Even so-called 'emerging markets' such as China are looking at UBI with increasing interest.

The UK-based Chartered Institute of Insurance (CII) also comments on the 'social benefit of insurance' in which they say that insurance:[4]

- 'Efficiently protects the public through innovative risk management techniques.
- Frees up businesses and professionals from everyday risks and encouraging innovation and competition.
- Relieves the burden from the state and providing comfort to individuals by providing safe, effective and affordable pension savings, (and) protection . . .'

The use of individualist, risk-sensitive and more granular underwriting does not appear to be at odds with the CII's view on the social benefit of insurance. Insurers are not in business to lose money – they never have been – and pricing a policy relative to risk is not unreasonable. In fact, this approach has been in existence since marine insurance started in the 17th century when different ships were rated according to their cargo, size and ownership.

As a corollary to the issue of the use of data at a granular level and whether it is correct or not to consider someone or something uninsurable is the issue of the ethical use of data. In their article 'What's Up with Big Data Ethics'[5] (Forbes magazine, March 28, 2014) Jonathan King (and others) provide a reminder of the ethical issues surrounding the use of data covering topics such as 'privacy, confidentiality, transparency and identity.' They suggest that Big Data is more than smart algorithms but is about 'money and power' relating to the profitability of the insurance carrier – and perhaps going forward, also to other related organizations which might become aligned to those insurers.

Whilst the article refers to the legal obligations which attach, organizations must give evidence of their trustworthiness by demonstrating transparency, honesty and confidentiality. The underwriting challenge may prove to be that although information is available to an underwriter, they may be precluded from using it. As insurers depend on underwriting guidelines to set the standards and ensure consistency, then it is only a matter of time before these guidelines will need to recognize the ethical position, and to draw lines which the underwriter may not cross in the search for better and more granular information.

To some degree these ethical guidelines may not be optional but rather might be enshrined in legislation. At the time of writing, the US-based National Association of Insurance Commissioners (NAIC) Casualty Actuarial and Statistical Task Force is looking in more detail at the question of rate calculations, and the topic of so-called 'price optimization' where rates are flexed dependent on matters not directly related to the physical risk, but rather related to 'elasticity of demand.' In other words, underwriters might consider the pricing of a risk, i.e., the premium, as being linked to the policyholder's propensity or need to buy, or to change insurer. Since December 2014, Maryland, Florida, Ohio and California have placed insurers on notice that they will not agree rate filings that use such a practice. 'Rate filings' are the process by which a State reviews insurance policy forms and their accompanying rates to ensure that consumers receive the protections and benefits required under local State law. The majority of filings fall into the categories of life, annuities, health, personal auto, homeowners and workers' compensation.

As underwriters come to terms with the Big Data and analytical environment, it is worth considering the additional information which might come into their hands, and the consequences (Table 4.1).

TABLE 4.1   Typical data available to underwriters

	Structured	**Unstructured**
External	Geolocation data	Competitive insights
	Government data	Analyst reports
	Research reports	Weather data
	Demographic profiling	Traffic data
Internal	Policy data	Policy documents
	Claims data	Emails
	Payment information	Proposals
	Customer data	Medical reports

4.2   UNDERWRITING FOR SPECIALIST LINES

There is a temptation to consider that analytics is for the 'volume' market, and to some degree that is true in so far as statistical analysis is usually based on the laws of big numbers. Notwithstanding, there are still important elements of the Big Data and Analytics agenda that apply to specialist lines, typically terrorism, High Net Worth, agriculture and transit, and these may apply more to the role of underwriter than perhaps to any other function in the specialist insurer segment (Table 4.2).

TABLE 4.2   Typical use cases for Big Data in specialist lines

Agriculture	■ Remote monitoring of crop damage ■ Microinsurance based on historic crop analysis ■ Claims paid based on remote weather monitoring – without site inspection ■ Risk management by crop, for each plot of land
Marine	■ Physical cargo monitoring ■ Pirate activity monitoring – use of satellites to track anomalies such as lost vessel signals ■ Product damage and consequent liability
Hostage	■ Hostage tracking devices ■ Network analytics connecting possible organizations involved ■ Political analytics – risk management
Cyber	■ Use of analytics to identify hidden patterns and unusual correlations
High Net Worth	■ Use of nano-technology to track high value artifacts ■ Improved profiling of customer base ■ Enhanced private risk services

4.3 TELEMATICS AND USER-BASED INSURANCE AS AN UNDERWRITING TOOL

Since 2010, the use of telematics in auto insurance has grown and it is no longer seen as a niche underwriting product for hazardous drivers such as the young, whose premiums are prohibitive, but rather as a mainstream alternative to 'normal' types of cover. The term extends to cover not only the black box technology but also the collection of data, its storage, analysis and ultimately how that translates into actionable insight about the risk relating to any particular driver, in a specific place and time and in a particular vehicle.

All this represents a genuine evolution in the pricing of risk which traditionally has taken 'class variables' as an indicator of risk or 'proxy,' whereby behaviors provide a much greater insight into risk. Historically insurers have tried to reflect behavior by reviewing accident history, no-claims bonuses and even in some early cases the distance which has been driven. This has evolved beyond 'pay as you drive' to 'pay how you drive.'

Other typical indicators might include:[6]

- How you drive
- When you drive
- What you drive
- What color is your car
- Where you drive to
- What else you drive.

Telematics is an example of the use of integrated technology at its best. The topic itself goes beyond technology but also extends to issues of culture, pricing, data ownership and risk management. Used effectively it also potentially allows insurers to move from a reactive mode where they are examining behavior and characteristics and retrospectively pricing the risk, to a potential position to be able to influence personal actions and in doing so to be *proactive*. One step towards this is the availability of data to the policyholder usually viewed through a portal. The consequence of this is the increased emergence of insurers as 'risk managers' rather than risk evaluators.

The access by underwriters to more data provides underwriters with considerable flexibility and control in setting premiums. The advent of systems which provide more data is likely to give underwriters considerably more insight. At the moment insurance underwriters seem only just to be coming to terms with their new-found capabilities. They seem in many situations to be viewing telematics (according to one recent UK job advertisement) as simply a new tool for collecting data, and from this to think about 'managing business volumes, gaining insight into profitability, product structure and rating, together with product development and distribution.' In effect the particular role appears to be as much about telematics product development as about better underwriting. Other insurers seem to view the role as some form of 'underwriting data scientist' which reinforces the point that data and analytics appear to be not only influencing existing professions and job roles but also creating new hybrid roles.

What becomes clear from the additional data available is that underwriters have access to much more data than before, but the real test is what they choose to do with it. It is obvious that they will benefit from greater segmentation and will be able to apply more dynamic pricing. This will also help with their product and segmentation 'mix' and ultimately their 'go to market' strategy. Underwriters can also improve the way that they apply discount rates and other incentives dependent on market conditions and the competitive landscape. Because of these variables and the differing risk appetite between insurers, premium rates can increasingly vary significantly between insurers for the same type of cover.

In many cases, current pricing for insurers seems to be restricted to retrospective review of telematics data, perhaps annually or at 90-day intervals. Discounts are then offered against the base rate and some insurers alternatively offer 'free miles' of cover rather than a financial discount.

As the use of telematics grows and the first signs of user-based insurance are emerging in other business areas, the indications are that the proverbial UBI 'genie' is out of the bottle as far as this approach is concerned. What has been demonstrated is that the technology has mainly proved to be robust, and that whilst some challenges might still exist it will be possible to resolve them. The growth in use suggests that, at least for some customers, this is an attractive proposition which will apply not only to the younger driver but also to the older driver or those who do less mileage. Experts anticipate significant continued impact on products and pricing.

It is clear that there is more development yet to happen in this space. If underwriting is ultimately to be at an individual, granular level then insurers will also need to think about how this extends to multicar policies, where a 'second' car is only used on a very occasional basis.

4.4 UNDERWRITING FOR FRAUD AVOIDANCE

With insurers increasingly using analytics at the point of claim to root out fraudulent claimants who are either opportunistic or organized, there is a natural tendency to consider whether these same tools can be used earlier in the insurance value chain process. At the point of claim the decision to investigate will generally depend on a number of factors, usually a combination of the event circumstances, the timing of the incident, the claims history of the policyholder and often also the demographics of the immediate environment.

As insurers look forward there may be increasing pressure on the current or prospective policyholder to allow the insurer to have access to all available information, much as a mortgage lender is entitled to check credit details before making a final decision on providing a loan. In fact, one insurer has recently started to consider creditworthiness as a key element of the underwriting process. The context of this is unclear and has stimulated some debate, it being argued that an individual's ability to pay a bill on time has nothing to do with their behavior behind the steering wheel. A contrary argument might be that the way an individual manages their financial affairs could be an indicator of their approach to personal risk and as such is a valid albeit slightly controversial metric.

Predicting fraud at inception opens up the possibility of an insurer 'pricing out' a prospective or existing customer based on what the policyholder 'might' do, rather than what they have done. There is nothing strange in this, in the same way that an underwriter might want to consider, for example, the potential for a teenager to have a crash in a high-powered sports car. In the case of predicting fraud, the underwriter not only anticipates the possibility of a fraudulent claim at some time in the future but also anticipates potential criminal behavior on the part of the prospective policyholder.

Naturally, were an underwriter to openly decline to provide cover on the basis of anticipated fraud, this would be a serious issue. A policyholder who has cover declined by an insurer is obliged to disclose this to other insurers when seeking new cover, as this is a question usually explicitly asked by the insurer at the time of proposal. For the potentially fraudulent policyholder to deliberately mislead is a matter of non-disclosure which also entitles the insurer to void the policy.

At the time of proposal, an insurer is not obliged to give any reason why cover is not offered but in the absence of any obvious material cause for declining insurance, the reason may be implicit. At what point will a potential customer be entitled to see the data on which they are being penalized? Will they understand it? Similarly, were a customer to discover that the offer made to them by an insurer at renewal or inception was deliberately uncompetitive, would they have a cause of action and if so what might that action be? Are there potential issues of discrimination to be considered? Will regulators view this as a matter of treating the customer unfairly or some other breach of consumer regulation?

4.5 ANALYTICS AND BUILDING INFORMATION MANAGEMENT (BIM)

If the insurance industry has to date focused on analytics relating to finance, risk and the customer then it will soon need to prepare itself for the next wave of information, that which originates from Building Information Modeling (sometimes also termed 'Building Information Management') but more commonly known as 'BIM.'

Originating in the USA, specifically in the US Army Corp of Engineers ('USACE'), the main intention of BIM is to provide an accurate record of data relating to the construction and maintenance of new buildings.[7] Already used in many USACE projects and missions, it is described as 'Smart 3-D,' differentiating it from the 3-D 'autocad' drawing capabilities already used by many architects. One of the criticisms of BIM is that whilst it provides a digital plan of the proposed construction, it is not always representative of the 'as-constructed' version due to construction changes and general modifications where records have not adequately been captured.

There is a useful (although slightly tenuous) comparison between BIM and the Solvency II program. Solvency II was intended to be a principle-based approach to the management of risk capital. As insurers increasingly asked questions of the regulators due to the uncertainty of the requirement, it became necessary to provide more detail to a point where the so-called Red Book became especially overcomplicated. The impact of this was to add cost and complexity. The same issue may potentially occur with BIM where the general principles of digitalization may well be overtaken by the degree of detail called for by practitioners.

Increasingly, major engineers and consultants are adopting the BIM methodology, specifically the PAS 1192 suite of information. PAS 1192 is the UK specification for information management for the capital/delivery phase of construction projects using building information modeling. One of BIM's strongest evangelists, Anne Kemp, a Fellow and Director at Atkins Engineering Consultancy, encourages her colleagues to look for the data points at each part of the construction process and capture information accordingly, a process which she describes as the 'digital plan of work.'

In reality, BIM has been relatively slow to take on in Europe but the decision by the UK Government to enforce the adoption of BIM in the construction of public buildings from 2016 will create an additional catalyst for change. The UK Government Strategy is to encourage 'fully collaborative 3-D BIM with all project and asset information, documentation and data being electronic.' The aim is for the UK Government to drive improvements in cost, value and carbon performance through the use of open sharable asset information.[8]

Whilst for many this will be viewed as another layer of bureaucracy, and for engineers it might be viewed as an unnecessary evil, it is nevertheless an interesting and important step in the digitalization of the Built Environment, and will be of enormous value to insurance underwriters. Skeptics who view this with suspicion must take into account the rapid development of the Internet of Things ('IoT'), and the ability to increase the amount of data through an increase in the number of devices and from this gain meaningful information. One useful definition of a device or transmitter contributing to the IoT is 'A thing, in the context of the Internet of Things (which) is an entity or physical object that has a unique identifier, an embedded system and the ability to transfer data over a network.'[9] Over the past five years, the speed of connection has increased by 200 times, the number of machines connected to each other by 300 times and the price of remote devices collecting information has fallen by 80%.

If BIM is likely to take a decade to embed itself in public buildings in the UK and beyond, and provide meaningful information from any data, then how long will it take to embed into commercial and residential properties? Changes often occur more quickly where they are least expected, or sometimes more slowly when there appears to be an absolute certainty of change. The speed and degree of engagement of the construction industry will be critical to change. It is only a matter of time before new construction reaches a 'tipping point' where all new buildings and their contents are digitized.

This BIM information naturally will be in a structured form but it will become more valuable as it is combined with unstructured information, typically climate conditions, weather and building usage such as customer footfall (for example in a retail scenario). Publicly funded building construction has the potential to provide the necessary proof of technology which leads into the digitalization of all new and, eventually, all existing buildings.

The absolute impact on insurers and underwriters is difficult to gauge at the present time. Clearly additional information will become increasingly available. This will help not only in underwriting decisions by providing greater levels of granularity but also in the claims process where investigations into policy conditions and warranties will perhaps also become more automated. BIM will also be one of the catalysts for the 'connected (or "Smart") building.'

The use of information collected through multiple data points will also help insurers gain a better understanding regarding building usage, behavior of visitors, physical conditions within the perimeter (and perhaps also in the surroundings), comparison with other similar buildings, and all in the context of codes and regulations. This will all lead to deeper insight and granularity regarding classes of risk. BIM when coupled with other data will also provide better insight with regards to compliance with warranties and policy conditions, and may even trigger alerts to building owners and managers that they are in breach of coverage requirements. Perhaps the use of BIM will also be another catalyst in the transformation of insurers from 'compensators' to 'risk managers.'

NOTES

1. Macedo, Lionel. 'The Role of the Underwriter in Insurance.' Primer series on Insurance, Issue 8. Published by The World Bank, 2009.
2. Taleb, Nassim Nicholas. 'The Black Swan: The Impact of the Highly Improbable.' *The New York Times.* April 22, 2007.

3. Joseph Rowntree Trust. 'Social Justice and the Future of Flood Insurance.' Published by Joseph Rowntree Trust, 2012. http://www.jrf.org.uk/sites/files/jrf/vulnerable-households-flood-insurance-summary.pdf (accessed February 12, 2016).

4. Chartered Insurance Institute. 'The Social Value of Insurance.' Posted February 26, 2015. Politics Home. https://www.politicshome.com/document/press-release/chartered-insurance-institute/social-value-insurance (accessed November 29, 2015)

5. King, Jonathan H. and Richards, Neil M. 'What's Up with Big Data Ethics.' *Forbes* magazine March 28, 2014. http://www.forbes.com/sites/oreillymedia/2014/03/28/whats-up-with-big-data-ethics/#7c0fa4aa2964 (accessed March 12, 2016).

6. Tindall, John. 'Telematics Movement in Behavioural Underwriting and Pricing.' Actuaries Institute. Presented May 20–21, 2013. Sydney, Australia. http://www.actuaries.asn.au/Library/Events/SUM/2013/8c-Tindall.pdf (accessed November 20, 2015).

7. Goodspeed, Rachel V. 'USACE introduces Building Information Modeling into Europe District projects.' Published www.army.mil., 2009. http://www.army.mil/article/29933/ (accessed March 12, 2016).

8 Department for Business, Innovation and Skills. 'Building Information Modelling.' URN 12/1327 Published by HM Government. London, 2012.

9. Techtarget. 'Essential Guide.' http://whatis.techtarget.com/definition/thing-in-the-Internet-of-Things (accessed March 12, 2016).

CHAPTER 5

Claims and the 'Moment of Truth'

For the customer, the most critical part of their relationship with their insurer is at the point of making a claim. Insurance is, after all, a promise to pay a claim subject to agreed terms and conditions, and legally endorsed by a contract. The way that the claim is handled affects the customer's propensity to buy at renewal, to purchase additional products and to recommend an insurer to a friend or neighbor. With customer advocacy representing a major part of the decision to buy, the claims experience becomes a critical part of the mix.

For an insurer, the situation may be somewhat different. Claims expenditure often represents the largest or second largest element of an insurer's expenditure (the other being reinsurance costs). Described as the 'loss ratio,' claims expenditure is generally expressed as the total losses incurred (paid and reserved) in claims, plus claims management (adjustment) expenses divided by the total premiums earned. In other words, if an insurer pays out £60 for every £100 earned in premium, then the loss ratio is 60%. Commonly the loss ratio will range from 50% to 70% although much depends on the mix of business, external conditions (e.g. weather) and the quality of the management team.

Claims savings go directly to the bottom line so there is considerable pressure on the claims team to avoid claims 'leakage,' an expression used to describe payments beyond the strict obligation of the policy. These claim savings, if pursued rigorously, may however have an adverse effect on the customer's experience so there is a degree of balancing that needs to be done.

5.1 'INDEMNITY' AND THE CONTRACTUAL ENTITLEMENT

The best starting point in considering the claims process in property insurance is to recognize the basic principle of 'indemnity,' that is, to put the policyholder back in the position they were in before the 'insured event' (as specified under the policy) took place. That event may have been a storm, flood, fire or whatever is specified in the contract wording (the policy wording defines which specific events are covered, with the exception of an 'all-risks' policy which covers everything other than what is excluded). The principle of indemnity is of long standing in the insurance industry. One of the leading legal cases on this topic is *Castellaine v Preston*

(1883) where it was held that insurance in a fire or marine policy is 'a contract of indemnity, and of indemnity only, and this contract means that the assured (insured) in case of a loss against which the policy has been made, shall be fully indemnified but shall be never more than fully indemnified.'[1]

Strictly speaking the policyholder is only entitled to have the status quo restored so wear and tear should be taken into account in the claims settlement. However, allowance can be made within the insurance cover provided to give 'new for old' cover, usually known as 'reinstatement' provided that there is no 'betterment,' that is to say, no improvement in the specification or quality of the repair/replacement.

The policyholder is not obliged to have their damaged property repaired or replaced but can also opt to take a financial settlement which reflects the 'loss of value' of their damaged goods. This alone can be contentious as 'value' may mean different things to different people and there can often be scope for disagreement. These disagreements can occur in many types of insurance, from auto to personal or commercial property, to bodily injury. In an auto write-off for example, the value may be the value that the (undamaged) car might have been sold for, as opposed to the amount which it was purchased for. In some cases, insurers also sell a form of 'gap cover' which meets the difference. A degree of compromise may be needed to achieve an amicable agreement. Intrinsic or emotional value is not a concern for insurers, although if matters deteriorate to such a degree that recompense needs to be awarded by the courts then an amount may be awarded by them for 'distress and inconvenience.' Even so, amounts awarded in that category often fall below the injured party's expectation.

It is against this background of relative uncertainty coupled with increasing propensity for individual or organized opportunism, that the topic of fraud rears its ugly head.

5.2   CLAIMS FRAUD

It is in the nature of human psychology that a proportion of the populace seeks more than their due entitlement assuming that they have any entitlement whatsoever. This principle is amply demonstrated in the case of insurance claims fraud.

It is suggested anecdotally that, in a room of ten people, two of them are likely to commit fraud and a further three of them are likely to endorse such activity. This is of course a generalization but the fact remains that insurers believe that for every £100 paid in claims, as much as £20 paid out is due to fraudulent activity, and in the UK at least, this adds an additional £50 to the cost of every annual premium.[2]

Fraud tends to come in two distinct forms:

■ Opportunistic, usually by an individual
■ Systematic or organized.

There is a third category which is not commonly considered, which might be called 'supplier opportunism' or supply chain 'leakage.' This occurs where a supplier working for an insurer, policyholder or intermediary optimizes the cost of work done either by overpricing, over scoping or using inferior materials. The topic of supplier management will be considered elsewhere but most probably relates indirectly to the rigid procurement policies adopted by many insurers. This has resulted in over-zealous unit rate reductions, low switching costs and ultimately an absence of a sustained relationship between insurer and vendor.

The UK Crime and Fraud Prevention Bureau annual report of 2013 indicates a total cost of fraud of £2.1 billion annually and their earlier reports suggest that there are four main types of misrepresentation:

- Completely false claims (12%)
- Deliberately misrepresenting the circumstances of the event (32%)
- Inflated loss value (39%)
- Claiming from multiple insurers (3%)
- Others (14%).

The UK Insurance Act 2015 gives additional entitlement to insurers where fraud is proven. There are three consequences:

1. That the insurer is not liable to pay the claim;
2. The insurer is entitled to recover sums from the insured already paid out on the claim;
3. That the policy may be terminated by notice from the date of the act which constitutes the fraud.

5.2.1 Opportunistic Fraud

For some individuals, insurance is viewed not as a protection but rather as an entitlement. They take the view that after having made payments over a number of years, an entitlement exists to repayment in some fashion from their insurer. Others view insurers as an easy source of funding perhaps to repay the cost of a holiday leading to spurious claims for the loss of a camera or theft of jewelry.

It is because of this that insurers have traditionally identified fraud 'triggers' which are indicative of fraudulent behavior. Typically, these triggers might include:

- Claims made just before renewal
- Claims made just after inception
- Claims arising from short-term policies often relating to travel.

Insurers are naturally reluctant to disclose all these triggers as it will aid the fraudulent policyholder, and it is in the spirit of that approach that this publication has also been appropriately discreet.

5.2.1.1 Analytics in Opportunistic Fraud

One of the main tools in fighting fraud is the use of predictive analytics whereby the 'triggers' identified by insurers as being typical of fraudulent behavior are applied to the claims notification process. If an appropriate 'red flag' occurs then the claim can be investigated by experts.

The plus side of this approach is that where these red flags do not occur, then the claim can be 'fast-tracked' to settlement. This improves the speed of the process, often reduces cost (there being a correlation between duration of the claim and the likely total cost) and importantly enhances the customer experience.

Predictive analytics is in effect a probabilistic approach – does this indicator suggest that 'fraud is possible'? Individual indicators are relative and simply summing up a series of indicators may give what is, in effect, a 'false positive.' That is to say, the circumstances suggest that a claim may be fraudulent when it is not. By wrongly identifying a claim as fraudulent, this usually results in the claim being passed to an investigator who may already have a heavy workload and this may create a bottleneck in the system. Even worse, it suggests to the policyholder that they are being treated like a criminal when in fact they are not.

Whilst insurers therefore may use fraud analytics as part of the detection process, arguably one of the main benefits is in the cost saving attached to rapid handling of non-fraud claims. It is unlikely that insurers would feel entirely confident in rejecting a claim based on analytics alone without some human intervention, even if this only comprises a telephone call to advise the policyholder that (for example) weather records show that storm conditions did not prevail on the date of the claim and inviting them to withdraw the claim.

5.2.2 Organized Fraud

Eighty percent or more of fraudulent insurance activity is due to organized or systematic fraud. Both the scale and the complexity of the problem lend themselves to analytical solutions. Such was the nature of fraud for insurers in the later 1980s and 1990s that a trend emerged for insurers to recruit ex-policemen, often retired, to investigate 'doubtful' claims. The word 'doubtful' is used deliberately in that issues of disclosure meant that insurers were (and remain) reluctant to call a claim fraudulent until the burden of proof has been established.

Based on Association of British Insurers figures, of the £2.1 billion of insurance fraud activity annually (2015 figures), this is allocated as follows:

- £1.7 billion as 'hidden fraud loss,' i.e., undetected
- £392 million as 'cash for crash'
- £39 million in identified fraud.

Nowadays organized fraud has taken on an entirely new perspective, especially (but not confined to) auto incidents. Staged accidents, 'cash for crash' and claims for 'whiplash' are prevalent especially as injury by whiplash is difficult to prove. The impact of telematics analytics is increasingly helpful in identifying whether the circumstances of an incident were sufficient to cause such an injury, but it is early days yet in that process.

Fraudulent insurance activity is not confined to auto incidents but potentially occurs in many scenarios including the deliberate fire-raising (or arson) of commercial premises where profits are down, or there are other adverse and doubtful issues arising. Increasingly insurers are seeing the same tools used by the police services in the analysis and investigation of organized crime. Network analytics and the use of new techniques to better understand the relationships between individuals and companies are used increasingly.

Even so, one of the main issues is that all that these analytics provide is an indicator rather than any degree of certainty. There is still a need for the foot-soldier investigator to carry out a detailed investigation and this inevitability builds in a delay. Effective investigation of fraud is likely to be an ongoing problem for the foreseeable future although improved use of analytics will help in terms of greater focus and fraud prevention.

5.2.2.1 Organized Fraud Detection through Network Analytics

With 80% of fraudulent activity being of an organized nature and often of higher value, this is naturally of particular interest to insurers. With many insurance fraud investigators coming from the ranks of the police service, it has been inevitable that techniques used in criminal investigations have found their way into the insurance sector, especially the use of network analytics, as illustrated in Figure 5.1.

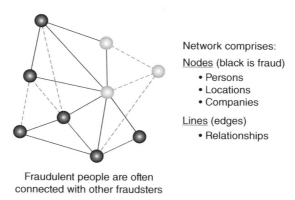

Network comprises:

<u>Nodes</u> (black is fraud)
- Persons
- Locations
- Companies

<u>Lines</u> (edges)
- Relationships

Fraudulent people are often
connected with other fraudsters

FIGURE 5.1   Fraud detection and network analytics

Network analytics helps insurers track between apparently disparate individuals or groups and identify linkages between them. Although it has always been possible to manually draw relationships onto a whiteboard, the modern reality is that often the relationships are too diverse and complex to bear manual tracking. Nowadays sophisticated software allows the user to draft elements of data onto a virtual 'palette' which looks like a drawing board on the workstation screen, and then to create links to other pieces of evidence. These systems allow new relationships to be explored, old ones perhaps down-selected, and to reflect changes when new evidence comes to light. Not only can this technology be used to identify linkage between parties, such as the flow of correspondence or money but it is even admissible as a tool in the courtroom.

Insurers should not underestimate the potential for organized fraud. It was discovered that vehicles damaged as a result of Hurricane Sandy on the East Coast of the US in 2012, and which were written off as total losses, were finding their way to the Baltics and Eastern Europe. Local insurers there were faced with dealing with exactly the same cars (with identity details removed) which had been newly burned out (to a total loss) in a fire.

5.2.2.2   Voice Analytics in the Claims Fraud Process

Another form of analysis is voice analytics which comprises a type of unstructured data. One fraud trigger is when the claimant becomes inappropriately nervous or aggressive during an interview process. This in itself is a relatively weak trigger as the nervousness might be due to a number of factors and aggression may be a reflection of frustration at delay. A skilled claims handler will often have the interpersonal skills to ensure the claimant is put at ease.

The use of voice or speech analytics can help insurers identify key trends or indicators which can be used to better understand customer sentiment, issues or operator training needs. In reality, real time analysis of voice is at an early stage as far as insurers are concerned. Some insurers are at the stage of transferring voice to text, and then analyzing (or 'mining') the text. Increasingly voice analytics APIs ('application programming interfaces') known also as 'software-to-software interfaces' are being recognized as an essential tool.

Currently the main use of voice analytics in other industries tends to be in respect of performance management of telephone call handlers, typically by identifying the amount of speech/non-speech, call hold times or periods of silence. The use of speech analytics also goes beyond matters of fraud and can help insurers and other organizations gain a better understanding of cost drivers, trends, market opportunities and strengths (or weaknesses) of particular product offerings.

The potential for improvement in this area is significant. The ability to incorporate voice, both in terms of tone and also content, into real time analytics and then to drive what is described as the 'next best action' would represent a step change in the way that agent/customer discussions are managed. That capability may be some way off yet especially in the mainstream management of claims fraud. The potential already exists for organizations to effectively search through voice or audio files and to automatically identify key parts of the dialogue, avoiding the need for manual searching.

5.2.2.3   Fraud Analytics at Inception

Another form of fraud is underwriting fraud. One key principle of insurance is that of utmost good faith, that is to say, at the point of purchase the policyholder gives an accurate description of themselves. It is on that basis that the insurer accurately gauges the risk. Misrepresentation therefore is, in effect, fraudulent behavior and if discovered would allow the insurer to void the policy from the start or 'ab initio.' Insurers would also therefore be entitled to avoid any claim subsequently made.

In its broadest sense, misrepresentation occurs when wrongful information is given which might have influenced the underwriter to offer different terms or perhaps even decline to offer insurance. Typical types of misrepresentation might include wrongful description of the property use, number of previous claims, who is the primary driver of a vehicle, or the profession of the individual.

Much of this information is obtained by the underwriter through the proposal form although there is an increasing tendency to reduce the size of the proposal form and ask 'simpler' questions. Historically the obligation has been on the policyholder to disclose relevant information but the burden has increasingly shifted to the insurer.

Technology already exists whereby the insurer can track changes by a prospective policyholder in an online proposal to see what changes have been made (for example to the described profession) in an attempt to manipulate premiums to the customer's advantage. Going beyond this, there are even some publically available websites which offer a service by suggesting what is a 'better' (i.e., lower premium) job to use as a description of profession, relative to the type of work an individual actually does.

In the era of Big Data, it is likely that much (although probably not yet all) of the information which an underwriter might need is already in the public domain, or could be made available with the customer's permission. Some questions in the proposal form such as whether a property has previously flooded start to become obsolete as insurers increasingly have access to location analytics which tell whether a property is in a location prone to flooding or not.

5.3   PROPERTY REPAIRS AND SUPPLY CHAIN MANAGEMENT

Originally, one of the key driving forces behind the use of supply chain management in the claims process was that of better fraud management. In this context the 'supply chain' comprises builders, repairers, restorers, replacement goods providers and any other white or brown goods vendor who provides a service to insurers by directly repairing or replacing damaged buildings or contents. The other major driving force was that of the scale benefit of purchasing where bulk buying from fewer suppliers allowed better deals to be struck.

Two decades ago in the UK, insurers would deal with property claims by inviting the policyholder to provide usually three estimates with insurers generally allowing repairs to proceed on the basis of the lowest estimate. In the days before 'word processing' it was often the case that the three estimates would be provided by the same supplier albeit under different letterheads. To add to this, payment processes by insurers were so poor that they resulted in the supplier asking if this was 'an insurance job,' in which case the cost would be inflated by 20% or more.

Even in this environment, fraud was recognized by insurers as a problem. The nature of the fraud and the tools used to identify this behavior were somewhat more rudimentary. For example, forensic analysis of 'typefaces' on individual estimates was compared to identify similarities and to see whether the allegedly different documents were created on the same typewriter. Ink tests were also used as well as other techniques straight out of the police forensic laboratory. In this rather less structured environment, there was always a risk of the potential for corruption between the suppliers and some of the less scrupulous claims inspectors and other third-party intermediaries, although on the whole the very great majority of transactions were probably both honest and above board.

Partly to regain control over this major issue of claims leakage, insurers increasingly took direct control of the repair process. It was quickly realized that this had the added bonus of not only providing an additional service to the customer but also potentially creating a competitive differentiator.

Insurers also realized that there were economies of scale to be obtained by directing larger volumes of work to a smaller number of suppliers. Not only did this allow scale benefit in cost but also greater control over the suppliers themselves who were increasingly managed by supply chain professionals. These supply chain experts are also known as 'category managers.' Beyond this, insurers increasingly directed their suppliers to where they would get their materials – a process known as 'second level supply management.' Procurement and supply chain management became part of the core competences of the claims department. Suppliers were 'sourced' using advanced category procurement concepts already well established in other sectors such as retail.

As part of the procurement process insurers were also entitled through RFI ('Request for Information') processes to gain a very deep understanding of a supplier's client base, their costs, overheads, systems, strengths and weaknesses. In the negotiation process following the RFI/RFP ('Request for Pricing'), insurers often had a clear idea of the optimal price point of the supplier. Advanced procurement techniques initially driven by the problem of fraud management had in effect moved purchasing *power* from the supplier to the insurer.

One added benefit of rationalization of the supply base was to allow insurers to insist on performance management information being provided in a specific format so that it could be incorporated into much broader databases. With such a deep level of insight, insurers increasingly recognized that they could use this insight to identify where value was added in the claims process and where unnecessary, i.e. avoidable, costs were being incurred. Gaining greater insight into the customer became increasingly important, leading to the identification of an 'emotional rollercoaster' (Figure 5.2). This graphically represented how a claimant reacted to the discovery of the loss, the point of notification, the investigation and eventual fulfillment (or resolution) of the claim. By tracking the expectations of a customer at the time

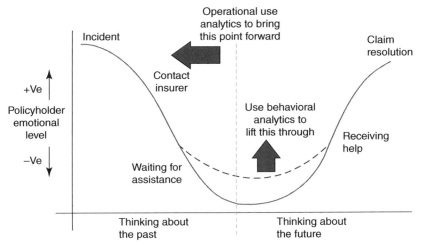

FIGURE 5.2   Customer's emotional rollercoaster

of the claim and what was needed to best resolve those expectations, it became possible to create a much more customer-facing best practice.

Comparing these ideas of twenty years ago to today's potential analytical practices, it might be argued that perhaps the same ideas remain very much in place. Insurers are increasingly thinking about the use of analytics to understand customer behavior at the time of purchase. This can relatively easily be taken to extend the understanding and behaviors of the customer at the point of claim, albeit that the tools available and insight derived are likely to be at a higher level.

As a result, this additional data allows new best practices for claims management to emerge. It also reinforces the point that insight and analytics are not the destination in these considerations but rather are key enablers in optimizing processes and adding value.

The move towards a more rigorous supply management and procurement process had some unfortunate side effects. Loyalty between the insurer and supplier was diminished. Suppliers recognized that any contract was only valuable for a short period (sometimes no longer than the notice period of the contract), that the contract was likely to be re-procured after a couple of years, and there was a reasonable chance that they would be replaced by other keener competitors. The switching costs of insurers between suppliers were generally low so there was little if any 'lock-in.' Where suppliers sought greater technological integration with insurers, this was generally resisted.

The overall consequence was that some suppliers sought to optimize the relationship with the insurer by overpricing, over scoping and underperforming. This did not occur at the corporate level which would strenuously deny such practices and work hard to prevent them but more often occurred at operative, subcontractor and sub-subcontractor level. Supervisors who were remunerated based on the productivity and profitability of directly employed tradesmen or subcontractors had little if any incentive to be accurate. This is 'generously' sometimes known as supplier opportunism but in reality it is also a form of fraudulent behavior.

As part of the procurement process, insurers insisted on detailed capacity planning especially for surges of work such as major flooding. With no reassurance of workloads beyond the end of the contract, repairers increasingly looked to subcontractors, and those subcontractors themselves in turn looked to sub-sub-contractors. At the so-called 'moment of truth' when a claim was being made, the repair work was actually being done often by suppliers or small companies who had no regard for the brand values of the insurer. Even worse, these suppliers and small companies were at the very end of the payment food-chain and payment terms were less than attractive. It was not unheard of for a tradesman to threaten to walk off a job until overdue payment was made.

Under the terms of the contracts, many insurers also provided 'delegated authority' to the suppliers to make decisions on their behalf. The repairer (who seldom had insurance training) would decide what was covered under the claim and what was not. Some suggest that this approach was tantamount to leaving the child alone in the sweet shop. Others viewed it as a direct challenge to the claims inspector and loss adjuster industries.

In reality these problems simply mirrored what insurers might have learned with a little more research from the public sector. They had already developed supply chain methodologies to manage and repair public property such as social housing. The public sector had adopted a turn-key methodology for the management of property repairs using fewer repairers operating within framework agreements to deliver services within agreed cost and service parameters.

In these comparable operating models, the expressions 'consumers' and 'citizens' are interchangeable. Poor service in the public sector supply chain impacts on the confidence of citizens who in turn express dissatisfaction not by changing their provider (as they have no direct choice in the matter) but by complaining to (and sometimes voting out) their public representative.

Within the public sector in terms of property repairs – with the same damage issues directly analogous to the insurance sector, such as flooding, fire and vandalism, operatives within the supply chain equally understood the transient and temporary nature of their relationship with their client. Work would be invoiced which was not done, for example, not removing the radiator and not decorating behind it (despite being paid for it). Invoices were raised for replacement of light bulbs and of valves which were impossible to check afterwards. As the tradesmen were paid not by the hour but by the unit of work, they had every incentive to misdescribe or enhance the work item.

Furthermore, their team leaders or managers were equally keen to retain their most motivated staff, especially if the work completed by the tradesmen (or at least charged for) was directly linked to the team leader's own remuneration. Improvement works would also be discreetly done for inspectors and in the tradesmen's homes, or for private weekend work done by the tradesmen, with the materials unknowingly funded by the insurer or local authority. Even inspectors and team leaders could not be absolutely trusted. *'Quis custodiet ipsos custodes?'* is an expression found in the work of the Roman poet Juvenal from his *Satires* and is literally translated as 'Who will guard the guards themselves?'

As a result, a whole new subsector of the insurance industry emerged. Insurance supply chain audit retrospectively managed the supply chain by measurement and analysis of repair costs, performance and complaints. Penalties for poor performance and overpricing were punitive. Repairers which the insurer's audit team had discovered overpricing by say 5% on a sample check might find the same 5% 'adjustment' across their entire month's invoice.

In a further attempt to drive down costs, insurers also introduced what is known as 'second-stage' supply chain management. This comprised the striking up of deals for the provision of materials with which the repairer would do the work. This allowed insurers to categorize, for example, the amount of timber or paint used and make a deal with a national merchant to enable these materials to be supplied at a discount. However, the impact on the tradesman was that the chosen merchant was not always optimally placed for the repairer to collect the materials, and time would be lost 'queuing' for materials each morning, assuming the materials were even actually available on the day. Time lost queuing would lead to later starts on site, loss of productivity and in many cases unhappy customers and unhappy tradesmen.

Beyond this was the matter of multi-tasking tradesmen. That is to say, plumbers who decorated and tiled, and decorators who did plumbing and electrical work. It was critical that tradesmen were suitably qualified for potentially hazardous tasks but on a relatively small job requiring multiple skills, there were issues of economy of scale involved. Was it appropriate to encourage multi-tasking and complete the work in one visit, or have multiple visits and cause greater disruption? The adage 'the bitter taste of poor quality lasts longer than the disappointment of delay' was never truer.

And finally, there was the issue of payments. Cash flow is king in the construction industry. The system had created an inbuilt complexity which led to delayed and incorrect payments and repairers threatening to walk off site if payments were not made. Where tax was able to be recovered by a commercial policyholder (such as Value Added Tax or 'VAT' in the UK), this added a further complication in that the insurance payments were made net of tax. The matter of the excess or deductible also needed to be considered in claim settlement. The onus was placed on the repairer to recover this directly from the policyholder themselves, even if strictly speaking the policyholder was not in direct contract with the repairer.

In what was intended as a cost-saving exercise, the fraud avoidance problem created a whole new set of costly operational issues. Beyond this, the fact that insurers had chosen and directly 'scoped' the extent of repair and chosen the repairer placed obligations on the insurer where anything went wrong or if there was a disagreement regarding quality.

In the same way that insurers recognized an emotional rollercoaster in the claims process, there was also a very clear pattern which emerged in respect of unhappy customers who initially escalated their concerns from complaining, to seeking compensation, and then when things really deteriorated to actively penalizing the insurer for the insurer's failure to live up to their promise at the 'moment of truth.' In the worst cases insurers ended up paying well over the odds from time to time to keep a policyholder satisfied.

With insurers increasingly placing cost pressure on their supply chain which was a side effect of overcapacity in the supplier ecosystem and insurer environment, this also placed pressure on the profession of loss adjusting. The loss adjusting and third-party inspection industry had traditionally enjoyed substantial revenues from major weather events such as ground subsidence and flooding but these events and revenue streams were becoming less reliable and more uncertain. As a result, external loss adjusting businesses also moved increasingly into the area of property repair management, providing insurers with a one-stop shop but equally inviting questions and criticism regarding potential conflicts of interest. Loss adjusters also saw their ability to provide such services as a key competitive differentiator. With the mantra of the loss adjuster being one of impartiality, how might that position be possible (or even tenable) if the loss adjuster is both investigator *and* repairer?

Questions started to arise in respect of the degree of 'added value' that the loss adjuster actually contributed, especially if the repairer themselves was allowed to self-scope the repairs which were merely 'signed off' by the adjuster. These are old wounds, but are still valid questions to be considered. Already it is recognized that the whole topic of Big Data and Analytics has the potential to help create new business models and revolutionize existing ones.

Property repairs will continue as part of the insurance process but to what degree will the process be transformed in this new analytical environment?

Whilst some of the legacy issues potentially remain, the industry now has the chance to rethink the issue. The supplier and adjuster may be less likely to be entirely independent in the future and both will be part of the insurer's virtual ecosystem. This will mean the effective flow of information up and down the supply chain in a more transparent way than the market has previously enjoyed. Trust will have been replaced by technology and transparancy.

Effective supplier auditing will need to remain in some form but will place more emphasis on analytical insight, increasingly removing the risk of subjectivity in the process. One insurer even identified a correlation between where an auditor lived, and his/her relationship with the supplier themselves; too close, and the relationship was too intimate; too far away, and the visits were hurried and too infrequent.

How this translates into greater freedom for the policyholder is unclear. The idea of earlier 'cashing out' is attractive for the insurer who can close out the claim more quickly and with a higher degree of certainty, but may be of cold comfort to the policyholder. There are pros and cons. 'Cashing out' potentially provides the customer with more flexibility and even the potential ability to rebuild or repair for less money than insurers calculated. Placing even an excessive amount of money in the pocket of the policyholder may be a small price to insurers for shifting the operational burden. If it becomes difficult for the policyholder to find a tradesman, then isn't it the customer's problem and not the insurer's?

The property repair industry has traditionally looked to auto repairs to provide some form of template for the customer experience. Property repairs are much more complex by virtue of the degree of their variation, the location of repairs (which is invariably on-site) and maybe also the degree of emotional attachment of the policyholder in respect of their own home. Nevertheless, there is some learning to be taken from this. What actually might that learning be and how can it best be applied?

5.4 AUTO REPAIRS

Traditionally auto repairs have been more advanced than property repairs, with proprietary pricing solutions and more effective workflow emerging at an early stage. Over the past two decades the insurance industry has moved away from the customer being left to make their own arrangements into a composite, coordinated repair and assistance solution (on which the property repair market has sought to model itself). This solution extends from roadside assistance through to repair and the provision of a replacement vehicle. The claims system has become increasingly automated with advanced workflow, virtualization and a more structured approach to pricing. To the consumer, this has been reflected in higher levels of service. To the insurer this shows itself in brand differentiation and claims cost containment.

But not everyone is happy, especially the smaller body shops which have borne the brunt of this transition. In many cases they have not been able to invest in essential technology to meet the demands of new processes and ever more complex vehicles. Reduced margins on insurable work have placed considerable pressures on this sector, and as a result, over the past two decades there has been a gradual reduction in the number of UK body shops, in both franchised and independent repairs.

According to UK-based *MotorTrader* in their report 'The Future of the Car Body Repair Market in the UK 2010–2015'[3] there has been a reduction in the number of UK auto body shops of 18% between 2009 and 2015, with (at time of writing) just over 3000 outlets remaining. They continue to paint a daunting picture in their report, going on to say: 'Further decline of the sector will ultimately disadvantage consumers and insurance companies, and erode the skills base needed to repair tomorrow's cars and assure their continued safety.'

This last point is particularly concerning. MotorTrader appear to be suggesting that the body shop industry is in a vicious downward spiral by virtue of the approach taken by insurers to operate through framework agreements rather than allowing the customer to make their own arrangements. But is it fair to consider insurers as being the 'bad guys' in all this? Insurers reasonably argue that by managing costs and improving service, they are satisfying their duty to their stakeholders and providing a more effective and competitive landscape for their current and future policyholders. On the other hand, body shops suffering from reduced margins and onerous service level agreements find themselves arguing that the playing field isn't level, saying that insurers are placing 'arbitrary' caps on material and other costs.

Even more to the point, body shop owners argue that insurers aren't actually entitled to follow the process which they adopt. They say that the contract of insurance is there to 'indemnify' the policyholder against costs which have been incurred and if those costs are higher than the insurer likes, well that's just too bad. It's an interesting but perhaps slightly naive viewpoint. It also fails to recognize that many insurance contracts allow the insurer to 'repair or reinstate,' rather than simply providing an indemnity (or cash) to the policyholder. In honesty, the auto repair process now looks pretty locked down and the expectation from the customer is now rather high. If there are any changes to the process, then these are most likely to emerge from new business models and the interaction of supply chains as a result the 'Internet of Things' rather than any pressure exerted by body shop trade associations.

Analytics is increasingly seen as a way of optimizing repairer networks, supporting decision management and adding value to the customer experience. Insurers can use analytics to identify the optimal body shop network, in an environment where there are a significant number of variables, typically:

- Different body shop types (insurer-owned, franchised, independent, dedicated)
- Size
- Location
- Capacity
- Vehicle complexity.

Any analytical approach becomes important to:

- Understand claims 'hotspots'
- Manage total claims volumes, including in surge conditions
- Process repairs relating to specific partnership arrangements (so-called 'affinity partners')
- Accommodate the effect of vehicle manufacturer warranties and other specialist repairs
- Manage repairs undertaken outside the network.

In addition, insurers also view the repair process time as a critical success factor, especially where they are funding the cost of an alternative vehicle. What is the trade-off between time and cost? Historically it has been impossible to do this accurately and effectively. Advanced analytics are increasingly an important tool in providing that holistic view.

There is also recognition that the customer has an expectation not only of what the response time to deal with a new claim should be, but also how long a repair should take.

Increasingly insurers and body shops aim to give an indication of repair times and are using messaging, usually SMS, to advise customers of progress. The indications are that customer loyalty can be enhanced at least by managing their expectation. It is much more likely that the customer will express dissatisfaction on social media for poor service rather than delight for good service provided. Social media analytics can provide insurers with insight into process issues rather than just be a record of individual dissatisfaction.

5.5 TRANSFORMING THE HANDLING OF COMPLEX DOMESTIC CLAIMS

The insurance industry has traditionally struggled with how to split their book of claims, either by:

- Personal or commercial
- High value, or low value
- Complex or non-complex.

In reality there are arguments for each option but for the sake of definition, this section has focused on segmentation of claims as complex/non-complex on the basis that a complex claim can be of low value but be technically complicated nevertheless. Complexity can also occur in either personal or commercial claims although invariably different skills are required to meet each type.

Three key developments are likely to occur in the future of handling complex domestic claims (such as fire, flood and subsidence) and also in commercial claims. These are:

- The emergence of the 'digital investigator'
- Changes in the process or business model
- Reinvention of the supplier ecosystem.

5.5.1 The Digital Investigator

The 'Digital Investigator' of the future will comprise a combination of technical (i.e., 'construction') skills and knowledge, insurance knowledge, will be more computer literate than at present and importantly will also have social media and data awareness. Not only will they have the ability to understand the ways in which properties are damaged and are repaired but also how the scope of damage relates to the cover under the policy. Beyond this, they will be aware of the availability of structured and unstructured data in their investigation process and the sources that this can come from. These sources may perhaps be open-sourced, structured or possibly specifically invited, such as from the use of drones which would allow experts to gain access to previously inaccessible locations. This might occur for example in the investigation of the cause or degree of damage of a major commercial fire involving hazardous materials.

Additionally, the investigator will be sensitive to the increasing importance of social media in the wider process and recognize that the customer (or third parties) may well express dissatisfaction on social media before complaining to the inspector or insurer. In fact, the investigator or insurer may well be the last person to know of a problem.

An interesting challenge looms and that is, to what degree might the investigator 'appease' the policyholder to avoid adverse social media? This approach is not unprecedented. Anecdotally even in the old model it was known that where a policyholder had been unhappy with certain elements of the claim, the scope of repair might be informally and discreetly slightly 'stretched' to avoid formal complaint. For example, perhaps this might include decoration which might otherwise have been considered borderline as far as policy admissibility was concerned. Historically, such matters have fallen under the broader title of 'negotiation,' but technology may start to limit the scope for *old-fashioned* negotiation as part of the mix.

What becomes clear is that the skills needed for this complex role in the future will be both broader and perhaps deeper than had existed in the past. These necessary skills may reside in the few, rather than with the many. Automation of the handling of complex claims may not be an option even if analytics may act as a useful tool. Large numbers of complex claims might also potentially and rapidly create a supply/demand imbalance amongst trained staff. As a result, it is critical that professional claims organizations understand the changing business environment and start to prepare for the future.

One interesting model which has been floated involves the use of technology which relays visual information back to what can best be described as a contact center, or center of competence. Based on remote imagery it might be possible to make technical decisions on the most appropriate action to take. Such a center of competence could be real, i.e., physical, or virtual, dissipated across multiple locations or even involving home workers. These home-based experts could even have a global mandate. The idea has its legacy in the auto claims industry although the difference is that there is far less standardization in property than in cars. The imagery of damaged property can be collected by a less skilled 'person' on the ground, perhaps even the policyholder themselves or an intermediary. Such a model appears to support economies of scale in the decision-making process even in complex investigations. It points not only to technology changing how work is done in terms of the approach to decisions but also where individuals are physically based.

Analytics can also be used to support inspector performance. This is important for three reasons:

- Understanding the impact on reducing the indemnity cost, in other words the cost of claims settlement and other claims expenses.
- Return on capital expenditure (ROCE), in other words, the cost of capital investment for the use of a field force relative to an outsourcing arrangement.
- Assessment of individual capability and competence. Who are the good and not-so-good performers, and what additional training do they need?

The location of inspectors/auditors also appears to be an important factor. Drive time analysis relative to average repair cost and notional cost deviance potentially provides an interesting and useful correlation in establishing the optimum inspection regime. Where inspectors are based relative to their duties can have a big impact on the outcome. Future employment considerations for this skill set might seek to take into account the location of the individual relative to the supplier network.

Inspection need not only be a reactive process. It provides an opportunity to collect information about the property, the circumstances of the loss and about the policyholder themselves. In doing so the inspection has the potential to provide significant added value. Obtaining such information does not come free of charge, and insurers will ultimately need to understand not only the cost of getting this additional information but also its eventual value. Whilst additional data and insight appear to have an *implicit* added value, it may become increasingly important for that value to be *explicit*. Understanding the true cost of acquiring extra information will allow insurers to better understand the trade-off between reduced productivity by the loss adjuster or inspector compared to the extra insight the insurer might gain from that additional data.

5.5.2   Potential Changes in the Claims Process

The prioritization process within a claim is generally known as triage after the process commonly used by doctors to attend to emergencies, as opposed to tending to lesser injuries and ailments. A similar approach can be used by insurers in identifying which claims need to be attended to first and which can be delayed.

The approach can take two routes. Firstly, the speed of response may be based on the value or importance of the customer. This might require the claims handler to understand the value of risk of the property which is often a good indicator of the size and value of the building, or the number of policies which an individual might have (in effect their 'value' to the insurer).

The second more likely approach is in respect of the incident itself or the physical property damage. Claims which are likely to need early attention include:

1. High value, i.e., when a substantial and costly loss has occurred.
2. Fraudulent activity, where it is important to quickly collect information.
3. Potential recovery/subrogation opportunities, where it is important to collect information to pursue a third-party action.
4. Specific types of claims, e.g., water or smoke damage where prompt action such as cleaning or drying can help to mitigate or reduce the scale of the loss.

With regards to the fourth example, insurers and restoration companies understand that there is a 'golden period' of 24 hours after an incident; early intervention within that time will help to reduce the degree of damage. Acidic soot starts to stain materials, water starts to seep into the fabric of the building and if moisture levels are left uncontrolled then mold starts to grow.

The information obtained at the notification of the claim will substantially help in establishing the prioritization process. In many cases the amount of information obtained at the outset – a process called FNOL ('First Notification of Loss') can be relatively sketchy. A claim may then be passed on by a call-center handler or agent to an inspector or loss adjuster who will need to establish the facts and make an appropriate decision on the speed of the response. There is often a duplication of information taken from the policyholder by the insurer and then by their intermediary which can be the source of some frustration. At that point, an external loss adjuster (if they are used) will often be seen by the customer as an 'extension' of the insurer. If the loss adjuster underperforms then that is perceived by the customer as underperformance by the insurer themselves.

There is a case for loss adjusters and other third-party experts having as good an analytics capability as the insurer themselves, albeit perhaps from a more specialized angle. External loss adjusters may argue that the cost of having these capabilities is considerable. However not only is it likely that costs will fall as analytics increasingly becomes commoditized or provided 'as a service' in the cloud, but more importantly insurers will ask for evidence of analytic capability at the point of renewal of contracts. Descriptive reporting alone is unlikely to be adequate, and increasingly insurers will ask for evidence of some degree of predictive capability.

As an adjunct to the use of analytics by loss adjusters and third parties, insurers will increasingly want to view the adjuster as part of their 'virtual enterprise' where there is a flow of information between the two, albeit with appropriate levels of security. Insurers historically baulked at the idea of the loss adjuster system being embedded in some way into the insurer's own system as this constituted a form of lock-in and the switching cost became higher. With the advent of easier information flow, this is now likely to be less of a worry.

In complex claims such as fire, flood and subsidence there is inevitably a degree of linear thinking. Such linear thinking creates so-called data points at each decision node and helps create a *digital process roadmap*. Each point of decision or 'node' allows a form of decision-tree approach to be created, perhaps through a set of business rules, and enables the claim to be navigated to the next optimal step. For example, is the property dry enough after flood damage to start decorating, or in the case of subsidence is it stable enough to be repaired?

Going forward, will there be a single linear process or will the process depend on the customer themselves? They may wish to take a much more active part in each decision (or all decisions) made. Perhaps one type of customer will choose to be heavily involved in each decision in the process and need to be consulted at each decision point. Another type may decide to delegate everything to the insurer to resolve. Perhaps a third type of customer will seek some hybrid depending on the importance of the decision involved, whereas another customer may be so concerned as to want to constantly seek a second opinion

The nature of the involvement may also be influenced by the age of the customer. Younger policyholders may behave in a different way and have different requirements to those of older customers. One size and one process are unlikely to fit all circumstances and this is likely to add further complexity to an already difficult working environment.

5.5.3   Reinvention of the Supplier Ecosystem

The existing process almost has an implicit hierarchy influenced by professional qualification, experience, ownership of the relationship, degree of direction and information flow. Increasing the speed of transfer of information and greater collaboration through the supply chain due to common shared data (both structured and unstructured) will start to revolutionize the supply chain, moving away from a linear approach to a more collaborative approach.

The current approach to procurement which involves term contracts coupled with standardized repair costs, usually discounted for volume (for example the 'unit cost' of painting 1 square metre of ceiling) could disappear in favor of so-called 'claims exchanges.' In such 'exchanges' repair opportunities could be offered to pre-qualified vendors to bid, based on their appetite for carrying out the work. This idea has been around for a decade but like telematics perhaps now the timing is better as there is a greater tendency for insurers to collaborate provided there is no evidence of anti-competitive behavior. For example, the Claims and Underwriting Exchange in the UK is a collaborative database dealing with the exchange of claims data as an anti-fraud initiative.

A 'claims exchange' potentially provides a new model for claims fulfillment. Using analytical approaches, work could be awarded to pre-approved vendors until they have reached their financial limits. Of course, this is not a fault-free approach. There may still be a tendency for vendors to underbid in the hope of winning work and then create profit for themselves through their subcontractor arrangements or through other efficiencies. It also undermines the idea that insurers can be differentiated by virtue of the claims service they provide, but the policyholder already has a minimum expectation in terms of the service they expect. In any event many of the leading claims management providers are acting for multiple clients already and any presumption to offer differentiated service is wishful thinking in operational terms.

What is likely to emerge overall is that the essential tasks required in the claims process may well remain, but may be redistributed through other parts of the ecosystem. Analytics could become the gatekeeper to avoid biases emerging. In the same way that insurers were forced to develop supply chain management as a core competence to avoid fraud, improve customer service and optimize purchasing leverage, the role of the insurance supplier manager is also likely to change.

Pre-approval of vendors might depend on:

- The technical capabilities of the vendor to undertake the work
- The ability to collaborate throughout the supplier ecosystem
- Appropriate financial controls and agreed limits
- Risk mitigation processes
- Customer-facing attitude
- Analytical capability.

Of all these it is likely that the capability to collaborate could be one of the most important. An element of caution must however be addressed for if insurers are viewed as being relatively traditional and slow to change, then the construction industry is arguably slower. At the end of the day, might the repair process still depend on the lowest common denominator, in effect the individual or 'independent tradesman' physically doing the work?

There are already signs of change. Major restoration companies are increasingly becoming digital in their outlook. New relationships will start to emerge which collectively comprise more than the sum of their parts. Participants might perhaps be more adventurous by partnering with organizations with *significantly* different skills and capabilities. The challenge will be for all those in the supplier ecosystem to demonstrate their value-add. If they cannot, then they are vulnerable. The age of the digital restoration vendor is approaching if it is not already here.

5.6   LEVELS OF INSPECTION

Outside those claims viewed as being critical for early inspection, insurers are still likely to maintain some inspection regime. The challenge is establishing at what level, what type of claims are best inspected, with what value and perhaps also what location. News that insurers pay without inspection often passes quickly amongst disreputable groups.

Inspection activities are not free of charge. If the inspections are carried out outside the organization, then there is usually a fee to consider which may be fixed or variable depending on the size and type of the loss. Inspections carried out by an internal field force also add to operating cost. There is also a further ancillary cost based on the return on capital expenditure

(ROCE), i.e., the loss of return on capital that could have been invested elsewhere. As a result, it is important for insurers to be clear regarding the Return on Investment or 'ROI' and how best to deploy the field force.

There is a tendency to establish a financial 'clip' level and have a different inspection regime below that figure. This broad brush approach lacks the granularity to provide an optimum outcome and an analytical approach provides greater sensitivity in the decision process as to whether to inspect or not. It is also dependent on the accuracy of the information provided at the initial call and on what basis the decision to make an inspection is based.

The ability to 'flex' these inspection arrangements, due perhaps to a weather incident, and to anticipate the consequences beforehand, clearly involves a process which is analytical in nature. Insurers can use predictive techniques to anticipate the impact of a change of inspection routine. They can also anticipate the outcome of modifying their practices on their loss ratio (which is a key business indicator). Insurance is not a static industry and continually suffers greatly from supply/demand imbalances especially in the field force. In time of crisis, for example in a major weather incident, insurers need to be able not only to be agile in their operations but also to anticipate the outcome of agility in advance to avoid surprises.

5.6.1 Reserving

One of the early parts of the claims process is that of setting the 'reserve' which in simple terms is the amount of money insurers put aside to meet their liabilities under the claim. This may represent a large single amount of money against a major single incident or an aggregate amount representing the cumulative total of many small (and sometime not so small) claims. They are important as they are considered as liabilities on the insurance balance sheet since they represent payments that have to be made sometime in the future.

Analytical approaches may be used to anticipate the probability of a loss per claim, a so-called 'automatic reserve,' which can then be refined going forward. The refinement can be based either on the claims handler's judgment or by predicting the future based on past trends. There are weaknesses in both these approaches, and these sometimes lead to the phenomenon known as 'reserve creep.' This is where the anticipated cost of repair creeps upwards and upwards as time goes on, usually due to a lack of control over the claims process or inadequate estimation at the outset.

Increasingly, the reserving process has been made more accurate through the use of estimating software which allows more detailed estimates to be created. These estimates may form the basis of a work instruction (or 'job order') but are equally likely to be used to anticipate the size of the loss and in doing so help set the reserve.

Most of these systems have emerged in the North American market and were initially aimed at ensuring that insurance was at the right level by being able to better predict the value at risk, and to ensure there was no lost premium.[4] Prediction tools for property damage costs are possible and can be localized to some degree for the European market but this has not been an easy transition. Property types and styles in North America are relatively more standard with less variation in materials, whereas in other parts of the world there is a much higher level of inconsistency due to the use of local materials.

Some software companies have sought to introduce an analytical approach which suggests that the likely cost of repairing a property under say 300mm of water is likely to be £x, and then advocates that the insurer focus on managing any cost outliers. It is reasonable to say that within a generation such capabilities, based on advanced analytics, are likely to be commonplace in some form.

Complications arise not only in the variety of construction materials and cost but also in the standards of quality. It is generally recognized that there are at least four levels of quality:

- *Economy* – where the property is built from standard plans which meet all required local codes with the intention to sell at low cost.
- *Standard* – construction from standard designs and plans, but with slightly higher levels of workmanship. They meet minimum codes and in some areas exceed them. Such properties are typified in the UK by having a dining room for example.
- *Customized* – usually these are non-standard homes with materials and workmanship exceeding the minimum standard, attractively decorated and often with special use rooms such as a dining room or 'family room.'
- *Luxury* – usually architecturally designed houses that exceed local codes and have expensive features, special trim, and special rooms such as media rooms and exercise rooms.

As the use of analytics progresses, increasingly it will allow insurers and other organizations to take into account the differences in standards between buildings and to allow for them either in the repair or reserving assessment. Whereas earlier it was possible to manage average costs and understand discrepancies, this was a relatively broad brush approach to the challenge of variation of property standards. The need for a higher level of granularity in the management of repair cost increasingly becomes critical.

When insurers consider the cost of a repair perhaps they also need to take into account not only issues of location, and supply and demand of workers and materials but also the standards which apply to the repair. Is the minimum standard one of simply meeting the necessary local repair code or does a degree of subjectivity start to creep in? And if subjectivity is an important element, for example the specific attitude of the property owner, how will this be allowed for in analytical calculation?

Perhaps as more information is gained about property types through open source data, insurers will be able to establish the 'standard' of a property without visiting it and where it falls between 'economy' and 'luxury.' It won't be possible to comment realistically on the quality of the inside of a property simply from an external examination but it may provide some form of indicator.

5.6.2   Business Interruption

Beyond property damage, insurers in commercial situations are concerned with the losses emerging from the interruption of the business. This is also known as consequential loss. Insurance cover is usually provided based on the nature of the business, the gross profit or turnover, and what is called the 'interruption period' by which is meant the period over which a business is likely to be affected. The impact of any *increased cost of working*, i.e., overtime working to maintain production, can also fall under this type of insurance cover.

Following a major incident such as a fire, the claim for business interruption can be affected by:

- The degree of damage to the building, which may require demolition and reconstruction
- Replacement of equipment and specialist machinery
- Replacement of stock
- Restoration of the supplier and customer base.

In the event of a claim occurring such losses are usually investigated by experts, often accountants. This is in reality a financial exercise (undertaken in the context of the cover available under the policy) and accountants and other experts often undertake their analysis using spreadsheets. Whilst usually providing adequate results from a tried-and-tested method there is often scope for discussion and negotiation around assumptions made of growth, market conditions, the competitive environment and other factors. The complexity of the negotiation process often leads to delay in the final settlement, and often it is this delay rather than the amount itself which is critical to a business re-establishing itself.

Increasingly businesses are using more sophisticated analytical tools to manage their businesses such as rolling forecasting and 'sandbox' analysis, and are able to cut and slice their data in quite sophisticated ways. Analysts such as Forester and others indicate a rapid growth in the use of financial performance management tools to address management, planning and forecasting processes. They make the point that financial professionals can no longer rely solely on spreadsheets[5] and indicate that this progression will increasingly be prevalent due to the availability of Software as a Service (SaaS).

It is important that insurers and their experts in analyzing the impact of a major incident are able to use analytical capabilities that are as good as, if not better than, those of the policyholder themselves. In a recent (April 2015) report by consultants Camford Sutton for the UK Financial Conduct Authority,[6] 100 interviews were carried out with SME ('Small and Medium Enterprise') firms following 'first party' claims of over £5000. All were commercial cases where there had been an expression of dissatisfaction and of these cases, 20 were subject to more detailed interview. This is a useful report (albeit rather limited in the number of participants) but indicates some trends seem to have emerged in claims handling:

- A lack of proactivity to resolve issues and drive claims to a conclusion.
- Delays pushing the claim beyond the 12-month 'indemnity period' beyond which the business could not claim.
- Effective use of interim payments but in some cases policyholders needing to 'plead' for cash and looking to their bank to support the business through the process.

Against this background report is the '80% myth' which is an anecdotal story according to which '80% of businesses close within 18 months of a major incident.' The myth was reviewed by Continuity Central, a site focusing on business continuity issues, citing 29 reference points and they concluded that the statistics 'have been heavily recycled,' more recent statistics seem to be 'less ambitious,' sources 'cannot be found' – and the writer even suggested that the '80% Myth had been busted.'[7]

There appears to be a correlation between time and cost in the claims process – the longer the claim goes on, the more expensive it becomes. One point being argued is that modern financial performance management tools, if used by insurers and their representatives, would not only speed up settlements but settle claims at potentially lower cost. In doing so, affected businesses might not suffer quite so much and start trading again more quickly. This can only be a good thing for everyone.

5.6.3 Subrogation

This process, otherwise known as the 'recovery' process, enables insurers to recover money from a third party if that third party has been in the wrong and caused the damage. In effect, as part of the contract of insurance, the policyholder signs away their legal rights and allows the insurer to stand in their place and pursue an action against somebody else. This action can arise against a third party in nuisance, negligence, contract or any other legal remedy. The process also prevents the policyholder from receiving an insurance payment and then separately suing a third party.

Such subrogation or recover actions are usually complex, although in their simplest form (for example) they occur whenever there is an auto collision in which case blame is attributed to one of the parties or shared. From time to time there are intercompany agreements but these can be contentious if one insurer has a larger book of auto business than the other, and the reciprocal agreement is unequal.

Outside auto claims, recovery actions may occur in claims for fire damage, water, nuisance and negligence. The success of an action will depend both on the circumstances of the incident and also the amount of evidence. Sometimes expert evidence from forensic scientists is used to try and determine causation.

Pursuing a recovery action is time consuming and costly. Insurers have often adopted the use of checklists to determine the likelihood of a successful action. The use of contingent fees by lawyers – payment only if successful – was seen at first as a panacea but is now viewed as an extension of the checklist approach. Lawyers quickly look at the facts and make an early decision as to whether to pursue or not. Whilst at face value this seems a sensible approach, sometimes the lack of a reaction to an incident means that a third party is not 'deterred' from repeating the action in the future. An analytical approach may help with the level of successful recoveries by providing greater insight into the likelihood of success.

The impact of Big Data in this context is also interesting. Additional structured and unstructured information may contribute to the strength of a subrogation opportunity in so far as that additional information is legally admissible. The test of 'negligence' in a legal case, put simply, is whether a person knew, or ought to have known, that their actions might cause harm or damage. The increasing amount of information in the public domain and the relative ease with which it can be sourced potentially starts to stress test that scenario. Will the amount of information available mean that a person is more likely to know that injury or damage might occur? Will the profession of a person and their internet usage increasingly be factors in determining negligence? How will the availability of more detailed insight at a personal and professional level change the legal landscape?

It is suggested that more effective use of data and analytics could help change the prospect of a successful recovery (or subrogation) process. Different to criminal activity which requires proof 'beyond reasonable doubt,' most actions by insurers arise as a civil liability which requires the burden of proof to be based on a 'balance of probabilities.' The increased availability of open data to support an action could add to the mix of information to satisfy that burden, but of course there may be issues regarding the legal admissibility of that information based on the 'rules of evidence.'

5.7 MOTOR ASSESSING AND LOSS ADJUSTING

Adjusting and automotive assessing form a critical part of the claims process, and they are also affected by Big Data and Analytics, albeit in different ways. Both professions are of long standing. Professional bodies are involved such as AIEA (Institute of Automotive Motor Assessors) and CILA (Chartered Institute of Loss Adjusters) who seek not only to represent their members but also to establish levels of qualification which are recognized as proof of capability in their respective fields. Of these two, automotive assessing may be the more likely to go through potentially the largest process of change the earlier of the two professions, due to the rapid 'digital transformation' of the motor car.

Historically it should also be noted that property claims management has tended to develop more slowly than auto in terms of technology. This is partly a matter of market maturity but equally reflects the lack of standardization of property stock (which is prone to modification and extension) compared to auto stock which nevertheless has greater similarity despite continual improvement. In fact, many auto components can be used across different brands, allowing a degree of standardization.

5.7.1 Motor Assessing

The traditional role of the auto or motor assessor, or motor engineer, was to inspect damage, agree scope and price with the body shop and agree final accounts. That function still remains although the process is much more automated and remote inspections are increasingly possible. The modus operandi is that the extent of obvious damage is agreed at the outset, any extras or supplementary costs due to unforeseen damage are considered, the final account is reconciled and then signed off.

With the continued development of supply chain management and procurement techniques, margins for repairers have been reduced and the supply chain is under pressure. The existence of intermediary network managers who take their cut of the total cost, coupled from time to time with retro rebates, adds further cost pressure on the body shop repairer.

Overall there are fewer repairs due to improved driving conditions and safety standards, but in addition there are other aspects that need to be considered, typically:

- Vehicle design: seatbelts, maintenance, stability control
- Road design: intersections, surfaces, lighting, signage
- Driver behavior: speed, intoxication, physical impairment, age, drug use, distraction.

Regardless of the exact cause, overall this has resulted in fewer repairs going into the repair network. A supply/demand imbalance has emerged in favor of the purchasers who are usually the insurers. Switching costs are low, competition is high, margins are poor, and there is limited loyalty. As a result, some disreputable body shops have been known to seek to optimize the potentially short time that they are under contract with an insurer or network by taking whatever opportunities exist to squeeze more money from the system. Effective use of analytics can play a major part in claims cost control in this area of business.

The role of the motor assessor has also changed from auditor to one which is much more forensic in nature. They provide a vital function in collecting evidence to investigate claims for personal injury obtained through a motor accident. Increasingly, telematics is also a component in that armory but is only one of the tools available.

Telematics is only one new technological development in the automotive industry. Typical elements in the transformation of the car include a variety of capabilities to improve safety but these add complexity to the vehicle itself. Examples of these are:

- Emergency braking and collision warning systems (e.g., 2014 Mercedes C Class)
- Improved night sight assistant, based on thermal imagery (Audi A8)
- Driver tiredness detection

- 360-degree camera
- Active park assist.

Beyond this there are multiple other software systems within the vehicle, the most obvious being the entertainment center GPS and telecom devices. Overall increasing complexity of vehicles is likely to continue. The 'Internet of Things' will inevitably have an impact as will the issue of integrating social media. All this will perhaps lead to currently unimaginable combinations and interactions between people, vehicles and the transportation system. It is no surprise that companies like Ford describe themselves as 'mobility providers' rather than as auto manufacturers, and that the age of the fully connected car is closely approaching.

It is tempting at this stage to briefly mention the topic of self-driven cars, although some may suggest that this is too speculative a subject for consideration at the moment. However it is intriguing to think that auto manufacturers may even link GIS and route mapping to advertising revenue and in fact one organization was granted a patent for 'Transportation-aware physical advertising conversions' (Patent 8.630.897).[8]

What this means to the motor insurance industry is that in an auto accident, visible damage alone is unlikely to be the only problem. Electronic components may have been jolted or disconnected within the vehicle and damage may only be recognized at a later time in the process, significantly adding to the cost of repair. As a result of cars becoming so much more complex than before, there is an increasing likelihood that repairing a car will become more like mending a computer. The skills needed by the motor assessor will invariably change to become a cross between forensic scientists and computer engineers. These changes are also mirrored by what is happening within manufacturers themselves with increasing development of analytical capabilities within the vehicles undertaken by groups of software engineers. Much of this focus is on warranty management and preventive maintenance but it is a sign of things to come.

These changes will not only affect motor engineers, but also the repair process. Some body shops with traditional focus on the physical repair of the car will find themselves out of their depth in terms of their ability to repair technology which is equivalent to an early spacecraft. In fact, there is probably more technology in a basic car today than was used in the early missions to the moon.

Three things may need to happen:

1. Massive investment of body shops to cope with technological change within the vehicles at a time when margins are low. This may drive further consolidation within the body shop industry.
2. The emergence of specialist subcontractors who focus on the technological elements of the vehicle repair.
3. Repairs will increasingly be done by the manufacturers themselves, not only to cope with the technology but also the matter of warranties.

If the latter occurs, which arguably is most likely, then this further reinforces the argument that the relationship between the insurer and the manufacturer will need to change.

5.7.2 Loss Adjusting

Although the loss adjusting industry claims that its heritage dates as far back as the 17th century,[9] the profession of the property loss adjuster started to emerge seriously in 1940 during the Second World War, in respect of enemy bomb damage with the formation of the

Association of Fire Loss Adjusters in 1941. The profession obtained a Royal Charter in 1960 and nowadays represents independent experts and many other experts aligned to or employed by insurance companies. Their role is to 'adjust' the loss, which may be by its nature due to fire, storm, flood and other insured 'perils.' The term 'adjust' is unfortunate in that it creates a false notion that any submitted claims will be 'adjusted' or reduced. In the early stages of the profession, many organizations described themselves as 'adjusters, valuers and surveyors.' Selfe and Co of London, one of the antecedents of Crawford who are currently the largest global adjusting firm, originally described themselves as 'licensed valuers.'

Nowadays as distinct from motor engineers discussed above, the role of the adjuster is both broad and deep, with their expertise ranging from the handling of large value, complex claims to property, issues of legal liability and the impact of consequential loss through interruption of business activities. The industry is split between mega vendors and many smaller independent companies with particular specializations.

The loss adjusting market is large. In their 2011 report 'View from the Ridge' Stone Ridge consultants estimated the size of the US marketplace for loss adjusting services, which includes specialist lawyers and claims management companies, to be in the order of $3.5 billion. In knowing that the US insurance market represents approximately one-third of the global picture, this places the total market size of the global loss adjusting market at around $10 billion. With Europe representing one-third of the total in aggregate, and the UK representing 25% of the European sector, this places the value of the UK loss adjusting market at $0.9 billion, or £450 million. (By comparison, this is about the same size as the UK Search Engine industry, at £500m pa.[10])

This is an industry which appears, on the whole, to be reactive rather than proactive in terms of the use of data and analytics. Certainly there is evidence of the use of analytics to manage individual adjuster and also branch performance, both in terms of revenue earning ability and ability to conform to agreed service level agreements dictated by insurers under the terms of their contracts. However, these analytics appear on the whole to be mainly descriptive rather than predictive. If there is any element of prediction within the claims process, then this is within the insurer themselves at the First Notification of Loss (FNOL). As insurers increasingly improve their analytical capability (as some are even currently considering cognitive capabilities), this will increase the operational gap between the insurer and loss adjusting companies. The consequence of this may be to make it less likely for claims FNOL, or the whole claims process, being outsourced to the loss adjusting community but rather to more analytically minded organizations.

With a major part of the adjuster's work being about visiting the site in a climate where workloads are always flexing and significant supply/demand imbalances emerge, more effective use of analytics within the adjusting process to effect a triage process would seem highly desirable. However as with other parts of the insurance supply chain, margins are relatively tight and investment in analytics needs to be soundly based. Forward thinking adjusting firms may need to consider alliances with analytic expert businesses rather than try to self-build new analytical capabilities.

5.7.3   Property Claims Networks

If the role of the adjuster is likely to change, then so too will the role of the property repair network manager. At the end of the day, there will still need to be someone who physically does the repair.

The development of repairer networks in the UK principally arose for two key reasons. Primarily it was to reduce fraud, and secondly to create purchasing leverage. A third reason, customer service, might also be considered but this was arguably principally to 'dress up' the key insurer priorities of cost control and fraud management. The template for property network management came from a combination of what was happening in the auto repair market and from experience in the public sector. In that sector, social housing repairs were carried out under term contracts with specialist repairers who were operating to schedules of rates and against strict service performance indicators.

Whilst bringing some benefits of cost control, this approach also brought some issues. With the cost of repair being in effect a combination of firstly establishing the scope of the work and secondly applying the correct rate, new challenges were set down by the repairers to the existing regime. Repairers said that, in effect, the adjuster or claims inspector was not adequately qualified or experienced to carry out the scoping exercise satisfactorily, and that this part of the claim was better left to the repairer themselves. This depended to some degree of course on whether the adjuster was a suitably qualified building professional, or whether the individual had come through a more general route to qualification.

By assuming responsibility for both scoping and pricing, the repairer argued, not only would the scoping be more accurate but the cost of sending out an inspector or adjuster would be avoided. For many, this would be seen as tantamount to putting the proverbial fox into the rabbit hutch. These concerns address the very real problem of understanding the claims value chain, where and how these are elements are best carried out, how this can be done efficiently and without conflict of interest.

A second major issue which affects service and quality is that of repairs being subcontracted. This creates key concerns, one of which being that the operative who actually carries out the work may be remote from the values of the network contractor, and even further remote from the values of the insurer themselves. Many network repairers place reliance on the subcontractor ecosystem to manage supply/demand imbalances in the workload, especially in times of surge.

At the end of the day insurers have increasingly come to realize that a large proportion of property repairs are carried out by tradesmen operating at the very edge of the enterprise. This remoteness from the center carries multiple operational weaknesses and risks. Their inability to digitally manage individual traders who are self-employed in many cases is questionable. Because of this the insurance industry may be some way from effectively operating a fully digital, and hence analytical, repairer enterprise. In addition, the opportunity to collect valuable data and information at the point of interface with the end customer may also be lost.

The third major problem is one of payment to the contractor, especially reconciling individual repair costs to individual claims. Granularity of payments to claims level is critical in order that insurers have visibility into repair costs by peril and location, which leads to better underwriting and more accurate pricing. In many instances this is done through spreadsheet analysis and manual reconciliation but this is both costly and of questionable accuracy. Delays in this reconciliation process inevitably led to delays in finalizing the claim, not necessarily for the customer but for the insurer themselves. This resulted in extended lapse times before the file itself could be closed, creating distortion in the records. Delays in payment also ensued, leading to supplier dissatisfaction.

All these issues are against a background of a part of the property claims process which is nearly three decades old. There is no doubt that in some cases the contractor network approach adds some value, but with greater insight and cost control going forward it may be found that it is a hammer to crack a nut.

Thinking forward, insurers may increasingly start to reconsider the value that the repairer network provides compared to the cost of managing the network. Analytical insight will increasingly allow insurers to predict the likely cost of repair with more accuracy. There may be an increased tendency to 'cash out' on the claim rather than adopt a repairer model which, after all, was primarily created as an anti-fraud solution. This appears at face value to follow the US model, perhaps more and more influenced by the US technology that is increasingly prevailing. Although not explicitly so, US insurers appear always to have been nervous in directly appointing repairers so as to avoid responsibility for any problems. UK and European insurers appear to have been less concerned with this burden of risk, but it is possible that improved analytics may be a catalyst for the end of property repairer networks as we know them.

Beyond this, in the field of customer analytics, different types of buying behavior have been identified. It is quite possible if not probable that these buying behaviors will also link in some way to claims process behaviors. Will policyholders keen on self-service at the point of purchase have a greater desire to be personally involved in the claims process, including choosing the repairer? Will dependent policyholders equally be prepared simply to leave matters in the hands of their insurers?

For those insurers who decide to retain repair networks as a service to the customer, the networks themselves (and their participants) are likely to change. Network repairers will become part of the virtual insurance enterprise with data and information flowing between as many parts of the key stakeholders as is practically possible. Repairers will be tracked and monitored in a way which is alien to them today and which may lead to some resistance. There will still need to be quality, scope and pricing controls.

Three potential shifts are likely:

1. The network manager will find it more important to be able to demonstrate that they are adding value. If they cannot show that value is being added without disproportionate risk, then their role and the entire network approach itself is inevitably under threat.
2. Secondly the repairer as part of the virtual enterprise will need to become more engaged, and because of this their direct relationship with the insurer will improve. This will have to extend to the subcontractor as far as practically possible. The linear, hierarchical relationship will increasingly flatten, and the repair process will increasingly democratize.
3. The third shift is that, unless property networks are transformed in some way, then insurers will seek to reduce operational risk by reverting to cash settlements.

For loss adjusting companies who have come to rely on repair network income as part of their broader financial mix, the possibility of this income stream being affected will be of concern to them. Some will invariably see the adjusting profession as being yet again under threat as it has been in the past. This is an entrepreneurial industry which through its history has constantly reinvented itself. The challenge of coping with a new analytical environment which will seemingly force more operational and financial transparency creates the potential for more forward thinking. Entrepreneurial firms and individuals will need to think harder about their own business model, and re-imagine what adjusting and property repair will look like within a decade or so.

Ford has moved away from being a motor manufacturer to becoming a 'mobility' company. What is the comparable transformation for the property repair industry?

5.7.4   Adjustment of Cybersecurity Claims

In their 2015 study for the UK Department for Business, Innovation and Skills, PWC carried out a survey of cyber security incidents and trends.[11,12] Their key observations were:

- The number, scale and cost of security breaches have almost doubled.
- Nearly nine out of 10 companies have suffered a security breach.
- That people are as likely to cause a breach as malware or viruses.

In 2015, only a small number of specialist adjusting firms offered a service in respect of losses stemming from cyber security. The threat of losses due to breach of cyber security is already with us. Cyber security insurance is still at a relatively early stage of maturity although it has existed in the US for a decade. Insurance cover has been available for loss of information but perhaps is still coming to terms with the impact of data leakage in this new era. In their review PWC identify the two main areas of concern as:

- Protecting customer information
- Protecting the organization's reputation.

Big Data appears to bring with it big risks and the potential for big losses. The report indicates that:

- For small businesses, the total cost of the incident on average was between £75,200 and £310,800, over 2–12 days.
- For large businesses, the total cost on average was £800,000–£2,100,000 over 4–11 days.

As incidents of cyber risk increase, so will the use of cyber insurance as part of the defense mechanism. Experts who currently practice in this relatively nascent part of the profession seem mainly to have come from an IT background and are principally conversant with matters of technology. However, future new losses are likely to have bigger impacts on the line of business and will be more complex in nature. Will the future bring cyber insurance investigators versed in, say, marketing, asset maintenance or supply chain management?

As was experienced in the early 1970s when UK insurers provided cover for the new risk of 'subsidence' (building damage due to ground movement), with hindsight it is now accepted that early policy wordings were somewhat weakly drafted. As a result, UK insurers ultimately found themselves making substantial claims payouts over the years for claims beyond the intention of the cover.

Underwriters will need to be equally careful that their new wordings for cyber risk provide appropriate protection to their customers but don't leave the door open for unintended claims. Where there is likely to be some uncertainty regarding policy wordings and interpretation, perhaps there is likely to be a need for the specialist adjuster – and lawyer – and in this regard a whole new series of market opportunities appears to be emerging.

5.7.5   The Demographic Time Bomb in Adjusting

The adjusting industry already recognizes that a demographic time bomb exists. Many existing practitioners are well advanced not only in their profession but also in years. New entrants are joining the profession but a long road to qualification lies before them if they wish to commit themselves fully to the industry. It is probable that by the time they are fully qualified, the claims landscape will have changed. The customer, i.e., the policyholder, will also have changed and will have become more digitally aware. Beyond this, the customer's attitude both to the insurer and to their intermediaries will also have moved on from what it is today. If we consider what are the 'digital customer' and the 'digital insurer,' then we should also think about the 'digital adjuster.'

Ideas already exist for the concept of the 'virtual adjuster,' that is to say, that images can be captured and relayed to a central adjusting bureau where experts assess the scope of damage and liability of insurers from afar. Remote inspections using drones are already technically feasible. New technology will open the door to having a non-qualified representative of the insurer located in each district with the ability to provide 'on the ground' presence. How the industry will respond to this apparent de-skilling, or reskilling, will be one of the great questions for this sector to consider.

How customers want their claims service to be in the future may also change and this will also have an impact on the adjusting process. The concept of 'self-service' claims management is already under consideration and there is a US pilot scheme in place. The proposal puts the control of the insurance claim adjustment process into the hands of the claimants by enabling live video, claimant-provided photos and audio. This new approach is said to remove the need for the adjuster, speed up claims settlement and apparently minimize fraud risk.

Cognitive computing may also provide one answer to the loss of skill from the adjusting industry as more senior members of the profession leave and are not replaced on a like-for-like basis. Liability decisions may become more automated, be made more quickly and with a higher level of consistency. The role of the professional adjuster could perhaps change to be one of validating the automated analytical decision, and/or providing the 'human face' of insurance.

As with other professions, it is critical that adjusters (and others) do not see these technologies as a threat but rather an enabling force. Adjusters are 'just one more' profession in the insurance industry who will feel the consequences of the data and analytics revolution.

NOTES

1. *Castellain v Preston* [1883] 11 QBD 380 at p. 386.
2. City of London Police's Insurance Fraud Enforcement Department, Detective Chief Inspector Angie Rogers. https://www.cityoflondon.police.uk/advice-and-support/fraud-and-economic-crime/ (accessed March 17, 2016).
3. Trend Tracker. 'The Future of the Car Body Repair Market in the UK 2015–2020.' England: published by Trend Tracker Limited, BA13 4AW.
4. Wells, Peter and the editors of Marshall & Swift/Boeckt. *Insuring to Value: Meeting a Critical Need*. Cincinnati: The National Underwriting Company, 2007.
5. Hammerman, Paul D., Gilpin, Mike and Angel, Nasri. 'The Forrester Wave Financial Performance Management Q3, 2013.' Published by Forrester Research, 2013.
6. Commercial Insurance Claims by SME's Report of Findings from File Reviews. Camford Sutton Associates for the Financial Conduct Authority, April 15, 2015.
7. Mel Gosling and Andrew Hiles. 'Business Continuity Statistics: Where Myth meets Fact.' http://www.continuitycentral.com/feature0660.html April, 24 2009 (accessed November 29, 2015).

8. Koehler, Thomas and Wollschlaeger, Dirk. *Digital Transformation of the Automotive*. Pattensen: Media-Manufaktur, 2014.

9. Cato Carter, E. F. 'Origins of the Loss Adjusting Profession.' London: (Unpublished – reproduced by Beryl Jolley. Copyright E.F. Cato Carter), 1979.

10. Hird, Jake and Warren-Payne, Andrew. 'SEO Agencies Buyer's Guide 2012.' Published by Econsultancy, 2012. http://econsultancy.com/reports/seo-agencies-buyers-guide (accessed March 17, 2016).

11. Simpson, Andrew G. 'ACORD Names 2 Insurance Innovation Challenge Winners: Livegenic, Insurity,' http://www.insurancejournal.com/news/national/2015/11/05/387535.htm (accessed November 30, 2015). See also 'Livegenic.'

12. H.M. Government and PricewaterhouseCooper. '2015 Information Security Breaches Survey. Technical Report.' London. Published by HM Government. Crown Copyright, 2015. http://www.pwc.co.uk/assets/pdf/2015-isbs-executive-summary-digital.pdf.

CHAPTER 6

Analytics and Marketing

It is said that any business requires only two functions – innovation and marketing. As with other parts of this book, the topic of marketing is an entire subject in itself and there are excellent textbooks and sources which exist to supplement the reader's knowledge. Analytics in marketing has become increasingly relevant to insurers as more customer-orientated information becomes available which complements an organization's insights into the most effective (and profitable) channel, product or service. Such information also helps to improve the customer experience.

Insurers increasingly have an understanding of the characteristics of the end consumer from information they have captured through their sales and service process. When added to other unstructured information such as social media these help provide a richer picture of their existing or potential client and the sales opportunity which might exist. Although customer analytics might seem at face value to relate to retail insurance, it remains valid to use analytics in B2B marketing by understanding:

- The role of the potential purchaser as an individual and the key drivers that affect them.
- Other key stakeholders within the organization that might be key influencers.
- The nature of the business and particular business issues which pertain and which are covered in the annual report or investors' presentation.
- Specific issues relative to the business client's operating environment, for example new regulations which might arise.
- The impact of the competitive environment, technological changes and general market trends.

Insurance marketers also need to have a clear view of the ambition of their own company in terms of revenue or profitability growth and how this is to be derived, as this will impact on the way that the marketing function effectively creates value for their own business. From this financial insight they will then be able to understand, either independently or in conjunction with others, how the additional revenue or profit needs to be allocated against business lines and start to create a 'go to market' strategy accordingly.

Analytics are often used in a retail insurance environment to understand buyer segmentation and to understand who might be the 'target' segmentation, perhaps by age, demographic or location. By having this insight marketers can start to craft campaigns accordingly and effectively measure against them.

The use of analytics in customer engagement is not unique to insurance and in fact it is a well recognized process. It is no surprise therefore that insurers and other financial services organizations look to retailers and other customer-facing sectors to understand how best to attract new customers and retain existing ones. In fact this thinking goes beyond merely looking – insurers also recruit analytically orientated marketing individuals from the retail, media and other associated sectors.

Chief executives of insurance companies understand that getting close to the customer is a critical success factor. The IBM 2010 CEO survey 'Capitalizing on Complexity'[1] indicated that 90% of insurance CEOs recognized that getting closer to the customer was at the top of their agenda. Now, over half a decade later, there is no reason why that mantra should have changed other than that there have been continued developments in technology and the Big Data agenda has gained a greater foothold. Beyond this, the customer base has also matured, achieving greater interlock with mobile technology and more avid use of social media to express concerns or satisfaction.

The advent of new approaches to insurance such as telematics has not only opened doors to new customer segments but has threatened existing ones. So-called 'one time insurance' for specific events such as single travel trips naturally also seems applicable to 'one time' lifestyle events. At the other end of the spectrum it remains surprising that consumers haven't been attracted to longer term property insurance policies which replicate in many ways the durability of life and pension products and are often provided by the same insurance group. Is it simply that insurers feel sufficiently uncomfortable about the future to be able to offer any form of longer term property insurance product? Can analytics in its widest form allow insurers to take a longer term viewpoint, and in doing so provide their customers with a more stable relationship (perhaps with some form of opt-out provision)? In taking this longer term approach can they start to mitigate the perennial challenge of customer churn and persistency?

Customer analytics in the insurance marketing space is multifaceted yet the purists might reasonably argue that the 'traditional' 4Ps of marketing – *Price, Product, Promotion* and *Place* – remain fundamental truths of marketing. The core of effective marketing is quite simply to put the right product in front of the right person at the right time and at the right price. The use of data and technology invariably allows insurers to gain greater understanding of these parameters within the new technological era and to flex these with greater confidence and success.

An integrated approach to modern insurance marketing needs to cover:

- Customer acquisition and retention
- Social media analytics
- Customer segmentation
- Promotion strategy
- Branding and pricing strategy
- The impact of service delivery
- Agile development of new product
- Influence of multichannel/omni-channel in the digital age.

6.1   CUSTOMER ACQUISITION AND RETENTION

One of the critical success factors for insurance organizations is not only to acquire new customers but also to keep them. Having kept them, they are also keen to ensure that existing customers are prepared to buy new and extended products from them. This process is known as cross-sell and upselling. In simple terms, this suggests that if a customer already has an insurance product with an insurance provider or 'carrier' and needs to buy additional cover due to a particular requirement such as a lifestyle change, then their original insurer is their first port of call.

Customer retention remains a big problem for insurers, especially in markets which are saturated and where, for many customers, insurance purchase remains a price-sensitive issue.

The 2008 Pitney Bowes report 'The Dynamics of Defection'[2] serves as a reminder that customer retention is a challenge for many industries, and is not confined to the insurance sector. Table 6.1 and Table 6.2 are taken from that report.

It is interesting to consider what it takes to make a customer loyal. In their 1998 report 'A Model of Consumer Perceptions,'[3] Cornell University worked with 160 retailers to identify

TABLE 6.1   Customer churn rates by industry

Churn rates	Europe (%)	US (%)
Your main supermarket	31.4	32.9
Internet service provider	26.2	38.2
Mobile phone provider	25.3	11.7
Car or house insurer	19.4	12.6
Bank	19.2	25.3
Main credit card issuer	9.2	20.6
Travel agent	10	2.9
Utilities provider	5.1	12.2
All sectors average	18.2	19.6

TABLE 6.2   Question – Which of the following providers (by %) have you changed in the last year?

	Italy	France	Spain	Germany	US	UK
Main supermarket	36	34	32.4	27	32.9	27.4
Internet service provider	25.7	22.6	29	29.2	38.2	24.6
Mobile phone provider	22.6	21.1	23.1	21.2	11.7	38.6
Bank	20.4	16.6	23.9	16.8	25.3	18.3
Car or house insurer	17.6	16.2	21.2	16.8	12.6	25.5
Main credit card issuer	5.9	7.3	9.2	7.1	20.6	16.2
Travel agent	12.8	7.7	14.9	6.5	2.9	8.1
Utilities provider	0.7	0.4	1.2	5.8	12.4	17.3
All sector average	17.7	15.7	19.4	16.3	19.6	22

the most loyal customers and worked backwards to identify three key reasons for their loyalty, which were:

- Store quality, for example in the case of retailers, the layout of the store and the quality of the assistance provided in specialized sections (e.g., bakery).
- Pricing and perceived value, especially if there were competing similar stores nearby, and where the ease of switching was high. (The corollary of this was that, if there was no obvious competition, then pricing became less critical to issues of loyalty.)
- Merchandise quality, which in the case of retailers was perceived as service quality. In other words, consumers formed a view on the quality of the merchandise through the quality of service in which that merchandise was provided. Even if the merchandise was the same, customer perception of the merchandise was poor if the service was poor.

The indications are therefore that regardless of the quality of the merchandise, if the service is good then customer loyalty will follow. The author of a review in *Business Psychology*[4] James Larson puts it simply: 'There are some lessons here, and they all harken back to service quality. Get that right, and customer loyalty will follow.'

One of the key metrics in measuring loyalty is known as the 'net promoter score' or NPS which in simple terms is the measurement by which an individual is likely to recommend the use of a particular supplier to another person. If an insurer's NPS is higher than its competitors, then it is more likely to outperform its competitors and therefore be more successful in growth. NPS is a relatively simple measure which comprises a simple response to a single question, for example: 'How likely are you to recommend this company/product/brand to a friend or colleague?' The reply may range from 0 (not at all) to 10 (highly likely). The net promotor score is the difference between the promotors (9s and 10s) and the detractors (0–6), with 7–8 viewed as neutral or passive. (These passives are viewed as being vulnerable to switching to a competitor.)

NPS is more than a simple metric. Used effectively, it can drive improvements in staff process and behavior and also support executives in prioritizing key activities.

There are however difficulties in directly comparing financial services with retailers mainly because of the intangible nature of the 'merchandise.' According to the Bain & Co 2013 report 'Customer Loyalty in Retail Banking':[5]

> On average, a bank's relative NPS explains roughly half of the variation in its relative win rate – a metric that shows whether a bank is winning more or less than its fair share of customers.

There are likely to be other factors affecting customer behavior, for example the cost of the service (usually represented by the fee), the location and convenience of the branch, and the degree of convenience in opening up an account in the first place.

The insurance proposition also finds itself with difficulties in creating customer loyalty because many customers see insurance as a grudge purchase, and also because of the low number of touch points which exist in the annual insurance cycle. To get over this many insurers try to improve the degree of customer engagement through:

- Adding value to their base proposition where possible, often through competitions.
- Increasing the number of contact points, for example by way of a regular newsletter.

- Constantly inviting feedback.
- Improving the quality and capability of customer facing staff.

Perhaps the most important factor is good service which reinforces the lesson of the retail survey mentioned above. Even so there are natural challenges in a call handler or claims advisor being adequately empathetic to a distressed policyholder whose possessions have been seriously damaged or completely lost. The situation can be worsened in the event of a major catastrophe such as flooding where there may be a surge of incidents creating pressures on the claims team.

In their 2014 Insurance report on Customer Loyalty[6] Bain reinforced the importance of NPS but suggested that too few insurers take action to respond to issues. Their suggestion is fourfold:

1. Identify where to focus.
2. Select key 'moments of truth.'
3. Acquire through price but retain through service and product innovation.
4. Accelerate digital transformation.

The increasing movement towards the use of mobile technology provides the insurer not only with more opportunities to gain data and insight but also to increase the number of engagements with their customer. This is a double-edged sword in that whilst initial contact might be notionally easier, it also presents a new burden on the insurer to ensure that contact is both timely and relevant. Excessive irrelevant contact is as likely to be a 'switch-off' for a customer as no contact whatsoever.

In a recent article in Forbes magazine,[7] Shep Hyken, who is an international customer services expert, adds eloquently:

Customer service is the new marketing. It really is. Create a better experience, at all touch points, and you give the customer a better experience. Customers come back, spend more, and tell their colleagues and friends.

The implication here is important. It is a reminder that *everyone* involved in customer service, both Front and Back Office, has a part to play in the success of the insurance business. Is marketing now too important to be left just to marketers?

Whilst issues of customer loyalty and retention had their traditional domain in the areas of general insurance, typically personal lines auto and property, matters have recently taken an unusual turn for the life and pension industry. In 2015 UK life and pension insurers were faced with reforms which allowed policyholders to withdraw, or 'draw down' funds after the age of 55. Companies who might have previously been confident of having virtually permanent access to deposited funds found themselves faced with many of the same issues as those of general insurers. They needed to understand and predict which customers might want to withdraw savings. In effect this was a similar problem to that of customer churn in other personal lines insurances. The ability of life and pension insurers in the UK to predict customer behavior has now become increasingly critical. They are keen to understand their customer's propensity to withdraw money, and to try and influence this behavior by proactively offering alternative easier access products.

All this appears to point to a greater need for all insurers to gain more understanding of their customers, not just in terms of the products they hold but also to anticipate those products which their customers will need in the future. They also need to have better understanding of the likelihood of a customer taking a certain course of action. These are not static behaviors but are dynamic in that a customer's behavior may be affected by lifestyle changes, employment conditions, health or the economic environment.

Behaviors or 'attitudes' are also prone to change with age. It is as yet unknown whether the Generation Zs will one day wake up and start to behave like Generation Ys, and so on, but analysts (and insurers) must recognize the shifting nature of the human condition. Perhaps as analytics evolves in the customer process there will be an increasing need for greater psychological understanding of decision drivers.

6.2 SOCIAL MEDIA ANALYTICS

If it is accepted that the customer experience is critical, then the importance of the customer in promoting a product or service becomes critical in the thinking of insurers. Net promotor scoring (NPS) is fundamentally about whether or not the customer is willing and able to become an advocate of the insurer, and to recommend a product, service or company to others. The increased use and availability of social media makes this increasingly important.

A 2008 survey by Harris[8] indicated that '87 percent will discontinue business with a company after a negative customer experience.' Beyond this, 84% will tell their friends about how they feel. In that particular report it is interesting to record the *personalized* human reaction to a negative customer experience. According to the study:

- 26% have sworn
- 17% have shouted
- 9% have felt sick
- 5% of males say they hit or break something
- 9% of females cry.

Nearly a decade on, it is almost certain that not only will they tell their friends but more importantly they will do it on social media. In an unhappy insurance experience, the emotional reaction may be even stronger. Policyholders may struggle to find a balance between a rational and an emotional approach to the problem. It is of little comfort for a policyholder to be told by an insurer that the volume of claims has led to a delay. The use of analytics to create a triage is important but the need to manage customer expectation is also a critical success factor.

The insurance claimant's 'emotional rollercoaster' reflects those sentiments which apply to each part of the claims process, from denial that the incident happened, to potential personal guilt that the individual could have done more, to acceptance of the position. Beyond this the customer reaction can be linked to poor performance on the part of the insurer:

- Firstly, seeking complaint through compensation.
- Subsequently, seeking punitive methods against the insurer.

All of these give rise to the potential for adverse policyholder activity on social media. If insurance is about anything, then it is about the 'moment of truth at the point of claim.' To satisfy that moment of truth, insurers must:

- Satisfy the customer – provided that it is cost effective to do so. (Some may argue that a degree of dissatisfaction is tolerable and 100% satisfaction equates to generosity.)
- Create an appropriate response but manage expectations accordingly.
- Ensure that any points of criticism are quickly and effectively responded to.

In considering the use of social media, the issue of demography is also a factor as clearly some age bands are more likely to be vociferous on social media than others and also may be significant influencers.

Social media analytics is the process by which large amounts of social data are analyzed to look for key trends. This information may come from blogs, on-line conversations such as Twitter and WhatsApp and from websites. The aim is to identify key customer sentiment from which a view can be obtained regarding issues of reputation, service, particular difficulties. From this information it is possible to create 'actionable insight' which enhances positive attributes and mitigates damaging issues. It is unusual for one personal expression of discontent to create sizeable consumer sentiment although perhaps a more generic issue such as data loss might trigger a flood of comment.

There are multiple social media analysis tools – some are free, some are available for a charge. These range from simple monitoring of online activity through to website traffic. As insurers increasingly enter the world of digital marketing, it becomes critical that they have appropriate tools at their disposal to measure digital activity and understand from this the impact of small but subtle changes on the attractiveness of a site.

6.3   DEMOGRAPHY AND HOW POPULATION MATTERS

Demography in its broadest description is the study of population, by means of which it provides a scientific and statistical viewpoint of the size, structure, distribution and behaviors of groups of people. In the context of insurance, we might take this to mean:

- Issues of market maturity in so far as it relates to insurance penetration.
- Use of technology, for example the extent to which individuals use mobile devices to effect purchases.
- The need for insurance products, and if there is such a need, what type of products are essential (if at all).
- Preferred distribution channels, for example the use of traditional agent channels.

These are complicated issues even when taken in isolation but when combined they create complex ecosystems. The need for global entities to understand local conditions becomes critical in optimizing 'go to market' strategies and often demands 'on the ground' knowledge. Detailed reports such as those provided by Swiss Re[9] set out in considerable detail those issues of insurance penetration relative to GDP. These and other similar key dependencies enable insurers to gain a better demographic viewpoint of market opportunities in terms of insurance market growth. Of particular interest at a macro level is the comparative saturation of the Western European insurance market compared to the growth markets of China and Asia Pacific. Some major insurers have taken into account this degree of saturation/penetration in formulating their strategy. Some are already looking to the Asia Pacific market as their growth engine rather than Western Europe.

Beyond this, insurers also need to consider the technological maturity of their potential and existing customer base. As in other areas, insurers are well advised to look outside their own sector for clues. Looking to the retail sector, the concept of 'showrooming' has emerged as a key buying pattern where potential retail customers examine goods in-store and then buy online. There is a very substantial difference in this behavior across territories, with Chinese purchasers 'showrooming' nearly six times more than North American and UK retail customers (Table 6.3),[10] and it is not unreasonable to suppose that the approach to online insurance purchases might be mirrored in some way.

TABLE 6.3 Propensity to 'showroom' before buying retail goods online (by %) (2013 figures)

Canada	1
US	4
Mexico	2
Brazil	10
Chile	4
UK	4
France	4
Germany	5
Spain	4
Italy	3
China	26
India	10
Japan	10
Australia	1

The indications are that different geographies have different attitudes to online purchasing. The role of the agent or third party who provides human intervention is greatly diminished in a geography where online activity is so prevalent, yet may still have some role to play. Insurers should heed the behavior of their customers in a retail environment and consider transposing that into the purchase of financial services.

6.4 SEGMENTATION

Not all customers are the same. Current approaches to segmentation seek to divide them into the following categories, as illustrated in Table 6.4:

TABLE 6.4   Segmentation of customers

		Characteristics
Gen Z	18–27	Low loyalty
Gen Y	28–38	Control but rapid response. Affected by 'life events.' i.e., marriage, family
Gen X	39–49	Longer term goals. Building wealth
Baby boomers	50–67	Conserving and preserving wealth
Seniors	68+	Multiple providers, conserving wealth, price

Segmentation not only drives behavior but helps insurers to better understand which distribution model is most appropriate to a particular segment. For example, the younger demographic of Generation Z appear more likely to be attracted to online carriers, whereas seniors are more likely to be attracted to agent-based insurers whose appeal is in providing individual and personalized treatment. (This may also be related to the complexity of their needs, and their personal risk appetites.) The implication is that insurers who focus on one particular distribution channel alone are likely to unwittingly (or deliberately) confine their growth opportunity to specific segment alignments.

Beyond this, the passage of time may also lead to a shifting of methods of access as well as the secondary impact of regulation. In the UK, for example, the Retail Distribution Review for insurers led to many independent agents leaving the market, forcing potential purchasers either to change adviser or to go down a different channel route, e.g., bancassurers.

Beyond these age demographical splits, in research IBM also identified[11] behavior segmentation which they called:

- Support seeking individualists (*'I need complete help'*)
- Product optimizers (*'I want a great product'*)
- Uninterested minimalists (*'Leave me alone'*)
- Price-sensitive analyzers (*'I want the best'*)
- Relationship-orientated traditionalists (*'I want someone I can trust'*).

There is some, but not absolute, alignment between these categories and age segmentations. In essence what insurance organizations are increasingly recognizing is that if they are to market to an individual personal level then each individual is a complex mix of these attributes, shaped by their own environment and circumstances. Marketers from all industries aspire to 'marketing to a segment of one' but in reality some degree of grouping appears essential if only to provide a systematic approach and obtain economy of scale.

Beyond the drive for granularity of marketing approach rest the further challenges of cultural and national differences. If one size does not fit all, then it may be impractical to customize each and every individual offering. Customization at its most basic definition means the ability to provide the right offer, at the right time, in the right way and at the right price. As cognitive analytic capabilities continue to mature, computing costs fall, and systems become increasingly automated, then the achievement of such ambition inevitably becomes closer.

6.5   PROMOTION STRATEGY

The expression 'promotion' refers to raising customer awareness of a product or brand, aiming to gain increased sales and loyalty. 'Promotion' comprises the set of activities which communicate the brand, product or service to the end consumer.

A major part of this relates to traditional advertising, either directly or indirectly through sponsorship. Social media analytics ('SMA') is effective in being able to associate sponsorship of sporting events, for example, with brand awareness. It is probably fair to say that the association between brand and event is not always as explicit as it might be and sometimes leaves much to the imagination. Social media analytics can be used to measure brand association to specific events and in doing so help to justify marketing expenditure. IBM's viewpoint on the activities of Chief Marketing Officers (2015) is that marketing spend on traditional forms is likely to fall whereas marketing spend on digital channels will increase, with this trend likely to continue.

Increasingly in this era of digital marketing, the task of promotion rests with those who are responsible for creating digital content on websites and outbound digital campaigns. These professionals are usually known as 'content marketers,' and need not necessarily come from an insurance background. The Chartered Institute of Marketing prepared a paper[12] which indicated how the most effective content marketers are using media to effectively promote goods and services (Table 6.5).

TABLE 6.5   Effectiveness of media to promote goods and services

	Most effective %	Least effective %
White papers	60	5
Blog posts	48	23
Earned media	46	23
Webinars	46	32
Infographics	44	18
News releases	44	64
Videos	44	27
Case studies	34	14
Research reports	32	0
Other	30	36

6.6   BRANDING AND PRICING

Brand is the sign, color, design, symbol or any other defining characteristic which differentiates one organization from another, and in financial terms can be considered an intangible asset.

Table 6.6 shows the World's most valuable brands in 2015, according to Forbes magazine.[13] In insurance or financial services, by comparison, the most valuable insurance brand in 2015 was Allianz, which was ranked 87th.

TABLE 6.6 World's most valuable brands in 2015 according to Forbes magazine (in US$ billions)

Rank	Brand	Brand value	1-yr value change	Brand revenue	Company advertising	Sector
#1	Apple	$145.3	17%	$182.3	$1.2	Technology
#2	Microsoft	$ 69.3	10%	$ 93.3	$2.3	Technology
#3	Google	$ 65.6	16%	$ 61.8	$3.0	Technology
#4	Coca Cola	$ 56	0%	$ 23.1	$3.5	Beverages
#5	IBM	$ 49.8	4%	$ 92.8	$1.3	Technology
#87	Allianz	$ 6.6	−6%	$131.6		Financial Services

Data Source: http://www.forbes.com/powerful-brands/list/

The caveat for these results is that Forbes only considered companies which are operative in the US, and therefore excluded companies such as Vodafone and China Mobile, which are the world's largest mobile providers.

The Forbes calculation was complex, and followed a series of key steps:

1. Determining earnings before interest and tax, obtained from company reports, research and experts, averaged across the past three years.
2. Deduction for capital employed which might have been earned elsewhere.
3. Applying corporation tax in the parent company's home country.
4. Allocation of percentage of earning to key brands based on the role brand plays in each country.
5. To derive the final 'brand earnings' number, applying average price to earning multiplier to arrive at final brand value.

In addition to this approach, analytic solutions already exist which measure 'brand equity,' otherwise described as 'the intangible value that consumers add to the value of a brand beyond its fair market value.'[14] As more data becomes more available, the computation of brand value and brand value 'fluctuation' will become easier to calculate in near-real time. The implication is that organizations including insurers will increasingly be able to understand their brand value and the impact, or potential impact, that external and internal events might have on that figure.

6.7   PRICING OPTIMIZATION

Price optimization is that process by which insurers might flex the price of a policy dependent not solely on issues of underwriting risk but also related to the time-driven demands of an existing or potential customer. Price optimization in insurance is analogous to the booking of airline flights where the cost of the flight changes dependent on the proximity of the request to the date of travel. The closer to the date of travel, the more expensive the cost of the flight until the airline recognizes a need to fill the plane in which case the cost usually falls.

In insurance, price optimization relates to the alignment of product pricing with the perceived value to the customer. It aims to balance the customer needs of reliability, brand, loyalty and convenience with the insurer's strategy, risk appetite, revenue growth and competitive environment. The key goal for insurers is to *optimize* the price of the insurance product whilst satisfying key corporate objectives such as business growth, revenue and retention. Proprietary optimization solutions comprise predictive analytics with patented algorithms. This provides insurers with greater customer insight in terms of what the customer might be prepared to pay for insurance products at any given time.

Beyond this, pricing optimization also recognizes the buying patterns of potential and existing policyholders and offers them different premiums based on their propensity to comparison shop even if the physical risk rating remains the same. As a result, the concept of pricing optimization is not universally accepted. Californian Insurance Commissioners (or 'regulators') ruled that the process was both 'discriminatory and illegal,'[15] saying:

> *'It is illegal for an insurer to charge people different rates based on their sensitivity to price increases or the likelihood they will comparison shop,'* (Insurance Commissioner) *Jones said in a statement. 'Price optimization represents a fundamental threat to fairness in rating.'*

In the UK, half of auto insurance is said to be priced using some form of price optimization tools but there is already some debate as to the appropriateness of this approach. The suggestion is that the consumer may see this as a form of exploitation of an already complex product. The implication is that as insurers increasingly rely on Big Data and the personal needs of an individual for matters of pricing rather than the underwriting risk, then this has the potential to further undermine the lack of trust the policyholder has in insurers.

The European legal case of *Test-Achats*[16] predominantly focused on the issue of gender but also reinforced the suggestion that insurance should be based on 'risk' rather than the nature of the individual. If this trend is followed, then it is suggested by some market experts that there is a possibility that consumers may 'call time' on pricing optimization but for the moment the analytical pricing process remains intact.

6.8   THE IMPACT OF SERVICE DELIVERY ON MARKETING SUCCESS

Customers are increasingly demanding effortless transitions across multiple touchpoints from the channel of their choice without having to repeat themselves. The indications are that insurance companies don't need to do exceptional things, but rather need to do the basics well. Anecdotally consumers appear to say they are likely to abandon their online purchase if they cannot find a quick answer to their questions.

At face value it seems a simple request. Do the simple things well, and companies are likely to keep their existing customers happy and win over prospective customers. Customers seem to say that their time is valuable and poor service comprises a waste of their time. Beyond this, customers want a unified experience across all channels, not only for consistency but also to avoid the time-wasting activity of trying to reconcile any differences in communication.

Whilst attitudinal differences in buying and support behavior are identified between different age groups, there is consistency between those age groups in intolerance to poor service. Older customers appear to be as intolerant as younger Generation Y customers when it comes to service failure.

Online services increasingly appear to meet the joint needs of rapid customer service, especially when coupled with cost reduction by the carrier through avoiding call center and other operational costs. This is dependent on the self-service process operating smoothly and effectively which is not always the case. Poor performance by online services may not necessarily result in a customer unfavorably differentiating against a particular insurer if everything else stacks up as being satisfactory, but it may create a disincentive for the user to try self-service in the future (for fear of again wasting their time).

6.9   AGILE DEVELOPMENT OF NEW PRODUCTS

The name of the game in product development now is 'agility,' which implies (amongst other things) the ability to bring new products to market more quickly in order to meet market and customer needs. The corollary to this is dropping market offerings when they are obsolete, or quickly modifying them in the face of competitive or other market pressures. The length of the product development lifecycle continues to tumble and this creates new and additional pressures. There is a constant drive for innovation but with this comes the issue of 'first mover advantage.' Those who move first have only a limited period before their competitors imitate them, provided they are not prevented legally from doing so.

The alternative to so-called first mover advantage is 'second' or 'last mover' advantage, a circumstance well known to the retail industry. Retailers often use own label branding to replace branded products once the need has been identified and the branded product has already been successfully marketed. Own label branding in retail is often less expensive and has minimal quality differences. As a result 'own label' products are extremely popular with the general public.

In their report 'The Myth of First Mover Advantage'[17] IHS Consulting cite a study showing that of 46 major innovations in the 20th century, the average timespan between introduction and follow-on declined by 90%, from 33 years to 3.4 years. It appears that reduction in the innovation cycle was already falling dramatically in the pre-digital age, so it is not unreasonable to expect the pace to pick up. Those companies that 'follow on' as second movers aimed to compete by improved operational excellence, improved offerings or innovative new formats. The IHS paper recalls that the first disposable diaper/nappy *Chux* lost out to Proctor and Gamble's *Pampers* product, and even companies such as Apple and Google built on the concepts of earlier pioneers.

Three key conditions apply for organizations to take advantage of first mover advantage:

- Learning/cost curves, which provide a barrier to entry for second movers who struggle to catch up with the innovator's initial development and subsequent scaling benefit.
- Scarceness of resources to implement a competitive strategy, although this is becoming less of an issue with the globalization of resource.
- Switching costs, where first movers lock in their customers, or alternatively followers need to incur additional costs to encourage change.

In insurance, those organizations who are adopting early mover strategies in the use of the Internet of Things may predominantly find their first mover advantage in the ownership and installation of the actual devices used to collect data. Alternatively, or additionally, advantage may rest in the know-how of how to use this information to gain particular insight.

Strategic partnerships will become increasingly critical followed closely by possible acquisition of those partners. As insurance becomes increasingly technologically orientated, the vertical acquisition by insurers of appropriate critical technologies such as analytical companies might seem more likely.

One potential downside of such vertical acquisitions may well be misalignment of culture. Large financial institutions priding themselves on legacy values find themselves unlikely bedfellows with much younger, dynamic technology companies which have very different cultures.

6.10   THE CHALLENGE OF 'AGILITY'

Customer-facing organizations including insurers aspire to be agile not just in product design and implementation but also in other business areas. 'Agile' development is often seen in IT development as an alternative to traditional project management, and as an alternative to 'waterfall' or sequential development. Development teams react to change through a series of incremental iterative changes known as 'sprints.'

'Agile' is not in itself a new concept but originated in 1970 when an American computer scientist Doctor Winston Royce presented a paper called 'Managing the Development of Large Software Systems.'[18] There he criticized the sequential process of obtaining all the requirements, creating the specification, then writing the code and so on. His argument was that as the requirements inevitably changed with time, this process impacted on the codes being written and therefore was inherently inefficient. As a consequence of this legacy process, developers were writing code for a process which by the time of delivery was inappropriate to the end-users' actual needs. (Some readers will recognize that scenario.)

In an 'agile' environment, every aspect of the development is constantly reassessed throughout the process on a shorter time cycle and thus there is a constant process of re-evaluation. If the end-user needs change, the process allows the development to change direction. The net benefit of this process is said to reduce time to market and thus costs.

One way of introducing 'agile' to a process is a technique known as 'scrum' which emphasizes feedback, self-directed teams and the building of reliable incremental changes within a short timeline. In this process, the team relies on three roles: product owner; team; and scrum master (which is a full-time facilitator role).[19] 'Agile' and 'scrum' are processes (or perhaps attitudes) which have predominantly originated in the technology sector. In theory, and probably in practice, there is no reason why this should not be able to be replicated in a product development or marketing environment. This may ensure better alignment between the role of marketing and the needs of the customer. Expert rugby players might argue that a 'scrum' approach to progress represents a team's effort to all push in the same direction. The analogy between intellectual processes and product development with the ultra-physical contact sport of rugby, from where the term 'scrum' emerges, is nevertheless slightly disconcerting. Those closest to the game will know that those in the 'front row' of the scrum are at the highest risk of physical injury.

'Agile Marketing'[20] describes the process in the following ways:

- Responding to change over following a plan
- Rapid iterations over so-called 'Big-Bang' campaigns
- Testing and data over opinions and conventions

- Numerous small experiments over a few large bets
- Individuals and interactions over target markets
- Collaboration over silos and hierarchy.

6.11   AGILE VS GREATER RISK?

There is no real consensus on how risk management should work in an agile environment other than that the idea of risk needs to be managed differently. If 'risk' is a measure of something negative which may or may not happen, then some suggest that in an agile approach it only becomes a problem when the 'risk' becomes an 'issue.' Furthermore, the iterative nature of the agile process means that unforeseen outcomes may even have a beneficial impact.

Even so, it is suggested that even an agile process should adopt some form of risk register which identifies risk, probability, impact and exposure (probability multiplied by impact). It is suggested that the risk register is reviewed at each sprint meeting.[21]

In an insurance organization which is naturally risk-averse, the adoption of such a 'fluid' risk-tolerant working environment creates specific challenges. By definition, this 'agile' methodology tolerates a degree of failure. Some non-insurance organizations run multiple 'sprints' simultaneously, maybe as many as 20, with the expectation that perhaps only one or two of these will develop to fruition. The real question is whether insurers can realistically operate in such an agile, risk-tolerant, and 'sandboxed' way (which allows entrepreneurism and innovation without threatening the main business). The indications seem to be that regulators may be tolerant towards innovation in a controlled environment.

6.12   THE DIGITAL CUSTOMER, MULTI- AND OMNI-CHANNEL

One development in more recent times is the advance of digital communications and in effect the 'digital customer.' These are customers who are influenced by the offers they receive on digital media such as on their mobile device. They then choose to act on the offer either by responding directly or alternatively by engaging with the insurer by telephone or on a face-to-face basis.

The process by which insurers aim to provide a consistency of offer and advice across all these channels is known as 'omni-channel.' Financial analytics in the form of financial performance management helps insurers to understand not only the cost of these channels but also their profitability when commissions and other costs are taken into account.

The use of digital media is a specific technique which is not related to insurers in particular but to all entities which place their offers online. The first part of the customer's journey is usually a targeted email, and authors recognize that it is not just a catchy title that is important but also the first line of the offer (as the first line is often also seen on the screen, even if the full page is not).

Web creation experts are keen to exploit the importance of color, font, visualizations and compelling text in their 'landing page,' and also to provide an easy to see click-through. They also recognize the need for conciseness and clarity in the text which has to demonstrate an understanding of the buyer's needs and challenges and provide reassurance that the offer from the insurer can meet those requirements. Prospective customers either need to be reassured by the brand or alternatively need some other sort of proof point to support the insurer's assertions.

These are complex issues and a prospective customer may still decide after opening the email not to proceed. Marketers are keen to understand why that should occur and may change one or more elements in the website or invitation to see if this makes a difference. The two main analytical processes which underpin this are called A/B and 'multivariate testing' (MTV). A/B testing is a simple approach whereby only one change is made, and the email offer is made again to see if this change has had any impact on conversion rates. The change may relate to something as simple as a single graphic or image. Some insurers might decide to run slightly different versions on a trial basis to see which version is the most effective. Multivariate testing, as the name suggests, involves a higher number of variants, and testing may include benchmarking conversion rates across a number of variations and then seeing which is the most successful.

Consumers also expect consistency across channels and no differences between operational silos. They view it as a fundamental requirement to be able to make enquiries across different channels in an effortless way, without the need to duplicate information and answer the same questions. 'Omni-channel' is described as a multi-channel approach to a single systematic customer experience.

Forrester, an influential research and advisory firm, suggests[22] that organizations should:

- Direct the customer to the channel of lowest effort for them to improve ease of engagement.
- Ensure that the technical infrastructure enables cross-silo movement.
- As far as practically possible, standardize workflows and processes across channels.
- Enable and empower agents and third parties.

6.13 THE IMPORTANCE OF THE CLAIMS SERVICE IN MARKETING

Whilst service often relates to the quote, purchase and policy administration process, service in the insurance industry is frequently best reflected by the claims process which for most insurance customers is the 'moment of truth.' The way in which a claim is handled is a critical success factor not only in terms of the indemnity process but in the perception of quality by the customer. Even if products are fundamentally the same, the customer's perception of quality is heavily influenced by the service delivery.

The ways in which an insurance claim is discharged are often affected by the number and quality of those involved who may be either inside or outside the organization. Service is affected by the key performance indicators ('KPIs') against which the parties are measured, and these KPIs often drive individual behaviors. Analytics provide insight from data points created in response to these key performance indicators which are obtained at critical decision points.

An alternative approach might be to contrast the measurement of customer satisfaction against each of these KPIs. By amending certain key measures and processes it may be possible to optimize the customer experience. In other words, perhaps a different approach might be to use analytics to obtain better understanding of what are the most appropriate, effective and *customer-satisfying* service delivery metrics and processes. This is in contrast to measuring achievement against existing internal financial measures. In doing so, insurers could have the potential to become truly 'customer-centric' by focusing on customer needs as the priority and building KPIs around those needs.

Increasingly the use of analytics can also help to integrate external providers and support them in becoming part of the virtual enterprise. The ability to consider the supply chain as part of the virtual enterprise of the insurer allows the collection of data from both inside and outside the insurance organization in a structured way. This lays the foundations for enhanced client/vendor relations of truth, trust and teamwork, all of which can only enhance the customer experience and also help with marketing.

Beyond this, insurers are also thinking about perhaps the ultimate in customer service – 'self-service' of claims. Indian-based auto insurer Bajaj Allianz General Insurance plans to allow customers to settle their claims on their own up to the limit allowed by insurance regulator IRDA. Managing Director and CEO Tapan Singhel describes the process as follows:[23]

> *A customer involved in an auto accident would download the company app and click photographs of the car. Based on the photos, the insurer will do the calculation of how much the loss should be . . . then the claim is settled on this basis. Nobody in between . . .*

Skeptics will invariably suggest that this process might open the door to fraudulent activity but by apparently cutting out the middle man in the process it would seem that the customer experience could be optimized. Such a process, suggests the insurer, could also be readily used on other simple claims.

Another form of disruptive 'self-service' claims handling process[24] allows for:

1. Inviting the customer to provide certain key elements of information.
2. Supplementing that information with imagery, e.g., photos taken by the customer themselves.
3. Adding external structured and unstructured data.
4. Remotely diagnosing the problem and instigating an appropriate remedy.

If it is accepted that customer service is critical and that insurance is ultimately about the quality of service at the moment of truth then new, innovative and perhaps even controversial approaches are likely to emerge. Whether they are successful or not will depend on the analysis of the data which yet further underpins the need for sound information around financial performance management.

One thing to be certain of is the increasing likelihood of transformational change in the insurance sector, not just in the acquisition and retention of insurance customers but also in the servicing of their claims.

NOTES

1. International Business Machines. 'Capitalizing on Complexity: Insights from the Global Chief Executive Officer Study' (Insurance Industry Executive Summary), 2010.
2. Pitney Bowes. 'The Dynamics of Defection.' London, 2008.
3. Sirohi, Niren, McLaughlin, Edward and Wittink, Dick. 'A Model of Consumer Perceptions and Store Loyalty Intentions for a Supermarket Retailer.' (1998) *Journal of Retailing* 74(2): 223–245.

4. Larsen, James. 'Customer Loyalty.' Customer Psychology Findings. Article 199. Pub Management Resources. http://www.businesspsych.org/articles/199.html (accessed November 9, 2015).

5. Bain and Co. *Customer Loyalty in Retail Banking: Global Edition.* Bain & Co., 2013.

6. Bain and Co. *Customer Loyalty and the Digital Transformation in P&C and Life Insurance: Global edition.* Bain & Co., 2014.

7. Hyken, Shep. 'IBM Conference Explains How Data Can Create a Better Customer Experience.' Published by IBM for Marketing Agencies, 2016. http://www.forbes.com/sites/shephyken/2015/11/07/ibm-conference-explains-how-data-can-create-a-better-customer-experience/ (accessed November 9, 2015).

8. Musico, Christopher. 'Customer Experience: Lifeboat for Today's Economy.' Published by Destination Cranblog, 2008. (Based on Harris Interactive Poll of 2112 adults over 18 years of age, October 6, 2008.)

9. Swiss Re Ltd Economic Research & Consulting. Sigma #3. 'World Insurance in 2012: Progressing on the Long and Winding Road to Recovery.' Published by Swiss Re, 2012. http://www.swissre.com/clients/Sigma_3_2013_World_insurance_in_2012.html.

10. International Business Machines. Institute of Business Value. 'Retail 2013 From Transactions to Relationships: Connecting with a Transitioning Shopper Study.' Published by IBM, 2013.

11. International Business Machines. Institute for Business Value. 'Creating New Value for Clients and their Customers.' Published by IBM, 2008.

12. Zinck, Barb Mosher. Results of CMO Survey. 'New Approaches for Content Marketing Promotion, Better Use of Marketing Analytics, and Leveraging Sensors for Improved Customer Experiences,' 2015. http://www.insidecxm.com/new-approaches-for-content-marketing-promotion-better-use-of-marketing-analytics-and-leveraging-sensors-for-improved-customer-experiences/ (accessed November 2015).

13. Forbes. 'Most Powerful Brands 2015.' http://www.forbes.com/powerful-brands/list/ (accessed November 10, 2015).

14. Joseph, Joy. 'Brand Equity.' Published by MetriScientist, 2010. http://metriscient.com/bequity.htm (accessed November 2015).

15. Insurance Journal (unattributed). 'California Commissioner Tells Insurers to Cease Price Optimization,' 2015. http://www.insurancejournal.com/news/west/2015/02/18/357788.htm (accessed November 10, 2015),

16. Case C-236/09, *Association Belge des Consommateurs Test-Achats ASBL et al.*

17. Pettit, Justin and Darner, Eric. 'The Myth of First Mover Advantage.' IHS Consulting: 2012.

18. Royce, Dr Winston W. 'Managing the Development of Large Software Systems.' Proceedings of IEEE WESCON 26 (August 1970): 1–9.

19. 'Agile methodology.' http://agilemethodology.org/ (accessed November 16, 2015).

20. Agile Marketing (unattributed). 'What is Agile Marketing?' http://www.agilemarketing.net/what-is-agile-marketing/ (accessed November 16, 2015).

21. Vethill, Satheesh Thekku. 'Risk Management in Agile.' Scrum Alliance Article, May 3, 2013. https://www.scrumalliance.org/community/articles/2013/2013-may/risk-management-in-agile (accessed November 16, 2015).

22. Leggett, Kate. 'Demands for Effortless Service Must Influence Your Customer Strategy.' Forrester, 2014.

23. Srivats, K.R. 'Now, settle insurance claims on your own via Bajaj Allianz app.' Published by The Hindu Business Line, 2015. http://www.thehindubusinessline.com/money-and-banking/bajaj-allianz-general-insurance-sharpens-customer-focus-with-tech-solution/article7864533.ece (accessed November 10, 2015).

24. 360globalnet. http://www.360globalnet.com/home (accessed November 10, 2015).

CHAPTER 7

Property Insurance

For the great majority of homeowners their experience of insurers at the moment of claim will be relatively minor. Perhaps a modest dent to their vehicle, a burst pipe (although in fairness, a burst pipe can be dramatic) or a few displaced roof tiles. They are the lucky ones. For the rest, perhaps their first experience of the claims process will be when their home has been burned to the ground, flooded or, in the case of the UK insurance market, has suffered major cracking as a result of ground movement such as subsidence damage. All these are traumatic and usually expensive events, sometimes technically difficult both from a property and from an insurance point of view, emotionally upsetting and all need to be handled accordingly.

At a time when emotions can run high the insurer will often attempt to empathize with a policyholder. This can be difficult as often the claims handler will never have suffered anything quite as dramatic in their own lives. It is impossible to understate the policyholder's emotion which is sometimes comparable to a bereavement. The loss of many or even all of a family's personal possessions can be a very painful event. These may include wedding photos, family documents and heirlooms. Often the incident may be accompanied by guilt – 'Did I really leave that cooker on?'

Insurers also need to view matters objectively. It became apparent through observation rather than analysis that where a pet owner deliberately set fire to their own home, then usually they also ensured that their pet had been safely removed beforehand. These 'triggers' and others often cannot be readily captured in the FNOL process yet to the experienced eye are sufficient to set in train a course of enquiry or a specific course of action. To what degree can an analytical approach identify these issues, if at all, and set in motion a different process?

In this section a selection of major domestic and complex claims will be discussed. First the context of each claim will be reviewed, then the impact of data and analytics will be investigated to help understand how loss types and levels can be predicted. Beyond this we shall consider how certain activities such as fraud management and restoration can be optimized by the use of analytics.

7.1 FLOOD

There is a specific insurance definition of 'flood' based on longstanding case law which talks about a sudden deluge of water as opposed to a gradual seepage (as in the case of rising groundwater). It's an expensive issue for insurers. The insurance costs of the floods of 2007 in England, the most expensive in the world that year, were over £3bn from 185,000 claims. The major flooding of New Orleans in 2005 as a result of Hurricane Katrina and the flooding of New York in 2014 appear to dwarf the UK event, but in reality there is no 'competition' involved here as each event is locally significant in its own right. Beyond the insurance aspect, these are deep and traumatic events which are both emotionally upsetting as well as economically disastrous. In addition to the impact on the home there is the impact on the local commercial community. Businesses cannot trade and sometimes need to relocate with a cost to local employees. Some stores and corner shops close on a permanent basis and whole communities are ultimately affected.

These are serious, painful and upsetting events for all involved. For insurers there are naturally the financial issues to consider but also the very personal and emotional challenges of those 'on the ground.' Claims adjusters and inspectors often find themselves in the most stressful of situations. They can be frustrated by lack of resource, sometimes feeling relatively helpless due to the scale of the incident yet also trying to provide ways that they can meet the needs of their policyholders at the proverbial 'moment of truth.'

Flood water is filthy. It is intrusive, destructive, often stinks and leaves a thick layer of sludge throughout the building. There are also significant health issues for the owners, inspectors of the damage and subsequent repairers. (Author's note: 'I remember being a claims inspector in 1987 when I visited a flooded property shortly after Christmas. The still-wrapped presents were floating in the water. It was heartbreaking.')

7.1.1 Predicting the Cost and Likelihood of Flood Damage

Insurers will soon be able to anticipate the likelihood of flooding taking place with a greater level of granularity than currently exists. There are considerable issues in predicting that a flood will actually occur. A '1-in-100-year flood' is only a statistical description of a particular flood event happening, and flooding can occur to a property on consecutive years. At best all insurers can hope to do is to understand the propensity of a property to flood at some time in the future and to rate the risk accordingly.

Typical factors to be considered include:

- Location of the property and its proximity to rivers and other water courses
- Height of the property above ground level
- Vulnerability of the building to damage
- Previous claims history
- Proximity and type of nearby defences
- Topography and water table
- Nature of policyholder, e.g., elderly
- Drainage systems which often back up and overflow
- Weather conditions.

Through weather tracking and rainfall/river measurements, insurers will increasingly improve their ability to anticipate and forewarn the policyholder at least in general terms before the damage occurs. As climate change leads to more and more flash flooding, such a proactive capability would increasingly appear to become a critical success factor for an insurer as a competitive differentiator.

Subject to appropriate approvals, insurers will soon be able to use remote real-time imagery or perhaps unmanned aerial devices (such as drones) to check visually that the property is under water. Liability will be triggered without further physical inspection and the claims process will swing into action. Understanding the probable depth of the water, the construction of the property, its location, the likely value and the likely expectations or behaviors of the owners or occupiers (which will give an insight into the quality of internal finishes) may even allow insurers, analytically, to place an initial estimate or 'reserve' on the loss.

It is useful to make a comparison between the US and Europe in this regard. The degree of diversity of building construction across Europe and indeed even in the UK alone is much more variable than that in North America which tends on the whole to be more standardized. The degree of diversification in Europe is influenced by available materials such as stone, timber, brick and also the much wider age bands of the buildings. Going forward this information is likely to be increasingly collected and perhaps shared, albeit at a cost.

There is an interesting question as to the value of this type of data in real terms. How much would an insurer or any other organization be prepared to pay to have a greater insight into risk and to be able eventually to obtain savings in both process and claims cost? Clearly this type of construction knowledge has some value (not only to insurers, but to government, property maintainers, and others with a vested interest). Might better analytics lead to improved monetization of data?

With data privacy currently focusing more on the individual rather than the property asset and with the increased movement towards 'digitalization,' it must only be a matter of time before there is a more comprehensive view of an insurer's asset base of property especially in mature environments. Is there a case for new data sources being set up which collate and distribute this information?

7.1.2   Analytics and the Drying Process

Drying is integral to the effective repair of a property which has been damaged by water. Permanent repairs cannot start until the property is dry. The drying process is heavily dependent on the nature of construction of the damaged building. There are many guides on the drying of a building yet many restorers still appear to rely on intuition and experience rather than adopting an analytical approach. It is a complex area. The quantity of water, its direction, the permeability of the construction materials and the length of time that the water has been standing in the property are all factors which need to be considered.[1]

Best practice for drying lends itself to a drying plan. Such a plan covers where to start, how to undertake water extraction, the containment of the problem (prevention of dampness moving from one part of the building to the other (causing secondary damage), how to compare moisture readings and how to implement an effective and scientific drying regime. All these issues appear to require an analytical approach.

Usually dehumidifiers are used to accelerate the drying process. These are machines which in essence remove the moisture from the air, collecting it as water (or condensate) which is then discarded. There are different types of dehumidifiers with different levels of efficiency and energy consumption. These may be 'condensing' appliances which act like a refrigeration unit, or alternatively absorption/desiccant dehumidifiers which have an absorbent 'desiccant' or absorption material which is exposed to the moist air. This is a major improvement from 20 years ago when the established method was simply to leave the windows open and allow drying through natural evaporation. As dehumidifiers became increasingly popular as a drying tool they were sometimes used together with having the windows open. This had the relatively useless effect of the equipment removing the moisture from the air outside the damaged building as opposed to helping with the drying process.

At the heart of effective drying is a requirement to understand the dynamics of drying. Manufacturers of dehumidifiers usually state the amount of water removal possible over a 24-hour period at a given temperature. It is then applied through a moisture management system, used to establish the number and required capacity of the driers and the probable duration of usage. With science at its core, effective drying certainly seems to lend itself to the collection of data either locally or remotely and then remote management of the drying procedure.

The development of the British Damage Management Association (BDMA) in the UK in 1999 was a major step in establishing and promoting best practices amongst the UK insurance industry. Its members now extend to flood restoration contractors, insurers and intermediaries such as loss adjusters. The BDMA Mission Statement[2] is 'to represent the interests of practitioners working in the damage management industry, to facilitate education, training, technical support, advice on standards and representation of members' interests in the public, industry and commercial domains.'

Elsewhere, flood 'schools' have also emerged to reflect the complexity of the flooding and subsequent drying process. The most advanced have custom-built structures which are deliberately flooded to allow operatives to gain first-hand experience of the problems and processes before they are allowed to work with the general public.

The challenge with flooding is that it often involves large numbers of properties across a wide area especially in the case of river flooding. This places enormous pressures on the restoration infrastructure as well as the insurance claims department. Such a problem of major supply/demand imbalance is unlikely to go away especially as the changing climate seems to point to a future of more frequent and perhaps greater flooding. Warmer wetter winters create a residual high water table and summer thunderstorms result in flash floods. Although the cause of climate change is disputed, government bodies such as the Intergovernmental Panel for Climate Change suggest an increase in winter rainfall of up to 25% by 2050, and an increase of up to 40% by 2080.[3]

If remote monitoring is viewed as the ultimate solution to the problem of the drying process, then it should be recognized that these changes will not occur overnight. Rather there will be a gradual shift, perhaps in the same way that the impact of the Internet of Things will become increasingly pervasive. As a result there might not be a 'burning platform' for change but rather the insurance industry will need to transition into a new operating model increasingly influenced by better data capture. In the same way that the innovators of remote monitoring devices of subsiding properties have found it a struggle to change established methods, those who innovate and introduce remote moisture sensors as a way of managing flood damage will also need to be clear, not only on the methodology but also on the return on investment, before they can capture the hearts and minds of the insurance community.

7.2 FIRE

Now that we have considered the problem of flooding, we should go on to consider that of fire which is equally destructive. Often extinguishment water is as damaging as the fire itself. In the same way that flood-damaged properties are affected in different ways as a result of age and type and construction, the effect of fire is significantly impacted by the nature of construction. Parts of the building not affected directly by fire may suffer due to the effect of smoke which is not only dirty but corrosive.

Beyond this a major contributing factor to the risk of fire damage is location. If the property is in a remote location or some distance from the fire station, then the probable impact of a fire will be significantly greater. Location of extinguishing services may present a growing problem to insurers

Like many other public services, the fire service is under pressure to reduce costs. In London for example, the Fifth London Safety Plan (LPS5)[4] recently identified £29 million of savings in London alone. Under the proposals which were approved by the London Fire and Emergency Planning Authority, it was successfully argued that the Brigade 'would still maintain its existing London-wide attendance target of getting a first fire engine to an emergency within an average six minutes and the second fire engine, if needed, within eight minutes.' The indicator therefore seems to be not necessarily one of 'absolute' location of fire stations, at least in London, but of how long it takes to get to the incident. Increased congestion of roads will inevitably add to the pressure of meeting these targets.

Sir Ken Knight in his report 'Facing the Future: Findings from the review of efficiencies and operations in fire and rescue authorities in England'[5] also suggested that there were further potential cuts of nearly £200m per year in the UK Fire Service principally as a result of the effect of fewer fires actually happening. There is wider discussion to be had on this topic and recognition that the Fire Service also attend to other incidents such as flooding and motor accidents but overall the indicators appear to be that there are fewer fires, which may place even greater pressure on resources.[6]

The US picture seems to reflect a similar story. According to the National Fire Protection Association 'Trends and Patterns of US Fire Losses in 2013'[7] US municipal fire departments responded to an estimated 1,240,000 fires in 2013. Structural fires totaling 487,500 accounted for 39% of all reported incidents. Reported fires fell 62% from 3,264,500 in 1977 to 1,240,000 in 2013. From 2012 (1,375,000 fires) to 2013, fires fell 10%. Home structure fires account for 85% of civilian fire deaths.

Clearly the use of fire alarms in the home has helped the situation. Working smoke alarm ownership increased rapidly from 8% in 1988 to 70% in 1994 in England, and has continued to rise in recent years, reaching 88% in 2011. From an analytical point of view, perhaps it would be interesting to have a 'connected' fire alarm that might be linked in some way to the Fire Service, apart from the potential problem of the number of false alarms that could be triggered as a result of burning the toast.

7.2.1 Predicting Fraud in Fire Claims

Many of those intent on fraudulent behavior recognize that the cause of a fire cannot always be readily identified with absolute certainty although often it is possible to speculate. Experts, more specifically forensic engineers, are able in some cases to identify the source of a fire by inspecting in great detail the degree of charring of timbers and the path of the fire generally. By working backwards, this allows them to move towards the 'seat' of the fire and from this form an opinion on causation. As many insurance reports are discoverable in court, should there be dispute on policy liability, inspectors and engineers often use the expression that the fire was 'doubtful in origin.' Claims managers reading between the lines will know exactly what this implies.

As with other types of claim, insurers often use 'fraud indicators' to help in the investigation process. These will differ depending on whether the fire is domestic or commercial in nature. Often insurers will want to 'reserve their position' until such time as causation is clear and therefore the liability of insurers can be established.

Usually insurers and their investigators look for a motive. In the case of a commercial fire, the clues may rest in the accounts. Were there cash flow or profitability issues? What was the position regarding stock and was this obsolete? And even if the insurer has a suspicion of fraud, can this be proven? The use of analytics as part of forensic accounting starts to become a critical part of the investigator's toolbag.

In a commercial environment, typical fraud indicators which might be associated with a potential fraudulent loss include:[8]

- Fire at night, especially after 11 pm.
- Commercial fire on a holiday, weekend or when business is closed.
- Fire cause is reported by the fire department to be incendiary, suspicious, doubtful or unknown.
- Failure of the fire alarm and/or sprinkler system at the time of the loss.

Deliberate fire-raising by the policyholder in a domestic situation is less likely but there are also indicators, for example:[9]

- Building and/or contents being up for sale at the time of the loss.
- Suspiciously coincidental absence of family pet at time of fire.
- Absence of items of sentimental value at the scene of investigation (e.g., family Bible, family photos, trophies).

It is unlikely that analytics will ever reach the point at which insurers will be able to say with any degree of certainty whether a claim is fraudulent or not, and to decline the claim accordingly. However, these 'indicators' if captured adequately may set the insurer or their advisor down a particular new line of enquiry which may reveal more information. Correlation between the circumstances of the event and other information, for example unstructured data relating to behavior or trading information, may present valuable clues which encourage insurers to dig more deeply. Beyond this, as insurance investigations become more analytical in nature there is a possibility that new correlations will start to materialize.

The issue of the behavior of individuals may be the most critical of all. Why would someone want to damage their own property? In 2002 the Australian Institute of Criminology considered motives and possible solutions,[10] suggesting that arson was due to one or more of the following factors:

- profit
- animosity
- vandalism
- crime concealment
- political objectives
- psychological factors.

With regards to the specific item of psychological factors, they suggest that the key indicators are

- schizophrenia
- personality disorders
- various forms of mental handicap
- substance abuse
- mood disorders.

To what degree might any or all of these symptoms be identified through unstructured information such as social media? It seems feasible to gain some insight into behavior from information which an individual might post on their social media site. Such techniques are often used, mainly with the benefit of hindsight, in investigating other types of criminal behavior.

7.3 SUBSIDENCE

If both flood and fire are viewed as traumatic and relatively instantaneous events causing major damage, the problem of subsidence is a quite different type of issue as the damage usually appears gradually. Liability for subsidence and ground movement damage first reared its head in the UK in the 1970s at a time when there was no real certainty as to what the peril was intended to cover. It arose as a need to protect lenders against loss of value due to foundation movement but transformed into a cottage industry in its own right. Over the course of 40 years, subsidence damage has cost UK insurers over £5 billion.

Subsidence is often but not always related to ground movement, usually clay shrinkage brought on by dry weather and tree root activity. The peaks in numbers of claims and cost to UK insurers correspond with significant periods of drought, i.e., between 1989 and 1992, 1995 and 1997 and in 2003. Over a 12-year period between 1989 and 2003 the total cost to the UK insurance industry was close to £4.8 billion, representing an annual average cost of £598 million. This is a relatively small amount compared to the average North American hurricane but remains an ongoing issue regardless. In recent years with milder weather the annual number of claims has reduced from 55,000 to 28,000 with an average repair cost of under £7,000.[11] Even so, the potential still remains for an extreme drought year where UK insurers could face the potential of claims costs of as much as £1.0 billion.

Insurers are obliged under the terms of the policy to indemnify the insured against 'loss or damage.' This usually results in a diminution of value (or cash) settlement, or the cost of foundation repair and making good above ground. The repair process itself can take months but the investigation process beforehand can take years. During this time the homeowner is often 'locked' into staying in that property even if the problem was first discovered when they were trying to relocate. In recent times insurers have become more proactive in the investigation and repair process through transferring the benefits of any outstanding claim to free up the sales process.

In the worst of cases the home can become unsaleable. As with flood and fire, these can be very emotional times. A sale may fall through and if the sale relates to relocation due to a job offer, then careers can potentially be affected. Marriages have been known to collapse as a result of the ongoing problem. Subsidence claims are often characterized by their longstanding nature and the emotional distress they involve.

The two main causes of subsidence damage to properties are:

- Tree-induced clay shrinkage, where moisture is taken from the ground by tree roots, often exacerbated by prolonged periods of dry weather.
- Influence of leaking drains on predominantly sandy or silty ground beneath foundations, causing a softening or washing-out effect.

7.3.1 Prediction of Subsidence

Subsidence damage to a property is complicated, involving multiple inter-related factors (as illustrated in Figure 7.1) typically:

- The fabric of the building and the materials from which it is constructed.
- The age of the building, which is usually related to the depth of foundation.
- The foundation depth and whether there is a cellar, which often acts as a natural 'pivot' upon which the remainder of the building hinges.

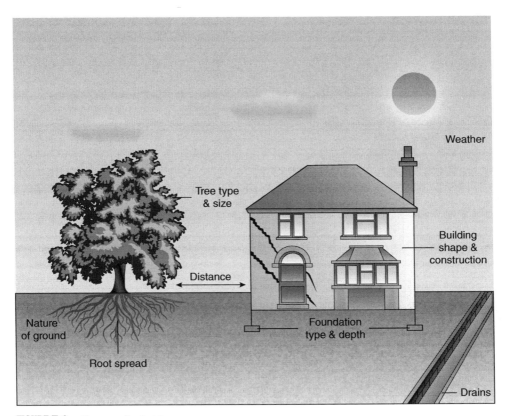

FIGURE 7.1 Causes of subsidence

- The shape of the building, in that those with extensions are often more vulnerable with the extension rotating away from the main part of the structure.
- The ground conditions – sand, clay, silty sand, sandy silt and many other combinations sometimes with very peculiar local characteristics.
- Location and age of drains, and their proximity to the foundations. Where the ground is especially silty or sandy, leaking drains can soften or wash away the substrata leading to a loss of strength in the underlying soil.
- Location and type of trees and their drying effect on clay soil strata bearing in mind that different trees have different 'thirsts.' The proximity of the trees to the affected building is a critical factor.
- The size of the tree canopy in that the thirst of the tree roots appears related to the size of the tree canopy and the degree of evaporation from the leaves.
- Weather conditions, typically heat and evaporation usually measured by average yearly temperatures.

The definitive guide to the challenge of subsidence is probably 'Subsidence of Low Rise Buildings' published by the Institution of Structural Engineers initially in 1994 but with further updates since then.[12] This guide represents the interests of multiple practitioners in the insurance market ranging from insurers to repairers. It remains an extremely strong example of collaboration across the wider marketplace. The foundational material ultimately led to the formation of the Subsidence Forum[13] which has published its own guide and is aligned to other agencies such as *Hortlink* which is a UK-based horticultural R&D organization focusing on the impact of trees on buildings.

The actual type of tree involved is important as different trees take in moisture from the ground to different degrees, and this has an impact on the likelihood of damage to nearby properties. Research[14] by tree experts, known as arboriculturalists, has discovered significant variation between different types of trees. Willow trees, for example, are considered to be especially 'thirsty' and most likely to cause clay shrinkage beneath the foundations of a building. Organizations such as the UK based Clay Research Group (CRG)[15] regularly and persistently look for patterns between trees, ground condition and weather. It has not been an easy task but intuitively there is a sense that they are on the right track by pursuing an analytically orientated approach to the problem.

The subsidence issue is particularly interesting in the context of analytics due to the number of variables involved. In addition, there are behavioral attributes of homeowners in their response to a problem with what is possibly their most valuable asset. Some homeowners react quite noisily to relatively modest degrees of damage, others are relatively complacent with severe damage if it is out of sight. Lenders and future insurers may also have rules in respect to their risk appetite in terms of whether this is a property they are prepared to provide a mortgage for, or provide future insurance cover.

The accuracy of prediction will improve with greater computing power and the use of better analytical capability. However, it is unlikely that the current low level and costs of claims will drive the required investment, nor the relatively localized nature of the insurance problem in global terms. Perhaps a niche opportunity exists for a start-up in this problem area.

Another question to consider is whether the ability to predict damage with absolute certainty is in fact critical for insurers. Underwriters only need to understand the likelihood of such damage occurring to allow them to rate the risk with reasonable accuracy. Is there a possibility that insurers will spend a disproportionate amount in seeking data and analyzing it before they realize that they are no better off than earlier in terms of their underwriting knowledge?

It is important that the insurance industry thinks about the concept of diminishing returns in their analytical investment. Insurers can look for additional data and insight but the real question may well be what degree of additional benefit or advantage might this give in terms of pricing or competitive advantage? Competition may well be 'at the edges of underwriting' but at what cost? Insurers need to understand ROI, even in an atmosphere of emotion, in deciding whether analytics is desirable or not.

The investigation and repair process has also changed considerably over the years. Where once the suggested approach was invasive, usually involving major foundation repairs known as underpinning, the preferred option now is to consider mitigating action and a 'wait and see' approach. This reduces the cost but extends the life of the claim. In the case of tree-related subsidence, trees are often cut back or removed allowing the property to stabilize and then repairs are confined mainly to the superstructure alone. The nature of tree management seems to be important but is still shrouded in a degree of uncertainty. If tree management is the panacea, then this also involves regular maintenance and ongoing cost.

One of the proof points of the investigation and successful remediation is whether the building is continuing to move and whether that movement is structurally significant. The ability to remotely monitor movement is increasingly replacing physical checking. However, the cost point of physical investigation remains low and in many cases is cheaper than a technological approach. Remote monitoring in an environment of the 'Internet of Things' is an effective solution if the cost of technology is attractive, but less so if it forces down the cost of the traditional methods and even potentially drives new business models.

One strong argument for continual remote telegraphic monitoring is that it provides an ongoing record of movement and distortion. This is in contrast to the infrequency of physical measurement where only the degree of movement or 'delta' since the last measurement can be captured as a record. Continuous monitoring may help the industry better understand the impact and influence of trees. Weather conditions and ground evaporation are also major contributors. More data may give us more insight into all these but in the case of subsidence damage how might it change the best practices of the marketplace?

At face value, subsidence provides one of the most difficult sets of circumstances in the insurance environment at least from a domestic claim point of view. Experts have collected and analyzed data for some years, and are still not yet in a position to accurately predict whether a building will suffer from subsidence or not. This is not a fault on the part of the experts nor the process by which the information has been collected. Rather, it is a feature of the complexity of the situation. The reduction in the number of subsidence insurance claims in recent years has removed any burning platform for investment. The impact of this may have been a temporary loss of focus but the possibility still exists for a major subsidence 'incident' at some time in the future when there may be a skill shortage or loss of talent.

This period of relative quiet in terms of claim numbers should not be an excuse for complacency. It presents an opportunity for revisiting the entire business model in a more controlled and less risky environment. New entrants have done this in the past but perhaps there is another radical approach which is both innovative and disruptive which has yet to be discovered.

7.4 HAIL

With hail often lasting no more than a few minutes yet with hail stones that can weigh up to 2 pounds, the cost of claims due to hail damage is significant. Underwriters are especially interested to understand where damage is likely to occur and the potential costs. The mechanism by which hail is created is complex involving evaporation, convection, and leading ultimately to a cloud phenomenon known as 'cloud topping' which is detectable by radar (Figure 7.2).

The annual cost of hail to crops and property in the US is about $1 billion dollars, according to the National Oceanic Atmospheric Administration (NOAA). There were 5411 major hail storms in 2015 according to US statistics, with a hailstone event described as 'major' when

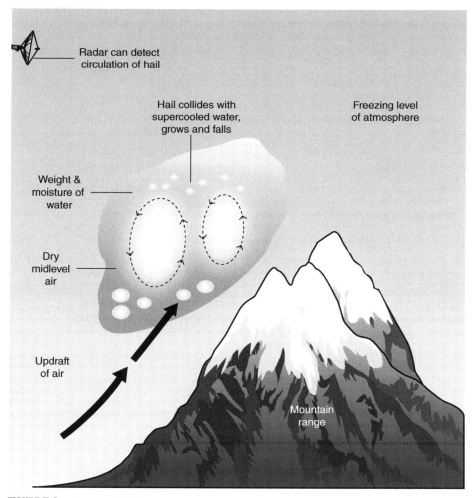

FIGURE 7.2   Causes of hailstones

comprising hailstones of more than 1 inch (25mm) diameter. Table 7.1 identifies the top five US States for major hail events in 2015. In the US, there were 5.9 auto damage claims due to hail per 1,000 insured vehicle years in 2011, compared with 2.9 in 2008 and 2009 and 2.7 in 2010.[16]

TABLE 7.1   Top five US States for major hail events, 2015

Rank	State	Number of Events
1	Texas	783
2	Kansas	519
3	Nebraska	458
4	Oklahoma	349
5	South Dakota	283
	United States	5411

Source: U.S. Department of Commerce, National Oceanic and Atmospheric Administration, National Weather Service

From 2000 to 2013, US insurers paid almost 9 million claims for hail losses totaling more than $54 billion. Most of those losses (70%) have occurred during the past six years.[17]

This is not just a North American phenomenon as China, Central Europe and southern Australia also experience hailstorms. In Europe significant hailstorms occur in southern and western Germany, northern and eastern France, and southern and eastern Benelux. In the three hailstorms of 2013 in northern Germany, the total cost to insurers was an estimated €3.2 billion (£2.5bn). In France in 2014 Hailstorm Ela cost insurers €2.3 billion (£1.7bn), affecting 190,000 vehicles and 140,000 properties.[18]

7.4.1   Prediction of Hail Storms

Prediction of hail damage can be done through understanding and analysis of:

- Hailstone size
- Existing loss data
- Eyewitness reports
- Weather databases
- Climate change models
- Remote sensing.

Beyond this, the cost of damage is affected by demographics, population intensity and also the time of the incident. One of the prime factors in the 'Wolfgang' hailstorm event, which cost insurers €115m, was the fact that the storm occurred at a time when there were more vehicles on the road. It was commuting time when the hailstorm happened with a great proportion of the damage being to cars. The increasing use of solar panels on the property roofs may also be seen to constitute a greater risk to losses.

In many cases, and as with other insured perils, data may not be directly comparable as it may relate to different study periods, levels of granularity and whether the information was obtained directly or indirectly. Increasingly, the use of radar and crowd sourcing helps provide more information. Work by expert institutions such as the Karlsruhe Institute of Technology (KIT) and conferences such as the 1st European Hail Workshop in Berne in 2014 are throwing more and more light on the topic and indicate that prediction from remote sensing is 'both practical and possible.'

7.5   HURRICANE

Not only do we happen to give hurricanes names like Katrina or Sandy, but also we give them numbers. These range from 1–5 and are taken from the Saffir-Simpson hurricane wind scale.[19] This measures the wind speed at 10m above ground at one point inside the cyclone. Category 5 is the strongest, with wind speeds of over 157 miles per hour. The description of Category 5 is dramatic:

> *Catastrophic damage will occur: A high percentage of framed homes will be destroyed, with total roof failure and wall collapse. Fallen trees and power poles will isolate residential areas. Power outages will last for weeks to possibly months. Most of the area will be uninhabitable for weeks or months.*

7.5.1   Prediction of Hurricane Damage

It is beyond the ability of insurers to prevent hurricanes but through the use of analytics the ability to understand the effects has greatly improved, both before the event and as a consequence of the damage. The ability to predict a hurricane occurring has existed for some time and the ability to model its effect is a core capability of some expert companies. The new challenge is how to do this more quickly and with greater accuracy.

The major damage in New Orleans as a result of Hurricane Katrina in 2005 repeated the flooding which had taken place in that city on five other occasions – 1915, 1940, 1947, 1965 and 1969. Improvements in catastrophe modeling had taken place following Hurricane Andrew in 1992, which was at the time of the incident the most destructive hurricane in US history.

Further improvements have been possible as a result of:

- Collecting more claims data from previous events
- Better incident simulation
- More accurate property information
- Consideration of the total impact of the hurricane over its entire lifecycle, rather than the landfall
- Simulation of failure of flood damage defenses.

The use of catastrophe risk engineering coupled with business continuity planning and emergency response procedures helps provide a more comprehensive catastrophe risk management program. Increasingly as defenses are replaced and properties are repaired following a major incident, they are being made more resilient, and refinements are being made in evacuation plans. Improvements seemingly can happen relatively quickly. When Hurricane Gustav occurred in 2008, 97% of customers evacuated on their own, and a total of 21,000 evacuated with the city's assistance.[20]

These are not insurance issues alone but rather reflect the need for an integrated public/ private collaborative viewpoint. This is not new thinking and the idea mirrors the challenges which already exist for flood damage.

For hurricanes, insurers are keen to understand current and anticipated wind field conditions, the current and anticipated location of the event and the likely impact of both on their customer base. From these factors they can understand the effect of a hurricane on their book of business. This helps them create a better understanding of both their solvency capital requirement and also how to optimize their reinsurance arrangements. Reinsurance and catastrophe bond companies are also keen to understand the financial impact of an event and to what degree their policies need to respond in an incident.

Insurers and reinsurers are anxious to predict the future as far as hurricane events are concerned in order to ensure that they remain both profitable and solvent. However, it is important to carry out effective post-event evaluation of predicted damage. Post-event review has the benefit of using additional observations which might not have been available in real time so as to give a greater insight into likely predictions in the future. One area of research at the moment is to better understanding the 'energy' within the hurricane in order to understand its destructive potential as opposed to relying on the Saffir-Simpson 'wind scale' approach which is in effect a 'point solution' (albeit a moving point).

Calculation of the energy of the hurricane is known as the Integrated Kinetic Energy (IKE) approach. This considers the hurricane as a series of concentric circles all having different wind speed and therefore different destructive powers. This approach takes into account the size of the hurricane as well as its strength. The total kinetic energy of a moving hurricane is known as 'TIKE,' named after a paper entitled 'Track Integrated Kinetic Energy of Atlantic Tropical Cyclones.'[21] Experts are currently examining data from historic hurricanes obtained from a variety of monitoring devices such as satellites, aircraft and radar to try to better understand the correlation between data and actual damage, and in effect retro-fit the new 'TIKE' model and improve it. Beyond this, satellite telemetry also claims to be able to measure the tiny capillary surface waves on top of the larger wind waves in the ocean as an indicator of potential hurricanes occurring.[22]

7.6   TERRORISM

By definition, terrorist events are intended to be unpredictable in order to cause the greatest threat and fear. Despite this, there is an analytical viewpoint both in terms of the assessment of risk and potential degree of damage.

Considering firstly the issue of the assessment of risk, analytics can be used in the measurement of terrorism and political risk, with specialist firms using a combination of levels of intelligence to assess political and violent incidents. Typical analytical capabilities include 'influence mapping, indicator identification, intelligence collection, qualitative forecasting for political risk, scenario analysis and modelling.'[23]

Political risks intrinsically also have a degree of uncertainty. With hindsight it is often easy to suggest that one risk was overstated whereas another was missed. Political risk is mainly a matter of experience and of judgment but increasingly social media has a part to play in understanding local sentiment. Specialist firms usually quantify the degree of risk in some form of metric or color coding if only to provide an element of benchmarking and better visualization.

Terrorism risk can apply both to physical damage and indirectly through kidnapping. Kidnap and ransom insurance (K&R) remains an important part of the specialist insurance portfolio, and some international companies even appear to have cover for key employees without actually telling them. Beyond this the *Lonely Planet* guide has even suggested to individual travelers that in certain areas they should not enter the country without having appropriate kidnap/hostage cover.

In the context of analytics, the quantification of political, terrorism or hostage risk appears to be no more than an attempt to quantify a probability of an event happening. This might be based on claims history, personal insights, media analytics, crowd sourced commentary or perhaps even just 'gut feeling.' Maybe this is one area where unstructured 'dark' information might be more used as part of the analytical mix.

7.6.1   Predicting Terrorism Damage

There is a tendency to associate terrorism with physical damage such as the effects of a bombing. Increasingly, the thinking seems to be moving away from terrorism being a single major incident, and towards it being a series of smaller consecutive ones with an aggregated effect. Insurers must unfortunately contemplate both scenarios, typically:

- A single large incident, affecting multiple properties nearby. In such a scenario, insurers will want to consider their accumulation of risk and which properties might be directly affected by a blast. What creates a particular challenge for some insurers is that they aren't always sure about the properties they insure. This often applies to major corporations which have subsidiaries with many trading names.
- Multiple smaller incidents designed to create disruption and distress but perhaps with less physical damage by comparison. The same issues relating to names of businesses and their locations also apply.

In the case of a single physical explosion, there is likely to be a single blast circle dependent on the size of the device. If a series of smaller events take place there will be a number of blast circles which may overlap, making the analysis of risk and hazard much more complex to calculate. Perhaps if such a pessimistic viewpoint is taken, then some portfolios of property could even prove to be uninsurable.

Contingency plans drafted for a single major incident may be of limited use in the case of multiple incidents as business disruption across a wider area may occur. In the case of a so-called 'dirty bomb,' access may be restricted for some considerable time. The problem would be exacerbated by multiple dirty devices. Can insurers really effectively plan for these worst case multiple incident scenarios either in terms of operational response, reinsurance cover or capital requirement? When regulators ask for stress testing, exactly how much 'stress' should the system be placed under in this current volatile environment?

What becomes clear is that prevention is better than cure. Increasingly insurers, brokers and risk managers have to consider 'worst case scenarios' and increasingly consider preventive measures rather than reactive solutions. Analytics has a major part to play in that discussion, especially the integration of Financial Performance Management tooling with location analytics. Perhaps this is not the capability that analytics and GIS companies might want to showcase on their websites but sensible discreet conversations might not go amiss. All this may not prevent the incident or incidents occurring but will help to mitigate the loss and improve the recovery process.

7.7   CLAIMS PROCESS AND THE 'DIGITAL CUSTOMER'

All these claim types take place in the context of the 'digital customer.' Whilst one viewpoint is that the concept of the digital customer relates solely to the sales, marketing and distribution process (covered elsewhere), the new capabilities of communication acquired by insurance policyholders have far-reaching effects. By way of example, let us explore one real-life case study relating to a family member of the author whose house was burned to the ground.

In this case, there were fortunately no casualties but it could have been very different. In the US, in 2013 there were 2755 civilian fire deaths in the home. By comparison, in 2013–14 there were 322 fire-related deaths in Great Britain, 20 fewer than in 2012–13, which is the lowest number recorded in the last 50 years. The highest number of fatalities recorded was 967 in 1985–86. Throughout the 1990s and 2000s there has been a clear downward trend in the number of fatalities. Even so, bereavement need not occur to stimulate a major emotional reaction on the part of the policyholder.

With fire especially in a timber building, there is a much greater risk of injury or death. Whilst a flood usually creeps up gently and forecasting can signal incoming inclement weather, fire occurs rapidly, dramatically and unexpectedly. A family with young children may find themselves standing in the dark with nothing more than the nightclothes they are wearing and some coats from helpful neighbors. They have lost their home and perhaps also many or all their photographic and sentimental possessions.

Such a dramatic event will also possibly be their first encounter with an insurance company. How the insurer and their representatives behave will be critical to the relationship going forward. When the dust has settled and the embers have cooled, there is sometimes a tendency to try and bring the claim to an early conclusion by way of a cash settlement by 'cutting a deal.' This is in effect passing the burden of responsibility to the policyholder to clear the site, design and arrange the reconstruction. The impact of this burden particularly on working and traumatized families should not be underestimated. Some affected policyholders might even see this as 'sharp practice.'

Adverse behavior by an insurer in a traumatic situation can very quickly become very public. Even if the home is destroyed, one of the first things to be restored by the individual is their connectivity. Whilst their original WiFi modem may be a melted blob in the corner of a pile of ashes, the homeowner will quickly make arrangements to telephone friends and to get online. It is at that point, as they get online, that the problem for the insurer potentially starts. Poor or inappropriate behavior by the insurer or their representatives is rapidly and extensively shared. Members of social networks will receive blow by blow accounts of offers, proposals, behaviors and responses. They will solicit sympathy for the claimant, anger at behaviors of intermediaries or perhaps, at best, provide advocacy of an insurer. Some claimants may only have a handful of contacts but others may have many hundreds, some even thousands. In such an environment, insurers should perhaps be aware of who they are dealing with. The upset digital customer at the point of claim is a formidable entity.

Insurers and their agents sometimes also implicitly take into account the 'value' of their affected customer. This value might be considered in terms of the total life value, i.e., the anticipated profit attributed to the future relationship with that individual, their commercial interests (for example their ownership of a business), their life and pension policies, or even from time to time their 'celebratory status.' Even so, many insurers still struggle to have adequate transparency across their businesses and to have a single viewpoint of their customer. Perhaps 'value' in the traditional way of thinking is also changing in the digital age, measured by the size of the individual's social network and their ability to influence others?

Not all fire-damaged buildings are 'write-offs.' Some may be structurally damaged while others which are more resilient will perhaps suffer from smoke and soot damage. Smoke and soot pervades the premises, getting into drawers and wardrobes, cupboards and soft and hard furnishings. It is important to start the cleaning process quickly – but there is also a trade-off between pressing ahead with cleaning and admitting policy liability. It is a weak (but sometimes understandable) excuse on the part of the inspector or adjuster to 'raise no objection' to the customer starting the clean-up operation but refusing to accept policy liability until investigations are complete.

Similarly, there needs to be sensitivity around the clean-up process itself. Where a property has been burned to the ground and nearly all possessions lost, the homeowner is likely to want to examine the debris carefully to see what can be salvaged. This is an emotional time which calls for sensitivity in this process-driven age. Key performance indicators are important but perhaps not at the expense of doing the 'right thing.'

How will this process transform in the digital age? Will there be a demand for quicker decisions at the speed of the internet and as a consequence will this start to transform the process? The ability to make a trade-off between availability of information and a decision regarding policy liability will increasingly become critical. Insurers are likely to need to commit to accepting liability more quickly and as a result become both more proactive and more sensitive in the remedial process.

Are decisions likely to be made based on both the observed and other available data rather than the physical evidence alone? Perhaps this will increasingly force the insurance industry down the road of automated decision-making.

NOTES

1. Lamond Booth et al. *Flood Hazards. Impacts and Responses for the Built Environment*, CRC Press, 2012.
2. British Damage Management Association (2015) http://www.bdma.org.uk/about/mission (accessed October 1, 2015).
3. E.P. Evans et al. 'An Update of the Foresight Future Flooding 2004 Qualitative Risk Analysis.' London: UK Cabinet Office, 2008.
4. London Fire Brigade. 'The Fifth London Safety Plan 2013-2015 (LPS5).' London, 2013. http://www.london-fire.gov.uk/Documents/LSP5-authority-version-18-july-following-september-authority-meeting.pdf (accessed May 17, 2016).
5. Knight, Sir Kenneth. 'Facing the Future: Findings from the review of efficiencies and operations in fire and rescue authorities in England.' London: HM Stationery Office, 2013.
6. Department for Communities and Local Government. 'Fire statistics monitor April to September 2012.' London: UK Government, 2013. https://www.gov.uk/government/uploads/system/uploads/attachment_data/file/141857/Fire_Statistics_Monitor_April-September_2012_final.pdf (accessed May 17, 2016).
7. National Fire Protection Association. 'Trends and Patterns of US Fire Losses in 2013.' One-Stop Data Shop NPFA No. USS47. Fire Analysis and Research Division, 2015.
8. Ohio Department of Insurance. 'Red Flag Indicators.' Ohio, NA. https://www.insurance.ohio.gov/Company/Documents/PropertyFraud.pdf (accessed April 11, 2016).
9. Department for Communities and Local Government. 'Fire Statistics: Great Britain April 2013 to March 2014.' London: UK Government, 2015.

10. Koksis, Richard C. 'Arson. Exploring motives and possible solutions.' Canberra: Australian Institute of Criminology. Trends and Issues in Crime and Criminal Justice. No 236, 2002.

11. https://www.localsurveyorsdirect.co.uk/tree-related-subsidence-damage (accessed October 6, 2015).

12. Clancy, Dr Brian et al. 'Subsidence of Low Rise Building.' London: Published by the Institution of Structural Engineers, 2000.

13. http://www.subsidenceforum.org.uk/ (accessed April 11, 2016).

14. Mercer, Giles, Reeves, Alan and O'Callaghan, Dealga. 'The relationship between trees, distance to building and subsidence events on clay soil.' (2011) *Arboricultural Journal* 33: 229–245.

15. http://www.theclayresearchgroup.org/ (accessed May 17, 2016).

16. Insurance Information Institute. 'Hail.' Published by the Insurance Information Institute. http://www.iii.org/fact-statistic/hail (accessed October 1, 2015).

17. Verisk Insurance Solutions. 'Property Hail Claims in the United States: 2000–2013.' Published by Verisk. http://www.verisk.com/verisk/cls/landing/hail/hail-claims-report-verisk-insurance-solutions-underwriting.html?source=iii (accessed May 17, 2016).

18. Willis Research Network. London, 2015. http://www.willisresearchnetwork.com/assets/files/WRN_kunz_201505.pdf (accessed May 17, 2016).

19. National Hurricane Center. Miami, 2015. http://www.nhc.noaa.gov/aboutsshws.php (accessed May 17, 2016).

20. Willis Group. 'Resilience Magazine.' London. Published by Willis Group, 2005.

21. Misra, V., DiNapoli, S. and Powell, M. 'The Track Integrated Kinetic Energy of Atlantic Tropical Cyclones.' (2013) *Monthly Weather Review of the American Meteorological Society* 141(7): 2383–2389.

22. Misra, V. et al. 'There are bigger and better ways to quantify how big and bad a hurricane is.' Published by The Conversation, 2015. https://theconversation.com/there-are-better-ways-to-quantify-how-big-and-bad-a-hurricane-is-40137 (accessed May 17, 2016).

23. Wray, Robert. 'Interview with Simon Sole.' Washington DC. Published by Robert Wray LLB, 2013. http://www.robertwraypllc.com/inside-exclusive-analysis-with-simon-sole/ (accessed May 17, 2016).

CHAPTER 8

Liability Insurance and Analytics

L iability insurance (as distinct from general insurance or business interruption insurance) in broad terms provides cover to a policyholder in respect of legal liability arising through matters of law such as statute, nuisance or negligence. Typically, payment is not made to the policyholder themselves but rather to a third party (or parties) who have claimed against the policyholder. Claims arising through a deliberate act or assumed under contract are usually excluded.

In the overall spirit of this book it is not the intention to discuss the topic of liability insurance in depth other than to consider how the topics of data and analytics currently play a part, or will play a part in the future.

Typical types of liability insurance might include:

- Employers' liability insurance, otherwise known as 'Workers Compensation' in the US.
- Public liability, which extends to members of the public who suffer loss or are damaged by acts or omissions of the policyholder.
- Product liability, relating to goods provided by a policyholder which prove to be unsuitable for purpose.
- Third-party liability, such as in the case of a car accident.

In addition, we will also briefly consider the issue of directors' and officers' liability especially arising from cyber security breach, although this is a relatively new area of interest.

8.1   EMPLOYERS' LIABILITY AND WORKERS' COMPENSATION

Employers' liability and in the US, 'Workers' Compensation' insurance is a type of cover intended to provide an employee who is injured at work with continued wages plus medical expenses, as an alternative to the employee seeking direct compensation from the employer. In reality it does not preclude such action taking place but may in certain circumstances reduce the likelihood of such legal action happening.

Turning to the specific topic of 'Workers' Comp' (as it is often abbreviated), it is currently the subject of some debate. These conversations are principally aimed at fitness for purpose and what is described as 'the spill of employer's obligations onto the general taxpaying public' by insurers delegating their obligations to public welfare.[1] As a result 'opt out' is gaining increasing attention, whereby companies opt out of workers' compensation and create their own compensation plans. The debate is principally over what is appropriate by way of compensation, and how this differs from state to state in the US. It is a complex and political issue but at the core of the insurance is the promise to compensate injured employees and protect employers.

Fraud is an issue which plagues workers' compensation – perhaps one of the biggest problems – and analytics has a key part to play in both mitigating and avoiding fraud. The increased use of Big Data as part of the analytics 'mix' will increasingly affect the degree of fraud captured going forward.

8.1.1   Fraud in Workers' Compensation Claims

Fraud potentially occurs at three levels:

- By the employee: Fraud by the employee usually relates to injuries not sustained in the workplace, the scale of the injury, pure fabrication (typically a back or neck injury, such as whiplash, which is difficult to accurately identify) or by extending the period of injury.
- By the employer: Fraud by the employer mainly comprises misdescription either of the employee, the size of the organization or the nature of the work involved.
- By the medical practitioner: Fraud by the medical practitioner relates to unnecessary testing or treatment, imagined treatment or wrong coding. In fact, many of the same traits that we have seen elsewhere in the property supply chain. In a medical scenario, this often includes excessive referral for MRI scans for example.

Statutory establishment of workers' compensation identifies the amounts which an employee is entitled to in the event of injury. These fall under five key categories:

- Medical treatment and benefits
- Payments for lost work days
- Compensation for permanent disability
- Supplemental job displacement benefit
- Death benefit.

The statutory amounts involved in themselves are also the subject of disagreement in that lawyers suggest these amounts are unrepresentative. Insurers on the other hand respond by saying that the degree of fraud in the system requires some type of capping process. As with other types of fraud it can be opportunistic or organized. Experts recognize that this approach is an imperfect science but is arguably a better way forward than the employee needing legal recourse on every occasion.

As with general insurance, there are certain key fraud triggers that should indicate concern under a Workers' Compensation claim. These may include:

- Lack of evidence or witnesses of the accident
- Nature of the work, for example seasonal or perhaps just before a layoff or end of contract
- Delay in notification
- Inconsistency between alleged work-related injury and actual symptoms
- Excessive recovery period.

In periods of economic volatility, especially downturns, there may also be a propensity for these fraudulent events to happen with more frequency.

The National Council on Compensation Insurance NCCI in their 2015 'Issues' report[2] not only looked at current claims but also claims made 20–30 years ago. They discovered that claims outcomes are quite different dependent on the age of the claimant. They explain the difference as being due to:

- Number of medical services needed
- Overall average prices paid for medical services
- Injury mix
- Prescription drug use, especially narcotics
- Quadriplegic and paraplegic claims.

There are three key analytical processes which apply in fraud detection for this category of cover:

1. Capture of information, both structured and unstructured. The aim is to seek as much information about the employer, employee and circumstances of the event as practically possible. Combinations of events or circumstances which seem out of order may raise alarm bells. Are the same medical practitioners involved? (Often, there is switching between insurers to try and avoid any trend being identified.)
2. Based on the evidence provided, what might be the predicted outcome, and how does the actual outcome align to the prediction? This requires some element of understanding of the recovery times for similar injuries and treatments. Has there been an escalation in treatment costs?
3. The triage decision and what the evidence has told us – does it align with what we expect, and what action should be taken? Early intervention will help in terms of medical treatment. This may be key not only in the recovery process in the event that the claim is legitimate but also in collecting evidence if there are doubts.

As with all analytic processes, the essence is not what the insight shows, but rather what changes an organization might make in terms of its best practice. The effective use of analytics allows insurers to modify current practices and thus improve effectiveness and profitability.

One of the biggest issues is that of fabrication or malingering. There are well-documented cases of special investigators 'stalking' and filming miscreants who claim that they are disabled or otherwise unfit for work. Increasingly, investigators use social media to identify discrepancies. This might typically reveal the employee who is too disabled to work but is well enough to ski, or has secondary employment.

There is a trend amongst fraudsters to try to remain 'one step ahead' of their investigators. In fact, many of these fraudsters are on the point of being 'professional' in nature. They make it their business to have an up-to-date knowledge of analytics and investigative techniques. It is natural therefore for insurers to be prudent in not giving all their investigative processes away, and this approach is respected in this publication.

Some may question whether it is legitimate to digitally 'snoop' individuals who may be innocent. In the days before current technology, insurers would routinely employ special investigators to follow and photograph individuals where claims were thought to be 'doubtful.' Today's use of technology simply brings an established investigatory process up to date.

Whilst the capture of fraudulent behavior is critical, the ability to quickly process 'honest' claims is also a clear benefit. Insurers have long realized that there is a correlation between time and cost. The longer it takes to resolve a claim, the more expensive it tends to become.

There are key advantages in raising awareness of the analytical capability within the fraudulent fraternity. It is unlikely to act as a complete deterrent but may influence those who are marginal. The Irish Insurance Association adopted an interesting approach by being very public in their approach to raising awareness about fraud. They made the point that insurance fraud affects everyone, and therefore it is in the 'common good' to work together. In doing so, they suggested, insurance premiums for all would be reduced, and they took this to the extent of exhibiting airport posters and a running a press campaign.

The problem of fraudulent insurance behavior is no less in growth markets. In South Africa, for example, the desire to provide insurance for the masses in the form of micro insurance, especially for funeral cover, spawned a new industry of forging birth and death certificates. As can be seen in many situations, systems are created but individuals still find ways of working their way around the system to their own personal advantage.

What all this seems to indicate is that fraud by employers, employees, supply chain and policyholders is likely to remain with us for the foreseeable future. Fraud is one symptom of our personal and sometimes quite mixed relationship with the insurance industry.

8.1.2 Employers' Liability Cover

In the UK there is an obligation for employers to carry insurance in respect of the injury, disease, or fatality of their employees during the course of work, or due to working conditions. There are similar statutory requirements in other geographies. In the UK, insurance must be provided by an authorized insurer and give cover up to £5 million. The requirement is enshrined in the Employers' Liability (Compulsory Insurance) Act 1969. Certain exceptions exist, typically for members of the family, and for public sector workers where the organization is funded through public funds. By law, cover is required for all those who operate under a contract of service including apprenticeships.[3]

As with Workers' Compensation provision described earlier, there are multiple opportunities for fraud to take place in the process. Fraud does not have geographical limits. The economic environment inevitably leads to trends emerging and 2014 saw a growing trend of claims stemming from assaults in the social care sector. This was mainly due to assaults by service users on employees or injuries sustained by employees.

During 2014 specialist insurers Markel identified a 15% month-on-month increase in claims for injuries sustained by carers following assaults by service users. There seems to be relatively little information on the amount of industry-wide fraud that takes place under employers' liability insurance. This might appear to be an area for further investigation in the future especially as tightening economic conditions could create a catalyst for less scrupulous behavior.

8.1.3 Effective Triaging of EL Claims

In both Workers' Compensation insurance and employers' liability, early intervention is critical to reduce the cost of the claim. Insurers increasingly adopt the use of analytically influenced triage to mitigate the consequences and cost of injury. The aims of the triage are to:

- Reduce time for advice in critical circumstances.
- Create early intervention for treatment.
- Identify the need for further detailed expertise.

The usual process is that a telephone assessment takes place by a trained nurse or medical expert to understand the nature of the injury, what has happened since and any treatment that has already taken place. Analytically based programs are often used to identify the most appropriate way forward. The essence of this approach is that it helps to move insurers away from a reactive claims management solution to one of proactivity.

Key benefits are described by one practitioner[4] as comprising:

- A consistent approach to injury and claims management process best practice.
- Reduction in lost time injuries and minimizing of 'lost productivity.'
- Decreased occupational rehabilitation spend and lower claims costs.
- Ultimately, a reduction in workers' premiums.
- For insurers, improved loss ratios and better profitability.

8.2   PUBLIC LIABILITY

The benefit of additional sources of data is increasingly an important issue in the consideration of what constitutes 'public liability,' that is, responsibility for loss or damage as a result of negligence, nuisance or statute.

If the focus of insurance in relation to public liability cover is the legal responsibility of a policyholder for acts or omissions leading to loss or injury, then a fundamental inference is that the policyholder was in fact legally liable. This requires evidential proof or strict liability which confirms this. For insurers, this means that all evidence collected and reference points obtained must be taken as if in a court of law. This approach is known as 'Rules of Evidence' and excludes for example hearsay and anecdotal evidence.

During the investigation process, it is possible that new or additional evidence may come to light which cannot be directly referenced especially if it has been sourced from an unstructured, anonymous or anecdotal source. Insurers may need to consider whether such information which may have been sourced from social media can be considered as evidence. If the evidence cannot be directly used, insurers need also to consider whether any insight that flows from such information can also be considered.

Anonymous evidence in court is already admissible to some degree, and one example of this is anonymous witness statements. As a basic principle, would-be witnesses can give evidence anonymously but this can be challenged. In the US, thinking about these issues appears to be more mature than in other geographies. Perhaps this is because of the advanced maturity of the US in terms of the use of technology. US courts already apply the Federal Rules of Evidence to digital content. Their view is that digital evidence tends to be more voluminous, more difficult to destroy, easily duplicated, potentially more expressive and more readily available. As a result, some courts have treated digital evidence differently for purposes of authenticity, hearsay and privilege.

A common attack on digital evidence is that it can be easily altered. However, in 2002 a US court ruled that 'the fact that it is possible to alter data contained in a computer is plainly insufficient to establish untrustworthiness,' but digital evidence is often ruled inadmissible by US courts as it is obtained without permission.

In the UK one key source of information is 'Digital Evidence, Digital Investigations and E-Disclosure: A Guide to Forensic Readiness for Organisations, Advisors and Security' published by the Information Assurance Advisory Council.[5] This is a lengthy and comprehensive document covering such issues as:

- Admissibility
- Weight of evidence
- Continuity of evidence
- Cyber evidence in practice
- Continuity of digital evidence.

By its nature, the increasing access to wider and more variable sources of data will have an impact on the volume and extent of evidence. The pervasiveness and increased accessibility of data will increasingly add to the volume of information to be considered as part of the liability decision. New investigation processes underpinned by technology are rapidly beginning to encroach, and it is important for insurers to consider how these new technologies are best accommodated by existing and future practitioners. New precedents will inevitably emerge which consider whether investigation as a result of inadmissible evidence will be acceptable to the courts. In the new era of Big Data, the law profession will have its moment and it's probable that new precedents will need to be set.

Traditionally and even until recent times, technology including analytics has been used to supplement existing investigation processes, for example by comparing physical evidence to other similarly modeled scenarios. The advent of the so-called 'fourth age of analytics,' cognitive analytics, starts to create an environment whereby technology will begin to move to a more central place in the investigation process. Although there is already legal discussion on the topic of data and the law, this has tended to focus on issues such as data privacy and cyber security. Perhaps consideration needs also to be given to what might constitute future admissible evidence especially given the lead by US courts. This may help insurers consider where best to search for additional information to prove or disprove liability, or where enquiries might lead them up a legal 'blind alley.'

It is inevitable that insurance investigators who focus on liability issues will also need to change and become more technologically savvy. This does not imply that investigators will be replaced by computers. However, as in other industries, an ability to research information and to use analytics as a complementary tool in the process, rather than a potential threat to their personal contribution, will become increasingly important.

8.3   PRODUCT LIABILITY

The essence of product liability insurance is to provide cover to the policyholder, which is usually a commercial enterprise, in the event that their product causes loss, injury or damage. Such liability may not be dependent on the policyholder actually manufacturing the product.

Liability can arise even if the name of the policyholder's business is on the product, or if the business repairs or changes a product.

Where foodstuffs are involved, the use of remote sensors and analysis of the forthcoming data can help in the investigation of a failed process. This may be both in terms of policy liability but also relative to a potential subrogation (an action against a 'third party'). In terms of policy liability cover for the defective product itself, analytics may be useful as a way of understanding the extent of the problem or defect in terms of distribution or customer reaction. The use of analytical methods to reach potentially affected customers may also have a part to play in this context.

One typical example of this is the use of telematics to monitor livestock, track it and categorize it in terms of age, condition and location. Whilst this gives insight into the livestock herd itself and can help with issues of health and condition, beyond this it allows interested stakeholders to better understand the food chain. Such information would be invaluable in the event of there being an outbreak of disease or contamination. The ability to understand storage conditions, transit and distribution inevitably adds to insurers' understanding. Through the use of analytics, one possible development is that of automatically creating alerts as a result of exceptions or discrepancies to normal processes within the supply chain ecosystem.

8.4   DIRECTORS AND OFFICERS LIABILITY

Directors and Officers (D&O) liability insurance has become progressively critical as directors and senior executives are increasingly in the firing line and held responsible for their actions. Over time, governmental interest in corporate activities has increased together with financial disclosure, both leading to a need for more insurance cover. Regulation and compliance are at the top of many organizational agendas. There is often more at stake because of the activity of institutional shareholders and smaller shareholders also look for greater involvement.

Gross mismanagement, negligence, fraud, dishonesty, libel and slander have gone hand in hand with corporate action. Spectacular bankruptcies have occurred, as well as disastrous takeovers and poorly managed acquisitions. Externally, environmental pressures, ethics and corporate social responsibility issues have all added to the mix. Behavior has become an important part of a company's reputation. An increased codification of directors' and officers' responsibilities is aimed to give greater clarification but in reality it is about making the directors and officers responsible for their actions.

D&O insurance is a highly specialist area. Claims can be brought in many areas including:

- Takeovers and mergers which are not in the best interests of shareholders or undertaken at inflated prices.
- Wrongful trading, for example if a business is trading whilst insolvent.
- Financial irregularities, e.g., insider trading.
- Contractual issues, including breach of confidentiality or breach of contract.

Additional access to data and analysis places greater obligation on the executives of any organization to be more aware of both the circumstances of the company and any legal reporting which has been carried out. The so-called 'democratization' of analytics, i.e., the ability to find analytical answers without recourse to the IT department, means that there is greater transparency throughout businesses. Because of this, directors and officers of organizations may have fewer defenses to the fact that they would not have been able to find out where there has been misconduct.

In effect what this means is that as the use of data and analytics becomes more widespread across all industries, the risk of claims under a D&O policy also may tend to increase. In addition, it will be possible to forensically examine the records of directors to see what information they personally sought and when. Or if perhaps, when there was a need to investigate, they exercised appropriate due diligence in researching the facts. Because of this additional duty, senior executives of all organizations may need to become more analytically minded as part of their normal role. This will also extend to non-executive directors who might reasonably be expected to be able to obtain access to, and investigate, the affairs of their business.

The capabilities of the claims investigator under a D&O policy will include the ability to interrogate the company's own analytical system to see what was accessed, when and by whom. This is another example of professionals affiliated to the insurance industry also needing to change to meet the advent of this new technology.

One of the major risks to most organizations is that of cyber security, and whilst many businesses are incurring cost in safeguarding information and systems, many others are using cyber insurance as one of the lines of defense as part of an integrated strategy. Affected stakeholders might reasonably ask executives whether appropriate cyber risk defenses and insurance cover were in place. It may be beyond individual executives at Board level to understand the precise details of cyber security in place but it should not be beyond them to have an analytically based operational risk dashboard before them. From this they should be able to understand in the broadest terms what protections are in place, and what contingent insurance cover has been arranged. Failure of either or both may in itself be sufficient to create some vulnerability under a D&O liability policy.

NOTES

1. DePaolo, David. 'Workers' Comp Is Under Attack.' Published online by InsuranceThoughtLeadership.com, 2015. http://insurancethoughtleadership.com/workers-comp-attack/#sthash.nUq1Uf5M.dpbs (accessed March 21, 2016).

2. National Council on Compensation Insurance. 'NCCI: Workers Compensation 2015 Issues Report,' 2015.

3. Health and Safety Executive. 'Employers Liability (Compulsory Insurances) Act 1969. Brief Guide for Employers'. Paper HSE40. Health and Safety Executive. First published 11/12. http://www.hse.gov.uk/pubns/hse40.pdf (accessed May 17, 2016).

4 Overland Health, 2016. https://www.overland-health.co.uk/minor-injury-triage (accessed March 21, 2016).

5. Sommer, Peter. 'Digital Evidence, Digital Investigations and E-Disclosure. A Guide to Forensic Readiness for Organisations, Security Advisers and Lawyers.' 4th edition. Published by Information Assurance Advisory Council, 2013.

CHAPTER 9

Life and Pensions

Life insurance, sometime known as life 'assurance' is a form of insurance which makes payment upon death, terminal illness or critical injury on the part of the policyholder. Upon the 'event' happening the insurer makes a payment usually by way of a lump sum. Where death appears suspicious in nature or there is insurance for a particularly large sum, insurers may want more than the death certificate and also want to look into the circumstances more carefully.

Endowment insurance is similar in nature to life insurance, other than that the policy is not 'triggered' by death but rather by the expiry of a defined period of time. In the UK, many house purchase mortgage arrangements are based on repayment of the interest on the loan only, with the capital being repaid at the end of the loan period as a lump sum underpinned by an endowment insurance.

The life insurance industry is complex with many parts to consider. The intention of the insurer is to predict the lifespan of the individual using actuarial sciences based on location, lifestyle and other factors, and then set a premium which adequately takes into account the eventual outgoings and administrative expenses.

Group Life Insurance is where a policy is taken out for a group of people, perhaps employees or members of a trade union or cooperative. In this situation the underwriter is unable to consider the individual but rather needs to deal with the group as a whole, usually taking into account the size and type of organization and its typical employee base. The use of selective questions allows the underwriter to manage any outliers.

Pension insurance provides for a fixed sum sometimes paid in installments, upon retirement from service or work. It can take the form of defined benefit plans, defined contributions or other combinations. The usual expression 'pension' represents the amount an individual receives upon stopping work or at any other agreed trigger point. Pensions can either be arranged by the individual or provided through a company scheme as part of the employee benefits package. Some pensions provide for disability where an individual who is incapacitated will be allowed to enter the pension plan at a time before normal retirement.

A 'defined benefit plan' is a pension which is based on a pre-set formula rather than based on investment returns. This formula may be based on the employee's age, length of work, age at retirement and other factors. Often known as a final salary scheme, the amount paid in pension is linked either to the actual salary at the time of retirement or the average salary over the few years prior to retirement. This is known in the US as a 'dollar times service' scheme.

Defined benefit schemes may be either funded or unfunded. In an unfunded scheme the employer does not put money aside but rather monies are paid – as and when. Most state schemes are unfunded in that payments for pensions are made from the income from taxes and social security contributions. Some countries such as France and the US operate hybrid systems where funds are held in reserve funds or, in the case of the US, in special US Treasury bonds.

In a 'defined contribution' pension, contributions are paid into a fund for the individual. This fund is invested in the stock market and the returns on investment are credited to the individual. Money contributed can either be by way of individual contributions, employer contributions or a combination of both. There is a high degree of uncertainty in this approach especially in a volatile marketplace. Although the amount of contributions may be known, the eventual benefits are not known. The risk and reward rests entirely with the individual who is heavily dependent on the advice given by their employer, who in turn is often responsible for the choice of asset manager and pension administrator.

9.1   HOW LIFE INSURANCE DIFFERS FROM GENERAL INSURANCE

General insurance is sometimes also known as 'non-life insurance.' In terms of how these two different types of policies are similar and different to general insurance, purists would reasonably argue that these are, in effect, two quite different industries. It is unusual although not unprecedented for individual professionals to cross over from one to the other. The two are similar in that both are reliant on premium income, invest that income, and make provision for claims payment and administration. They differ however in terms of the long-tail nature of the policy with general insurers needing to manage their business on a much shorter cycle of time.

Both may also be subject to misdescription, either innocent or fraudulent, in that each type of insurer is dependent on having an understanding of material facts ('facts which would influence the underwriter and the terms or pricing of the policy').

Both may also potentially be subject to fraudulent behavior at the point of claim. Such behavior is perhaps more apparent in general insurance but can also show itself in life insurance. One version of life insurance is that of funeral insurance, where for a small premium the insurer funds the cost of funeral expenses. This type of funeral or 'burial' insurance is very old and there is some evidence that the Greeks and Romans even had a type of provision through 'benevolent societies.' In more recent times the so-called Friendly Societies also had cheap cover available. Burial insurance has also shown itself in the micro-insurance market. Micro insurance is a form of insurance designed and distributed for low income families in accordance with their wealth and conditions. With administration costs being necessarily low, claims are often paid based on the evidence of a birth and death supported by appropriate documentation, spawning a new industry of forged birth and death certificates.

Both non-life and life insurers are vulnerable to major events. In the case of property, the impact of a major weather incident will give rise to many damage claims of varying types, complexities and values. In the case of life insurers, they too are concerned with major incidents especially where there has been loss of life. Generally, their greatest concerns are of an entirely different nature, typically events such as pandemics which cause widespread death. Examples of this might be Asian influenza or Ebola, although fortunately neither of these has proved to be a major problem for insurers (or the general public) in recent times.

In their report 'Facts and Perspectives on the Ebola Outbreak,' dated October 2014[1] the Insurance Information Institute describe the impact of an Ebola outbreak in the US – even if affecting tens of thousands – as 'quite manageable.' They suggest that the life insurance market is well capitalized and reinsured, and at worst this would result in a reduction of profits. The report also considers, incidentally, the major impact of such an epidemic on health insurers by way of reminder that the costs of care of an Ebola patient are estimated at $1000 per hour. They also consider the potential for liabilities that might arise under Workers' Compensation cover where inadequate provision for safety of employees might have rendered them vulnerable in some way to infection.

In terms of the differences between general and life customers, at face value there appear to be two different types of customer behavior. General customers (for personal lines, for example) are more concerned with the short term in that they consider renewal annually and there is a greater likelihood of customer churn. The life insurance customer is more likely to take a longer view, often making provision for events or lifestyle changes which may occur many years hence. Even so, the economic environment may affect the amount which they are prepared to invest. Recent changes in UK legislation, for example, allowing individuals to withdraw their pension fund as cash over the age of 55 may serve to 'move the goalposts' in terms of customer behavior. Issues of customer loyalty and retention which traditionally have rested in the general insurance market are now increasingly finding their way into the life and pensions sector. Life insurers are increasingly keen to understand potential customer behavior and be able to offer alternative more flexible pension plans.

The topic of telematics has tended to reside in the area of auto insurance (although to some degree the auto industry itself has served as a useful catalyst and willing participant) and telematics is increasingly breaking out into other areas of property business. Life insurers are also seeing the potential benefit of increased insight into their customer, through the use of mobile fitness devices and information gained from the gym. Telematics for cars is being complemented by telematics for people with both capabilities increasingly providing insurers with an excuse for more frequent interaction with their customers.

The final area to consider in terms of similarities and differences between general and life insurance is the issue of asset and liability management. As evidenced by the implementation of Solvency II, general insurers have different considerations compared to life insurers in terms of their risk management and capital profiles. General insurers are more concerned with short-term liabilities although they recognize that in some more complex claims there are 'long tails' to consider. Life insurers need to take a much longer term viewpoint with all the uncertainties that attach to that.

9.2   BASIS OF LIFE INSURANCE

The basis of life insurance is simply that in the event of the death of a person insured under the contract, a payment is made to an agreed beneficiary. Other versions of this exist, typically critical illness. The 'life-based' insurance policy often falls into one of two types – a protection policy which pays out a lump sum, or alternatively an investment policy. In an investment policy the intention is to grow the amount contributed either by way of regular payments or a lump sum, and which through shrewd investment on the part of the insurer will result in the growth of the capital amount contributed. The insurer calculates the price of insurance taking into account the costs to be paid, plus administrative expenses.

The key concerns of life insurers are:

- What is the best way to forecast future mortality rates and build for uncertainty?
- How do insurers find and retain customers?
- How are future cash flows valued?
- What hedging strategies are appropriate?
- How can risk be mitigated?

9.3   ISSUES OF MORTALITY

Analytics has been at the heart of life and pension payments from almost the very beginning. The first 'mortality table,' also known as a 'life table' or 'actuarial table,' was created in the mid-1600s. The mortality table shows for each age the probability that a person of that age will die before their next birthday. From this information can be inferred:

- The probability of surviving to any particular age
- The remaining life expectancy of people of a given age.

One of the roles of the actuary is to compare the actual death rate with that which was projected through mathematical modeling and to come up with the probability of death at that particular age. The age of Big Data allows much more information than was ever available before, and to create much more detailed life expectancy models which take into account items more specific to the individual, allowing a higher level of granularity.

In their book *The Analysis of Mortality and other Actuarial Statistics* by Benjamin, Haycocks and Pollard,[2] created as a textbook for the Institute of Actuaries, the writers set out that the risk of dying varies with a number of factors – 'sex and age, and other factors which influence the physical constitution or the environment of the people, such as birthplace, geographical locality of residence, occupation, marital condition.'

Death rates for females are lower than males at all ages. This is explained as follows:

- That boys in infancy are more vulnerable and also run the risk of injury as they take part in more vigorous activities.
- In early and middle life, men are more at risk of dying through accidents and violence and also have a higher propensity to die due to respiratory diseases such as cancer and bronchitis.
- At more advanced ages men appear to physically deteriorate more quickly than women, with cerebral haemorrhages, arterial disease and cancer taking a higher toll on men than on women,

They also indicate that mortality rates appear to vary with marital condition suggesting that those married fare better and live longer as a result of mutual care and protection by the marital partners. Ethnic origins are also addressed. To what degree these generalizations, which were formed two decades ago, remain valid is a moot point, and analytics may ultimately have a major part to play in overturning such broad statements.

Personal risk management is also a factor when linked to a standard risk profile based on severity and frequency of risk. This may comprise giving up smoking or extreme sports, having regular checks and scans, improving diet, better exercise and appropriate medication. At the core of this proactive approach is better education and training in terms of reducing the risk.

In terms of behavior, it is likely that there is a correlation between a person's risk aversion and their propensity to purchase life insurance products. This connection is described by Stephen Diacon of the Centre for Risk and Insurance Studies (CRIS) at Nottingham Business School in his paper 'Protection Insurance and Financial Wellbeing.'[3] There he refers to personal prudence as being one of the key behavioral issues in the insurance buying process.

Other behavioral issues include 'vitality,' a term used by Diacon to describe the individual's incentive to take mitigating action. There is a high level of uncertainty in behavioral issues partly influenced by the value that people put on their own lives. Table 9.1 summarizes the risk aversion level across demographic and behavioral groups in the US in 1992 by way of example.

TABLE 9.1   Risk aversion level across demographic and behavioral groups US 1992

Attributes	Low (more risk-tolerant)				High (dislikes risks)
Age group	Young	Old			Middle Aged
Sex	Male				Female
Race	Asian	Hispanic	Other	Black	White
Religion	Jewish	Catholic	Other		Protestant
Behavior	Currently smokes		Quit smoking		Never smoked
	Drinks				Doesn't drink
	No life insurance				Owns life insurance
Income	Lowest	Highest			Medium
Wealth	Lowest	Highest			Medium

Source: Barsky et al. (1997)[4]

Many life and pension insurance arrangements are sold as a group scheme as opposed to being at an individual level. The underwriter has a more difficult job in that they are not able to consider risk at a granular or individual level, but has to take into account the group as a whole.

As with all other parts of this book, the intention is not to give a detailed treatise on life and pension insurance (although recommended reading is provided). Rather the intention is to consider what developments will arise in respect of new capabilities available relative to Big Data and Analytics.

9.4   THE ROLE OF BIG DATA IN MORTALITY RATES

Mortality mainly depends on a series of locational and behavioral issues. The question is, to what degree might additional information give us greater insight in terms of lifespan and health? Additional information might come from the following sources:

- Location devices which identify how 'mobile' an individual is, and may be a reflection of fitness.

- Membership of clubs and societies, some of which may have greater risk than others.
- Professional activities in connection with work, for example a civil engineer may work either on-site or in an office, with obviously different risk.
- Social behaviors.

Additional information gives more insight into the 'risk appetite' of the individual which may be a better indicator of their behavior. Evidence of affluence would also be a contributing factor, as might religious views or ethnic background. Some individuals may be reluctant to give away such granular data as this but we have seen already that there are demographic differences in response to sharing information. For example, Millennials (those born between 1979 and 1999) are more prepared to share location information provided there is some benefit to be accrued. Would they also be prepared to share additional more personal information for similar benefits?

Life insurers are exposed to catastrophe mortality risk via pandemics. This can lead to larger payments and solvency capital issues. Mortality catastrophe bonds[5] are an actuarial tool to help provide additional risk management. Distinct from traditional reinsurance, they do not provide a 'credit risk' as they are triggered when mortality rates of the general population reach a certain level. Some reinsurers have been prepared to combine natural catastrophe and mortality risks into a single bond offering.[6]

9.5   PURCHASING LIFE INSURANCE IN A VOLATILE ECONOMY

Insurers have key challenges in persuading people to spend money on events which may not occur until many years hence, e.g., retirement. Sometimes known as the Peter Pan syndrome based on the literary character who remained a boy forever, the seventh annual Scottish Widows UK pension report dated 2013, based on interviews with 5200 adults, showed 'widespread and ingrained inertia' across the country in respect of non-state provision for old age. Interestingly, they discovered that savings levels have remained broadly consistent during the past five years regardless of the economic downturn suggesting that the volatility of the economy might not be a factor in purchasing life insurance. If that is the case, then there is a greater need to understand the behavioral drivers of purchasers.

Overall the propensity of the younger generation to invest in their future is relatively low, and this seems to be consistent with the findings of 'Risk Aversion' investigations (Table 9.1 above). Perhaps surprisingly, more young people than ever are contributing to pension insurance as a result of the UK Government's automatic pension enrolment scheme. According to the UK Office of National Statistics, the number of UK employees in pension schemes increased from 50% in 2013 to 59% in 2014.[7]

The greatest level of growth in UK membership of pension schemes was amongst young people in the 22–29 age bracket, leaping from 36% in 2013 to 59% in 2014. A process known as auto-enrollment was aimed at all those between 22 years and pensionable age, and earning over £8000 per year. Beyond this, people in the 16–21 age bracket who didn't fall under the auto-enrolment scheme also increased their participation in insurance products, increasing from 3.5% to 4.4% between 2013 and 2014. For actuaries this becomes rather challenging territory. Revenue growth is welcome but perhaps insurers would have preferred it not to come from the demographic group who are most likely to want to take risks.

This growth appears to offer a different view to comments made in 2012 by Michael Johnson, a research fellow at the UK-based Centre for Policy Studies, who suggested 'that private pensions will cease to exist within years because young people see having immediate access to savings as far more important than putting money aside for their retirement.'[8] The actual level of increase could point to the fact that it might be more a matter of legislation than behavior or opinion which drives growth in the number of life policies. There is still however a potential issue of cross-selling and up-selling. Might behavioral data collected as part of the mortality issue potentially even be reused for sales and marketing purposes if the customer allows it?

By way of a caveat, reusing data for multiple purposes can create issues. At the very least, the rules of use may change from country to country and even within one country it may be possible to get different opinions from one person in the Regulator's Office to another. In some countries an insurer can only use the information provided by a customer for the specific reason intended, unless they give specific permission. As a result, most insurers obtain permission at the point of sale although there is an argument as to whether this should comprise an 'opt-in' or 'opt-out.' There are other complications particularly for financial services companies. For example if a customer allows an insurer to directly mail them, does this also allow the same company to market them with other products in the group, e.g., banking or healthcare products? This is especially relevant in the case of bancassurers and can become more complex where the insurance and banking business operate under entirely different brands.

The same question may apply where there are different lines of business – cross-selling a pension to someone who has auto insurance. The problem is exacerbated where a group acquires another company. Does the permission stand, or does it have to be renewed?

9.6   HOW LIFE INSURERS CAN ENGAGE WITH THE YOUNG

Increasingly analytics are being used to better understand the customer, gain insight into lifetime value and apply this to decisions which affect their loyalty and likelihood of purchasing more products and services. Lifetime value assessment of individuals becomes even more critical when considering younger age groups whose total lifetime value is much higher, especially those from professional groups or potentially high-earning industries.

One additional factor which is becoming prevalent is increased transparency. Young and old alike have an ingrained suspicion of insurers especially life insurers where funds appear to be 'locked away' perhaps for decades. Millennials are of course the 'new' digital customer. The way that they interact with life and pension insurers will inevitably be different from older established customers. Analytics allows greater transparency of outcome and the ability to create customized solutions which are appropriate to particular needs. These solutions may also need a degree of agility as lifetime needs change over time.

In the same way that specific insurance offerings have emerged for the older customer, it is likely that new trendy brands will start to emerge for younger age groups. These new brands will be analytically orientated in nature, and focus not only on the actuarial elements of the life and pension solution but also on the different buying behaviors that the millennial purchaser will use. Millennials are 27% more likely than the average adult to consider themselves sophisticated; 45% of Millenials would say that they are risk takers and 44% think they live a lifestyle that impresses others. Although these are not trends that are necessarily attractive to insurance underwriters or actuaries, they nevertheless remain a market opportunity.[9]

If other parallel markets are considered, it is observed that Millennials tend to buy with three things in mind:

1. They are image conscious, looking for something which is 'cool,' probably technology orientated and easy to use. This equates to the top of the range smart phone. Is it too difficult a stretch of the imagination to think about how any insurance product might satisfy any of these ideas? What does 'cool insurance cover' look like?
2. They want to be where the fun is. Old age probably doesn't really fit that scenario.
3. The third and probably most critical and relevant, is their social media persona. Millennials on the whole want to be viewed as sensible adults, to be taken seriously and have their views heard and appreciated. It may even improve their position in the 'partnership' race, by being able to demonstrate that they can provide care for later years. (In reality, this might not be a good opening chat line.)

What this means, taken in the round, is that to capture the millennial sector of its own accord rather than through the back door of legislation, the life and pension market will need to rethink its 'go to market' strategy and create a new set of relevant, flexible, exciting products for a new generation.

This may have to go beyond simply adding value to existing core insurance propositions but rather rethinking the ethos of the insurance cover. There is a temptation to suggest that this is impossible – but as has been seen elsewhere, analytics has a propensity to change business models (e.g., 'Uber'). There is no reason to think that the life and pensions industry could not undergo the same transformation.

9.7   LIFE AND PENSIONS FOR THE OLDER DEMOGRAPHIC

At the later stage of life, investment decisions become more critical and relevant. One key factor to consider is that of longer lifespans, and improved healthcare and support.

Work by IBM and others identifies the reality of the multi-modal customer[10] as being one who has moved beyond using a single point of interaction with their insurer, to a customer searching through multiple points of contact ranging from agent to website. Much depends on age and location and there are cultural issues to consider. If the Millennial creates new challenges and opportunities for insurers, then those at the other end of the age spectrum might also expect new ways of thinking from their providers. Those approaching retirement are more likely to be beneficiaries of pensions rather than contributors, but recent legislation now entitles earlier drawdown of retirement fund. There is also the opportunity for investment of lump sums to take into account such as from recently deceased parents.

If the Millennial has created a new category of 'buyer' for the pension insurance market, then there are also the Generation X and Generation Y buyers. 'Gen X,' or 'Generation X' is an expression used for those born in the years 1965–1979. It was coined by the famous photographer Robert Capa and popularized by the Canadian author Douglas Coupland when he wrote about young adults in the 1980s. Generation Y are recognized as the demographic group coming after Generation X, and are generally taken to mean those born between 1980 and 1997, although there appear to be no hard and fast rules about when Gen X ends and Gen Y starts.

Both Gen X and Gen Y can be further divided into buying attitudes – so-called attitude clusters – ranging from 'security-orientated individual' (I know what I want and can organize myself) to 'informed optimizer' (I take time to research and find the best). Different locational behaviors are increasingly being eroded as global behaviors are replicated across continents. For the older generation, personal contact and interaction (normally with some form of insurance agent) remains important, but there is often reluctance to pay for advice.

Analytics plays a critical part in how insurers interact with all customers, be they at the start of their working life or at the end. If the post 2000-born Millennial is digital and risk-taking, then at the other end of the spectrum the Gen X is analog and wary. They have become far too cynical to be spoon-fed with figures on how much they *might* get in retirement. Surely it should be possible for insurers to create customer-facing solutions which help individuals navigate their way better through the financial uncertainties of old age?

An interesting exercise was carried out by Skipton Building Society,[11] the fourth largest mutual (or cooperative) lender in the UK, who wanted to gain greater understanding of the decision drivers for their 785,000 customers. A high proportion of their customer base falls into the over-45 age bracket, and Skipton's particular interest was to consider the mid-way ground between investments and pensions. The building society commissioned a three-stage research project that combined traditional research with information obtained from biometric devices using a third party, Sensum, who have expertise in capturing, consolidating and analyzing information from data streams from wearable devices.

Sensum measured customer reaction based on 'galvanic skin response' which is the electrical conductance to sweat on the skin. This allowed them to identify physical responses which interestingly appeared to be at odds with what participants had actually said. In the survey 64% of participants recorded a difference between the conscious requirement and the subconscious desire, with most participants being unhappy with the notion that retirement was necessarily 'golden years' or the 'end of a chapter.'

Further detailed screening by Sensum identified five key personas in retirement:

1. Activity seeker
2. Adventurer
3. Comfort seeker
4. Knowledge seeker
5. Worker.

With individual personas comprising a blend of all these, Skipton describe this combination of characteristics as being 'like DNA,' with each set of characteristics being individual to the participants. They are currently equipping their advisers with a 'Retirement DNA' app to better understand individual customer needs. This case study launched to media in November 2014 presents a strong and innovative example of how data and analytics could improve on the financial services offerings by providing more granular and customized offerings.

9.8 LIFE AND PENSION BENEFITS IN THE DIGITAL ERA

The Digital Era will be radical: An explosion of Big Data; advanced and cognitive analytics; unconstrained agility from the cloud; insight on demand from our mobile device; greater consumer empowerment; new forms of competition; different business models; multiple and continuous disruption. Whether this is this a vision of Utopia or Orwell's '1984' is perhaps in the eye of the beholder.

Retirement benefits are often considered in terms of what they will buy an individual at the time of need. Participants wonder if the available funds will support a particular lifestyle, medical care or allow them to run their car. In reality, the speed of transition is such that there is no clarity of what life will really be like in 20 or 30 years' time. If the rate of progress is measured by the amount of data being created, then what will the world look like by the time these pension benefits are called on? Will the funding of car ownership be an issue if we live in a world of car-sharing, perhaps even with the cars self-driving?

To what degree will our health insurance be linked to our individual behavior? Will the individual have signed away their rights to their health insurer seeing what has been bought at the supermarket checkout? Should we anticipate a world where the checkout, in collaboration with our healthcare insurers, refuses to allow us to make purchase because too many units of alcohol or highly saturated fats have been purchased? One alternative could be that 'flexible' insurance premiums may reflect customer eating behavior and be adjusted in near-real time – telematics meets diet. Dietmatics?

Analytics may have another contribution to the digital age, that of the more rapid development of treatments that support longer lifespans. Even today, cognitive analytics is being used by cancer researchers in the early identification of cancer symptoms and earlier and more appropriate intervention. Time magazine recently described cognitive analytics as being the next tool in the cancer toolbox.[12]

There is no doubt that life expectancy is increasing. Life expectancy in the 21st century increased from 50 years to 75 years in developed countries, and it is thought that it will probably level off in the mid-80s. UN statistics show that for the period 2005–2010, Japan (82.6 years) has the world's highest life expectancy followed by Hong Kong (82.2 years) and Iceland (81.8 years). By comparison, the world average is 67.2 years and the UK average is 79.4 years.

It also appears that there will be more people who hit 100 years of age. In their 2011 report detailing life expectancy, the UK Department of Work and Pensions compared generations at 20, 50 and 80 years old. Table 9.2 illustrates the likelihood of becoming a centenarian. They indicated that 20-year-olds are three times more likely to reach 100 than their grandparents, and twice as likely as their parents. Girls born in 2011 have a one-in-three chance of living to their 100th birthday, boys have a one-in-four chance. Compared to a baby born in 1931, the children of 2011 are almost eight times more likely to become centenarians.[13]

The full table of centennial expectancy by year of birth is included in Appendix B. It is important to recognize that this data is UK-specific and that different locations may have different projections influenced by diet and other local considerations.

UK Pensions Minister Steve Webb interestingly expressed the problem in these terms:

> *The dramatic speed at which life expectancy is changing means that we need to radically rethink our perceptions about our later lives ... We simply can't look to our grandparents' experience of retirement as a model for our own. We will live longer and we will have to save more.*

The London-based Cass Business School, with the International Longevity Centre, are a little more bullish in terms of life expectancy suggesting that age at death will increasingly cluster in the 90s and that the life expectancy of men and women will converge.[14] There are downsides to this longevity. The International Longevity Centre (www.ilcuk.org.uk/) says

TABLE 9.2 Likelihood of reaching 100 in the UK, by year of birth

Likelihood of reaching 100

Year of Birth	Male, %	Female, %	Both Sexes, %
1915	0.3	1.2	0.8
1920	0.6	1.8	1.2
1925	1.2	3	2.1
1930	2.3	4.6	3.4
1935	4	7.3	5.6
1940	5.4	9.6	7.5
1945	6.6	11.1	8.9
1950	7.9	12.8	10.4
1955	9.1	14.4	11.7
1960	10.2	15.9	13.1
1965	11.5	17.4	14.5
1970	12.8	19	15.9
1975	14.2	20.7	17.4
1980	15.7	22.4	19.1
1985	17.3	24.2	20.7
1990	18.9	26	22.4
1995	20.5	27.8	24.2
2000	22.2	29.6	25.9
2005	23.9	31.5	27.7
2010	25.7	33.3	29.5

Source: UK Department of Work and Pensions

that by 2060 many Eastern European countries will have less than two working age adults per dependent – Japan currently has 1.61 working age adults per dependent.

These issues of extended life expectancy will in time clearly create issues in terms of economic growth, reduction in GDP, decreased savings and other side issues. A useful report by the UK-based Chartered Institute of Insurance, in conjunction with Cicero[15] entitled 'Curve Balls: Global Political Risks in 2015 and Beyond' makes the point that 'we are not equipped politically, economically or socially' to handle the effects of old age. If that is true of wider civilization at the moment, what is the level of preparedness of the insurance industry?

9.9 LIFE INSURANCE AND BANCASSURERS

Bancassurance is the term generally used to describe the relationship between a bank and an insurance company, which sometimes can both be entities within the same group. In effect it enables the insurance company to use the bank as a distribution channel. This allows the insurer to sell through the bank to the bank's customers and leverage the bank's own brand but also to sell to the bank's own staff as well.

Traditionally the bank and the insurance company share the commission, but this can also extend to a share of the profit of the insurance company. This means that the bank may have an interest in the way that the insurer settles claims, with the risk of over-generous settlements especially in general insurance products eroding overall profitability. There is an interesting balance to be found here as banks are fiercely protective of brand, but are also keen to improve income through insurance-based commission. Equally they are brand-protective in terms of the service that the policyholder receives from the insurer. If banking seems to many like a homogeneous offering across the wider marketplace, it is in the area of bancassurance that perhaps true differentiation can be obtained and where banking battles may ultimately be won and lost.

Banks usually place specific service level agreements on their third-party insurance service partners in order to obtain a differentiated service. Many insurers are willing to sign up to this as the volumes of business acquired through bancassurer deals create quicker growth than simple organic growth. Often insurers pass on these service level requirements (which are sometimes onerous) to their own supply chain without the benefit of any price differentiation. The point of service delivery, for example, in claims handling or fulfillment ultimately appears to rest with a small number of organizations which are seldom compensated for differentiated service. Those in the supply chain and who are at the sharp end generally seem to adopt the principle of 'all are equal, but some are more equal than others.'

In terms of the wider bancassurer model, the global process tends to be that firstly a banking infrastructure is set up, then life and pension products emerge, then general insurance follows. Banking tends to be the vanguard of the bancassurance process and generally without banks it is unlikely that there would be insurance. There is little evidence of an insurance industry setting up where there is no banking infrastructure already in place. By way of example, banks in Africa lead the way in helping develop the economy with insurance following behind.[16] There is every reason to think that the rate of change will lead to much more rapid acceleration of that process.

Although often grouped broadly as 'financial services' and reasonably argued that banking and insurance have more in common than they have differences, in reality these are two different industries. This is reflected in the fact that regulation is split between banking and insurance (Basel III and Solvency II, for example) and that capital management of each needs to be separated. There is some discussion that, downstream and at some time in the future, there will be a degree of coming together but this is unlikely except within the broadest parameters. Banks are concerned with the 'here and now,' insurers (and especially life and pension insurers) with future scenarios.

However, one cannot help but feel that, regulation aside, there is a natural convergence of capabilities. If an individual is prepared to trust an organization with the contents of their paycheck or savings, then shouldn't that same trust extend to provision in older age through pension arrangements? Are life and pension insurers intrinsically trusted more than banks? Rather than banks selling insurance products, perhaps it is for insurers to sell banking products?

Or as a third alternative, perhaps it will be for new brand-led offerings possibly emerging out of retail, to create innovative customer-centric propositions in both insurance and banking. If that were the case, these retail brands might provide nothing more than a brand 'vanilla' as the core investment expertise would still remain in the financial services sector.

What would be interesting is that these retail brands would bring retail-orientated customer analytics into the financial services space.

In 2013 in London, the author arranged a presentation by a high street retailer to a group of financial services organizations about the use of customer analytics, loyalty cards and discounts. The retailer, a well-known high street pharmacist, spoke about what, where and when their customers prefer to buy. The reaction of the banking and insurance attendees was extraordinary – 'How can we reach out to, and influence our customers in the same way as our retail industry colleagues are able to do?'

In a similar vein, at a major international conference featuring the use of analytics for multiple industries, the head of innovation at a global insurer spent all of his time looking at other industries such as retail, telco and banking. To paraphrase, his approach was that he 'knew everything that his peers were doing, but the real innovation came from learning about what was happening in other industries.' Policyholders benchmark the quality of insurance service against that received from banks, retailers, utilities and telco companies, with the service provided by insurers often coming out a poor second.

So, what might this mean for bancassurers?

1. Banks are very well positioned to understand the requirements of their customers in terms of their insurance needs, not only in respect of life and pension but, in due course, to provide safety and security in respect of their possessions. This requires banks to have a clearer view of the current – and future – needs of their customers.

2. Banks and insurers need to benchmark their service activities, and their ability to bundle new solutions, not with each other but with other providers outside the financial sector. Of course, it is unlikely that a retailer will readily be able to understand matters of capital management but perhaps in time the task of complying with regulations may become more of a hygiene factor rather than a differentiator.

3. Thirdly, there are matters of trust to be considered. Many of the issues that have affected the trustworthiness of the banking industry recently have related to investment activity and have not involved retail banking where much of the insurance distribution would take place. There is inevitably a contagion issue to contend with, but where banks seek to ensure separation between retail and investment offerings to the general public, then a degree of clarity and greater public trust is likely to ensue.

What this might mean overall is that whilst banking and insurance remain two sides of the same coin, there is no reason why greater convergence should not occur. Indeed, there are strong reasons why they should be encouraged. Were this to happen, then analytical insight into customer needs would increasingly be crystallized and a broader response to the wider financial needs of the customer could result.

NOTES

1. Weisbart, Dr Steven N. 'Facts and Perspectives on the Ebola Pandemic.' Insurance Information Institute. 2014. http://www.iii.org/article/facts-and-perspectives-on-the-ebola-pandemic (accessed March 21, 2016).
2. Bernard, Benjamin, Haycocks, H.W. and Pollard, J.H. *The Analysis of Mortality and Other Actuarial Statistics*, 3rd edition. Institute of Actuaries, 1993.

3. Diacon, S. and Mahdzan, N. *Protection Insurance and Financial Wellbeing.* Nottingham University Business School, 2008.

4. Barsky, R.B., Juster, F.T., Kimball, M.S. and Shapiro, M.D. 'Preference parameters and behavioral heterogeneity: an experimental approach in the health and retirement study.' (1997) *Quarterly Journal of Economics* 112(2) 537–579.

5. Huynk, Alex, Browne, Bridget and Brishu, Aaron. 'Catastrophe Mortality Bonds. Analysis of basic risks and hedging effectiveness.' A. Huyne, Booz and Co, Australia; B. Browne and Aaron Brishu, Australian National University. 2013.

6. Press Release. 'Swiss Re places first bonds to combine natural catastrophe and mortality risks, obtaining USD 200 million in protection for North Atlantic hurricane and UK extreme mortality risk.' Swiss Re. New York, 2012. http://www.swissre.com/media/news_releases/nr_20121106_Swiss_Re_Mythen_bonds.html (accessed May 17, 2016).

7. UK Office of National Statistics. 'Occupational Pension Schemes Survey: 2014.' HM Government, 2014.

8. Hall, James. 'Pensions will not exist by 2050, expert warns.' *Daily Telegraph,* 2012. http://www.telegraph.co.uk/finance/personalfinance/9741893/Pensions-will-not-exist-by-2050-expert-warns.html (accessed May 17, 2016).

9. Denterprise, R.B. 'How Millennials Buy – Some Motivating Factors.' Retail Business Development, 2013. http://retailsalesmarketingmanagement.com/how-millennials-buy-some-motivating-factors/ (accessed May 17, 2016).

10. International Business Machines, Institute of Business Value. 'Stepping up to the Challenge.' International Business Machines, 2014.

11. Chartered Institute of Marketing. *The Marketeer.* March/April 2015, pp. 22–24.

12. Saporito, Bill. 'IBM Watsons Startling Cancer Coup.' *Time Magazine,* 2014. http://time.com/3208716/ibm-watson-cancer/ (accessed May 17, 2016).

13. Department of Works and Pensions. 'Differences in life expectancy between those aged 20, 50 and 80 – in 2011 and at birth.' HM Government, 2011. https://www.gov.uk/government/uploads/system/uploads/attachment_data/file/223114/diffs_life_expectancy_20_50_80.pdf (accessed May 17, 2016).

14. International Longevity Centre-UK. 'A jam-jar model of life expectancy and limits to life.' International Longevity Centre-UK, 2015. http://www.ilcuk.org.uk/index.php/publications/publication_details/a_jam_jar_model_of_life_expectancy_and_limits_to_life (accessed May 17, 2016).

15. Cicero. 'Curve Balls: Global Political Risks is 2015 and Beyond.' Chartered Insurance Institute, 2015.

16. Christiansen, Benedicte. 'Financial Integration in Africa. Implications for Monetary Policy and Financial Stability.' Department for Business, Innovation and Skills. Paper #76. http://www.bis.org/publ/bppdf/bispap76c.pdf (accessed May 17, 2016).

CHAPTER **10**

The Importance of Location

'Everything and Everyone is somewhere.' This expression could have been written specifically for the insurance industry which is perhaps one of the most location-orientated industries of all. In general insurance, all property is somewhere, with insurers continually considering whether there is a likelihood of storm or flood to these properties. Equally, in both life and non-life insurance, insurers recognize that all their policyholders are somewhere, thus making the topic of location critical in terms of sales and underwriting.

10.1   LOCATION ANALYTICS

In describing Big Data by the '5 Vs' (volume, variety, velocity, value and veracity), the final 'V,' that of veracity or 'truthfulness,' is absolutely underpinned by the topic of geography and location. The map never lies and location is arguably an absolute truth in terms of the Big Data agenda. In fact there is an argument for dropping the expression 'map' in this context. A map is 'just' a pictorial record of location-specific data and provides no more than a snapshot of information by way of a form of visualization, in much the same way that a dashboard is only a record of events at a moment in time.

Unlike analytics, location addresses itself in many ways and in many names: location analytics, spatial analytics, GIS, geographic information systems, spatial temporal analytics and others. At the end of the day it is an element of Big Data which, through geocoding, adds another critical dimension to our understanding.

10.1.1   The New Role of the Geo-Location Expert

As the location element is seen as being more and more important in the analytics mix so the importance of the location specialist has also increased. For many years a back-room niche task, location specialists are now coming out of the dark and recognizing they have a part to play in the Big Data agenda.

Interestingly, their role models are not from the insurance industry but from other sectors. The smooth operation of the London Olympics 2012 and the Commonwealth Games in Glasgow in 2014 was due in no small part to the skills of geo-location specialists. One of their GIS leaders tells an insightful story about the fact that, in discussions with business leaders, he led with the business issue (of the mass movement of people) rather than GIS as the solution.

This is a good approach – individuals, in describing themselves as analysts of a particular genre, run the risk of pigeonholing themselves into technical or 'capability' roles. It is much better to present themselves as key contributors to finding business solutions by effectively using analytics, and thus being able to support operations or align the business to strategic objectives. In the same way that the analytical expert must be able to communicate with line of business in language both understand, without jargon, the niche location specialists must be able to do the same.

Professional institutes have a role to play in this transformation. Too often professional conferences are capability-orientated rather than having one eye (or both eyes) on the business issue. The round of applause which sometimes follows the launch of a new GIS capability is often more akin to the 'Church of Mapology' rather than an analytical capability of value to the business community. In what seems a break with tradition, the UK-based Association for Geographic Information recently included business leaders as keynote speakers in their 2014 and 2015 conferences and it is hoped that this approach will continue. It is a significant recognition not only of the impact of location on businesses but also that the method of engagement with business also needs to change.

10.1.2   Sharing Location Information

A recent survey of US mobile consumers indicated that they were prepared to give away details about their location provided that they got something in return by way of relevant content and promotion.[1] This was further backed up by a more recent UK survey which indicated that 84% of UK 18–34-year-olds were comfortable sharing personal data provided that they received some benefit. Research of 2000 adults indicated that nearly two-thirds were willing to share information about themselves provided they were aware what it would be used for, and that social media log-ons gave them the opportunity to be selective in that sharing.[2]

The Chief Executive of the funders of the particular research, Gigya (who are a provider of customer analytics solutions) makes the point that 'Social login gives customers control over what they share with brands while offering them convenience and saving them time.' Both these surveys, and others, were undertaken in the context of consumer goods rather than financial services, but the point is clear. There appears to be a trade-off between sharing information against the benefit of receiving value-add propositions. With consumer goods this may equate to offers and discounts being pushed to a prospective buyer, encouraging them to visit a nearby store or even a department within a store.

Equivalent offers are not unheard of from insurers. Single trip travel policies are typical in the holiday industry. However, to add a location 'dimension,' one large Japanese insurer piloted the concept of 'one time insurance' for the golf course. The background is that golfers who successfully hit a hole-in-one are obliged to buy gifts for their fellow players. Through location analytics it was possible to identify that the prospective purchaser of the policy was on the golf course, and an offer was pushed to the individual inviting them to purchase 'one time cover' as a contingency against the hole-in-one happening (with purchase effected through their telephone account).

10.1.3   Geocoding

Geocoding is the process of transferring the description of the location of a place (or a person) into a set of coordinates such as latitude and longitude, to provide a unique locator. By adding additional descriptions known as 'attributes' it is possible to identify, for example, the number of particular properties at risk (e.g., from flood) in a specific area. Reverse geocoding allows the use of coordinates to find a particular postal address, for example. A 'geocoder' is that piece of technical middleware which allows a geocoding process to be implemented.

At its most straightforward level it assists in grouping numbers of properties against specific geocoding indicators. There is an element of generalization in this approach as 'blocks' of properties are usually considered rather than individual buildings. However insurers are especially keen to obtain greater granularity given that within a group or 'block' of properties, there may be variations in the risk from one end of the group to the other.

'Point-level' geocoding is especially critical to insurers to help them understand issues of risk associated with precise location, for example proximity to a river or precise location within a flood plain. As with other parts of this book, the broad-based information provided is principally to raise awareness and does not seek to provide a deep dive into the topic. An excellent guide to the topic of geocoding is available from the University of Southern California GIS Laboratory in their paper 'A Geocoding Best Practice Guide.'[3] The particular interest of the authors relates to gaining a better understanding of the link between location and illness.

10.1.4   Location Analytics in Fraud Investigation

Insurance fraud is complex and analytics generally has a role to play both in its prevention and its detection. It is useful to separately consider the location component in that discussion.

It is perhaps tempting and maybe obvious to equate the location of greatest fraud with areas of deprivation and crime, and in effect 'mash' together information from third parties such as crime agencies. This certainly is one key indicator, but only one, as criminals are known of course to 'commute' from a poorer area to one with 'richer pickings.' Equally, in staged road traffic accidents, there is some evidence to suggest that certain locations are better than others for this, for example accident hotspots.

In 2010 the UK organization ActionFraud, the National Fraud and Cyber Crime Reporting Centre, reported on an Insurance Fraud Bureau investigation which indicated the major 'hotspots' for fraudulent car accidents,[4] the top ten in the UK being:

1. Birmingham
2. Liverpool
3. Blackburn
4. Manchester
5. Leeds
6. London East
7. Oldham
8. Bradford
9. London North
10. Bolton.

Organized fraud is however often more complex involving more 'players' who are networked together. Network analytics can help in those investigations but it would be wrong to overlook the location component. Work by organizations such as Ordnance Survey in the UK coupled with the UK Fraud Agency indicate that there is much to be done in this area yet, and few would argue that effective deterrent strategy is essential.

10.1.5   Location Analytics in Terrorism Risk

As has previously been covered elsewhere, insurers often model acts of terrorism as single large events such as a major explosion. In such modeling, it becomes possible to understand the area of impact of the blast sometimes in models as relatively simplistic as concentric circles. The degree of damage, simply put, is a combination of the degree of the blast and the vulnerability of the building.

Increasingly, it is being recognized that another possible risk is one of concurrent, perhaps – but not necessarily – smaller incidents. As a result, insurers need to consider the cumulative effect and location analytics plays a critical part in that. In such scenarios risk accumulation becomes a critical consideration and the location of individual properties, for example, plays a critical part in that topic.

Whilst growth of revenue is always attractive, this cannot be at the cost of deviating from the overall risk appetite of the insurer. Insurers need to have a clear line of sight of their existing locational risk exposure as part of their operational decision-making. Such levels of modeling require significant analysis and computing power, and at the heart of this analysis is the interlock between location intelligence, financial performance management and predictive analysis.

10.1.6   Location Analytics and Flooding

With evidence of climate change there appear to be more incidents of flooding and with greater frequency. The cost of flooding in recent years has been significant. UK flooding in 2013 cost insurers £1.2bn, and is currently estimated (2015) to be as high as £4.5bn. Over the last decade the annual cost of flooding in continental Europe (defined as mainland Europe excluding European islands such as the United Kingdom, and Greece) has been €4.5bn and is estimated to increase to €23bn per year by 2050.[5]

Flooding continues to be a major issue not just for insurers but for mankind as a whole. Major flood events which come to mind include:

- 2004 Tsunami in Asia
- 2005 New Orleans
- 2007 United Kingdom
- 2010 Pakistan.

Flooding is the most frequently occurring natural disaster and over the 30 years leading up to 2006 has killed over 200,000 people[6] as well as causing untold misery and illness. The topic of flood is also covered elsewhere but from a location aspect it is helpful to provide more background to the subject.

Flooding can occur due to many causes:[7]

- From river flooding or 'alluvial'
- From watercourses such as rivers and ditches or 'fluvial'
- From surface water flooding from overflowing drains operating beyond capacity
- From rising groundwater levels
- From the failure of artificial water systems
- From the sea, including coastal and estuarial flooding.

Although knowledge of the impact of flooding has increased and continues to do so, aided by more data and better analytics, there are still challenges in the quality of prediction. The main issues seem to rest not in the quality of the captured data, or even to some degree the ability to predict when rain might accurately occur. Rather they rest with the ability to fully understand how all the data comes together to provide a single clear view of what flood conditions may (or may not) lie ahead.

The ability to forecast whether or not a flood will occur is not simply a matter for insurers, albeit they have a vested interest in being able to do so, but for governments as a whole. There has been some improvement in approach. Today operational flood forecasting centers are changing their approach and moving away from what is called a 'deterministic' forecast ('will it flood or won't it?') into a combination of forecasting which matches the probability of individual elements occurring, and what their relevance is in context. This process is known as a 'Hydrological Ensemble Prediction Systems' or 'HEPS,' and seems to have some commonality with advanced analytics in so far as the process considers the combination of structured and unstructured data, and arrives at some sort of probability analysis.[8]

Moving away from a 'will it/won't it' approach to flood prediction implies issues not just of technology and analytics but also how this information is to be acted upon. If there is only a *possibility* of flooding, rather than a probability, then is this enough to act? The manner in which this information is communicated, perhaps through a form of traffic light or RAG status warning, is critical. 'Traffic lights' seem on balance to be a crude but effective representation of the potential for major damage and disruption.

The question of whether or not flooding will occur is an issue of probability and insurers are veterans in managing probability. The issue is not so much that of minor flooding but of predicting major floods which fortunately are not regular occurrences. Predictive models are possible but these also need to be calibrated against real life occurrences. In the context of location and insurance, deciding that a property is prone to flooding or not based mainly on geographical location seems at face value to be a crude tool. Even taking into account the possibility of flooding of nearby properties may be misleading, as much may depend on the exact location and height of the affected buildings and the precise reason for the nearby flood.

Tempting as it is for insurers to find a location-based flood model, this is not a problem that is likely to be solved by the insurance community in isolation. The benefits of finding an effective flood model will be of interest to insured and uninsured alike. One question to address is whether such a flood model should first evolve in mature markets with a density of soundly built properties, better data and greater potential economic loss. The alternative is to start in immature markets where building codes of practice may be weaker (or maybe even relatively non-existent) and where data quality is poor. In those places the economic loss is not as great but the human cost is greater. It is in these relatively underdeveloped locations that many manufacturing supply chains are based. What starts to become apparent is that the answer – somewhere – rests in the topic of Big Data and Analytics, and in the sizeable computing power that will need to sit alongside these attributes.

In the UK it has been assessed that one in six properties are prone to flooding, according to the UK Public Affairs Committee of the House of Commons,[9] a situation thought by some to have been made worse by cut-backs in flood defenses due to economic austerity measures and the need to find savings. Following the 2007 UK flooding which caused £3.0bn of damage, affected 44,000 homes and left 13 dead, the UK Government commissioned an independent report from Sir Michael Pitt.

The Pitt Report[10] made 92 major recommendations for the UK including:

1. Confirmation that the Environment Agency should take on a national overview of flood risk.
2. Further development of modeling tools and techniques.
3. Making flood visualization data more accessible.
4. Better interlock with Weather Agencies.
5. Creation of a more specific flood warning system for infrastructure operators.
6. Improving work with local responders to raise awareness in flood risk areas.
7. Working with telecoms companies to issue telephone flood warning schemes.

The insurance community should continually remind themselves of Pitt's recommendations. In the same way that his report called for public and private enterprise to sit alongside each other as a response to the UK flooding issues, insurers need to recognize that the way forward with issues of flood prediction and management is through more collaboration and not necessarily through independent thinking. Suggestions of anti-competitive behavior should not get in the way of what is clearly in the public good. The reasoning for this is that the problem frankly is too complicated and too big for one single insurer to cope with (regardless of scale), in the same way that insurers work together to combat the problem of insurance fraud.

The recent introduction in the UK of FloodRe, a government-sponsored and industry-funded backstop, mirrors PoolRe which is a mutual set up by the UK government to provide terrorist cover. At the heart of FloodRe is a desire to provide affordable insurance to consumers and offer a degree of financial protection to insurers. This is not a 'catch-all' as there are many exceptions to the scheme but the idea is well intentioned and represents another element of public/private collaboration in this particular space.

10.1.7 Location Analytics, Cargo and Theft

It is natural to want to consider location devices working in an environment of the Internet of Things as providing a cure-all for tracking and tracing stolen cargo or vehicles. In addition, there are multiple anecdotal and reported stories of vehicle owners being informed through tracking devices that their car had been stolen whilst they were away on vacation, and the cars had been taken out of the country.

Location analytics is critical to such capability but it is not infallible. Recently the US Georgia Bureau of Investigation recovered jamming technology after executing a search warrant in respect of suspected cargo theft.[11] These GPS jamming capabilities are not in common use by criminals but are available nevertheless and their existence serves as a reminder that effective security needs to be in place to reduce such risks.

Beyond this, the ability of underwriters to understand the location of cargo is desirable. At its most optimal, it could allow insurers to place a limit on the amount of cargo or number of vessels passing through a particular place. Whilst piracy cannot be entirely prevented, its effect may be mitigated. Many of these risks are placed with specialist insurers but the question must be asked: how many of these are ready to be proactive rather than reactive?

10.2   TELEMATICS AND USER-BASED INSURANCE ('UBI')

One of the more recent and exciting developments in the field of Big Data and Analytics is the advent of telematics, often also known as 'pay as you drive' but increasingly taking on the mantle of 'pay how you drive.'

In practical terms, a device fitted in the vehicle either in the factory or later allows insurers to record information such as driving duration, speed, severe braking, time and location. The idea is that insurers can better understand the behavior of the driver and underwrite, or price, the insurance cover with greater accuracy. This can lead to either a reduction or an increase in premium. Whilst marketers suggest savings to the policyholder, an increase in premium is equally possible dependent on driver behavior.

One of the main marketing propositions of telematics is that it rewards the younger driver for good behavior behind the wheel, but with older drivers increasingly being disadvantaged by higher premiums, this is a capability that would also seem to apply to all generations and different user types.

In addition, insurers recommending this technology seek to add value by suggesting that telematics can also act as a tracking device in the event of the car being stolen. Also, the device can potentially help act as an accident alert device, where the driver is alone in remote locations.

In effect telematics comprises four key components:

1. A location system, allowing insurers to understand where and when the car is being driven. This can be correlated to the type of road being used, e.g., a motorway.
2. A device such as an accelerometer which provides information about the motion of the car – rapid acceleration or braking for example. This helps insurers better understand driving behavior.
3. A transmittal device.
4. Analytic capability which allows insurers to take into account all the key data and from this to gain better insight into the underwriting risk, and the appropriate premium.

10.2.1   History of Telematics

The term telematics appears to go back as far as 1978 when the term *'telematiques'* was coined by Simon Nora and Alain Minc. Then it referred in a report[12] to the French government to the convergence of *'telecommunications'* and *'informatique'* as being a methodology by which information could be transferred by telecommunications. At that time the principle had not been considered to apply to cars although the idea had initially gained attention in the tracking of cargo containers and trailers.

In terms of the use of telematics for vehicle insurance, this was invented and patented by a US insurer, Progressive, who first brought the idea to market in 1996[13] described as a 'motor vehicle monitoring system for determining a cost of insurance.' Examination of the patent itself makes good reading and is a wonderful example of forward thinking about a 'big data and analytical' world which at that time had yet to mature to the level of today's capability and imagination. The patent establishes the potential for pricing insurance based on a foundational or 'base cost' with additions or savings 'representative of an operating state of the vehicle or an action of the operator.'

The patent itself is forward thinking in its ideas suggesting that beyond simply being a process for managing insurance premiums, it adds considerable value in terms of vehicle and driver safety. The patent explains that the technical capability could also be used where there was:

- Excessive speed: In effect the reading of the vehicle speed sensors would tell whether the vehicle was exceeding any speed limit. The measurement of time would show whether this was consistent practice.
- Presence of alcohol: The use of an air content analyzer or breath analyzer might show the level of alcohol taken by the driver.
- Non-use of seatbelt: Sensors would detect the use of seat belts and this would be reflected in the premium.
- Non-use of turn signals: Low or no use could result in a premium adjustment.
- ABS application without an accident: High use could indicate erratic driving even without an accident.

Beyond this, the patent provided for other 'extras,' to include:

- Accident occurrence
- Roadside assistance needed
- Lock-out assistance needed
- Driving restrictions in dangerous areas.

In reality, this was a broad-based and ambitious set of descriptions which seem at face value to create a vision of motoring in the future. Retrospectively, the scope of the thinking was both ambitious and audacious. One of the people behind this patent was a Spanish inventor, Salvador Minguijon Perez, who had captured these ideas in his own personal European patent[14] in 1995, over 20 years ago. Today Perez potentially stands as one of the unsung giants of technology.

Progressive's 'Snapshot' device had by 2013 contributed over $2bn to the company's auto premium revenue but these patents were overturned in 2014 and this has increasingly opened the door to market development. By agreement telematics was first brought into the UK insurance market in 2005 by Norwich Union principally as a mechanism for improving the affordability of insurance amongst young and risky drivers. It is interesting to compare the market maturity of the North American and UK markets. By 2013 insurers in the UK were still considering this as a niche market for high risk drivers whereas the North American model had made this a mainstream option in terms of insurance choice. There is an interesting comparison between the US and Europe, in that by 2013 Progressive were describing telematics as a 'hard sell.'[15] Perhaps it hasn't been as hard as they suggest. Progressive's competitors Allstate started their program six years after Progressive and participants have racked up 3.0 billion miles of data across 39 states. About one-third of new customers apparently sign up for the discount program where it's offered.[16]

The current position is that in the UK, insurance online aggregator sites usually actively invite the consumer to choose if they are interested in a telematics-type offering. Telematics has become mainstream albeit that the level of penetration remains relatively modest. Looking forward to 2021, analysts IHS suggest the two main markets for UBI will be the US and China. According to Ivey Business Review 'In 2012, 11.4% of cars shipped globally possessed some type of in-vehicle telematics unit; this is projected to increase to 60% in 2017 . . .. Additionally, it is predicted that by 2020, more than $30B or 25% of the entire US auto insurance premium revenue will be generated via telematics.'[17]

10.2.2 Telematics in Fraud Detection

With one of the major areas of auto injury comprising whiplash, which is virtually impossible to diagnose with any degree of accuracy, the use of telematics is increasingly a tool in the armory of insurers. Whiplash is the term used to describe a neck injury caused by sudden movement of the head backwards, forwards or sideways, as might happen in the case of an auto accident. It is a serious problem for insurers. In 2007, 430,000 people made a claim for whiplash, allegedly adding 14% to the cost of everyone's insurance premium.[18]

Whilst the soreness of whiplash injury may resolve itself in a few days and can often be helped by anti-inflammatory medicine, it is suggested that 50% of those affected may have some degree of ongoing problem. Much has been written on this topic already. There appears to be a correlation between injury and age, with those in their forties and older more likely to be affected.[19] In addition it is suggested that whiplash occurs at speeds of 15mph or even less. This also inevitably involves low speed 'shunts' which are either accidental or fraudulent in nature. Use of mobile phones in low speed traffic may also be a contributor.

The topic remains contentious. It is suggested that MRI, CT scans and X-rays are not able to identify whiplash.[20] On the other hand, one major insurer has sought mandatory MRI scans in all whiplash claims which caused a furious reaction from legal experts.[21]

Notwithstanding, it remains helpful to understand the connection between whiplash and vehicle accidents in a telematics context:

- Speed of impact appears to be a factor.
- Location may be important, in that it may be possible to correlate the location of the incident with a known accident hotspot.
- The age and type of vehicle are indicators.
- Previous insurance experience and claims history of the individual involved may point to heightened awareness of the insurance process.
- Previous medical history of the claimant may identify some earlier injury.

Whilst telematics may not prove to be the ultimate solution for fraud investigation in motor incidents, it is likely to remain an important part of the insurer's toolbox.

10.2.3 What is the Impact on Motor Insurers?

Traditionalists may have viewed telematics and user-based insurance initially as a gimmick, but the rapid take up and increasing adoption of this approach must be more than a temporary or partial approach to the issue of auto insurance. Nowadays telematics and user-based insurance must be viewed as a viable option and one which needs to be put before prospective purchasers as a reasonable alternative. In fact, some are suggesting that the development and rate of take-up of telematics might herald the end of auto insurance as we know it.

The relaxation of patent issues and the apparent reduction of cost of implementation coupled with new entrants must make user-based insurance including telematics a threat to traditional players. Devices can be retrospectively added to vehicles or, more likely, will be embedded from manufacture making the vehicle manufacturer in effect a new distribution channel for insurance products, or even allow motor insurers to create insurance products in their own right.

Technology would not appear to present a barrier, the major issue perhaps being that of regulation. Were ABC Motor Manufacturer to create an auto insurance proposition, how well placed or qualified would they be to meet the issues of Solvency II, RMORSA or other local regulatory regimes? New skills, competencies and relationships will inevitably emerge. In the same way that property insurers discovered the need for supply chain management as a core competence, auto manufacturers may also discover the need to develop insurance capability in all its widest forms, including risk management and compliance as an adjunct to putting wheels on chassis. This will not have been an entirely untried path – motor manufacturers have long since been intimately engaged in auto financing and the provision of insurance may simply prove to be an extension of their financial services thinking and capability.

10.2.4 Telematics and Vehicle Dashboard Design

Telematics, or more properly described, user-based insurance is already beginning to influence the ergonomic design of vehicle dashboards. Some readers will remember the use of a fuel efficiency indicator – for want of a better name – on certain German and Scandinavian cars in the 1990s. In effect as the driver pushed their foot harder onto the accelerator and made the engine work harder, the dashboard provided a mile-per-gallon indicator. The more brutally the driver worked the accelerator, the more challenging it was on the driver's wallet. It was a simple device which linked driver performance to cost and provided very clear evidence that it was possible to modify driver behavior by simple analytics. It rather depends on whether the driver is personally paying for the fuel – or whether perhaps it is a company account – but the point is made.

In a similar approach some motor insurers are already thinking about the practicalities of putting some form of 'cost of premium' indicator on the dashboard. The more violently the car is driven, the higher the premium. One suggestion is to have a simple Red/Amber/Green approach, as clearly it is difficult to calculate premium in absolute terms in real time, but the ambition is clear.

One question which arises is to what degree such an indicator might change driver behavior. An indication of fluctuation in monthly premium is interesting or it could be by way of an annual adjustment, but can this somehow be done in 'real time'? Notwithstanding the technical architecture 'beneath the bonnet,' one key consideration appears to be the size and location of the 'premium indicator' – let's call it the 'insurance gauge' for convenience. The greatest impact is likely to be when the driver cannot help but see the indicator – giving rise to ergonomic issues of size and location. If too discreet, then the indicator will not make an impact. If too obvious, then aesthetically it may be unacceptable. In this new world of data, analytics, and telematics it seems that ergonomics has a place as well.

In the wider context such an approach may also depend on the vehicle itself. Some owners of high performance, high value vehicles may scoff at the idea of an insurance premium indicator on their dashboard because for them the insurance element doesn't matter. Other more cost-conscious individuals may be grateful as lower premiums may help fund the repayments on the car purchase. Amongst the general public, insurance is a key component in the cost of running a car and as has been seen elsewhere, consumers are increasingly willing to trade information for benefit that can be realized. To what degree insurers and vehicle manufacturers take advantage of this trade-off remains to be seen.

10.2.5 Telematics and Regulation

As user-based insurance becomes increasingly popular, or at least needs to be considered as a viable option, then there will also be a regulatory angle to consider. Auto manufacturers who think about entering the insurance world directly without partnering with established insurers will need to consider the vagaries of capital management, evidenced through Solvency II and other equivalent regimes. Auto manufacturers have not been deterred from offering finance and the more committed will not see insurance regulation as a barrier to entry in terms of offering their own insurance products. Manufacturers and insurers also will need to reflect on issues such as ownership of data and whether this can be used for reasons other than the purpose intended. Police may insist on access to telematics data as part of a legitimate legal enquiry, and UK insurers for example may have no option but to share this information.[22]

In the US, insurers will also need to comply with local commissions who may take a tougher stance. Their role is to protect the consumer and have the autonomy to make individual laws to ensure that issues such as risk and consumer protection are adequately represented and catered for. Dealing with 50-plus sets of regulations makes the management of issues such as telematics highly complex especially given that by its very nature telematics involves most US drivers potentially travelling from state to state. Nevertheless, insurers must deal with this complex environment and the effective work of the National Association of Insurance Commissioners (NAIC) helps to provide a degree of consistency.

Eric Nordman, Director of Regulatory Service and speaking on behalf of NAIC, usefully points out:

> *We view telematics as the next evolution of risk classification and as being perhaps more accurate. It has the potential of recording information at a very detailed level. However, insurance regulators and legislators look at telematics as just one more tool in the toolbox.*[23]

Telematics in Europe potentially finds itself in the same fragmented position, perhaps more so in that whilst there are EU Directives encouraging the adoption of user-based insurance these are at a lesser level of maturity. Currently the European Union strategy on the use of telematics might even be being driven by the medical profession – the European Medical Agency – which takes us back to the very real linkage between data, location and illness.[24] Many life insurers view a pandemic as being one of the greatest insurance threats of all. Telematics – or the use of location, tracking and analytics to track and manage medical epidemics across boundaries – is viewed as a major priority for the medical profession.

Beyond this, the new EU data privacy laws will add greater impetus to the need to ensure that data collected is used for the purpose intended. In addition, whilst first-mover advantage has its benefits, EU law prevents organizations – and this includes insurers – from taking advantage of dominant business positions. This may include some insurers having significantly more telematics data than their competitors and therefore offering substantially improved terms or premiums. The implication is that those in control of, or with a monopoly on, data insight may in effect raise the barriers to entry of other potential insurance providers and this would be, in effect, unfair practice. Against a background of fierce competition, overcapacity in the market and brand assertiveness, European insurers might still be obliged to ensure that the 'playing field' remains more or less level.

Overall it's a complex landscape. In the US there seems to be a divergence of thinking amongst states, for example Washington appears more forward-thinking and has policies to encourage user-based insurance compared to more conservative states. One size may not fit all in respect of the ability to implement a UBI strategy taking into account a regulatory viewpoint.

Beyond this, insurers and motor manufacturers also need to reflect on the alignment of insurance and improved management of claims with other wider initiatives, for example the concept known as 'V2X.' This concept is at the heart of the idea of the 'connected car.' Two particular aspects are considered under V2X:

1. V2V (Vehicle to Vehicle), – Communication between vehicles
2. V2I (Vehicle to Infrastructure) – This typically comprises roadside units but can also include advertising and travel-related information.

The key takeaway from this thinking is that if a vehicle is able to communicate better with its surroundings, including other nearby vehicles, then there is also scope for improvement in safety and other benefits. V2X has applications in the management of traffic flow, toll collection, freight management and alerting cars to the condition of the road surface beneath. If the market is not quite ready for self-drive cars, then it is probably closer to being ready for the V2X approach.

Whilst these capabilities are naturally dependent on location analytics there are other issues to consider, typically the manner in which this information will be transmitted and also the rate at which devices will be incorporated into the environment to make the information meaningful. Juniper Research suggest that a take-up of 97% is needed to make the process viable, and clearly we are some considerable distance away from that at the moment.[25]

As these systems become increasingly available perhaps there will also be a knock-on effect in driver behavior. To what degree will driving skills start to change when there is greater reliance on the embedded system within the car to help the driver in the process of moving from A to B? Over time, will driver judgment and reaction speeds start to be affected? In the same way that the use of physical maps (and ability to use them) seems to have declined in favor of drivers following the directions of their 'Sat-Navs,' perhaps there will be a similar change in driving capability. One analogy perhaps rests with mountain walkers in the UK who are increasingly abandoning paper maps for satellite navigation devices, resulting in a fall of 25% in the sales of paper maps between 2005 and 2012, yet at the same time an increase in the need for mountain rescues of 52% over the same period. Does this suggest a shift in capability and dependency?[26]

10.2.6 Telematics – More Than Technology

In considering telematics as an alternative pricing structure fueled by data and analytics, it is tempting to think that it is a technology solution alone. The technology which underpins a telematics solution is naturally complex in nature but the solution is more than technology (Figure 10.1) and needs to take into account:

- The cost, ownership and installation of the device, and what the situation is if the insurance is transferred or the vehicle is sold.
- The business operating model and what the go-to-market is.

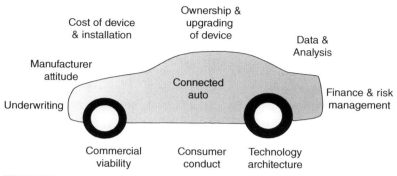

FIGURE 10.1   Telematics is more than technology

- The commercial viability of the telematics solution.
- Consumer acceptance, which may be linked to other added-value attributes.

Insurers need to understand and recognize the differences (and probable potential improvement) in loss ratios, taking into account the initial outlay and reduction in premiums and the impact this may have in the re-pricing of their book of business. Some telematics solutions already place caps on their premium discount because of the technology but some consumers may feel entitled to ask whether these caps are reasonable.

Telematics also fundamentally shifts the relationship between the insurer and the policyholder, giving the policyholder much greater control than ever before over their insurance premium. It also potentially moves the insurer from being reactive to proactive. These value propositions are startlingly simple yet fundamental to this new form of relationship, and it is important that this approach is not lost in the technology or the pricing. User-based insurance represents a significant disruption in the traditional insurance process and has ramifications in many areas including capital management.

Entry level insurers will also want to consider the cost of implementation, to include the cost of data capture, storage, analysis, underwriting and customer service, and whether these complexities may present some form of either real or perceived barrier to entry. Hybrid systems may help in that regard, such as the use of OBD-II devices. The expression 'OBD' means 'On Board Diagnostics,' and these are computer-based systems built into modern cars that monitor emission-related controls and access to numerous parameters and sensors from the Engine Control Unit.[27] When coupled with some sort of mechanism for data transfer this appears to provide a basis for cost savings which insurers may find attractive. The recent disclosure[28] of diagnostic manipulation of emissions by a major motor manufacturer affecting 1.2m cars in the UK and 0.5m cars in the US is unlikely to have any long-term impact on the use of this type of technology but skeptics are likely nevertheless to have some worries and will perhaps demand greater transparency.

10.2.7   User-Based Insurance in Other Areas

Whilst at a relatively early stage of maturity, it is possible to envisage telematics-based usage in other types of insurance, for example life and pension or healthcare. At a personal level there are already a number of commonly available devices which record personal activity such as walking or running. Some are standalone and others are embedded into android devices. One issue with standalone devices is the risk of the user not remembering to carry the device. The recent news that a UK-based boutique jeweler is to embed this type of capability into certain jewellery, including watches, might open the door to more regular usage.[29]

As in the case of auto insurance, it will be interesting to see how device manufacturers change the behavior of individuals and incentivize them to change their level of activity. In the case of one particular standalone device, for example, the device shows a smiley face if a certain level of activity has been undertaken although such an approach may be a little crude on an expensive watch or piece of jewelry.

Consideration is also being given to the use of telematics in healthcare and the broader concept of telemedicine. The changing demographic and the greater number of people who will reach old age will increasingly place burdens on traditional methods of care, and telematics-type devices will almost certainly have a part to play in any new operating model. The concept of Remote Patient Monitoring (RPM) is a process which allows remote access to the patient outside normal care facilities and is considered to be one way of reducing cost and improving service. Beyond this, patients and families have the comfort of knowing that the patient is being monitored and able to receive appropriate care treatment including remote provision of medicines. In the case of patients with dementia, RPM coupled with tracking devices can help in the detection of falls or perhaps where an elderly person has wandered from their normal place of residence.

The core components of RPM are recognizable from other telematics areas, typically:

- Wireless-enabled sensors.
- Data storage – perhaps some form of local datamart which provides more local and speedier access to information, together with a larger central data repository with greater reach.
- Analytical capability including but not confined to diagnostic capability.

The concept of the 'connected home' is also more than speculative, as utility providers and others start to instrument and analyze individual properties to measure usage of energy, water and other critical attributes. Insurers need to be careful that these discussions and developments do not take place in isolation but that issues are considered 'in the round.' A sudden loss of pressure detected by a water utility may also provide a signal to an insurer that a burst has taken place. What is the process by which such information might be passed from one type of organization to another? Might new legal liabilities arise if the water company fails to act to mitigate the loss?

The ongoing development of the Internet of Things, where devices have the ability to communicate with each other without human intervention, will almost certainly have a telematics or *location* component. The insurance version which may evolve will probably in time provide some degree of automation in the claims process, where for example the rapid deceleration of a vehicle coupled with some form of impact will trigger a set of activities. These may range from an outbound call from the insurer to the policyholder to check for any injuries, to arranging a tow truck and a replacement vehicle.

10.2.8 Telematics in Commercial Insurances

It is tempting to consider telematics mainly as a consumer-orientated, personal lines tool. However, it is equally feasible to consider telematics-type tools in a commercial environment.

Such capabilities might tend to focus on optimizing productivity, efficiency, cost reduction and profitability. Where used in fleet and transit management, for example, or even by making the employee carry devices, the use of telematics could normally extend to cover safety and sustainability issues. For insurers this represents a reduced risk and is therefore potentially reflected in lower premiums especially in employers' liability/Workers' Compensation cover for instance. How employees feel about such micro-analysis is a matter for conjecture.

TechNavio, a technology research and advisory company, forecast the market for commercial telematics principally in vehicle tracking to grow in the US by 16.7% between 2015 and 2019[30] driven by increased globalization, high fuel prices and greater competition, especially in the growth of the Asian market. Visiongain suggests the current 2015 value of the commercial tracking market to be about $13.21bn.[31]

The use of telematics in insurance potentially goes considerably beyond fleet management and accrued insurance advantage. Any processes or 'things' in commercial enterprises which are mobile would seem to have an application for some form of a 'telematics' solution within the widest meaning of the expression. If it moves and it is capable of being insured, or the consequences of failure give rise to an insurable loss, then there is probably a 'telematical' opportunity.

This might extend from the obvious, for example in the case of aviation or marine risk, to the less obvious such as:

- Machinery failure and the potential impact on product liability.
- Excessive bridge deflection leading to roads and railways being closed, and the consequent knock-on effect on business.
- Agriculture and the impact of events or incidents in the food chain.

In effect anything which moves and where a failure to move occurs, or even where it moves in the wrong direction (and which therefore gives rise to a legal and potentially insurable liability) might in the future become matters of attention to the insurance community. Of course, insurers will be concerned with 'direct' economic losses bearing in mind the long string of legal precedents such as that of *Anns v Merton London Borough*[32] which demanded a sufficient level of proximity to the loss.

Insurers will also want to keep a watchful eye on the increased attention given to Building Information Management ('BIM') and how this also might give rise to new liabilities. What this seems to imply is that whilst insurers may gain greater insight from data and analytics, on the other hand new liabilities might arise as a result of the availability of information and the so-called democratization of analytics. One typical example (mentioned elsewhere) is the increased pressure and scrutiny on directors and non-executive directors of organizations either for failing to effectively implement analytical enterprises or even worse failing to act on the insights which these analytics are providing.

If data and analytics have the capability to provide greater insight, then the other side of the coin is that this places greater responsibility on those who can access – or should have accessed – this information. At executive level, this invariably involves Directors and Officers Liability insurance cover for those who may have a duty not only to know what their company is doing, but also where employees are and what they are up to. The Big Data and Analytics era appears to be a double-edged sword in that whilst it provides insight for insurance organizations, it also potentially creates a new regime of claims. Stakeholders of companies may perhaps quite reasonably ask why the officers of the company, with all the technology and data around them, did not (or chose not to) advise them of issues which might affect stock value. Employees might equally ask how the company allowed them to undertake risky activities in hazardous locations.

All that aside, what starts to become clear is that the topic of Big Data and Analytics is not a matter solely for retail insurers focusing on auto telematics who might perhaps choose to rely on the laws of big numbers but also it will impact on specialty lines, commercial insurance arrangements and other areas. Possibly this new era may also encourage, or perhaps even force, underwriters to think about their wordings before the courts place them in compromising situations.

NOTES

1. JiWire. 'Mobile Audience Insights Report,' 2011. http://www.thelbma.com/files/124-JiWire-Q2 .pdf (accessed May 17, 2016).
2. Davies, Jessica. '84% of young UK adults are willing to share personal data with brands via social logins, says Gigya report.' The Drum, 2014. http://www.thedrum.com/news/2014/10/06/84-young-uk-adults-are-willing-share-personal-data-brands-social-logins-says-gigya (accessed March 25, 2016).
3. Goldberg, Daniel W. 'A Geocoding Best Practices Guide. North American Association of Central Cancer Registries.' University of Southern California GIS Research Laboratory, 2008.
4. Action Fraud. 'Car crash scam hotspots revealed,' 2010. http://www.actionfraud.police.uk/car-crash-scam-hotspots-revealed-aug10 (accessed March 25, 2016).
5. Jongman, Brenden et al. 'Increasing stress on disaster-risk finance due to large floods.' (2014) *Nature Climate Change* 4: 264–268. http://www.nature.com/nclimate/journal/v4/n4/full/nclimate2124 .html (accessed May 17, 2016).
6. Guha-Sapir, D. 'Climate change and human dimension.' International Workshop on Climate Change Impacts. Brussels, 2006.
7. Lancaster, J.W., Preene, M. and Marshall, C.T. 'Development and Flood Risk – Guidance for the Construction Industry.' Construction Industry Research and Information Association. London, 2004.
8. Wood, A.W., Thielen, J., Pappenberger, F. et al. 'The Hydrological Emsemble Prediction Experiment.' American Geophysical Union, Fall Meeting 2012, abstract #H43A-1313, 2012.
9. Press Association. 'One in six UK homes at risk from flooding, says MPs report.' *The Guardian,* 2015. http://www.theguardian.com/environment/2015/mar/25/one-in-six-uk-homes-risk-from-flooding-mps-report (accessed March 25, 2016).
10. HM Government; Sir Michael Pitt. 'The Pitt Review: Lessons Learned from the 2007 Floods.' Cabinet Office. London, 2010. http://webarchive.nationalarchives.gov.uk/20100807034701/http:// archive.cabinetoffice.gov.uk/pittreview/_/media/assets/www.cabinetoffice.gov.uk/flooding_ review/final_press_notice%20pdf.pdf (accessed March 25, 2016).
11. Fleet Owner. 'GPS jammers recovered from cargo thieves, says FreightWatch,' 2015. http://m .fleetowner.com/technology/gps-jammers-recovered-cargo-thieves-says-freightwatch (accessed March 25, 2016).
12. Nora, Simon. 'L'informatisation de la société: Rapport à M. le Président de la République.' Seuil, 1978.
13. McMillan, Robert J. 'Motor vehicle monitoring system for determining a cost of insurance.' U.S. Patent 5,797,134, 1998. https://www.google.com/patents/US5797134 (accessed March 25, 2016).
14. Minguijon Perez, Salvador. 'Individuelle Bewertungsystem für das Risiko an Selbstangetriebene Fahrzeuge.' European Patent EP0700009B1. European Patent Office, 1995. http://worldwide .espacenet.com/publicationDetails/originalDocument?CC=EP&NR=0700009&KC=&FT=E (accessed March 25, 2016).

15. Golia, Nathan. 'Progressive Finds Telematics a Hard Sell.' Information Week, 2013. http://www.insurancetech.com/progressive-finds-telematics-a-hard-sell/a/d-id/1314702 (accessed May 17, 2016).
16. Voelker, Michael. 'Telematics: Carriers expanding tools beyond usage-based insurance.' Property-Casualty360. 2014. http://www.propertycasualty360.com/2014/08/12/telematics-carriers-expanding-tools-beyond-usage-b (accessed March 25, 2016).
17. Xu, Danielle. 'A new lifeline for General Motors.' Ivey Business Review, 2014. http://iveybusinessreview.ca/blogs/dxuhba2015/2014/11/09/new-lifeline-gm/ (accessed March 25, 2016).
18. BBC News. 'Warning over whiplash epidemic.' BBC News, 2008/11/15, retrieved 2010/04/06. http://news.bbc.co.uk/1/hi/health/7729336.stm (accessed March 25, 2016).
19. Barnsley, L., Lord, S. and Bodduk, N. 'Whiplash injury' (1994) *Pain* 58(3): 283–307.
20. Farnworth Rose. 'Whiplash Injury and Compensation.' Compensationwhiplashinjury.co.uk. http://compensationwhiplashinjury.co.uk/Whiplash_information/whiplash_diagnosis_and_scans/ (accessed December 8, 2015).
21. Rose, Neil. 'MASS hits back at "biased" AXA whiplash report.' Litigation Futures, 2013. http://www.litigationfutures.com/news/mass-hits-back-biased-axa-whiplash-report (accessed March 25, 2016).
22. Martindale, John. 'Insurers admit telematics data shared with police.' Telematics.com, 2014. http://www.telematics.com/insurers-admit-telematics-data-shared-with-police/ (accessed March 25, 2016).
23. Kuchinskas, Susan. 'Insurance telematics: US state regulators tackle UBI.' TU Automotive, 2012. http://analysis.tu-auto.com/insurance-telematics/insurance-telematics-us-state-regulators-tackle-ubi (accessed March 25, 2016).
24. European Medicines Agency. 'EU Telematics.' Ref EMA/289808/2014. European Medicines Agency. http://www.ema.europa.eu/ema/index.jsp?curl=pages/about_us/general/general_content_000116.jsp&mid=WC0b01ac0580028c2b (accessed March 25, 2016).
25. Juniper Research. 'V2X: Good Concept, How Long for Reality? Juniperresearch.com, 2013. http://www.juniperresearch.com/analystxpress/march-2013/v2x-good-concept-how-long-for-reality (accessed March 25, 2016).
26. Copping, Jasper. 'Warning over decline in map skills as ramblers rely on sat navs.' *The Daily Telegraph,* 2012. http://www.telegraph.co.uk/news/earth/countryside/9090729/Warning-over-decline-in-map-skills-as-ramblers-rely-on-sat-navs.html (accessed March 25, 2016).
27. OBD Autodoctor. 'OBD Auto Doctor is the advanced car diagnostic software.' http://www.obdautodoctor.com/ (accessed March 25, 2016).
28. Ruddick, Graham. 'VW emissions scandal: 1.2m UK cars affected.' *The Guardian,* 2015. http://www.theguardian.com/business/2015/sep/30/vw-emissions-scandal-12m-uk-cars-affected (accessed March 25, 2016).
29. Trenholm, Richard. 'Kovert connected jewellery is high-tech and high fashion.' CNET, 2014. http://www.cnet.com/uk/news/kovert-connected-jewellery-is-high-tech-and-high-fashion/#! (accessed March 25, 2016).
30. PR Newswire. 'Commercial Vehicle Telematics Market in the Americas 2015–2019.' www.Reportbuyer.com. 2015. http://www.prnewswire.com/news-releases/commercial-vehicle-telematics-market-in-the-americas-2015-2019-300023023.html (accessed March 25, 2016).
31. Visiongain. 'Commercial Vehicle Telematics Market 2015-2025.' Visiongain. https://www.visiongain.com/Report/1412/Commercial-Vehicle-Telematics-Market-2015-2025 (accessed March 26, 2016).
32. House of Lords. 'Anns v Merton London Borough Council.' [1978] AC 728. http://www.bailii.org/uk/cases/UKHL/1977/4.html (accessed March 25, 2016).

CHAPTER 11

Analytics and Insurance People

As far as the topic of analytics in insurance is considered, there is a tendency to think of it as being only 'outwards facing,' that is to say, concerned only with data and issues outside the insurance organization. If an insurer is to become truly analytical and have analytics as part of its DNA then it also needs to be inward looking. This means that it needs not only to understand the capabilities necessary for success but also to create or develop a talent pool to ensure that those capabilities are:

- Aligned with the strategy of the organization
- Able to realistically understand the current situation
- Have the ability to prioritize development.

11.1   TALENT MANAGEMENT

Whilst not specific to insurance, it is nevertheless appropriate to consider talent analytics in an insurance context if only to allow us to examine the application of analytics across the entire insurance enterprise. The concept of talent management and talent analytics is not new. It has been around for a couple of decades and to some degree the terms are interchangeable. However in recent years, the maturing of analytical software for employee management has continued and has led to greater sophistication.

The insurance industry is a major employer. The US Bureau of Labor indicated in their 2008 report that US insurers employed about 2.3 million people[1] with insurance carriers accounting for 62% of US insurance industry jobs, and with brokers, agents and other intermediaries accounting for the balance. By comparison, the UK insurance sector which is the largest in Europe comprises about 290,000 employees,[2] representing one quarter of all jobs in the financial services sector and twice as many as employed in the combined water, gas and electricity industries.[3]

The majority of organizations are relatively small but some of the larger organizations, especially the major insurers and brokers, employ over 250 people. Major global insurers have staff levels measured in tens of thousands. In 2014, Allianz Group worldwide employed 147,000. Zurich Insurance Group employs about 60,000 people working in 140 countries. Unemployment levels in the financial services sector are in the order of 3% according to 2008 records.

In the 1990s the concept of talent analytics emerged in the guise of employee management as a way to transfer the burden of staff management away from the HR department to the managers of the staff themselves. Talent management now extends to the tracking of training which is delivered through online modules and capability monitoring measured against key success factors attributed to roles, productivity and attrition management.

The ability to effectively visualize trends through reporting in the form of dashboards also helps organizations understand key trends in employee behavior, for example, if there is any pattern in staff leaving an organization.

11.1.1   The Need for New Competences

Traditional competences of understanding and being able to apply the basic principles of insurance form the bedrock on which the insurance industry is founded. At face value this is a simple statement but the insurance industry seems to be increasingly reaching a point where traditional competences are becoming overshadowed by the need for new technical capabilities. As a result, it is unlikely that the traditional competences will be adequate any longer if insurance professionals are to survive and thrive in this new era. The ability for insurance professionals to interact with and exploit data and information is arguably becoming as, if not more, important than a detailed understanding of *Rylands v Fletcher* and other insurance case law. Traditional insurance skills are being supplemented and in some cases replaced by the ability to understand and manipulate new technologies.

For many professional insurance organizations, technology is seen not as an enabler but as a risk (in other words, a problem). For some, it is also a potential new line of business as underwriters and claims adjusters offer cyber risk policies and cyber claims management skills.[4]

As the insurance industry changes, so the competences of individuals within that industry will need to evolve. This is not a unique situation as similar developments have occurred in other industries which are more technologically developed in the analytics space. By comparison the motor manufacturing industry has been transformed by analytics, robotics and continuous engineering. The result is better engineered vehicles of higher quality and reliability and with higher levels of customization. This has also created other issues – the modern vehicle is a computer on wheels with over 100 million lines of code embedded, which is a far cry from a decade or two ago and opens up all manner of issues relative to servicing and repair. There is no reason why the insurance industry should not be transformed in the same way and to the same degree.

Many professional organizations for insurance and other industries remain adamant that traditional learning still has a place, and it is difficult to disagree with them. After all, the 'foundations' are critical and provide a bedrock on which the structure becomes stable. However, the rapid advance of technology is increasing the pace of insurance industry change and it is important that professional organizations not only keep up to speed, but provide thought leadership (and in some cases an ethical compass as well). Big Data, analytics and new methodologies are not simply a set of tools but rather a whole new way of thinking. It requires individuals and organizations to approach problems and challenges within their business not only with technical expertise and market understanding, but with a sense of imagination as well.

Later sections of this book will consider issues of implementation in more detail, but aligned to this are the competences required of professionals in the future. New roles will emerge and are already doing so. These are likely to be a combination of insurance knowledge and analytical ability, and may perhaps even be better suited to a particular age group or aptitude. One question to consider is what is the best 'starting point' for this new breed of individual? Are they likely to be 'insurance people' who learn new technologies – or savvy IT experts who start to understand insurance-specific business decisions? Who is best placed to occupy this new middle ground? Perhaps the future of the insurance industry will find itself resting in the hands of young 'challengers of the truth,' possibly even from other industries such as retail and auto, who seek out different ways of transacting the business of insurance and risk transfer.

But what of the traditional roles? These changes do not mean that the role of the traditional claims director (for example) is completely dying out, but rather that the traditional roles as we currently know them will need to evolve. They will probably need to evolve rapidly to take into account the changes which are actively happening. If, for example, one particular concern of a claims director is that of claims fraud, then he or she will not only need to be aware of new counter-fraud technologies but also how best to implement these in practice. This will extend not only to the technologies but also to issues of data protection, security and regulation.

This may not mean that a claims director needs to become an expert in the use of predictive or network analytics for fraud detection. Rather it means that there is sufficient knowledge and awareness and an ability to have effective dialogue with someone who does. The risk of the claims director not doing so is that the fraudster will become increasingly ahead of the game, with greater insight and ability to manipulate the system and take advantage. If insurers need to stay ahead of their nemesis, then they need to be not only as good as their adversary but better than them.

Beyond technology, when the UK Insurance Act comes into force in September 2016, thought by some to reflect the greatest change in insurance contract law in the UK for over 100 years, it is critically important that the claims director or vice-president is aware of the implications if not the exact wording. For example, in the matter of utmost good faith/non-disclosure in a business scenario (consumer insurance having already been dealt with in other legislation) the insured party (the policyholder) will be deemed to know information about their business which 'should reasonably have been revealed by a reasonable search' (section 4(6) of the Act). What this means going forward in a new landscape of greater and more accessible data has yet to be fully understood.

The Act also places a positive duty of enquiry on the insurer as well. Under section 5(2) they will be presumed to know things which not only are common knowledge but are pertinent to particular classes of business. This indicates a much greater dependence on the insurer being able to have access to greater levels of insight. Perhaps the world of Big Data will 'move the goalposts' in respect of what the insurer is 'presumed' to know.

11.1.2 Essential Qualities and Capabilities

In the new era of Big Data and Analytics, it is likely that some generic qualities and capabilities are likely to emerge, as illustrated in Figure 11.1. The most important of these might comprise the following (in no order of priority):

- Foundational insurance knowledge
- Technology insight
- Quickness to learn and adapt
- Problem solving
- Collaborative and communication skills.

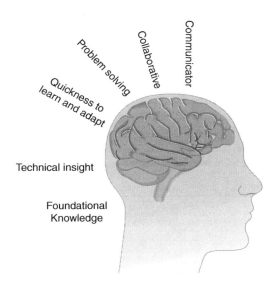

FIGURE 11.1   Qualities and capabilities for success

11.1.2.1   Foundational Insurance Knowledge

It is a matter of fact that probably no-one in insurance knows everything about all aspects of insurance. General insurance is very different to life and pension insurances, and even within the *general* sector there are different behaviors. Take for instance the London Market which has different processes and skill sets relative to the retail insurance sector. As a result there is always likely to be some need for the skilled individual to understand the rudiments of insurance knowledge which are underpinned by the:

- Principle of *utmost good faith*, where there is a duty on the policyholder to disclose all appropriate facts to an insurer which might influence their decision on price or whether to accept the cover, and under what terms.
- Principle of *insurable interest*, whereby the policyholder has some interest in what is being insured at the time of purchase of the cover.
- Principle of *indemnity*, whereby the policyholder may not be compensated with an amount exceeding the insured's economic loss.
- Principle of *subrogation*, whereby the insurer has the right to recover money from a third party who may have caused the loss or damage.
- Principle of *proximate cause*, usually taken to mean the most dominant and effective cause of the loss or damage.
- Principle of *dual insurance*, whereby if there are two policies in place, then the insured party cannot recover more than the actual loss, and cannot claim the whole amount from each insurer.

11.1.2.2   Technology Insight

By the same measure, no single IT expert will be expected to know everything about everything but rather a degree of focus starts to emerge depending on their specialization or the market segment they are operating in. An IT professional working for example in a marketing environment within an insurer will start to hone their skills on predictive analytics as far as it relates to customer retention and growth. That is not to say that some of these technical skills are not transferable to other parts of the business (predictive analytics being also commonly used in fraud detection) but rather that a degree of expertise through familiarity with specific technical capabilities is likely to dominate. As a result that particular expertise can be stretched to other parts of the business.

It is tempting to propose what might be the technology equivalent of the Principles of Insurance, which might comprise:

- The principle of *cloud and storage*, which recognizes issues of size and type of data, where and how this is best stored with due regard to access, regulation and security.
- The principle of *analytics*, whereby analytics is recognized as a way to extract value from data and does not in itself comprise the 'destination' but rather is a means to improve efficiency, reduce cost and improve customer service.
- The principle of *mobile* technology, recognizing the ubiquitous nature of mobile devices including those used directly and indirectly.
- The principle of *security*, understanding the risks of data loss and the challenges of data security in an increasingly malicious world.

11.1.2.3   Quickness to Learn and Adapt

Unlike insurance knowledge and technical capability which are a combination of academic and technical understanding, the next three desirable capabilities are mainly behavioral.

The speed of change is likely to be significant going forward – a problem which the insurance industry is not entirely used to. New technical products and solutions will become increasingly available, costs of usage may fall, and innovations will occur more rapidly. The increasing emergence of disruptive financial technologies – so-called 'FinTech' or 'Insuretech' companies – has yet to find significant traction in the insurance industry, but when this happens the impact could be traumatic for established models.

Some insurers are already thinking about the impact of disruptive technologies such as 'Blockchain' and 'Sidechain' (in effect the architectures underpinning Bitcoin) and their impact on the distribution channel. Coupled with this, the overall pace of change within the industry is likely to speed up with new business models emerging. Although the most successful insurance professionals may have one foot in the past, their line of sight will need to be clear into the future.

11.1.2.4   Problem Solving

With new market conditions and customer behaviors often influenced by other industries such as telecom and retail, new problems may emerge which need to be tackled with either existing tools or only partly available data sets. New partners may also need to be sought. New sources of information, for example from the 'Internet of Things' may become relevant to solving insurance problems. As a result, a degree of creativity and imagination may be needed.

This seems to imply that new entrants to the insurance sector may not necessarily be from a technical or financial background, but perhaps from a sector whose recruitment and training may have been more influenced by creativity. The suggestion that individuals are either 'left brain' thinkers (who are meant to have more maths and logic) or 'right brain' thinkers (who are meant to have more creative capabilities) is increasingly being de-bunked and is now viewed to be outdated. Nevertheless it is clear that individuals do have particular blends of strengths and in the new world of insurance it is probable that *problem solving* will be a key attribute.

11.1.2.5 Collaborative and Communication Skills

This is not likely to be a world where analytics leaders as individuals sit in the back room, crunching figures and reporting to senior management, but rather the most successful insurance professionals of the future will be both collaborative and able to evangelize the power and capability of the Big Data story. This will be one of the most important aspects. Traditionally and within many industries, there has been (and sometime still is) a disconnect between the business and the IT department. As the industry reaches the tipping point where analytics is infused throughout the entire insurance organization, then the relationship between the business and IT will also need to fundamentally change and this change is likely to occur as much at a personal level as through organization realignment.

Furthermore there is a likelihood that the collaboration will not occur through established organizational hierarchies or even in the same room. Task-based individuals will increasingly operate in virtual teams, perhaps seldom physically meeting, and using collaborative tools. A 'sprint' approach to change may be increasingly prevalent with multiple short projects in play across cross-functional teams. The ability of an individual to personally operate in that environment as opposed to an office-based, face-to-face relationship may also prove to be a critical success factor at an individual level. Beyond this, a certain degree of personal resilience would appear to be beneficial as the individual negotiates their way through the mire of a 300-year-old industry which is being impacted by 300-day-old technology.

This new breed of insurance professional will be increasingly self-seeking in terms of new techniques and information. This also places a burden on technology vendors to ensure that there is up-to-date and relevant information which is digitally available. These new insurance professionals are likely to have strong market and technical awareness and an ability to source the solutions they need. External vendor websites will increasingly need to be easy to access, simple to navigate and be both relevant and up to date. As the industry goes forward, the level of complexity of solutions, the speed of change and the cost of maintenance will be such that 'buy' (or 'rent') as opposed to 'self-build' is increasingly likely to be the preferred option.

These attributes may well generate positions of leadership, and may also be influenced by new approaches such as cognitive computing which support the leader's decision-making. The call to action is one of personal transformation in the same way that the insurance industry as a whole is changing.

'Leadership' is often accompanied by 'Followership' which implies that it is for a single individual to set the agenda and for others to follow. One cannot exist without the other, but in the new paradigm of data and analytics it may well be that a degree of levelling will happen brought about by the empowerment of analytics. In such a new environment, leaders will set the strategy as they always have done but there may be much greater freedom around operational delivery. New freedoms will bring new risks. This transformation will need to be supported by education and learning provided by professional organizations and companies, foundational, technical, behavioral and perhaps even ethical – but the most important driver will be the attitude of the individual themselves and their personal motivation and capability for change.

11.2   TALENT, EMPLOYMENT AND THE FUTURE OF INSURANCE

As multiple reports emerge on the future of insurance in the era of Big Data and Analytics and against a backdrop of the 'digital customer,' there is a general consensus that one of the key barriers to change is the availability and adequacy of skills. In their 2014 report 'Transforming Insurance,' KPMG consultants cite the fact that 'half of respondents identified human barriers to implementing a data and analytics strategy rather than technical constraints.'

What is perhaps less clear is the impact that the data and analytics revolution will have on employment levels within the insurance industry. With insurance purchasers keen to drive value from their analytical and data investment, value will be driven not only through greater agility but also inevitably through greater effectiveness.

There are no obvious statistics which help understand the impact on employment levels in the insurance industry going forward. Perhaps we must look to other industries to see how they have been affected by automation which inevitably must be one by-product of insurance transformation. One of the most striking examples of automation is in the car industry where curiously the records of employment during the period 1995–2006 indicated a modest growth of 1%.[5] If this is a reliable comparison then there is a real possibility that with effective talent management, there may not be a significant loss of headcount from the industry, if at all.

From this it might be inferred that the insurance industry has the potential to grow in employee numbers in the decades ahead even if there will need to be some degree of redefining of roles and responsibilities. This may be consistent with the indications that the Big Data and Analytics era will be a net contributor to the workforce and economy rather than a detractor.

11.2.1   Talent Analytics and the Challenge for Human Resources

In their 2013 report,[6] the UK-based Chartered Institute for Personnel and Development describe talent analytics as a 'must have' capability for Human Resource (HR) departments and indicate that there are two key elements to implementation:

Firstly, a strategic viewpoint – which recognizes analytics as a key enabler for people development and:

- 'Develops analytics as a continuous improvement strategy
- Puts people analytics at the center of business priorities
- Accelerates the requirement for analytical bandwidth up the HR capability agenda.'

Secondly, a tactical viewpoint, which considers issues of implementation and focuses on the need for greater skill development in talent analytics, the need to recruit new skills such as occupational psychologists, and greater alignment between the 'people agenda' and actionable insights.

The report, written in conjunction with Oracle, also covers what the authors describe as 'suspicions and skepticism' amongst the HR community (which they describe as 'backwards looking' with regards to the use of talent analytics). The concerns of the Chartered Institute of Personnel and Development also focus on:

- Data reducing people to units of analysis
- The 'treadmill' of continuous expectation
- HR being 'left behind' in the skills race.

These are genuine concerns and emphasize the particular skills of the HR department which are described as being relationship focused, and more used to dealing with ambiguity than the accuracy of analytics. They also recognize that whilst the HR department operated in a particular way historically, this is inevitably set to change and that this will lead to some degree of redefining of the HR profession.

11.3 LEARNING AND KNOWLEDGE TRANSFER

Having initiated a process of transformation or perhaps even just part of that process, it is important that the insurer considers how to ensure that staff are kept up to speed with current analytical capabilities and technological developments. This section aims to consider the learning and knowledge transfer process and its application in an insurance environment.

There is inevitably something of a generic approach to this topic. The challenges of an insurer towards transformation are arguably no different to a bank, major retailer or utility company. A useful place to begin is to consider the different ways that people learn as this may provide good insight into the best ways of implementing the learning process.

The starting point is to recognize that, on the whole, everyone's brain is wired differently. As a result one approach does not fit all in terms of learning and training. Good teachers know this and consciously or unconsciously implement an approach commonly known as 'brain friendly learning' which adjusts the teaching process to the needs of the individual. Brain friendly learning is partly about the manner in which information is conveyed but also extends to the environment in which the teaching or training takes place. It considers whether learning is better achieved in a safe or stressful environment. At its core is a recognition that people of all ages have different learning styles, basically categorized as aural, visual or tactile. These are extremely simple expressions of what is, in effect, neuroscience – the science of understanding how the brain works.

Increasingly, commercial organizations are taking the concepts of brain friendly learning on board. In their 2014 research report 'Neuroscience in action: applying insights to L&D practice'[7] published by the Chartered Institute of Personnel and Development, the authors explore how such techniques not only help to provide greater insight for staff members but also help improve customer service and staff retention.

A selection of case studies are included within that report including one insurer, Unum, which is a US-based Life and Protection company recognized as a leading disability insurer and employing around 9000 employees. The case study specifically refers to the UK subsidiary which in 2013 provided protection for 1.6 million people. Chaucer Syndicates, a leading Managing Agency at Lloyds of London and part of the Hanover Group, a top 25 US P&C insurer, is also mentioned.

Interviewees for the research report identified four key methods of learning:

1. Reading materials including books, press, white papers and journals.
2. Formal certification and training either by way of qualification or structured education.
3. Face to face meetings and networking.
4. Social media and technology, including LinkedIn, Twitter and TED talks.'TED' (Technology, Entertainment, Design) is a global set of conferences run by the private not-for-profit organization called the Sapling Foundation.

11.3.1 Reading Materials

The printing press was invented in 1440 and much has changed since then. Printing is more scientific, the ink and paper are better, and books are available worldwide and can be ordered online. The digitalization of the process continues and access to historically printed materials online is increasing. The fact that the reader is accessing this text either as a physical object or as a digital image is evidence to the fact that it still has validity as a channel of communication and learning. The issue is not the future of the printed media but rather the use of this specifically for learning about analytics.

For many, there are too many sources of information, which are also too diverse, on the topic of analytics. The volume of information is still likely to grow. Entering the words 'insurance analytics' into some search engines will give 64 million results. As a result, it is important to think of books and printed media as part of the entire data and information universe. Entrants to this topic often need a source of foundational learning such as the printed word which permits them to read or study at their leisure, to dip into areas which are of specific interest or to gain an understanding of the breadth of the analytical opportunity in insurance.

If it only does only one thing, this publication will hopefully show the depth and breadth of analytics in the insurance business. It will hopefully persuade the reader that analytics will ultimately be both pervasive, enterprise-wide and a fundamental part of the insurance industry going forward.

Some insurance publications including those with an 'online' presence are also creating specific 'technology editions' which focus on technology rather than purely business. To their credit the publications are framing their text in the context of business need, e.g., fraud or customer retention. The risk is that business readers will view the 'technology edition' as not being relevant to them and perhaps pass over it. They need to appreciate that the insurers of the future will have technology and analytics absolutely embedded and there will in effect be little or no differentiation between the business of insurance and the technology which enables its operation.

11.3.2 Formal Qualifications and Structured Learning

Formal qualifications have a critical part to play in the insurance industry, providing individuals and organizations with evidence of appropriate credentials. These can vary from foundational generic qualifications to high level qualifications in relatively specialist areas. The role of insurance organizations is to support and develop their members, maintain professionalism and enhance the standing of the insurance industry.

In many cases the qualifications provided by professional organizations are based on what might best be described as a 'legacy' approach to the industry, discussing foundational issues such as underwriting, contract law and investment planning. Generally speaking, these fail to recognize the impact that technology and analytics is currently having and will continue to have. If it is truly believed that these factors will have a transformative impact on insurance, then isn't it incumbent on professional organizations to provide at least some foundational training and guidance on these new methods?

The insurer of the future will comprise new 'hybrid' roles combining business knowledge and technological capability. With that in mind, it is likely that professional insurance organizations will need to respond by having some form of technology work stream. This is more likely to be driven by insurance institutions and trade bodies rather than the IT sector. It is critical that industry-specific knowledge becomes embedded in the learning process, even if business models for the insurance industry in the future may be somewhat different.

Structured learning, i.e., training courses, may sit either within or outside professional organizations. They are often provided at no charge by technology vendors and can be either general in nature or with specific business outcomes in mind. Such events, which can be physical or virtual, for example webinars, have much to commend them but attendees are often keen to avoid being influenced as well as educated. Technology vendors often provide an educational service which would not otherwise exist.

It may be argued that company events are self-serving and viewed as a form of marketing, but on balance this might be a fair trade-off and such an attitude does a disservice to discerning attendees. Professional bodies may be nervous about getting too close to technology vendors for fear of showing bias or preference, but there needs to be recognition that this can be a win-win situation for both provided that the technology vendor is not too explicit in their commercialization of the event.

For many the essence of structured training is that it allows individuals and organizations to see demonstrations of particular solutions which may meet the particular current or potential need of the insurer. Demonstrations should be both relevant and appropriate. In the past there has been criticism of some vendors that they have shown, for example, a retailing demo to an insurance audience, and vice versa. As insurers look to other industries for ideas and as a basis for innovation, seeing examples of analytics in other industries may still have some validity. Might a demonstration of asset management in the utilities industry showing solutions which result in reduced maintenance costs and downtime also have some relevance in terms of insurance risk management? Aren't demonstrations of sales performance management in the banking sector equally valid in the insurance sector as evidence of general sales force optimization?

Looking forward, there needs to be greater collaboration between professional bodies and technology vendors in a relationship of respect and education. Technology vendors have much to learn from the professional insurance institutions, and vice versa.

11.3.3   Face-to-Face Training

There are three ways in which this might be considered:

1. Individual mentoring
2. Smaller, round-table events
3. Larger, conference-type events.

All three have value but for different reasons. The circumstances of the participants, their individual and corporate aspirations all influence the best way to transfer knowledge and information. Expanding on these three ways:

- *Individual mentoring and training* provides an intimacy of relationship which allows knowledge transfer to take place at the pace of the individual potentially allowing questioning, validation, and verbal testing to ensure understanding.
- *Round-table events* comprising perhaps a dozen or so people still provide a degree of intimacy but will reflect the varying levels of knowledge of individuals within the group who may be at different stages. This is inevitably challenging for the trainer due to the

combination of intimacy and diversity. On the plus side this type of smaller event does allow scope for discussion across the table, exploration of ideas and expression of common concerns.

- *Conferences* comprise the third type of face-to-face activity. In analytics as with many other types of business, the conference process is an industry in itself. Such events help individuals and companies validate their own positions and network with peers. Conferences are normally substantially funded by sponsorship which provides a platform for demonstrations and introductions and to that extent they are useful. If sponsors did not find a return on investment either in terms of soft or hard benefit, then they would not support this type of format.

Conferences provide a useful albeit an expensive function in education. If individuals in a smaller round table are concerned about asking questions, expressing concern or just general uncertainty, then the problem is magnified in a larger forum. In terms of format, the idea of smaller break-out groups as part of a larger conference has validity. There are some who might argue that conferences are there as much for the speakers as for the attendees. Conference events give oxygen to industry experts and thought leaders who use the events to raise their personal profile or that of their business. For this reason alone, it might be arguably a legitimate trade-off especially when speakers attend at their own time and cost.

The future of conferences must also be open to some debate. There are clearly pros and cons, and as purchasing decisions for analytics and technology increasingly shift to the line of business then perhaps the type and seniority of attendees will change. An argument exists to suggest that those likely to make decisions are probably already well aware of what is happening and what is available in the marketplace as a result of their own 'digital self-service.' As a result, conferences are unlikely to enlighten them to any significant degree. Overall it is important that conference organizers recognize the changing needs of their audience in the 'digital age' and respond accordingly.

11.3.4 Social Media and Technology

Social media can be either intrusive and worrying, or insightful and compelling dependent on the viewpoint of the individual. Certainly there is no doubt that social media creates a very large amount of information. Some of the information is critical, some is useful, some is duplicated, some is provocative – the rest is just 'noise.'

The impact of social media for the user is that it is increasingly easy to network, operate within peer groups and be less constrained by geography or industry. It is likely that as analytics progresses, the sourcing of relevant information will become easier and easier. Analytics will help identify the topics that the reader is interested in, and push information and contacts to them in a relevant and timely matter. The use of mobile devices, one of the megatrends of technology, will increasingly make this information available anytime, anywhere. Cognitive computing will in time transform our interaction with data and the device and will inevitably impact on training and knowledge transfer. Perhaps less training will be needed, who knows?

There is no shortage of thought leadership articles, white papers, opinions and commentary available for the insurance market. Unlike the printed page, the relatively low cost of participation and ease of access makes everyone a potential participant. Once the individual has got over the initial fear of openly expressing an opinion on a particular topic they are only limited by their imagination (and sometimes also by their corporate rulebook). Provided that certain legal, ethical and moral bounds are not crossed there is potential for almost endless input.

Thought leadership can sometimes appear to be achieved as much by the volume of contribution as by the content. The ability of some individuals to 'tweet' tens of thousands of contributions can only be described as staggering. Perhaps with such volumes of content it is becoming harder to identify who actually are leading lights in terms of forward thinking and who are just 'echo chambers.' The ability to use social media on an industrial scale is yet another new capability of the modern age.

Perhaps there is light at the end of the tunnel. If the industry is being overwhelmed by sheer volume and variety of content, the increasing use of analytics to help identify trends can also provide a filter by allowing individuals to rise above the 'noise' and allow users and observers to get a feel for what is really important, and what people are commenting about en masse. This is otherwise known as their 'sentiment.'

In considering brain friendly learning we identified that individuals might learn by aural, visual or tactile methods. Social media and technology provide an approach for doing all these things. Articles can be read, videos watched, podcasts listened to and the individual can even 'have a try' with online demos. Social media and technology may not be the panacea for learning and knowledge transfer but they are almost certainly a key component going forward. Gaming techniques which are familiar as entertainment are likely to increasingly find their way into learning activities.

The ubiquity of this information will inevitably change the way insurers (and other industry professionals) buy analytical solutions. More and better access to information will increasingly allow insurance experts to become self-serving in terms of seeking the analytical products and services they need and from whom they will buy.

Those individuals with more imagination will also work out for themselves the synergies between industries allowing them to migrate capabilities from one industry to another and also probably be able to identify the development needs of existing solutions. Complaint has the capability to be transformed into crowd-sourced constructive advice. Perhaps helped by analysts or other third parties who may help set evaluation criteria, the relationship between customer and vendor may be also be set to change and in many cases this will affect the sales process of technology vendors.

11.4 LEADERSHIP AND INSURANCE ANALYTICS

Leadership is generally well understood. Each year there are hundreds – perhaps thousands – of books written on the subject. The thrust of leadership is to harness the key attributes of:

- Vision
- Culture
- Values
- Strategy
- Personal standards.

These attributes then need to be coralled into a single coherent approach to a problem or opportunity. Some might argue that successful leaders only emerge because of the qualities of those who support them. Others suggest that the most successful organizations don't have just one leader and a group of followers, but operate a group where each member of the team is a leader in their own right. Another alternative is that the main role of the leader is to set the strategic framework and all else will naturally follow.

What is increasingly clear is that the era of data and analytics starts to alter the view of management, bringing about a change in the order of decision-making guided by analytical insight and 'data-driven' decisions. What then is the role for insurance leaders of the future?

11.4.1   Knowledge and Power

The expression 'Knowledge is Power' is a term which increasingly seems confined to a previous time. A democratization of information increasingly exists in a world where, as a result of technology, insight and information are increasingly available to those who need them. If the printing presses of Caxton and others made knowledge available to the masses, this is multiplied endlessly by the effect of the internet and the presence of Big Data and Analytics.

One of the effects of this is to create inclusiveness rather than knowledge being the domain of a few. As a result, the relationship between senior management and the 'worker bees' is being transformed, protected only by a hierarchy of access to levels of productivity information and commercially confidential issues. What does this mean for those who rely on their personal experience as a differentiator?

The role of the so-called 'knowledge worker' is likely to change in all industries and insurance will be no different. The scale and speed at which information is emerging means that knowledge within individuals is becoming less valuable, and as a result the 'intellectual capital' of knowledge workers will be reduced, especially if we accept that cognitive analytics will be increasingly pervasive. Knowledge is becoming a commodity. For some it would seem a natural defense not to share that knowledge but resistance is probably futile. In most cases the knowledge worker is most respected for their willingness to share that knowledge. But knowledge in itself is no better than an uncut diamond and perhaps the essential skill will increasingly be how to *apply* the knowledge, not the knowledge itself.[8]

Beyond knowledge, industries including insurance continue to look for fresh thinking. This is usually known by another name – 'disruption' – and this shows itself more and more in the guise of disruptive technology. Disruptive technology is often identified with small entrepreneurial start-ups. It is very difficult to distinguish between an established organization and a start-up just from their webpages which are often professionally and attractively created. The more careful will check for references, financial statements and track record and then form a judgment. This should not exclude start-ups from being considered to be 'in the running' in adding to the knowledge pool especially in this increasingly agile business environment and the *climate* of FinTech. These new entrants approach traditional problems with a fresh set of ideas and the ability to execute through new, effective means. Established organizations can give legitimacy to start-ups through their relationships with them and the willingness of each diverse party to accept the other's culture.

11.4.2   Leadership and Influence

Leadership is often about seniority and ownership but it is also about the ability to create influence. At a time when data and analytics are creating a paradigm shift in thinking, the challenge may increasingly be the ability to 'influence' rather than to 'direct.'

If leadership equates to having influence, what does having influence actually mean? Normally it comprises:

- The ability to affect decisions
- Having the knowledge and skill to affect individual perceptions
- Knowing how and with what to influence a meeting or group of individuals.
- Knowing how to position an argument in the most effective way.

These are all standard leadership issues and there are good sources to review elsewhere, typically from writers such as Aryanne Oade[9] and others.

Leadership and innovation are not only about having a 'Eureka' moment in the bath but also about having the ability to put new ideas in motion, and maneuvering through organizational politics to bring ideas to fruition. Part of this can be achieved through being 'directional,' i.e., through giving instruction or direction by virtue of a position of seniority within the organization. Another approach can be by having a level of 'thought leadership' which allows personal expression and perhaps a degree of freedom as well, as is also seen in the current role of the 'knowledge worker.'

Organizational status or 'power' of individuals is critical in many situations. Power allows an individual to give direction on the values and objectives that a business, department or individual needs to adopt. It also allows them to define their personal workloads, the extent and quality of their customer relationships, and their own interactions across the wider business.

Power can be measured by either one, or a combination, of:

- The skill to influence, supported by strength of character.
- Hierarchical positioning within the organization and the ability to reward others.
- Expert knowledge which may also bring a level of insight to the business.

The challenge is that in this new era of Big Data and Analytics, senior individuals in insurance and elsewhere need to cope with new levels of information that they themselves never had the benefit of. Whilst they may have power by virtue of the traits mentioned above, they are now faced with a new issue – how to be effective 'influencers' without the benefit of the experience of this new era of data to lean on. Not only do leaders need the capability to recognize the challenge of uncertainty in a volatile economy, but also they need to understand the impact of democratization of information on their colleagues and the broader effect of analytics in the new business world of the future.

In such an uncertain world, the expression 'trust me' isn't strong enough. Insurance leaders inevitably look for proof points to support their argument and to reassure their critics. Proof points remain critical but insurers especially should not solely look to each other for evidence of the next thing to do, but rather think about the expectation of their own customers.

Leaders and influencers need not only to know what is happening within the insurance sector but also what is happening in the wider business environment. Customers are already using capabilities like Amazon and Uber but don't immediately see a large scale insurance equivalent on the horizon, even if there is some evidence of new smaller scale start-ups which are beginning to break established rules.

At Board level there are multiple mechanisms to start analytical transformation but the key mechanism is that of finance and budget. This is why the Return on Investment (ROI) issue is so critical. Even so, the debate is moving away from 'whether' organizations should do this, towards 'where first'? ROI is being used more and more to identify where the starting point is and how an enterprise-wide transformation towards being an 'analytical insurer' can take place. The insurance CFO remains the gatekeeper of finance and investment but the weight of opinion increasingly is towards the right investment. The reality is that 'if' is not an option for insurers in terms of whether to become an analytical enterprise or not. It is a question of 'when' and 'how.'

Some individuals might even feel that they don't have the seniority to carry the Big Data and Analytics message. Perhaps they believe that they don't have the influence, the network, the status, or are just being outnumbered by non-believers. For those in that position, the important thing is to ensure that individuals are in the right place at the right time to act quickly and decisively. In the interim, those concerned should continue to gain knowledge, evangelize and to build trust and reputation in the workplace.

In terms of how to become a trusted advisor to the business, based on work by Tom Peters[10] and others, trust is won through integrity, reliability, goodwill and dependability. At a time when new technology looks to be undermining traditional thinking, this can be a delicate and sensitive journey. For senior decision-makers the new era can be especially daunting. They still have their 'day job' and an obligation to keep the 'ship afloat,' but at the same time are faced with the challenges of a new working environment. They must not only recognize the issues with the industry and their own business but also cope with the potential changes and challenges to their own roles.

In a volatile economy, rapidly changing and with all the pressures of shareholder management, customer expectation, risk and regulation, senior insurance executives must have all the personal and technical attributes to allow them to stand at the top of the lighthouse and to look as far as they can towards the horizon. They not only have to anticipate change but to be prepared to actively move towards it. It is insufficient for them as individuals to be at the foot of the lighthouse, on the rocks, being battered by the waves of change and hoping to survive. Big Data and Analytics is not just a series of 'waves' but a tsunami coming towards them. Executives must not only develop coping strategies but also have the foresight to take advantage.

It is essential not be sensitive about this. Many current executives were brought up in a time of modest technology and even now view social media with an element of suspicion. The world has moved on rapidly. There is more and better technology in a mid-sized modern car than was there to place a man on the moon. Insurance executives as well as the entire insurance industry need to be prepared to step outside their comfort zone. If transformation of the industry and of individual companies is to take place, then this starts with the transformation of individuals.

11.4.3   Analytics and the Impact on Employees

It is important to reflect on how the use of Big Data and Analytics will impact on the staff and employees of insurance companies. Organizational change does not occur in a vacuum. Whilst there is an argument for empowerment and more insightful decision-making at the point of delivery, there are inevitably potential downsides which need to be considered. Overall it is important that employees should not be too anxious about this as individuals, or certainly no more anxious than about other issues which affect their day-to-day lives. It is in the nature of commerce, industry and to some degree civilization itself that change will happen.

What might be the impact of such change on insurance employees and is this likely to be a good thing? It is impossible to say with certainty. Perhaps indicators might come from other industries and parts of history where industrialization has helped transform business models. One obvious area to consider as evidence of the impact of change is the transformation of the automotive production line which has been covered elsewhere. A different, perhaps better example might be the transformation of the cotton industry as a result of automation.

Like insurance, the cotton industry was (and still is) a global industry but one which was perhaps most affected by what is described as a 'New Era,' created in the 18th century on the basis of man-made components – the machine and the factory. During that period, Great Britain (as it was) 'went through a change so fundamental and traumatic that we can find nothing comparable in the whole of written history' says Anthony Burton in his book *The Rise and Fall of King Cotton*.[11]

At that time the whole world either benefited from – or some might say was a victim of – the Industrial Revolution. Globally there emerged a land of 'haves' and 'have-nots.' Anthony Burton's book discusses an epoch that, pre-Industrial Revolution, was mainly concerned with keeping itself alive and with individuals living a 'hand to mouth' existence. Post-Industrial Revolution, there was a transformation of the way business was done and who did it.

He submits that the transition from pre- to post- was traumatic and comparable to having a tooth taken out without anesthetic, suggesting that it feels better afterwards but that the exercise of removal can be very painful indeed. The question is whether the insurance industry in their transition from a pre-analytics world to a post-analytical world will find the transition painful. And if pain is to be anticipated, how might this best be mitigated? Not all employees are tolerant of pain and some may positively resist it.

As we look back at the history of cotton, it too was affected by technology. The flying shuttle and the spinning jenny are terms as alien to us today as the expression 'predictive analytics' might have been to our own forefathers. Both these two pieces of 'technology' resulted in the cottage industry of the textile business being transformed, or industrialized, into the factories and workshops that we commonly associate with the cotton industry today.

Beyond this, the way of life of cotton workers also changed from what is seen as an idyllic trade into mill working and conditions that were so different to what they had known in the past that they could never have anticipated them. There is no suggestion that the development of insurance analytics will take us back to the technological equivalent of William Blake's 'dark Satanic mills.' We simply need to reflect on the fact that the potential change may be completely transformational and the insurance industry as a whole might need to prepare itself for dramatic consequences.

11.4.4   Understanding Employee Resistance

Perhaps in the same way that the older hands in the insurance industry might resist change, so too did the cotton workers. The expression 'Luddites' was used for the group that resisted industrialization to the point of rioting and destroying equipment. The name is taken from their leader who adopted the name of 'General Ludd' to create the impression of military authority. Today 'Luddism' is mostly thought of as opposition to progress and antipathy to change.

In fact, Luddites did not have an argument with the machines themselves but rather with the owners and the manner of implementation. Their arguments were linked to low wages and apprenticeships. When they had tried unsuccessfully to resolve these matters through the courts, they then took it upon themselves to damage the machines. There is a message here in that the advent of analytics in insurance will not only transform business models but also will change working practices.

In many countries, the power of unionization or collective bargaining has diminished or disappeared entirely as a result of economic pressures. Some might say that it never really applied to insurance professionals, or perhaps it is just a symptom of harder economic times. Overall will there be challenges in how employees stand up and offer a collective voice in terms of how the individual is affected by the advent of analytics? If so, how will this materialize? Or will the Tsunami of Change wash over the insurance industry without resistance?

For the sake of completeness in the story of 'King Cotton,' it is appropriate to reflect on the historical position one final time. The American Civil War led to reduced volumes of raw cotton being produced overall. As a result India developed new capabilities and resources and textile manufacture increased in India and collapsed elsewhere. The cotton industry today is now entirely different both in terms of skills, outputs, capacity and geographic location. That provides at least one long-term question: if the insurance industry is projected forward by 100 years, how will it look? Then perhaps anticipate that the speed of change might be much quicker, and that this is perhaps how the insurance industry might look within a few decades.

Overall some might argue that it's not a pretty picture or maybe that there is not even a realistic comparison between manufacturing and financial services, even if others describe insurance as a form of manufacturing of products and policies. Nevertheless, maybe it presents a picture of how industrialization, automation and 'analyticalization' of the insurance industry might have the capability to transform an industry with a 300-year-old history. Perhaps there will be as much change in the next 20 or 30 years as in the past 300 years.

How will insurance companies, intermediaries, professional institutions and individuals prepare themselves for such change? In the same way that insurance companies themselves need to think of technological roadmaps which move their organization from descriptive analytics to cognitive analytics, so too they need to think about the impact on their own internal affairs. This demands an ability to be able to take a longer term view of their organization and to shift away from the 'here and now' with the current focus being on short-term deliverables.

Insurers who declare an intention to become 'digital' or 'analytical' need to think about all the knock-on effects on their staff and to manage the transition process accordingly across both the depth and breadth of the enterprise. Those who have not yet declared an intention will almost certainly need to go down that road sooner or later.

Part of such staff engagement in the change process may include staff/employee councils, workshops and other representative bodies – often enshrined in local employment regulations. Overall this goes beyond relatively simple internal and external stakeholder management but rather involves a genuine desire to understand the true impact of analytical transformation on insurance employees generally. In doing so not only will this help to set the boundaries and timeline of change but also recognize the issues, coping strategies, personal capabilities and workforce metrics of the broader team.

Failure to do so runs the risk of uncertainty, fear and resistance. Modern-day Luddites will not break the machines as their forefathers did but will resist discreetly rather than overtly, which could perhaps be just as damaging if not more so.

NOTES

1. Casale, Jeffrey. 'Number working in insurance industry drops.' Business Insurance, 2009. http://www.businessinsurance.com/apps/pbcs.dll/article?AID=9999200015356 (accessed March 26, 2016).
2. Office for National Statistics. 'Economic and Labour Market Review.' Vol. 5, No. 2. London: Office for National Statistics, 2011.
3. Association of British Insurers. 'UK Insurance Key Facts 2012.' Association of British Insurers (ABI), 2012.
4. Chartered Insurance Institute. 'How Technology Could Make or Break our Future.' Technical paper. London: Chartered Insurance Institute, 2012.
5. Ward, Terry and Loire, Patrick. 'Employment, skills and occupational trends in the automotive industry.' Alphametrics/Grope Alpha, 2008.
6. Chartered Institute for Personnel and Development. 'Talent analytics and big data: the challenge for HR.' London: Chartered Institute for Personnel and Development, 2013.
7. Chartered Institute of Personnel and Development. 'Neuroscience in action: applying insights to L&D practice.' London: Chartered Institute of Personnel and Development, 2014. Reference: 6620 c.
8. Donkin, Richard. *Blood Sweat and Tears: The Evolution of Work*. London: Texere Publishing, 2001.
9. Oade, Aryanne. *Managing Politics at Work*. Basingstoke: Palgrave Macmillan, 2009.
10. Peters, Tom. *Reimagine. Business Excellence in a Disruption Age*. London: Dorling Kindersley, 2003.
11. Burton, Anthony. *The Rise and Fall of King Cotton*. London: Andre Deutsch Ltd, 1984.

CHAPTER 12

Implementation

Big Data and Analytics are with us. The genie has been let out of the bottle and it is now a matter of implementation. Where to start, what to do first, how to approach the problem. Or perhaps wait and see whether with time things will get either cheaper or easier. It is tempting to think about first mover advantage in these matters, and one would do well to remember that some of the most successful brands came along second, as imitators of the innovators.

There is also the notion of 'second mover advantage' in effect learning from customer reaction and competitor problems to create a follow-up offering. First mover advantage doesn't always guarantee success. Who remembers 'Archie,' the world's first search engine in 1992, or SixDegrees.com, the first social network in 1997?

Doing nothing is a tempting proposition but not one to be recommended in the case of Big Data and Analytics. There is sufficient evidence even in the short term to show that those who embrace the idea start to rapidly and positively differentiate themselves and move away from their competition. Using data and analytics to transform an organization is not a task to be undertaken lightly. To paraphrase a famous Chinese saying, the hardest part of a 1000-mile journey is in taking the first step. Readers may be consoled to some degree to realize that reading this book alone, or even parts of it, might comprise that 'first step.'

Throughout this publication the impact of analytics has been considered on particular types of insurance and also in respect of particular insurance issues such as claims and underwriting. Some views will be expressed about what 'might' comprise a vision for the future for different categories of insurance. The intention is to allow the creative juices to flow in terms of the analytic potential for the insurance industry.

In those 'visionary' comments, an arbitrary timeframe of 2025 has been chosen which may or may not be realistic. Things have a nasty habit of occurring sooner or later than expected, with the timeframe often driven by market and competitor behavior, customer demand, innovation and leadership. It is important to consider the issue of implementation not only because it is a critical part of the mix but because it can be one of the simplest, or if approached incorrectly, one of the hardest areas to address.

The implementing organization needs to have a high level of awareness not only of its own business and the attitude of key stakeholders, but also the behavior of competitors and also other industries. Analytical maturity is more advanced in industries such as telco and retail. Insurers would be well advised to understand the true benchmarks that their customer is judging them against. As the use of analytics has the potential to change business models and allow new entrants to emerge, insurers may even potentially need to consider analytical implementation as a defensive strategy.

Within many organizations (and insurers are no exception) there is often a disconnect between the C-level and the individuals tasked with day-to-day operations. Executives are often told what they want to hear and not what they need to hear. Whilst thought leaders within organizations might be spending at least some of their day reflecting on new business models and the impact of disruptive technology, others on the 'front line' of service are still struggling with spreadsheets, pivot tables and basic technology. They view cognitive analytics and robotics with a mixture of skepticism, concern and disbelief. Communication and evangelism become critical components in the implementation storyboard.

It may be helpful to also consider the role of conferences in relation to implementation. Conferences may be either vendor organized, or organized by a third party with multiple speakers who have often paid (sometimes handsomely) to have the advantage of a shop window for prospective clients. Despite the fact that there are many analytics conferences taking place, there is often concern that these represent inadequate value for money for participants and presenters alike. As a result, it becomes critical that conference content is well crafted, meaningful and relevant. Additionally, it becomes increasingly critical that attendees have the opportunity to network and debate, and conferences need to specifically plan for those issues.

One reason for this is that buyers appear to be better informed than previously and are more aware of what is available to solve their problems. There will always be those attendees who are at an early stage in their learning but it is unlikely that these individuals are going to be true *economic buyers*. Vendors sponsoring third-party events find it harder and harder to directly identify opportunities and secure a return on investment unless the prime intention of the sponsor is just to raise brand awareness (which arguably might be done in more efficient ways digitally).

One of the special challenges of this topic of data and analytics is that it is already evolving so quickly. Users and technology vendors are innovating at the speed of WiFi. Think of it in these terms. Imagine you are standing on a railway platform at the station. 'Big Data and Analytics' is like an express train coming towards you and on that train are all your customers, and perhaps also the future of your business. The train isn't planning to stop at your platform, so there are two choices: to jump on while it's travelling and maybe hang on for dear life or to wait for the next train (which won't stop for you either!). It isn't much of a choice but there are things which can be done to make the decision to commit easier.

This section is intended to help with a roadmap in terms of implementation. It is written for the layperson, rather than the IT professional. By necessity it avoids (and deliberately omits) some of the depth of complexity which inevitably is involved.

The following four areas will be considered:

- Culture and organization
- Creating a strategy
- Management of the data
- Tooling and skill sets required.

These are not offered in any suggested sequence. In fact, there is an argument for considering many of the aspects concurrently. There is always a temptation to start with the data. After all, the old adage 'rubbish in, rubbish out' may still apply but perhaps that adage is on its last legs. Organizations face the inevitable ambiguity of unstructured and variable data of uncertain quality. Starting with the data has its own problems. Vast amounts of money and time can be spent on the data, and at the end of the day there may be little to show. Through a data-led approach the organization loses confidence. Funding slows down and analytical projects get in a rut.

A different starting point is the emotional one. There, an organization, or more likely an individual within an organization, realizes that data and analytics are critical to progress and as a result either canvasses stakeholders or otherwise wins support to gain funding. Sometimes even funding is not essential with the keenness of many vendors to lend a helping hand.

Understanding the business issue and then working back into the data to find insight allows organizations to create a data prioritization process and to achieve real value much sooner. Low key projects can be undertaken either as proof of concept with vendors doing work at low or no cost to gain a foot in the door, or alternatively the use of 'Freemium' analytic offerings quickly make the user familiar with new analytical capabilities. ('Freemium' is an expression for providing limited software to a user at no cost for personal or limited business use in the hope that they will be 'hooked' and upgrade, and eventually buy some licenses.)

There is also a move away from the financial constraint of the budgeting cycle which depends on the purchase of analytical software licenses as part of capital expenditure ('Capex'), towards obtaining analytical software 'as a service.' In effect it moves the customer to paying for it on a monthly or similar basis. The advantage is that this now becomes an operating expense ('Opex'), and makes the funding process very much easier. Capex to Opex significantly moves the goalposts for the client in terms of analytical implementation.

Starting to view the problem from an emotional position is also an interesting proposition, especially for decision-makers who are trained not to be emotional but rather rational in their decision-making. Emotion conjures up a picture of irrationality, but in fact it is quite the contrary. It represents the coming together of experience, intuition, competitive behavior and an eye on opportunity to recognize that certain steps need to be taken.

The seminal book on this topic is Daniel Goleman's *Emotional Intelligence – Why it can matter more than IQ*[1] which considers the skills and characteristics which drive leadership behavior. Goleman also advocated the concept of EQ 'Emotion Quotient' as a method of measurement, but this idea had been around since the 1960s. IBM were later to put a slightly different but familiar spin on things by inviting customers to consider their AQ or 'Analytics Quotient' as an indicator of analytical maturity.

In this context it is assumed that someone, somewhere in the insurance organization recognizes that there is a need for a data and analytics solution. This could be at the most senior level or perhaps at a lower level within the business where there is a specific tactical problem to be resolved. The catalyst may even be a new recruit or someone from a different industry who has recently joined.

It is critical that those with seniority do not see this as a fad or hype. Or even worse, that this is an extension of a management information ('MI') project, and that the whole Big Data and Analytics approach is nothing more than 'MI with a coat of lipstick.' The reality is that data and analytics have the capability to transform the organization, to be the difference between success and failure, to be the sentinel that helps strategic objectives be met and on which reputations are won and lost.

Insurers should not just compare themselves to their peers in such matters. Consumers are alive to levels of service in other sectors such as retail, banking, and telecom for example. Insurers therefore need to be as cognizant of what is happening in those other industries as in their own, and see both the opportunity and also the threat. Data and analytics brings with it the power of organizations to rapidly enter markets, and equally rapidly leave them when they recognize the truth about profitability and the business environment. Analytics can bring order out of chaos, but by its very nature can also be disruptive, which is an uncomfortable thing for a 300-year-old insurance industry.

According to 2014 research[2] from BearingPoint consultants, 'The Smart Insurer: More than just Big Data' only 10% of insurance firms have implemented a company-wide Big Data strategy. 30% were still exploring the possibilities, and nearly a quarter had some form of departmental implementation. Their research revealed that 71% said that Big Data will be a top priority by 2018, but a skill shortage was a problem in implementation according to 53% of insurance executives across Europe. Beyond this, their report indicated that 16% don't know enough about Big Data; 53% said this was an IT rather than a line of business issue, and only 37% viewed their company as in a position to implement new ideas because of the availability of additional data and analytical insight.

12.1   CULTURE AND ORGANIZATION

One of the major steps in transforming an insurer is the issue of changing the culture from one based on experience and intuition to one which recognizes the importance of data and analytics. This is not to say that there is no place for experience and intuition but rather that those critical intuitive attributes must now increasingly take their place beside more scientific methods.

At a recent insurance event, an underwriter asked to what degree underwriting decisions would in the future be *fully* automated through the use of Big Data and Analytics, and as a result was the underwriting profession under threat? It was a fair question, but in reality a better question to have asked might have been how the underwriting profession is likely to change going forward in this new analytical environment. It is entirely possible, even probable, that some traditional insurance roles will disappear in the future but equally likely that new roles will emerge. New business models will arise which will change current practices and ways of working. This is already starting to happen and the pace of change may accelerate over the coming years.

The first consideration of an insurer contemplating change should be to imagine what transformation might ultimately look like, limited by the confines of current knowledge and technology. If an insurer imagines itself to be an 'analytical insurer,' what does that mean in reality? Even exploring that issue takes us into interesting new territory. Perhaps an analytical insurer means different things to different people within the organization.

One definition might be:

An analytical insurer is an organization which effectively integrates data, analytics, and experience to create a differentiated offering which meets the need of their customer.

Before an analytical insurer starts to make a difference to their customer base it is often prudent to think about the internal impact on the organization. Almost all parts of the organization are likely to be affected from executive level downwards. New skills are likely to be needed, new roles created and personal targets set. An analytical insurer starts to see internal silos breaking down, new relationships formed and greater interdependency between the workforces.

It is unlikely that all the new skills needed will already exist within the organization and external recruitment may be needed. This 'new blood' will bring not only analytical skills to the insurer but perhaps other viewpoints from other industries. The insurer needs to help these new recruits understand insurance, so that their work can be done 'in context' but also the insurer should understand what innovation can be obtained within their own organization as a result of cross-fertilization of ideas from other sectors. Whilst some ideas clearly are not directly transferable such as retail loyalty cards for example, insurers may want to offer some added-value benefits to loyal customers beyond a no-claims discount.

It is inevitable that in the recruitment process, insurers will be attracted by candidates with what seem to be appropriate job titles. Typical ones might be 'data scientist' or 'Chief Digital Officer.' In the overall scheme of things these jobs might be at best transient roles, suitable for the current time but perhaps unlikely to be enduring as the technology evolves.

To expand, 'data scientist' is a role which has emerged in response to the difficulties of working with data and analytics, a role which differs from the role of 'data analyst.' A data analyst works with data provided to him or her in pre-configured analytical models whereas a data scientist is someone who creates their own models or derives information directly from the data itself.[3] By comparison, Chief Digital Officer (CDO) is a position which has emerged in recent times to reflect the increasingly digital nature of the insurance customer who increasingly buys online, or seeks more information about their insurance product from online sources. The acronym 'CDO' (for Chief Digital Officer) is also unhelpful as it can be confused with the Chief Data Officer which some might say is fundamentally an information management role.

Suggesting that the new roles may not be enduring compared to say an underwriter role which is over 300 years old implies that:

- The nature of rapid change in the technology means that data management and governance will become increasingly automated.
- Cognitive computing will ultimately provide the most appropriate analytical capability rather than the individual needing special analytic skills.
- All customers will eventually become 'digital' which will become the standard method of connecting (and why then would you need a special CDO role, for example?).

This might be a gross overstatement but simply seeks to emphasize the point that, during a recruitment process, insurers should recognize the transient nature of the roles, and in many cases understand the lack of formal qualifications that exist for the tasks associated with this new paradigm.

Perhaps the most likely change that will occur in insurance and other industries is the notion of a person who sits *between* the line of business decision-maker and the IT department. This individual will usually have an understanding of the key business drivers of the department in which they operate, the most appropriate technologies to help support and optimize those business decisions and the most appropriate data to fuel that decision-making.

This line of business/IT professional may sound like a new concept but in reality already exists in many places. Arguably it is also an interim role until disciplines take analytics fully on board. These people are in effect analysts who have attached themselves to departments of the insurance business for example in the area of marketing, perhaps starting with spreadsheets but maturing into the use of more sophisticated and functionally specific tools.

One burning question relative to this type of new role is how it is best created. Which is the easier path; for a person with insurance knowledge to learn technology, or for a technologist to learn insurance? At face value, it might be argued that it is easier for a technologist to learn insurance than vice versa. For an insurance professional baffled by the jargon of the technology department, it may be easier for a proverbial camel to pass through the eye of a needle than it is for an insurance person to learn IT.

There is an element of 'horses for courses,' and both sides of the house – IT and line of business – create artificial and unfortunate barriers through the jargon they use. Whilst insurance professionals may be confused by the 'jargon soup' of Hadoop, SQL and Hive, IT professionals will be equally uncomfortable with the insurance case law intricacies of *Rylands v Fletcher* (1868) which is one of the foundation stones of English tort law and helped establish the law of nuisance. (The US legal viewpoint of strict liability for the escape of 'hazards' from a neighboring property is fundamentally based on *Rylands*.)

Those experienced in data management might simply argue that data is data is data, and that there is no industry application or perspective. As a result they might suggest that foundational insurance knowledge is simply irrelevant. To some degree they are right, although certainly there are industry nuances which need to be taken into account especially in the area of risk and compliance, or for fraud analytics at the point of underwriting.

Going forward, the role of professional insurance institutes will also be important. At the moment many insurance institutes recognize technology as being a new source of business for their members. This is principally in the underwriting of cyber security policies for loss of data and the increased liabilities that this new era brings upon the obligations of executives protected under Directors and Officers Insurance. This entrepreneurial approach is entirely fair as the new era of data brings with it a new era of risks. It goes further than that. The loss of Big Data through poor data security may ultimately bring with it losses of a type and size never before encountered. This is also new territory for the insurance industry with limited precedents and experience (although this appears to be growing). Cyber security has been underwritten for nearly a decade. Equally or arguably more importantly, professional insurance institutes also need to recognize the great impact of technology on their members and adequately reflect this in the future syllabus of professional qualifications.

Some insurance institutes might feel that the need to learn technology is a matter for technology institutes (and equally technology institutes might feel that their members need not learn about business drivers, or how marketing campaigns work in practice, for example). However, the working environment will increasingly require people to sit in that middle ground.

Some organizations seem more mature than others in their thinking. The Insurance Accounting and Systems Association ('IASA') in North America have a technology viewpoint and a separate work stream at their annual conference. In recent times the Chartered Insurance Institute has also released some data-orientated discussion papers. How long will it be before strategic alliances start to emerge between quite disparate but increasingly complementary professional organizations and institutes?

Will the new era of data and analytics not only lead to new business models in the insurance community, but new professional bodies? Will we see an Institute for Telematics, an Association of User-Based Insurance and professional qualifications in Insurance Analytics?

Universities and colleges are following the money and gearing up for the new analytics age. Those specifically interested in Big Data analytics as applied to insurance and financial services might want to look at the University of Illinois where State Farm, one of the largest insurers in the US, has a research center that offers tuition assistance and internship opportunities.[4]

Insurers should also try to understand the skills and capabilities which *already exist* within the organization, and see how these can be leveraged across the wider business. Some tasks are already mainly analytical in nature, for example actuarial work, and it may be that individuals within those departments could create a bedrock of skills for the new analytical enterprise. Larger organizations in multiple geographies may find that these individuals are geographically diverse, and consideration will have to be given to finding a way of these people working effectively together to maximize the impact of the transformation project. They may already be using some analytical tools for tactical reasons in dark corners of the organization and perhaps on a piecemeal basis.

Having a series of isolated tactical tools spread around the business can also be problematic. The 'not invented here' syndrome can occur resulting in internal resistance to change, lack of standardization and an inability to obtain scale benefit across the business when more strategic decisions around tooling and vendors need to be made. Individuals become comfortable with the analytic tools they are using, some having adopted those tools whilst at college or university. Even so, the level of use of analytical tools within an organization will help better illustrate the readiness of the wider organization for change.

Most insurance organizations expect to see a tangible benefit in a relatively short time, usually within a year. Some more aggressive organizations outside the insurance sector look for tangible evidence within three months. Not only is this important in terms of providing financial justification for change but also helps to win hearts and minds within the business as well as additional funding. Insurers seldom embark on a 'big bang' transformation but rather create an implementation roadmap, with a series of incremental projects within an overall program, each project having a definable ROI and set of deliverables. Beyond this, there is an increasing trend for 'agile development' which comprises a series of short 'sprints' as proof of concept.

It follows that if demonstrating progress in financial terms is a key objective then the insurers need to have some clarity and certainty of the current starting position so that the delta of change can be effectively measured. Without some degree of certainty regarding the starting position there will always be some uncertainty about the true level of benefit obtained.

Successful implementation needs a program of change and there has been much already written about change management in its broadest sense.[5] As with any transformation or re-engineering process there must be sufficient incentive for people or organizations to want to change. Typical barriers to change might include:

- Cultural constraints and barriers – company structures that support management in a silo approach.
- Confrontation – including potential industrial relations problems.
- Political resistance – where managers see change as undermining their power base.
- Corporate backsliding – where new practices are not pushed fully, and people revert back to their 'old ways.'
- Rejection of the 'New Order' – not everyone is cut out for the new world of data and analytics.

All of these barriers and others can be dealt with specifically through a change management process with an agreed mitigating action but each element should not be treated lightly but rather within an integrated program of activities.

12.1.1 Communication and Evangelism

Effective communication is critical and not only comprises the creation and 'selling' of the vision of an insurer's journey towards becoming analytical but also provides a series of internal checkpoints through regular and frequent updates. All too often, organizations hear about change through external news. Communication ideally should be bi-directional and take into account all media currently available including video, social media and face-to-face. In effect this is a form of internal marketing of a transformation so it would seem entirely appropriate to use the marketing skills of an insurer to help the internal journey along.

Effective communication goes beyond keeping the top people involved but extends into other layers of management. Ineffective communication can breed resentment and resistance. Analytics by its nature is empowering and it is important that those to be empowered are also adequately informed. It is critical that communication starts as soon as possible in the program as fear and uncertainty are insidious and create a breeding ground for resistance.

Not all the information about what constitutes an 'analytical insurer' will be known from the outset. It may simply be no more than a statement of intent but ideally it may be helpful to share insights such as the following:

- What does the future look like?
- Why is change needed?
- What are the organizational changes?
- What roles and responsibilities are involved?
- What does transition look like – i.e., the 'roadmap'?
- The speed of change – how quickly will it happen?

Effective change management demands that other issues will need to be considered, for example rewards and recognition. This may be difficult in an area of activity which is both innovative and unprecedented. The topic of analytics seems to be fast moving as evidenced by the amount of online content and rate of innovation by vendors. To remain 'cutting edge' and competitive with new entrants, an insurer may need to take risks – but how might risk-takers be recognized (and rewarded) in an industry which is, on the whole, risk-averse?

There is a role for *evangelism* in communication. Although the term has its roots in religion, in effect converting someone to a particular set of beliefs, it is now often used in business to express the way that both customers and employees are brought around to a particular way of thinking. It is a way of eradicating existing beliefs and replacing them with new ones, and encouraging people to adopt behaviors and practices which differ from the ones they had previously. It is critical that this is done in such a way as not to suggest that the old ways were 'worthless' – to do so may result in resentment.

Evangelism and leadership often go hand in hand with the leader not only providing sponsorship and support but also helping create a vision for the future. Creating such a vision is partly an emotional message but it is important to support that message with coherent facts, appropriate personal behaviors and a strong call to action.

12.1.2   Stakeholders' Vision of the Future

One of the more interesting 'open' questions to engage existing and potential stakeholders is that of asking them what their vision of the future is. Through such a process, individuals can be encouraged to express their hopes, ambitions and concerns with regards to the concept of an analytical insurer. Issues may arise which are common to many parts of the organization, typically the impact on brand or reputation especially if there have been recent rocky times. Alternatively, there may be issues relative to a particular department or location.

Viewpoints expressed can often be tied back to Maslow's famous *Hierarchy of Needs* with those who feel most confident about their personal position and future perhaps being most optimistic in respect of change. On the other hand, those individuals who feel they are most likely to be at risk and might be adversely affected by 'technology' in terms of automation of tasks, de-skilling and changes to working conditions may feel the most negative. Some demographics may have a 'take it or leave it' attitude, especially those in the lower age band, whilst those at the upper end might simply use the idea of change to reinforce their own personal exit strategy from the company.

There are no right or wrong answers in inviting questions about the future, but an exercise of visualizing the future will be helpful in better understanding existing and potential issues and ultimately contributing to a more effective internal communication strategy.

One particular form of stakeholder management is through the use of representative workers' groups which present a cross-sector, broad representation of the staff who are likely to be affected. Such group discussions may be best done off-site, without distraction from day-to-day issues and using an impartial, informed and independent facilitator.

One specific issue to address is the degree of secrecy in such conversations. In reality there are few things which are absolutely secret within an organization and often secrecy breeds uncertainty and lack of trust. Whilst individuals may be duty bound not to disclose to colleagues that they are working on a special project that they cannot describe, the very fact that they are working on something secretive and special is often enough to raise interest and perhaps concern. There is a need for discretion where there are commercial issues to consider, new partnerships to be formed or new strategies to be announced but secrecy within organizations tends on the whole to be divisive at a time when a degree of unity is a critical success factor. Such issues are especially highlighted when new projects emerge with secretive names known only to a select elite.

12.2   CREATING A STRATEGY

The strategic purpose of an organization sets out its goals and priorities. So too the creation of an analytics strategy sets out the large-scale objectives of an analytical transformation in relation to the improved performance of that organization.

This section considers the foundational actions required and aims to look further and in more detail at strategies which will ultimately make an implementation sustainable. In doing so it provides help and gives the organization lasting value.

Creating an effective strategy requires some key steps, typically:

- Program sponsorship
- Building a project program

- Stakeholder management
- Recognizing analytics as a tool for empowerment
- Creation of open and trusting relationships
- Forming a development roadmap.

Addressing all of these issues will help organizations move more quickly and effectively to a successful and sustainable outcome. Although issues of leadership have been considered earlier, the leader may not necessarily come from the highest levels of the organization, for example Board or 'C' level, but rather may come from lower down the hierarchy.

He or she may have such skills and understanding as to recognize the value and importance of an analytical viewpoint. This may have been developed as a result of experience in a related field or perhaps outside the organization. Possibly they may have been recruited because of their different experience, may already have a relationship with the eventual project sponsor or have been directly or indirectly recruited by him/her.

12.2.1 Program Sponsorship

One of the most critical parts of the implementation process is finding a sponsor who provides organizational support for change. This support may be:

- Direct, as in the case of holding financial or budgetary control
- Indirect, such as an influential and trusted member of senior management.

The role of the sponsor is critical in that they provide appropriate and timely support to the program management and also exist as a person of 'last resort' in the event that internal issues create roadblocks to progress. The role of the sponsor also carries personal risk in that by supporting a particular initiative such as an analytical mandate, they may be politically injured if the analytical solution does not provide what it has promised to do.

With regards to the management of the analytics program, the sponsor should be viewed not only as a critical part of the process but also as a possible resource to support appropriate mitigating actions if unwelcome developments arise. It is important also to consider what might be the impact on the analytics implementation if the sponsor were to leave, or become discredited in some way.

For the sponsor, there are often methods which can be used to influence fellow executives. Raising awareness of competitor behavior is typical and thus driving a course of action which is 'defensive' in nature. A more appropriate and proactive strategy is to encourage the gaining of competitive advantage – through improved profitability, reducing cost or reducing risk.

Increasingly executives are looking outside their own insurance industry to gain better insight into the behavior of customers from other sectors. Many executives also encourage the use of external consultants to support a strategy, or at the very least to ratify one which is already drafted and in doing so provide some line of personal defense if things don't work out.

Traditionally the approach has been one of understanding the return on investment of a project and the financial benefit of proceeding in tangible terms measured by hard or soft benefits, or a combination of both. With the pace and momentum of the analytical age, things are becoming less clear and organizations and individuals are starting to make more emotional decisions as to whether or not to implement change. It might be argued that for some insurers an emotional decision is infinitely more valuable than a financial one as insurers are on the whole cynical by nature, and have the capability to create many barriers to change.

They might argue that:

- Their own business is significantly different to those seen in other case studies.
- The customer or product mix is different.
- Their own company has unique qualities in the marketplace.
- Promised improvements are at best optimistic.
- Or at worst the promises are entirely unrealistic.

Greater credence may be placed on the advice of trusted advisers especially industry experts who have been in practice for many years.

At some point in the process, the individual – who will ultimately be the sponsor – reaches a 'tipping point' when they realize that the adoption of an analytical agenda is no longer optional, but essential. In effect they have become 'believers' in the Church of Big Data and Analytics. Their responsibility means not only that they will support but also evangelize both within their organization and outside, and encourage others to do so.

12.2.2   Building a Project Program

One of the most effective means of implementation is to create a program of activities against which progress can be planned, measured and appropriately resourced. The nature of an analytical program is such that it will invariably comprise a combination of interdependent tasks which combine to provide a solid final outcome. It is critical to have a competent and experienced program manager but in the case of analytics this may be easier said than done as the industry is in a new phase of thinking. The challenges of this new analytical agenda, its relative speed of take-up and its application across multiple sectors mean that suitably skilled and experienced professionals may be hard to find. Much of the industry focus to date has been on technical data skills but there is also a need to develop robust and specialized project management skills for this quite special and innovative working environment.

Because of these difficulties it may well be that program management does not rest with an individual but rather with a small group of people who are aligned and hold a single shared vision of success. The title of such a group might differ from business to business and perhaps from industry to industry – typically an 'Analytical Center of Excellence' or 'Competence Center' – but often these groups are as concerned with running a Business as Usual Model as about creating and maintaining an implementation agenda.

The nature, breadth and depth of creating an implementation program will differ from organization to organization and depend on the line of business, the geography, the complexity and many other attributes. The creation of a detailed project program is a critical success factor.

One of the key elements of the program is to have a base-line study of the status quo. Without this, it is impossible to measure progress. The measurement must be done in such a way as to make future assessments of the improvement beyond reproach. If 'improvement' is a criterion for success then an ability to measure and agree on the level of improvement would appear to be essential. Notwithstanding, insurers operate in a difficult and volatile environment and change due to the use of analytics alone may be difficult to measure.

Results may not be achieved for multiple reasons for example:

- Physical (as in the case of a single big claim, or weather event)
- Economic (as in the case of a volatile economy)
- Legislative (due to new insurance regulation)
- Client behavior (such as a response to a reputational issue)
- Competitive behavior (for example new entrants or offerings).

For example, if improved profitability is the target, then the release of technical reserves can also give that impression. All of this serves to remind us that if analytics is about creating improvement then sometimes the measure of that improvement may be more difficult to demonstrate. Perhaps analytics best shows measurable improvement by being able to use data and analytics to demonstrate to regulators and rating agencies alike that the business is under sound control, leading to improved credit ratings and in turn ultimately helping with stock value.

It is worthwhile also to consider the ambition for change within insurance organizations. Whilst insurers may increasingly describe themselves as aspiring to become 'digital insurers,' few if any are prepared to provide a blank cheque book to recruit, implement and tool up the business. There is no such thing as a 'big bang' implementation but rather usually a series of sequential projects which form part of a longer term roadmap. Each of these projects tends to be shorter in duration, less complex to implement and have a defined deliverable.

There are pros and cons to this approach:

- On the positive side, each incremental step ensures that the business moves at a pace that is manageable. Risk is reduced, control is maintained and potential failure can be mitigated.
- On the negative side, a piecemeal approach may create internal pressures in terms of the prioritization, and competitive or other behavior may prejudice existing plans. Momentum may be lost and tactical decisions may not always be in the interests of the wider organization.

Perhaps one of the greatest weaknesses to an extended roadmap is its duration. The reality is that the most successful insurance organizations are likely to be the ones who transform themselves quickly, demonstrating innovation and agility. This may ultimately be done not through an organic, incremental response to change but rather through multiple step changes which may be undertaken through either a single or multiple strategic alliances, probably some significant outsourcing and most probably also reinvention of elements of the existing business model.

Increasingly the trend is one of 'agility' with organizations moving in short sprints, with a higher tolerance of failure. This does not align with the mood of many insurers nor even exist in their DNA. Beyond this, new operational risks might emerge which may not be tolerable either to the organization or to the regulators. Ring-fencing of these agile activities is usually seen as the ultimate solution to risk so as to avoid contagion of the wider business.

The rate of progress of analytics is such that self-built systems by insurers are unlikely to be able to keep up with progress. The situation is reminiscent of two decades ago when UK insurers considered 'build or buy' options in the choice of claims software and mainly opted for 'build' despite scalable claims systems already in operation in North America. This

UK and European trend is now progressively being reversed as US software companies find greater foothold within insurers. Moving forward there is increasing probability that insurers will need to form major strategic alliances with analytics platform vendors to achieve essential step changes.

12.2.3 Stakeholder Management

Effective stakeholder management is a critical component of all implementation programs. An analytics implementation is arguably no different, were it not for the fact that for many insurers (perhaps all of them) the critical stakeholders will also be in uncharted territory. Change is always difficult to cope with and creating an analytical transformation may bring special challenges associated with greater transparency, new tools and techniques, new roles and the likelihood of changing existing ways of business.

With analytics affecting different parts of insurers in different ways and with individuals (and demographic groups) having a different response to the digital age, there are inevitably going to be different reactions. How might a seasoned underwriter or asset manager react to the possibility that in the foreseeable future, their role may be replaced at least in part by a computer which has the ability to undertake cognitive analysis? At the least, some will be in denial – after all, how can 'their' experience be replaced by 'buttons and bytes'? Some will possibly feel threatened especially as new technologists enter their business area using terminology and technical capabilities which established insurance practitioners don't really understand.

In addition there is already the likelihood that new job roles will emerge which are perhaps not entirely suited to the capabilities of current incumbents. These new job roles with job descriptions are yet to be quantified but will invariably sit somewhere between technology and the line of business. But at an individual level, what will this mean? To what degree will the established hierarchy be diminished or even overturned? Some may initially think this to be an over-reaction to change but the reality will be that methods will change perhaps to an unimaginable degree. Compare the business world 'pre-mobile' and 'post-mobile.' When a famous drinks manufacturer coined the phrase 'Anytime, anywhere, any place . . .' they almost certainly didn't have insurance analytics in a mobile environment in mind.

Interestingly at a recent London event when analytics were presented to a group of senior insurance professionals, they also raised an ethical perspective. 'Isn't insurance about the protection of the individual through contribution of the premiums by the many?' they suggested. At a time when the insurance industry is arguably at its most threatened both by commercial pressures but also by pervasive technology, it is both interesting that the industry still looks to its roots and still wants to consider an ethical angle.

There are many issues for the insurance individual to ponder. If insurance individuals are not personally engaged in operational or organizational transformation, then the business runs the risk of silent 'terrorism' paying lip service to change but without fully engaging. Such an approach undermines the process and transformation albeit in a discrete and subtle way. Different cultures and organizations have different approaches to change. Some are more 'democratic' and inclusive than others; some will perhaps simply present transformation of any type as a 'take or leave it' approach; for others, there will not be any debate.

The essence of stakeholder management is that whilst it appears to be a 'soft' issue in terms of a transformation program, it still remains critical. If people at all levels of the organization understand and buy into change, then the prospect of success is greatly enhanced. Part of this 'buy-in process' is through an effective and multi-channeled approach to communication.

Often as a result of poor internal communications, employees look to the outside for better information. What for some insurers is an exercise in external positioning and marketing becomes a critical source of information for staff. As a result staff become misaligned with messaging, they present conflicting viewpoints to their customers and are not adequately engaged. Internal marketing of change is as critical as external marketing, and maybe more so. Because of this, the quality of communication becomes a key success factor.

A communication strategy needs to be planned and implemented as effectively as any technological change. Even if there is an element of uncertainty as to the eventual outcome – and in reality who *really* knows what a fully effective analytical insurer 'truly' looks like – it is critical that internal positioning places such transformation as a positive thing rather than a threat.

One alternative approach is that insurers can quite deliberately position change as a *provocative* statement of intent. This may work more effectively with larger organizations than smaller ones especially when linked to cost-cutting but the challenge of stakeholder engagement in a nervous environment creates its own issues. Marketing of these new ideas must inevitably accentuate the positive – greater empowerment, more transparency – but the individual also needs to believe that this means greater personal security. Maslow's Hierarchy places personal security at the foundations of personal achievement. If an individual feels personally uncertain about their own position, it will impact on their ability to take advantage of the changes happening around them.

The reality is that if the world of insurance is to change as a result of Big Data and Analytics then the world of work for insurance employees at all levels is equally likely to change. The other reality is that we cannot be sure by how much. At an individual level, for some this can be deeply unsettling.

12.2.4   Recognizing Analytics as a Tool of Empowerment

One of the key perceived attributes of an analytical insurer is that of staff empowerment especially as information from trusted sources becomes increasingly available. The expression 'democratization of information' is often used.

In an analytical enterprise there will inevitably be levels of access and security so it will not be a 'free-for all' in terms of information or the creation of reports. Beyond issues of confidentiality of information, controls are exerted on individuals because when (depending on the deployed system) staff members have been allowed to create their own reports using random requests, it is sometimes seen that the complexity of the report request is such that the system starts to respond more slowly. This in itself becomes a source of frustration and annoyance – and often ultimately of complaints to the IT department.

To avoid this, some companies only allow their staff to interrogate the system within a prescribed framework, often supported by a datamart or data layer sitting below the reporting layer, as opposed to allowing staff access to the main data source. This speeds up the response speed of the system. Whilst arguably limiting some of the information available to the individual, on the other hand this limitation offsets individual frustrations and improves the experience of the user.

As technology develops and insurers become more interested in external data which is likely to be unstructured in many cases, businesses will need to consider how best to empower their staff to navigate their way through a sea of information without becoming distracted.

Some insurers and other companies already prevent their staff from accessing the internet during the working day on the basis that it affects productivity. This internet access often relates to checking personal emails but in the new Big Data world it is likely that new rules of employee behavior will need to be drawn up.

At the end of the day, individuals are most likely to be looking for greater 'insight' to enable them to carry out their work. The door will increasingly open to the concept of 'insight as a service,' often also described in general terms as a 'cloud based, action orientated, analytically-driven application.'[6]

Empowerment also potentially brings its own problems typically in the conduct of individuals. As empowerment grows, so perhaps do operational and conduct risk. Conduct risk is loosely defined as the way that individuals in all parts of the company behave in terms of the discharging of their duties but also especially in relation to the customer. As empowerment grows, so becomes a need to put in place appropriate controls and practices and the creation of new risk frameworks.

If an analytical insurance enterprise seems to create new risks, greater risks or a combination of both, it is also through the use of analytics that additional controls can be put in place. Operational risk dashboards help executives understand whether adequate processes are in place and what steps might be needed to ensure that any risk is mitigated.

12.2.5   Creation of Open and Trusting Relationships

Creating an analytical insurer and infusing analytics throughout the organization is for many insurers the equivalent of stepping into unknown territory. There is an impact on business models, commercial aspects, customer relations, supply chains and other elements of the insurance business. Also it has been suggested that roles will change, new jobs will be created and individuals will need to interact with the system in new ways.

New skills will be valued; skills of innovation, radical thinking, thought leadership and ability to collaborate as well as the essential technical skills to operate these new tools.

Beyond this, the traditional staff hierarchy may also need to change:

- Organizational structures will become flatter.
- Experience will become less valued, in favor of cognitive analytics.
- Intuition will be replaced with insights.
- New behaviors, and new risks will emerge.

How quickly this occurs will be less a factor of the technological development than how quickly the insurance industry reaches the tipping point of change. The rate of knowledge sharing, across disciplines, industries and geographies is taking place at an unprecedented rate. Perhaps certain individuals are hoping that the regulators will somehow slow down the process. This may ultimately prove to be the case to some degree.

This 'era' of Big Data and its description as the 'new natural resource,' is sometimes compared to the era of the steam-driven industrial revolution of the 1700s (and also the electricity and oil eras of the 1800s and 1900s respectively). It is a curious coincidence that the same expression – 'regulator' – is used as being a critical component in two quite different eras but with relatively common meaning. Nowadays insurers are required to satisfy the Regulator (as an official body) to demonstrate that they are solvent. The expression 'regulator' has its origin in the era of steam when it had a very different meaning. The 'regulator device' reduced pressure in the steam engine and prevented the system from overheating or stalling. In the first circumstance it is used to prevent the steam engine from exploding; in the second circumstance it represents a function which ensures the insurance company does not 'collapse' through insolvency.

What all this seems to point to is that the entire system for an industry founded in the coffee houses of London nearly four centuries ago is on the point of transformation. Those insurers which do not transform in one way or another will not survive. Effective transformation is absolutely dependent on people – even in this increasingly analytical and technological age – and one key element for success will be the nature of interpersonal relationships. If there is likely to be a single effective mantra which needs to be adopted, it will need to be that of 'truth, trust and teamwork.'

As organizations increasingly focus on change, additional time will need to be dedicated to the sociological impact of creating an analytical insurer. Individuals increasingly work in a performance-orientated environment measured by sales or inspections and this in turn drives particular behaviors. If analytics has at its heart insights based on data points, and those data points are in effect measures of performance, then an analytical world will drive new types of behavior. Will employees feel under more stress? Will employers be able to identify employee stress through outliers in performance? Will employees who clumsily implement change, or poorly operate in this new environment find themselves open to workers' compensation and liability claims?

In this 'Brave New World'[7] it is essential that time is put aside to reflect on all the consequences. Insurers and perhaps the industry as a whole might usefully consider the role of 'Devil's Advocate' in their deliberations.

The expression comes from a religious process whereby the Catholic Church, in considering whether to canonize an individual, would appoint someone to try and find reasons why the person involved should not be made a saint. In effect the Church introduced a policy whereby they would deliberately seek to consider the alternative, contrary view.

Whilst for them this was a deliberate process to avoid being misled, in today's parlance it is used to promote discussion in a non-adversarial way. It is unlikely that such contrary views would result in an organization changing its strategy especially in regards to the adoption of an analytical enterprise. However, it may open up new lines of conversation which may need to be addressed, if not immediately then further along in the process.

The new operating paradigm for insurers and almost all other industries will inevitably bring up new personal issues for all involved. There is a risk that by focusing on the technological and organizational issues, the industry fails to see the proverbial elephant in the room. The 'elephant' in this case is the impact of change not only on the organization but also on the individual.

12.2.6   Developing a Roadmap

Insurers usually initially adopt some form of analytics as a tactical tool to meet specific needs, typically fraud, customer retention or perhaps better management of the call center. For insurers working in multiple geographies, the same tactical issues may be being addressed by different parts of the organization using different analytical tooling. This was seen in the case of regulatory compliance for Solvency II where in the early stages some global insurers initially adopted a federated model of implementation and initially missed the opportunity to leverage scale and learning across the enterprise.

Where the same problem is being addressed in different ways using different analytical tools, the natural thing (one might imagine) would be to benchmark each solution and then make a decision to standardize. Unfortunately, this doesn't often happen and a 'not invented here' attitude starts to emerge, ultimately resulting in a divisive, tactical approach. The same capability might be needed across different departments. For example, the marketing department might use one predictive tool while another department such as claims uses a different one. Interesting questions emerge at this point, typically is it better to standardize across the whole enterprise using a single technical vendor, or alternatively to have multiple vendors who provide 'best of breed' solutions in each area?

Perhaps the question of using multiple analytical solutions will become less relevant in the future. Competing systems are increasingly able to work with each other and exchanging of data from one system to another is more easily achieved. The new environment is likely to be more forgiving in terms of multiple best of breed systems working alongside each other. As analytical technology continues to evolve, those in control of purchasing decisions within insurers will end up with a need to manage multiple vendors who will have multiple and numerous complexities. If managed incorrectly, multiple tactical solutions to operational problems will result in a fragmented transition to the new analytical world. Will this create escapable delays and avoidable consequences?

All that aside, as organizations step back and think about what might be an effective, managed implementation program, a 'big bang' approach is less likely than a series of incremental improvements with each having a return on investment. Insurers increasingly know that they need to jump onto the analytics train because they cannot afford not to, and as a result the decision to become 'analytical' is almost an emotional one.

Where an emotional decision to become analytical has already been made, the ROI process will help insurers understand where to start first on their analytical journey. Understanding the benefit case for change will help with the prioritization process and ensure resources are effectively deployed.

There are three schools of thought as to where an insurer might start their analytical journey.

1. The first is that the insurer has to gain analytical control of their finances, and therefore the natural starting position is in the office of finance. This is often the case with other industries as well who see firm financial control and planning as fundamental to their business success. In reality many insurers already have a firm grip on their financial analytics but the opportunity remains to improve efficiency and reduce cost.

2. The second alternative might be to start at a place where there is a particular pain point, perhaps in fraud analytics for their motor or healthcare business. Claims leakage is a major problem for insurers directly affecting the bottom line, and insurers might naturally want to start in a place which immediately saves them money.

3. The third place to start might best be decided upon by reference to the insurer's own strategy. What type of analytics and where might it be optimally seated to best assist the insurer in meeting its strategic objectives? This may drive the insurer towards the use of a particular capability or insight.

Any and all of these options are sensible but the office of finance is perhaps the most sensible of the three. Without effective control mechanisms in place, an insurer is simply flying in the dark without having clear visibility of which products, geographies or channels are profitable. Without this clarity of insight, they will be weaker in terms of their capability to effectively plan and budget.

Perhaps there is an argument for slightly more radical thinking. It is not inconceivable for an insurer to recognize that within a decade, possibly sooner, the nature of insurance will have changed. Analytics and technology will have become infused into the industry, the customer will have changed, products may be significantly different and the delivery mechanisms will have been transformed out of all recognition.

The competitive landscape will also be filled with new insurance brands underpinned by technology companies. If one buys into that line of thinking, then an insurer might want to step beyond an incremental approach into something which is somewhat bolder – perhaps a strategic partnership with an existing analytics vendor at joint-venture level or even maybe some sort of acquisition.

With a partnership such as this, there would still be a need to think about an implementation roadmap but it would allow the insurers to be somewhat bolder in terms of both scope and speed to implement, and also give them greater control.

12.2.7   Implementation Flowcharts

A set of suggested implementation flowcharts are provided in Appendix C. They enable the reader to consider specific issues of implementation at a place that is most appropriate to them, allowing them to dip in and out as and when the need arises.

12.3   MANAGING THE DATA

If there is any part of this publication which focuses on Information Technology (IT) in its purest sense, then this is it. It is impossible to consider Big Data and Analytics as far as it relates to insurance without having some rudimentary understanding of the technologies which sit at the data layer within the analytics process.

Technology experts will probably scoff at the relatively superficial nature of the following sections which are presented with an appropriate apology. This topic at its heart is hugely technical with the IT department having its own jargon and specializations. For the insurance expert coming to this subject afresh or even with some limited understanding, it will be helpful for them to understand some of the core technological issues at the data and platform layer. This book also carries a list of recommended reading for those who wish at some later stage to dive more deeply into the data element of the topic.

At the heart of the Big Data and Analytics agenda is the data. It is the source of all insight, the proverbial spring at the source of the river. Traditionally the data was obtained in a controlled structured way and then with the benefit of spreadsheets was transformed into management information (MI) or as business intelligence. This was comparatively simple in nature compared to the more complex data management that takes place today.

Data can be considered as falling into one of four quadrants:

- Structured and internal to the organization, such as information held in data warehouses or spreadsheets.
- Structured and external to the organization, such as third-party government data and records, or geo-coded information.

- Unstructured and internal, such as information obtained from internal social media.
- Unstructured and external, such as social media or streamed information from videos.

There are a number of key criteria that need to be considered as part of data management and there are also other books that cover these data issues in considerably more detail. However, for the purposes of completeness, the following areas will be briefly considered in the context of insurance:

- Master data management
- Data governance
- Data quality
- Data standardization
- Storing and managing data
- Security.

12.3.1 Master Data Management

Master data management or 'MDM' is the process by which duplicate data is removed, data is standardized and rules are incorporated to prevent incorrect data from entering the system. This is needed in order to create a single version of the truth with regards to the source data, or in other words the 'master version.' Errors in data collection often stem from the fragmented nature of the organization, with the same customer data being provided by different channels and product lines. Also 'redundant data' often remains within the system which further complicates the problem.

Master data management is the framework that provides a method of collecting, aggregating, matching, consolidating, quality-assuring, maintaining and distributing such data through the organization in such a way as to provide a consistent outcome. It also provides control in maintaining and using this information. If analytics extracts the value from the data, then MDM is the 'central bank' which provides the currency.[8]

12.3.2 Data Governance

This term is used to mean the control environment by which data entered by an individual or as part of an automated process meets the agreed standards of the business, such as business rules, agreed data definitions and agreed qualities of data.

According to the Data Governance Institute, a US-based vendor-neutral group set up in 2003 to establish data best practice, data governance is a 'quality control discipline for assessing, managing, using, improving, monitoring, maintaining, and protecting organizational information. It is a system of decision rights and accountabilities for information-related processes, executed according to agreed-upon models which describe who can take what actions with what information, and when, under what circumstances, using what methods.'[9]

Data governance is the process by which the veracity or truthfulness of the data is established. This became especially critical for insurers in areas of regulation such as Solvency II where accurate reporting is dependent on accurate figures. Such was the state of some data sets that very considerable expense was incurred by insurers in the data governance process as part of Solvency II programs. Some suggest that 80% of the overall cost of Solvency II compliance was in the data organization and governance area.

12.3.3 Data Quality

Data can also be of different qualities, and poor quality data can create risks on interpretation. The expression 'rubbish in, rubbish out' is often heard. On the other hand, even weak data may be better than no data if those interpreting it have an understanding of the data quality. One major international bank takes into account the uncertain quality of data by giving it a weighting or score so as to reflect the confidence level. Additionally, more sophisticated analytical tools can give source data a confidence score.

According to Joseph Duran (1904–2008), an influential management consultant and evangelist in the area of quality management, data (plural) are of high quality if 'they are fit for their intended uses in operations, decision making and planning.'

Data quality in insurance often manifests itself in issues of customer and address data. Misspelling or data entry can often lead to multiple entries for the same individual or location. This has multiple impacts for insurers with different levels of impact, typically:

- In a Big Data world which aims to have a 360-degree view of the customer, insurers end up with incorrect data preventing appropriate and timely offers being made.
- Offers are duplicated to the same address or household which adds unnecessary and avoidable cost to the marketing process.
- The customer themselves may be irritated by multiple contacts, coupled with misspelling of names, affecting loyalty, which may also be a factor in customer retention.

Data quality tools already exist which identify misspelling and address duplication. These have been criticized for their inability to deal with the very large amount of data which is becoming increasingly available in the Big Data environment. Reduced data quality may simply become a byproduct of the Big Data explosion. If data quality was difficult in an era when data was simply internal and structured, significant challenges must lie ahead as insurers consider the external and unstructured data which represents 80% of the total.

12.3.4 Data Standardization

As with many industries, standardization is that process which seeks to reduce or remove completely the degree of customization of individual processes. In effect customization is a form of compromise – the parties agree on a common set of rules for mutual benefit and this results in a more consistent output. The ability to standardize helps ensure that data entered in one part of the organization is also of benefit to other parts.

In insurance, one key benefit of standardization is around customer data where information obtained through marketing can also help the customer service process. In finance, standardized data not only helps insurers satisfy regulatory requirements but also allows them to understand the profitability of products and distribution channels with greater certainty.

Data matching or 'record linkage' is also an important process for many business applications. It involves linking of data records from multiple sources that don't have a mechanism to draw them together naturally. In insurance, the most typical uses are in creating a single view of the customer or sometimes in the investigation of fraud networks.

At the heart of data matching is the standardization of the data entry which needs to happen at the point when data is entered. As policyholders increasingly 'self-serve' by entering their details online, there is sometimes a lack of care as they enter even their own data. Spell-checking tools do not yet seem to exist in self-service tools, and even if they did it is unlikely that such tools would capture mistakes in addresses or names. If standardization doesn't take place at the outset then problems inevitably arise downstream or in the back-end process.

Beyond this, data merge or consolidation is often needed to try and create a consolidated single viewpoint from multiple source systems. According to recent surveys by leading analyst firms,[10] 'close to 20% of the data in an enterprise is duplicate information. A good percentage of this data is "inexact" or fuzzy duplication making the process of detecting and eliminating them complex.'

The problem of duplicate data has a major impact on insurer reputation and operations:

- Duplicate data records showing differently named customers at the same address add to the cost of posting.
- Customers are miscommunicated with or inconsistently contacted.
- There can be missed sales opportunities due to the absence of a single version of the truth.
- Compliance/audit issues become more complicated.
- It becomes more difficult to detect fraudulent activity, especially through network analytics.

All these aspects relate to internal data issues, but there is a major issue also in terms of external data recognizing that the majority of useful information may rest outside the organization. There will inevitably be data quality issues in the external environment which are more difficult to reconcile.

ACORD[11] is a global non-profit organization working to improve data quality and information exchange specifically for the insurance industry. As an organization it is committed to helping insurers achieve the goal of straight-through processing by offering many public standards specifications and documentation. In addition, they provide 'Members Only' documentation to aid member organizations in implementing the specifications.

12.3.5   Storing and Managing Data

A data warehouse is used for storing current and historical data for the purpose of analysis. Data may also be held in an operational data store or 'datamart' prior to it being used for focused analytics such as regulatory reporting or customer analytics.

A data warehouse focuses on the specific business problem of data storage which in its broadest description also includes the retrieval or 'extraction' of the data, its transformation into a usable form and the loading of the data into other analytical systems in a usable form. This process is known is 'ETL,' or 'extract, transfer, load.' In addition, data warehouses often have 'data dictionary' capabilities to ensure that data is consistently recorded.

12.3.5.1   Industry Data Models

An insurance data model is a pre-built physical data model which helps insurers capture data from multiple source systems and business processes such as claims, underwriting and policy at a granular level. It is usually accompanied by data definitions. The benefits of this capability include:

- Easier support to analytical requirement
- Reduction of inconsistency of data
- Improvement of auditability.

12.3.5.2 Data Platform

The 'data platform,' sometimes also known as a 'data management platform' or 'unified data management platform' is a centralized part of the computing system which collates, integrates and manages large data sets from multiple disparate sources. Often described as the 'plumbing' of the system, it provides the critical function of collecting data, translating it, indexing it and storing it.

Data Management Platforms do three things:

- Importing of data.
- Finding of segments
- Sending of instructions.

12.3.5.3 Cloud Computing

Cloud is a recently evolved computing expression meant to reflect the shared utilization of computing assets. It involves deploying groups of remote servers and software networks that allow centralized data storage and online access to computer services or resources. Clouds can be classified as public, private or hybrid. The whole principle is to maximize the use of these shared resources for all users. The availability of these resources can also be dynamically allocated dependent on the user's demand, for example where different organizations are working in different time zones, or where perhaps there is a particularly high computation demand for specific incidents of short duration such as regulatory reporting.

Not only does the cloud approach optimize the use of computing power but there are other 'green' issues to consider such as the reduced environmental damage due to the use of less power.

From a financial point of view, the use of cloud for insurers allows them to move away from a traditional capital expenditure ('Capex') model where they buy the required hardware and allow the asset to depreciate over a period of time, to an 'opex' approach where insurers use a shared cloud infrastructure and pay for it as it is used. With increased pressure on insurers to be more agile and bring products and services to the consumer market more quickly, the concept of cloud computing is becoming more attractive especially as security concerns are progressively being resolved. Increasingly the concept of the 'hybrid cloud' is gaining attention, which is a combination of on-premise storage of data and off-premise analytics for specific capabilities.

12.3.5.4 Computer 'Appliances'

Named after the concept of a household 'appliance' these are generally self-contained storage devices with integrated software. The complete 'bundled' solution is often created to meet a particular functional need. Appliances usually contain a pre-configured combination of analytics and mapping capabilities, for example. In insurance, their use is particularly appropriate for specific functions such as catastrophe modeling.

What they lose in flexibility, they make up for in speed and 'time to value' – in effect the speed that data can be fed in and useful output obtained by the client.

12.3.5.5 The Lexicon of Technology

In the same way that it is impossible to cover all the elements of insurance in a publication such as this, the depth and breadth of technology means that dictionaries of IT terms exist which describe themselves as 'covering thousands of IT terms.'[12]

Such sites are both useful and confusing. The casual reader will potentially be faced with multiple terms and expressions such as Hadoop, Java and many others. It is way beyond the scope of this publication to explain these terms other than with one specific exception. Hadoop is an open source shared industry initiative for distributing large data sets. It is generally accepted that mainstream users don't need to know exactly what it is or how it works, only that it removes the constraints around the management of Big Data. If readers manage to get their heads around Hadoop, then Apache Hadoop is waiting around the corner for them.

One of the expressions of the moment is 'BYOD' which is an acronym for 'Bring Your Own Device.' This is a company policy of allowing individuals to use their own personally owned devices for work-related issues, whilst at the same time getting company support, especially around data security. Providers such as Pluralsite[13] provide information on the '20 Most-Common Terms Entry-Level IT Professionals should know.'

12.3.6 Security

Data security is the expression used for protection of data from theft, damage or tampering by unauthorized users. In the context of insurance, the issues are as great as other industries in terms of the potential for physical and reputational damage. As with other parts of this publication, it is too large a subject to be covered in depth other than to comment on the special circumstances in which insurers potentially find themselves going forward.

The future of insurance will be a 'connected' one. Current developments indicate that solutions like telematics and other forms of user-based insurance (which are entirely dependent on external devices) will continue to grow. With much of the current emphasis being on security of internal systems and increasingly security of cloud-based storage, the attention of cyber intruders may now turn to the vulnerability of the devices themselves and how those devices supply data to the Big Data 'mix.'

Beyond this, as structured and unstructured data are combined to provide unprecedented insight then the security of the systems which provide the unstructured data will come under increased scrutiny. According to PWC's 2016 'Global State of Information Security Survey,' organizations reported a 93% increase in security incidents between 2013 and 2014.[14] Insurers remain very much in the firing line for cyber theft as evidenced by the massive leak in a US healthcare insurer in early 2015 involving a database of 80 million customer records[15] and a second smaller leak in the UK in the same year.[16]

12.4   TOOLING AND SKILLSETS

Chapter 1 summarized the generic analytical tooling or capability needed under the following headings:

- Descriptive
- Predictive
- Prescriptive
- Cognitive.

All these comprise mainly unique combinations of skill sets and are not necessarily interchangeable. An expert in descriptive analytics is unlikely also to have skills in predictive analytics, although these additional skills can be acquired. Additionally, individuals may also focus on particular segments of analytics, for example risk or financial performance management.

12.4.1 Certification and Qualifications

The measurement of such skills is usually by certification in particular branded tools, which for the individual can gain demonstrable professional recognition. This allows insurers or any other potential employer to recruit with confidence. In many cases employers themselves are keen to support an individual's journey towards professional competence, recognizing that it improves both individual productivity and also staff loyalty.

Usually certification can be done either virtually or in the classroom in a way which is least disruptive to the employee's normal work. Personal 1-2-1 training is also an option. Training towards certification may be done by the technical vendor or by approved intermediaries.

As an alternative to certification, individuals may choose or be encouraged to gain industry-specific knowledge by joining a professional institution such as the Chartered Insurance Institute (CII) in the UK or the Insurance Accounting and Systems Association in the US (IASA) to name but two. With over 115,000 members in 150 countries, the CII describe itself as the 'world's largest professional body dedicated to insurance and financial services.' In the US there are over 40 professional bodies for insurance that invite membership either at a group or personal level.

Beyond direct insurance professional groups, individuals might also be attracted by other professional associations such as the Chartered Institute of Marketing with a meagre 34,000 members, or the American Marketing Association with around 30,000 members. Both of these, and others, will help an individual understand what is topical in the world of digital marketing for example and allow them to contextualize their analytical learning beyond their immediate employer's environment

12.4.2 Competences

In Chapter 11 the topic of the desired skills and capabilities of individuals was considered in detail. This section aims to briefly recap them and to consider the tooling needed for the successful analytical insurer.

Successful implementation of an analytical solution within an insurer depends not just on technical ability but also on a broad range of behavioral issues as well, including:

- Quickness to learn and adapt
- Problem solving ability
- Collaboration and communication skills.

Employers should be careful about trying to understand different thinking skills of their employees through psychometric analysis alone. According to *Blood Sweat and Tears, the Evolution of Work* by Richard Donkin,[17] much of the work on behavioral prediction harks back to 1949 and the '16 Personality Factor' questionnaire based on 180 questions and taking 40 minutes to complete. By the 1990s, psychologists were suggesting that they could see 'precious little evidence' of the ability to predict behavior. Donkin suggests that the controversy over testing is likely to 'run and run.' This is especially so as customer analytic vendors are increasingly looking to include behavioral elements within their solutions.

The expression 'competences' was created to reflect the attributes of the most successful crews of US naval ships, for example. They have been described as 'a bit higher than a skill, more of a motive and a trait, a human characteristic that distinguishes outstanding from typical performance.'

Donkin concluded that both knowledge and skills can be developed but that the 'motive' to work was much more difficult to grow. If successful implementation is really about 'motive' at the end of the day, doesn't the burden inevitably fall on the leader to 'motivate' and encourage the individual to combine the analytical, practical and creative?

NOTES

1. Goleman, Daniel. *Emotional Intelligence*. New York: Bloomsbury Publishing, 1996.
2. Bearing Point Institute. 'The Smart Insurer: More than just Big Data.' Published Bearing Point Institute Report, Issue 004, 2014.
3. Voulgaris, Z. *Data Scientist, the Definitive Guide to Becoming a Data Scientist*. US: Technics Publications, 2014.
4. Henchern, Doug. 'Big Data Analytics Master's Degrees: 20 Top Programs.' Information Week, 2013. http://www.techweb.com/news/240145673/big-data-analytics-masters-degrees-20-top-programs .html (accessed April 9, 2016).
5. Harvey, David. *ReEngineering: The Critical Success Factors*. London: Business Intelligence Ltd, 1995.
6. Simoudis, Evangelos. 'Big Data and Insight as a Service.' Trident Capital, 2012. Sandhill.com. http://sandhill.com/article/big-data-and-insight-as-a-service/ (accessed April 9, 2016).
7. Shakespeare, William. 'The Tempest.' Act V, Scene I, ll. 203–206.
8. Millman, Ivan, Dreibelbis, Allen and Hechler, Eberhard. *What is a Master Data Management System*. US: IBM Press, 2008. http://searchdatamanagement.techtarget.com/feature/What-is-a-master-data-management-system (accessed December 11, 2015).
9. The Data Governance Institute. 'Data Governance Framework.' US, 2013. http://www.datagovernance .com/dgi-data-governance-framework/ (accessed April 9, 2016).
10. Infosolve Technologies. 'De-Duplication.' US. Published by Infosolve, 2015. http://www .dataqualitysolution.com/duplicate-detection-and-consolidation (accessed December 11, 2015).
11. ACORD. 'Data Standards.' Published by ACORD, 2015. Acord.org/standards/downloads/Pages/ default.aspx (accessed April 9, 2016).
12. Whatis. 'Find a Tech Definition.' Published by Techtarget, 2015. http://whatis.techtarget.com/ (accessed December 11, 2015).
13. Sumastre, Michael Gabriel. '20 Most-Common Terms Entry-Level IT Professionals Should Know.' Pluralsight, 2015. http://blog.pluralsight.com/20-it-terms (accessed December 11, 2015).
14. PWC. 'The Global State of Information Security® Survey 2016.' US, Published by Pricewaterhouse-Coopers, 2016. http://www.pwc.com/gx/en/issues/cyber-security/information-security-survey.html (accessed April 9, 2016).
15. Riley, Charles. 'Insurance giant Anthem hit by massive data breach.' US, Published by CNN, 2015. http://money.cnn.com/2015/02/04/technology/anthem-insurance-hack-data-security/index.html (accessed December 11, 2015).
16. Kroll Ontrack. 'Aviva reveals details of second data breach.' London, Published by Kroll Ontrack, 2015. http://www.krollontrack.co.uk/company/press-room/legal-technologies-news/aviva-reveals-details-of-second-data-breach-584.aspx (accessed April 9, 2015).
17. Donkin Richard. *Blood Sweat and Tears*. Knutsford: Texere, 2001.

CHAPTER 13

Visions of the Future?

Pick up most books about quotations and they have pithy lines about the future. Many if not all of them could find a place here. Two useful famous lines come to mind:

> *'You can never plan the future by the past.'*
>
> Edmund Burke, British statesman (1729–97)[1]

> *'It is a mistake to look too far ahead. Only one link of the chain of destiny can be handled at a time.'*
>
> Sir Winston Churchill (1874–1965)[2]

It is probably possible to find a quotation to fit any particular personal point of view. If one is worried, then someone somewhere will already have expressed that in some form. Alternatively, if one is optimistic then equally there will be words but overall it's important that quotations are kept in context. When Shakespeare in his play *The Tempest* referred to a 'Brave New World,' it was with a sense of irony. Context is everything.

So it is therefore with a slight element of trepidation that a number of analytical visions of the future are suggested which involve insurance. The intention is to stimulate, reflect and challenge. Perhaps within a very short time some of the ideas which have been suggested will have crossed the finish line whereas others may not even have got across the starting line.

If we are to think about what makes an 'analytical insurer' then it will be the way that the insurer behaves both internally and externally, how it is connected between departments, with its supply chain, with its partners, with its customers and perhaps even with its peers.

13.1   AUTO 2025

By 2025 the auto insurance industry had undergone major changes as the so-called Internet of Things had really kicked in. Ever since the beginning of the century, vehicles had become increasingly dependent on computerized systems. Long gone were the days of needing to check the oil in the engine with a dipstick as the vehicle dashboard told the driver that an oil service was needed. Beyond this, the instruments not only told the driver when fuel was running out and the distance that the vehicle could travel until it ran out of fuel, but also a whole number of peripheral items such as tire pressure, driver behavior and how both of these – and other relevant factors – influenced fuel consumption. Low pressure tires adversely affected the performance of the vehicle not just in terms of road performance but also in respect of engine efficiency.

Increasingly, motor manufacturers recognized the importance of running costs in the purchase decision, and therefore the issue of insurance premiums as part of the overall cost of vehicle ownership. Companies such as Ford and Mercedes had, by the mid-2010s, started to reinvent themselves as mobility providers rather than motor manufacturers. This had increasingly led to bundled financial services offerings as part of the car purchase but also in respect of running costs. To most of the general public, the idea of cars being an asset had started to fade in favor of a more utilitarian approach to travel. This had created major issues for brand-led motor manufacturers, especially those in the prestige brand sector, and as a result they had increasingly extended their brand attributes beyond the vehicle itself and into lifestyle purchases such as jewelry, clothing and watches.

By 2025, user-based insurance for autos had increased and now represented nearly 80% of the auto insurance industry. The doubts and relatively slow take-up of the middle of the previous decade had been put aside. Insurance marketers had increasingly and successfully sold the benefits, and had downplayed the fact that for many customers the price of insurance had gone up rather than down. For insurers, the ability to improve the accuracy of underwriting by linking premiums to performance had become more and more attractive, and increasingly adversely priced against policyholders seeking the 'traditional approach' to pricing.

In 2019, an insurance company who represented the 20% of one country's book of auto business had decided not to provide auto insurance in the form of the traditional annual premium as an option but rather provide only a user-based 'telematics' solution. It was viewed by some as a brave move, but paid off not only in respect of profitability but also through significant increase in market share. Other insurers were to follow, and like the demise of the old 'penny pension' schemes of the previous century where an insurance agent would collect money on the doorstep on a weekly basis, the traditional method of selling insurance on an annual basis had now been left behind.

Auto manufacturers had also recognized the imminent change and had formed deeper strategic alliances with insurance carriers whose actuarial insight into asset and liability management had helped new insurance propositions to be crafted. For the regulators, it was critical that whoever carried the insurance risk would remain solvent and the role of the traditional insurer became increasingly one of capital management.

Solvency III in Europe had also got off to a slow and uncertain start much like its immediate predecessor. It was not until 2018 that insurers really gained control over the issues relating to Solvency II, and by that time the insurance models were already beginning to change. As motor manufacturers increasingly provided variations of user-based motor cover, they relied on the insurance carriers to manage the risk element of the proposition. In a market which was progressively and rapidly changing and consolidating, no-one had really anticipated the merger of a global motor manufacturer and a global insurance company.

For the driver, the changes in business model were equally unsubtle. Motor manufacturers understood the relationship between driver behavior and insurance premium, and to reflect this had started to show how the insurance premium changed in real time by having a 'premium optimization' gauge on the digital auto dashboards. 'Prem-Op' was first announced at the Motor Show in Frankfurt in 2020 and had proved an immediate attraction.

The idea of an insurance premium gauge was in many ways a throw-back to the Volvos and Saabs of the 1990s, cars which had a gauge showing worsening fuel consumption if a driver was too heavy on the pedal. One of the biggest issues was that of ergonomics on the dashboard. Should the gauge be large and conspicuous so as to influence driver behavior, or should it be small and discreet? Ultimately there proved to be a correlation between car value and size of gauge. The reality seemed to be that if one could afford a prestige vehicle then perhaps insurance premium was not as much an issue of concern.

The embedding of sensors into vehicles increasingly helped in reducing the number and frequency of impacts. Automatic braking linked to distance sensors had become increasingly prevalent. Whilst the use of self-driving cars had failed to take off in the developed world as much as expected, technology had helped not only in reducing the number of accidents but also their severity. The ability to interrogate car systems increasingly helped investigators to understand any collision incident, apportion blame but equally have a clear understanding of the likelihood of whiplash injury. By 2025 fraudulent whiplash claims had been virtually eradicated.

In the event of an incident, the 'connected' vehicle would self-report the event to the insurer and also to the recovery provider if the impact was of appropriate severity. An appointment would be automatically made with the body shop, to be subsequently ratified with the owner's diary. A replacement hire car would also be automatically scheduled. The damaged vehicle would be able to identify which other cars were involved. Linked to digitally-held car registration, ownership and insurance details would trigger straight-through claims processing, resulting in 100% success in subrogation (monies recovered from a third party).

There was however a downside to the increased amount of technology in autos. Where an accident had taken place, the cost of repair to damaged vehicles soared. The profession of auto assessor had necessarily been transformed into the role of inspector of virtual mobile computers. For this profession, what had once been the relatively simple task of observing dents in bodywork had become an altogether more sophisticated operation. Bodywork still needed to be repaired, but this also had become much more complex as manufacturers increasingly used hybrid materials to improve performance and reduce weight. Traditional body shops had become obsolete in favor of new, advanced repairers where not only could physical damage be rectified, but the vehicle could also be 'plugged in' to self-diagnose any electrical faults.

A new form of fraud had started to emerge. Vehicle diagnostics solutions were recoded and 'hacked' to show alleged defects that did not exist in reality, and creating the supposed need to replace components unnecessarily. Such work might be invoiced but never actually carried out. Fortunately, central management of repair costs and trends by insurers was able to help identify outliers, supported by automatic forensic analysis of data.

The complexity of the repair process had also inevitably resulted in fewer and more specialist body shops. Traditional term contracts between insurers and body shops were replaced in favor of a new 'claims exchange process' where repairers where allowed to bid automatically online dependent on their capacity, current work in progress and their appetite to do the work. The role of the supplier manager and procurement team had been transformed.

The issue of auto complexity also created issues in terms of repair capacity management. Insurers had needed to be 'locked in' to certain repairers who were experts in particular brands and technologies. This, together with the increase in switching costs from one repairer to another, represented a shift of power from insurer to repairer as a result of the increasing complexity of the repair process.

Self-drive cars had never really lived up to the hype of the mid-2010s. The concerns about liability and responsibility in the event of a collision never really materialized. Discussions about whether fault rested with the manufacturers, the driver or some other party proved to be academic rather than real. Some self-drive cars did come into production but these were mainly used in the new city developments of the Middle East and China where traditional vehicles were kept off the road. These vehicles travelled only at relatively modest speeds as a substitute for public transportation. On reflection, self-driving cars were more of a proof of technology than a realistic and deliberate plan to transform the auto industry.

Satellite navigation techniques also evolved from their early start in the mid-2000s. The increased number of devices in the public space inevitably led to greater insight about optimizing the journey not only in respect of time, but also in respect of customer value. A patent taken out by one major technology vendor to direct the vehicle along specific routes where advertising billboards were more prevalent came to operational fruition and whilst there was some initial public disquiet, this had led in turn to an 'opt-in, opt-out' model for sat-nav. The *opt-in* model meant that a driver would allow the vehicle to be guided along particular routes and in return would also be provided with purchasing discounts. *Opt-out* meant that the purchase would pay a non-discounted price for goods purchased, but would have the benefit of a shorter journey. The retail and transportation industries had increasingly found ways to create 'bundled' offerings.

13.2   THE DIGITAL HOME IN 2025 – 'PROPERTY TELEMATICS'

It was inevitable that homes would become digitalized, so the big questions were how, why and when? Of course, the expression 'telematics' was not the most appropriate for a structure which did not move but it was the one by which the capability was best known.

The advent of telematics as a mainstream option for auto insurance had become increasingly common towards the end of the decade. Despite the early expressions of concern, telematics for people, initially in terms of healthcare, had also became increasingly common. The early mover statements by some US insurers had created plenty of debate with some degree of interest over the use of brightly colored bracelets containing the monitoring device. This eased off as mainstream jewelers increasingly added monitoring devices as an option with increasing frequency. Within a short time, remote devices were not only commonplace but fashionable especially for those who sought to be seen as trendsetters.

The use of so-called aggregator sites had increased despite efforts by carriers to resist the trend by refusing to engage. This increased use of aggregators had occurred mainly as a result not only of the behavior of the buying public who were eager to make price comparisons but also aggressive and effective marketing by the aggregators themselves. Regulators' earlier concerns that prospective purchasers might not receive enough information at the point of purchase proved to be capable of resolution. As these sites grew, the impact on intermediates and agencies proved to be a problem especially for smaller businesses. Technology not only had changed the distribution model but was to affect livelihoods as well, much in the same way that the Retail Distribution Review of 2015 had done in the UK by driving out many of the unqualified independent insurance brokers.

Big Data and Analytics had been able to give the insurance underwriter greater access to relevant information. As a result, the rating of risk could be done automatically with a higher level of granularity than ever before. The extent of the risk could now be accurately assessed not only on the basis of a property location but also taking into account the location of the insured premises in terms of height. This was especially important for multi-story properties where the risk was above ground level. Open source data and better property information, coupled with agency records such as crime and societal research provided the underwriting process with deep insight into the propensity of a property to suffer loss. The UK Government had stepped in with FloodRe almost a decade before when the risk had been deemed too high to be normally insurable. This had become an increasing problem as the continued impact of climate change had repeatedly caused flash flooding.

The level of sophistication of the underwriting process was such that not only could assessment be made of ground levels and topography in the case of flood plains, but insurers were also able to model the impact of flash rainstorms taking into account the geology of the ground and potential water table fluctuations.

One of the bigger flooding issues came from overflowing of surface water drains. Over-development in many urban locations had meant that the drainage infrastructure had reached capacity and even relatively modest amounts of rainfall could lead to backing up of drains and localized flooding. Pressures on costs had also led to reduced drainage maintenance which had aggravated the problem. Earlier efforts to create natural drainage to avoid flooding, so-called 'SUDS,' or 'sustainable urban drainage systems,' had not become popular despite their natural attraction. The approach had not adequately resolved the problem of inadequate drainage even if other benefits such as reduced water pollution were achieved.

So as cars and people became 'connected,' then the advent of the connected home was simply a matter of time. The initial forays into connectivity related to power, heating, security and lighting. The ability to turn on the heating from a distance had become desirable as fuel costs increased. The adverse economic climate had created some social problems leading to a short-term surge in burglary and property theft. Homeowners were reassured by being able to check on the status of their alarm system from the luxury of their android device. They were even able to see whether the home had been entered or not, even if there was little that could be done about it by that time. Cuts in policing resources had also meant that domestic burglary had become less of a priority for them.

The digital home allowed all manner of insurance-related benefits. If a sudden reduction in water pressure was detected consistent with a water leak or burst pipe then not only would the water system be turned off automatically, but restoration experts would be automatically mobilized to be in a position to carry out drying. Insurers had long recognized the relationship between claims cost and early intervention and were increasingly keen to start the drying process sooner rather than later. Similarly, with smoke alarms where action had not been taken by the homeowner to disable the alarm (and in doing so demonstrate that the 'smoke event' was under control), an alert would be simultaneously sent to the insurer, the fire brigade and also the restoration specialists. The linkage between smoke alarms, insurance and extinguishment services felt to some like a modern equivalent of the system of insurance firemarks in the 18th century, where the attending brigade would only take action if the appropriate mark was on the outside of the affected building.

The claims process had also been transformed. On the domestic front, the role of the claims adjuster had evolved and now was mainly concerned with specialist and commercial incidents. The loss of so-called 'volume claims' due to increased automation, which were a cash cow for many independent adjusting firms, had forced industry restructuring and the creation of new business models.

As there were more, older insurance professionals looking for limited part-time work, this had allowed the major insurers and independent adjusting firms to now have a representative in each area, sometimes each village or district. These local representatives would be 'on call' in the event of an insurable incident taking place. They would be able to quickly visit and using effective imagery would transmit pictures back to the insurance command center, where a trained expert would advise online the extent of any coverage and what else might need to be done other than involving restoration experts.

In the case of burglary or theft, records of high value contents were already electronically held by the insurer and proof of ownership was immediate. In earlier days there had been a bit of a problem where hackers had created 'phantom' assets on the insurer's site, and had claimed for stolen items which had never existed or had been sold. This had been an ingenious attempt at fraud but one which National Cyber Security had passively detected, advising the Special Investigations Units of insurance companies accordingly.

The Special Investigations Unit of the insurer had also evolved. Once the domain of retired policemen, it had been transformed into a highly technical and extremely well-funded center of excellence. For some time, insurers had been able to figure out which policyholders were most likely to engage in fraudulent behavior – from misdescription at the point of policy inception, through to the claims process itself either by way of opportunistic or organized behavior.

The traumas resulting from the economic crises of the previous decade had never gone away – if anything they were worse. Analytically fueled automation had resulted in job losses amongst blue collar workers and left many of the traditional white collar professionals behind. Full-time employment had decreased although there were more less well paid part-time roles available. The lost power of employee unions and their reduced activity had meant that there was little scope for fighting against change. In fact, apart from isolated incidents, there hadn't been any major employee strikes for a decade.

By 2025 insurers were able to predict whether an individual had a propensity to be fraudulent or not and to price the risk accordingly. At the point of claim, insurers remained reluctant to decline a claim based on analytical insight alone but had a higher level of confidence in their decision to investigate with more care. The consequence was three-fold:

1. Special Investigations Units were much more efficient in their operations.
2. Investigation techniques used were more sophisticated and lent themselves to a younger Intelligence Officer, rather than a retired policeman.
3. Insurers were able to act with more confidence with non-fraudulent claims, improving the friction-free process and reducing cost and time. Customer experience as a result had reached an all-time high.

All this had come about through additional investment by insurers in the area of fraud management, an area previously considered to be a relatively niche part of the business.

On a contingency basis, the potential need for alternative accommodation as a result of serious property damage would be automatically handled. The days of the policyholder needing to find their own alternative accommodation had long since passed. Strategic partnerships between insurers, hotels and rental agencies allowed accommodation need and room availability to be automatically matched

The transition to the digital home had not been easy but was encouraged by the premium discounts which insurers offered to homeowners for becoming connected. This was no different to the approach taken by auto insurers and healthcare providers who also discounted their premiums provided that the car or person was 'wired up.' It had been relatively easy to create 'digital homes' in the case of new build properties where the changes in building codes and regulations meant that the devices had to be included as part of the design. It was a little trickier with existing properties but government incentives and utility providers led the way. As the insurance ecosystem continued to mature, new and previously unheard-of partnerships began to emerge where a collaborative approach started to provide a win-win for all concerned including the homeowner.

The management of claims incidents had been affected by the increased use of remote devices, not only in the property but also outside with the use of remote imagery and aerial devices such as drones. Redundant military technology had become increasingly available for commercial use and high definition photography helped insurers understand the scale and extent of a problem. Even virtual 3-D imagery was possible as cameras 'shot' the same property from different angles. The computer was now able to reconcile location with direction to give a 3-D effect. The need to visit the site became less and less critical, especially where the main problem was external damage such as to roofing.

The management of major incidents such as floods had also gone through a step change. Insurers already had the ability to anticipate weather conditions and send an 'added value' warning to their policyholders but sometimes this hadn't been enough and for some homes damage was inevitable. Insurers not only had the capability to understand how much of their book of business was affected, but also what reserve they might usefully hold, and whether their reinsurance arrangements were likely to be triggered (or indeed, if they were adequate).

The ability of claims systems to anticipate likely loss costs had developed throughout the decade. Insurers now knew what the likely property repair cost would be if a property was flooded to a particular depth of water, and increasingly managed the claims process by the management of outliers. In other words, if the claims cost fell outside the anticipated estimate, then it would be investigated. Inside that agreed financial threshold it would be rapidly processed. The system had worked much better in those locations where there was greater standardization of property.

By 2025 it had become almost impossible to buy a white-label device such as a fridge, freezer, or washing machine or any form of communication device like a TV without having embedded connectivity. Even in 2015, the ability of a fridge to identify the number of eggs in the tray had become a reality although these gimmicks were not in common use. Homeowners had not yet reached the point where the fridge would automatically re-order foodstuffs but by 2025 that was close to being on the horizon.

More importantly for insurers, household equipment had the capability to self-diagnose failure. More often than not, failure was electronic rather than mechanical. The appliance itself would trigger an insurance-backed warranty claim. Repairs would be carried out by approved agents of the manufacturer thereby ensuring the warranty was restored. The by-product of this was that the smaller independent repairer had been largely driven out of business, although in fairness the technology had moved on to such a level as to make it harder and harder for them to understand and attend to the problem.

The first mover in this 'integrated appliance' space had been a major Asian manufacturer with an insurance sidearm. Increasingly, appliance brand names had partnered with financial services providers to create bundled solutions. It was a win-win for everyone. The appliance manufacturer ensured that repair components were original parts, the insurer had created a new distribution channel and the homeowner benefited from improved service.

What became especially intriguing was the ability of the appliance to self-diagnose that there were issues in its operational performance suggesting an imminent if not an actual failure. This prediction of anticipated failure took some getting used to. Most households had historically 'reacted' to a breakdown of their appliance rather than anticipating failure and avoiding it. As with many issues of change, the challenge was one of cultural perception and changes to traditional behavior rather than the capability of the technology.

13.3   COMMERCIAL INSURANCE – ANALYTICALLY TRANSFORMED

With 60% of commercial claims historically taking up to three years to settle and placing enormous pressure on affected businesses, the increased use of analytics by expert claims staff and adjusters allowed claims for business interruption (formerly known as consequential loss) to be settled in a fraction of the time previously taken.

By 2025 many large and even mid-sized businesses had already become accustomed to advanced methods of financial performance management (FPM), using these tools not only to understand why they had obtained the results achieved but also gaining greater insight into product and channel profitability and being able to model anticipated outcomes. It had become essential that insurers and adjusters were up to speed with these not-so-new techniques.

Complications had also emerged regarding the increased take-up of what were called 'zero hours' contracts in terms of what an organization's actual ongoing costs might be. Zero hours contracts had been a legitimate (although for some a slightly doubtful) response by employers to the management of supply/demand imbalance in the workforce. This approach to employment avoided guaranteeing employees any minimum hours of work per week. However, it equally reflected the approach of many older workers who were less inclined to adopt a full-time or even regular part-time role if it resulted in personal inflexibility and adversely affected their 'work-life' balance.

Most advanced financial performance management tools already had a predictive component and had the capability to 'sandbox,' or create models of business scenarios. By insurers using the same tools and capabilities, it had been possible to create a much more accurate and speedy assessment of the likely loss of revenue and therefore loss of gross profit on which basis the policy normally provided cover.

Being able to more rapidly calculate financial loss with greater accuracy also allowed insurers either to resolve complex financial claims more quickly or to make advanced or 'interim' payments with more confidence. The beneficial impact on affected commercial policyholders had been substantial and they had now been able to restore their business more quickly.

As in many other professions impacted by the advent of more sophisticated analytics, these new capabilities had a knock-on effect on the claims management and adjusting professions who had to move on from the traditional spreadsheet analysis of interruption claims to more advanced methods. An understanding of policy terms and conditions remained critical – how else would a claim be 'adjusted' within the terms and conditions of the wording? But now the claims professional needed to be at the same level of skill and competence as the analytical skills in the claimant's own Office of Finance.

Greater transparency and the use of standardized analytical methodologies also allowed swifter and less contentious negotiation. This was just as well as by 2025 the marketplace had become even more economically volatile than just a decade before. For a business with global reach and dependent on global distribution and a global supply chain, some of the bigger issues to resolve for insurers were more in the nature of the impact of macro and micro economics. How might an entity which was out of business in full or part for an extended period cope with such global volatility? Invariably there was always likely to be some degree of uncertainty in calculating what might be the final loss, but analytics had significantly reduced the degree of doubt in the calculation.

Within a further five years, sophisticated algorithms would also be created which allowed the claims department to 'ask' the cognitive system, using natural language rather than coding, what the extent of the loss might be (relative to the cover in place) and the degree of confidence in the calculation.

Better insight into consequential or business interruption losses also allowed insurers and businesses to better consider the cost benefit of accelerating the repair or rebuilding work. This allowed them to fund the cost of materials at premium prices and where appropriate encourage overtime working to ensure earlier completion. The global nature of supply chains and the 'just in time' approach to manufacture meant that the cost of steel and therefore the cost of building repair, for example, might be impacted by other international construction projects. Whilst the Internet of Things had provided more data and insight, at the same time the degree of connectivity and the global supply chain had also led to greater interdependencies.

In the same way that many insurers had developed supply chain management as a core competence in the mid-1990s and later, insurers had also increasingly understood the impact of commodity prices on repair and claims. Some sophisticated insurers with significant buying power had started to use 'hedging' of material costs. Although initially considered as a claims cost management approach, it also provided a useful alternative to investment management when market conditions continued to fail to provide adequate investment yield.

It was not only in the area of claims that change had taken place. The risk inspector had more information about the property, risk category and policyholder history than ever before. The use of remote imagery had become commonplace. Where there was any degree of uncertainty perhaps due to inaccessibility it was now possible to use a remotely controlled drone to provide a clearer picture.

Recommendations by risk inspectors such as storing warehouse materials a certain distance above ground floor level or the maintenance of sprinklers were more easy to check through the use of remote devices. Where such requirements took the form of a warranty, endorsement or special condition to the policy, it allowed insurers to automatically see whether a breach had taken place and whether this breach was material to the damage occurring. Insurers were also able to identify in real time where a breach was taking place and proactively advise the policyholder, even before any loss had occurred.

Such remote devices were not intended as a punitive measure. In fact, it was just as much in the interests of the policyholder to ensure that all warranties were being complied with. The degree of operational interlock between insurers and their clients had now reached a point whereby insurers were no long simply the carriers of risk but also played an effective part in risk or loss mitigation. Aligning such operations to predictive maintenance of sprinklers and other systems further reinforced that now-matured relationship.

Many insurance brokers through whom most of commercial insurance is placed had been relatively slow to take on board the broader analytics agenda, with the exception of those providing risk management services. In much the same way as adjusters had transformed, the broker community had increasingly started to use analytics to understand their client's maximum probable loss and risk exposures, and to optimize insurance and reinsurance arrangements.

13.4 SPECIALIST RISKS AND DEEPER INSIGHT

Insurers of 'Specialist Risks' such as terrorism, marine, aviation and 'high net worth' for example had been relatively slow to take on the topic of Big Data and the application of analytics, having been mainly of the view that they were already well placed to have deep understanding about the nature of the risk and how best this could be written. Their view was that data and analytics were most effective when applying the rules of 'big numbers,' i.e. volume claims, and that this was a different marketplace to the niche specialist risk industry.

For many their view was changed due to a small number of severe incidents which had not been anticipated and had forced them to consider a shift in their thinking.

The challenge of terrorism in major cities had existed for many decades but the capability and inventiveness of the perpetrators had increased bringing the risk to a higher level. As a result, the potential severity had become much greater. Insurers had already modeled their risk on a major single incident and its impact on neighboring buildings, and had used a combination of analytics and location to anticipate and avoid risk accumulation.

Terrorists had however increasingly recognized the much more disruptive influence of a number of simultaneously timed incidents in multiple locations. Such an approach was much more difficult to model and whilst insurers would inevitably view this as several incidents rather than one (even if planned by the same group), this had made the prediction of probable maximum loss much more challenging.

Some experts had even gone so far as to suggest that by adopting an approach of multiple simultaneous incidents, some portfolios of property had become almost uninsurable. As a result of this insurers had increasingly worked with their policyholders to improve the management of risk and had become proactive by helping them in the design and maintenance of their buildings and other assets. This had resulted in specialist insurers and some major brokers adding property design as a new core capability to mitigate terrorism losses. The relatively small number of reputable expert companies who already were very busy safeguarding public buildings found their value quickly increasing. Those specialty insurers and brokers who acquired such expertise were able to create significant differentiation in the marketplace.

Elsewhere major engineering practices with these skills also found themselves forming strategic partnerships with insurers and developers where such relationships had not previously existed. The major recognizable trend of specialty insurance by the mid-2020s had been one of new collaborations emerging between previously disparate types of organizations.

For the marine market, insurers had also recognized the issue of risk accumulation and had been able to use special analytics to understand where insured vessels and cargo were at any time. The use of RFID (Radio frequency identification) tagging had allowed them to monitor movement and insurers had become more proactive in directing cargo traffic. This was another shift from insurers being reactive to becoming proactive, and was in effect the marine equivalent of what had been seen in auto telematics in the earlier part of the previous decade.

Aviation insurers looking not only to understand the cause of failure but to reduce risk had also identified that they could use analytics to better understand maintenance schedules and more deeply embed the concepts of predictive maintenance into their insurance proposition. Passenger airlines and major fleets already had a rigorous approach to the issue of maintenance but this had not been as rigorously reflected in smaller private aircraft.

For high net worth insurers, the ability to create a secure online record of valuables had proved useful for insurers in terms of insight regarding value at risk and had allowed insurers to better understand the impact of fluctuations in value of individual items. This had also helped in the assessment of a loss where there were poor records or no record of purchase, or perhaps a property had suffered a major devastating loss such as in the case of a fire.

An unwanted by-product of this approach had been that cyber-criminals had identified a new opportunity for identifying the most appropriate targets for crime. Beyond this, developments in nano-technology had led to the creation of an extremely thin and undetectable membrane which could be applied over expensive items, and which allowed them to be tracked in case of loss. However, the take-up had been affected by valuers indicating that this impaired the value of the item itself. Nevertheless, insurers had increasingly started to insist on it as a condition of cover.

Those policyholders who were sufficiently attractive as targets to merit kidnap cover suffered the disadvantage and indignity of needing to accept the installation of a small tracking device discreetly installed under the skin. This was not hugely different to what had been implanted in their dogs over a decade previously as a response to the theft of pedigree animals.

13.5   2025: TRANSFORMATION OF THE LIFE AND PENSIONS INDUSTRY

The link between lifestyle and longevity had always been recognized by insurers. The age of data and analytics had extended the desire by insurers to influence personal behavior in terms of exercise, diet and even sleeping patterns.

There were many people who viewed this intervention as a step too far but were eventually convinced by insurers being able to add additional value in terms of premium reductions, which were now being collected on a much more frequent basis. The premium increasingly reflected policyholder 'behavior.' Evidence of insufficient exercise alone had been enough to push the premium up. By 2025, annual health checks had become a mandatory part of the life and pension process. This comprised firstly an online test followed if necessary by a personal assessment and interview.

Insurers had increasingly been able to collect data on the individual through multiple personal devices. Insurers in the US had been early movers and this approach spread as devices became more commonly embedded into more attractive jewelry and watches. There were always those individuals who thought that they could fiddle the system but sophisticated analytics allowed unusual behavior to be identified as an outlier and managed accordingly. It seemed that the challenge of fraudulent behavior had never gone away – it had just entered the new cyber era.

One issue which had prompted considerable debate had been the question of who owned the data. Cyber-security and data ownership had remained high on the agenda and was to continue to do so for the foreseeable future. Was the data owned by the individual, the insurer, the device owner or even the manufacturer? What was the position if an individual moved their insurer either by design or as a result of a new employer who had provided a company scheme and had changed the arrangements?

A series of high profile legal cases with global implications had also helped in setting the ground rules, as well as the impact of local regulators. It had become clear that the new era of data and analytics had forced many types of organizations, including insurers, to re-evaluate their stance on the collection and use of data and information. Regulators in some US states had created the precedent by restricting the use of data to that purpose specifically obtained unless the customer gave express permission.

By 2025 the issue of general longevity of lifespan had placed governments under significant financial strain. Some governments had not created a pot of money to fund state pensions but had relied on money coming into the system from the existing workforce. This was in effect a sort of 'Ponzi Scheme' (named after Charles Ponzi who used the technique in the 1920s – although Charles Dickens of somewhat older pedigree had also written about it in *Martin Chuzzlewit*). Ponzi had operated an investment scheme which relied on money coming into the system to pay benefits to existing members.

Despite the age of retirement increasing where it was now possible to work into your late seventies or older, there were fewer people in full-time employment. So-called 'zero hours' contracts had become more widely used by employers to manage workload fluctuations. As a result the individual had become more dependent on insurers to fund their lifestyle into older age, supplemented by informal work arrangements, but also in some cases it provided scope for contributions into the insurance 'pot.'

For many the nature of work had also changed. Analytics and rules-based automation of many processes had largely eradicated the blue collar worker. A major divide had emerged between white collar workers who focused on thought leadership (and of whom there were fewer) and other less-qualified workers in the service industry. Manufacturing was now largely carried out in Asia, Latin America and especially Africa.

Some life and pension insurers had also embraced the health insurance industry. Like life and pensions, health insurance was heavily regulated and contained many of the same characteristics relative to personal behavior. Health insurance had also gone through significant growth as a result of the increased pressures on state-funded treatment. Consumer sentiment reflected the delays in treatment and poorer service. In the US, 'Affordable Care' had become the genie that could not be put back into the bottle although had operationally settled down from the early days.

For life and pension insurers, their main focus had been on their relationship with the customer. Improved segmentation had reaffirmed that 'one size did not fit all' as different customer demographics had quite different purchasing and loyalty characteristics. Younger people still had little interest in pension provision for what was, for them, a long time in the future. Linkage of pension products with other trend-setting brands had helped but not to a significant degree. 'Nike Life Insurance' had proved to be one of the more successful due to the strong brand and interlock between longevity and fitness.

For the older generation, i.e., those closer to retirement or in a position to withdraw funds, insurers were concerned not only with customer retention but also with being able to provide online visibility of the available funding benefit upon policy maturity. Insurers wanted to be able to give relatively realistic assessment of benefit by the policyholder changing their risk appetite and benefit timings. One solution to this problem was found in the use of cognitive analytics which by 2025 had increasingly become mainstream in providing investment advice. Customers also now had the opportunity to draw down partial benefits with flexible timing and at an amount which was most convenient, as opposed to a fixed amount at regular intervals, but with greater insight into the consequences.

The other big issue which dominated the thinking of life insurers was that of a pandemic either by natural, accidental or deliberate causation, and the risk of widespread death within a short period. Fortunately, the increased use of data and analytics in both the surveillance and medical industries had significantly lessened the likelihood of a pandemic but the possibility had remained.

More accurate modeling had helped insurers better understand their exposure and as in the case of Ebola and Zika, government agencies had become much better at contagion control. Even so there was an operational gap between analytics and immunization. The Ebola scare of 2014–15 had led insurers to state that even in a worst-case scenario, the scale of any losses would be 'manageable.' Some however thought that this viewpoint had led the industry into a sense of false security.

13.6 OUTSOURCING AND THE MOVE AWAY FROM NON-CORE ACTIVITIES

For those insurers of all types with critical mass, most non-core activities remained mainly under direct operational control as an in-house function, either in full or in part. This included services relative to First Notification of Loss (FNOL), inspection and adjusting services, payments, and even some elements of claims management. The impact of taxation on these services was also a key element in their consideration.

For others, the ability of insurers to more effectively outsource non-core activities had been transformed by the extension of third-party suppliers such as loss adjusters to become part of the 'virtual enterprise.' More immediate and transparent data was increasingly being shared with insurers so that the insurer had high real-time visibility of supplier workloads, performance and other critical KPIs. This improved control of their suppliers by insurers had been achieved without compromising any 'lock-in' between the relationship of the insurers and the third party, providing the insurer with flexibility to switch suppliers in the event of non-performance.

This improved analytical visibility allowed individual insurers to better create and monitor service level differentiation. In doing so they were able to retain competitive advantage in service delivery. In addition, insurers no longer had the burden of needing to consider their return on capital expenditure (ROCE) but rather could operate a much more flexible operating model. This was also helped by the emergence of the 'Super Supplier.'

There were still some insurers who operated a hybrid model comprising a mix of insourced and outsourced services. One main difference which had emerged was that where previously there had been a degree of (arguably unfair) selection to keep in-house services fully utilized, it was now possible to more accurately benchmark comparable internal versus external services.

Because of this there had been a significant increase in the number, size and type of outsourcing companies who themselves had embraced data and analytics as a way of improving efficiency and creating greater profit. The shedding of non-core activities by existing insurers had also allowed them to focus more on core issues of risk and capital management, product development and agile innovation.

New entrants to the insurance marketplace also started to emerge more quickly and create greater competition and increase choice. Increased competition between insurers had led to continued softening of premiums which created yet further cost pressure, forcing them to look even harder at reducing their operating costs.

As analytics had become more complex and volumes of data had increased, some insurers had also been prepared even to outsource their analytical capability. This had increasingly shown itself in the form of 'Analytics as a Service.' The ability of the insurance user at any point of usage within the organization, subject to appropriate authority, to interrogate the analytical system in natural language had remained. However, the role of procuring, maintaining and upgrading the analytical system including all the hardware and software had increasingly lent itself to outsourcing. This had the added benefit of transferring a capital expense to an operating expense.

Whilst larger complex insurers with critical mass had retained analytical capability primarily as a form of internal shared service, they had increasingly viewed this not only as a cost center but also as a potential profit center. Sharing this with others was attractive to non-competing insurers. The nervousness of unwittingly sharing customer data with competitors was sufficient to cause worry, but operational and cost benefit made the use of shared services compelling.

13.7   THE RISE OF THE SUPER SUPPLIER

As insurers continually sought to reduce their operating costs and where possible to adapt their business model, one impact was continued pressure on their supply chain. This typically affected loss adjusters, inspectors, body shops, restoration contractors and others. Where term contracts remained, this pressure continued and revealed itself in lower unit rates and volume discounts. Rather oddly, despite all these processes and controls the cost of repair had actually increased.

Insurers had started to participate in a 'Claims Exchange' where claims reinstatement work was offered to the supplier community, and vetted suppliers were able to bid to do individual pieces of work, with their price reflected in the supplier's own appetite for business. The advantage for all parties had been to optimize the cost of the work based on market conditions. The main 'downside' had been a reduction in some elements of customer service differentiation. Promises to make the customer central to the proposition had been outweighed by the need for greater profitability.

Regardless of which approach was adopted, members of the supply chain also sought to reduce their own operating cost. Often this was by outsourcing to sub-contractors which increasingly removed the insurer further and further away from the point of delivery of the service. This was not a new phenomenon but one which consistently impacted on the customer experience.

It had become critical for suppliers providing an outsourced service to insurers to have analytical capability. Whilst at first this had required relatively cash-strapped suppliers to invest in technology, the use of 'analytics as a service' had also gained in appeal. This allowed the supplier to improve analytical capability to an equivalent level to that of their insurer clients but as an operating cost rather than capital expenditure. The ability of suppliers to be 'analytical' had become a key differentiator in a competitive marketplace.

A new question therefore had arisen on insurers' procurement documents, typically: 'Please provide details of your analytical capability and any outsourced analytics provider you are using.' This had indirectly led to the recruitment of 'analysts' within the supply chain, adding to the shortage of adequately qualified and experienced people.

One impact of this change was that suppliers themselves not only needed to create new analytical competence but also were being increasingly asked by their clients to collect more information at all the key data points. There was an operational cost to this, which suppliers had to absorb to remain 'in the game.' This analytical competence went far beyond analysis by spreadsheet but rather reflected a much more mature analytical and reporting environment, including predictive and cognitive intelligence in the suppliers' own systems.

As a result of these new capabilities, suppliers could more effectively triage their service. Typically for restoration companies involved in water or fire damage, this had allowed them to operationally engage more intimately with insurers. More importantly they could transform the service which the insurance industry provided to customers.

Ironically, for a process that was fundamentally driven by insurers in an attempt to reduce cost, this had led to suppliers enjoying both the autonomy and respect that they had sought for three decades. Analytics had created a tighter interlock with their insurer clients without either's position being compromised. At the end of the day these changes were creating a step change in improvement in customer service.

As the development of cognitive analytics became increasingly infused into industries, processes and individuals, the concept of 'contextual analytics' became ever more important. Contextual analytics is a form of analytics which gives greater understanding of outcomes by placing them in the context of external circumstances. This includes macro and micro economic factors, competitor activity, market behaviors and consumer sentiment. This broader viewpoint had led to insurers and their super suppliers gaining a better perspective into why they had achieved certain outcomes. In the words of celebrated MIT professor and serial inventor Alan Kay, 'Context is worth 80 IQ points.' On reflection, it was disappointing that it had taken so long for this particular penny to drop.

NOTES

1. Burke, Edmund. Letter to a Member of the National Assembly, 1791.
2. Churchill, Sir Winston Leonard Spencer. Speech, House of Commons. February 27, 1945.

CHAPTER 14

Conclusions and Reflections

When Tom Peters in his book *Re-Imagine*[1] invited us to think differently about ourselves and our business environment, he might have had the world of Big Data and Analytics in mind. His book was written in 2003 when the Big Data story was still in its earliest stages and many industries were still in the relatively dark ages of the information revolution. He described a future upheaval in the work done by blue collar workers and placed a spotlight on 'White Collar world' which talked about 'automation of white-collar business processes within the firm and amongst its business partners.'

Beyond this he also painted a picture of a world where a micro-chip would replace a $35,000-a-year staffer who does mundane paper processing by automating the system, and even threatens the $150,000-a-year manager that the £35k staffer used to report to. It is easy to be cynical as predictions can be either right or wrong. Correct predictions are viewed with reverence; wrong ones are explained away or just forgotten. But Peters went even further when he described (in 2003) that the next 25 years would bring 'astounding' advances for the organization and for individuals. That was over 10 years ago and if he is to be proved right then there are only 10 years or so left.

The potential contrasts between the old world and the new are significant. Each represents a sea change in thinking, operations and behaviors, e.g., as shown in Table 14.1. Collectively they comprise an industrial tsunami.

TABLE 14.1   Insurance analytics – was and will be

Was	Will be
Spreadsheet	Insight as a service
Mainframe	Cloud
IT as a threat	IT as the key enabler
Professionally qualified	Technologically enhanced

The use of enterprise-wide analytics is set to transform the way in which work is done, how employees relate to each other, how they depend on each other, and this will all be underpinned by the Big Data and Analytics agenda. Before very long, insurance businesses will have obtained mastery of the data under their direct control and sitting within their own organization. Beyond this they will have gained control over data available from their virtual enterprise, for example from their supply chain.

As a result, insurers will have fundamentally changed their relationship with their suppliers from one of suspicion and concern to one of trust and empowerment. Elsewhere other data will have become cheap and increasingly available, although some unique data will still command a price. Perhaps the true value will be in the data itself, with the analytics itself coming free of charge as a means to access the data. (As a comparison, imagine taxi rides being free of charge and solely funded by advertisements inside the cab.) Interaction with data and analytics in natural language will exponentially increase access to the common user. The inevitable impact of all this will be one of improving customer engagement and service. Because of this, these impending changes should not be viewed as being threatening to insurers but rather as a catalyst to transformation.

What is currently considered as cutting edge will increasingly become the norm. Advanced analytics including forms of artificial intelligence will one day become commoditized. As with all new technologies it will not be a matter of the technology itself but rather the manner in which it is applied. Perhaps even the way these new technologies are operationalized will be quite different to the traditional ways that are currently known and understood. It is not simply a matter of using technology to optimize existing processes but rather that entirely new workflow processes and ecosystems will start to emerge.

Insurers will increasingly evolve from remedying losses and being the providers of compensation to a model whereby loss prevention and mitigation (as far as practically possible) becomes a core competence. Some insurers and brokers already practice degrees of risk management especially in the commercial sector, but this is often seen as a side issue and in any event the benefits of avoiding losses are sometimes difficult to quantify. How will this approach extend to the life and pensions sector, and how also will it change personal lines insurance? Perhaps analytics will ultimately help the industry gain a better understanding of the true consequence of an event through using 'what if' scenarios. Such modeling will help insurers gain a better understanding of the impact of avoiding or mitigating a risk.

Traditional hierarchies will also start to change. If knowledge is no longer power, then relationships will inevitably change. As Rick Levine said in his internet commentary, 'Hyperlinks subvert hierarchy.'[2]

Insurance organizations are on the cusp of obtaining incredible improvements in service and efficiency, typically:

- Customized insurance cover
- Alignment of insurance cover with lifestyle needs
- Flexibility of benefit, not rigidity
- Seamless integration with the supply chain
- Absolute consistency of offering, regardless of channel.

Beyond all these, the novelty of technology will wear off. All of us will come to expect high levels of service from future insurers which today we might view as extraordinary.

As the use of customer analytics increases to enable the industry to better understand the customer, it is important to recognize that the customer is also likely to change. If insurers are thinking about the 'age' of data and analytics, then equally the 'age' of the informed customer has yet to fully show itself. Customers are unlikely to be prepared to be pushed around, will be less tolerant of poor service and more likely to share their experiences through social media. As a result, insurers cannot afford to be complacent.

Without significant industry consolidation and restructuring, the current relative over-capacity of the 'mature' marketplace means that insurers are ultimately unlikely to remain in the driving seat. One impact is that the insurance industry will be increasingly measured against other industries and not just against itself. The recent acquisition of shares of an insurance company by major Chinese retailer Alibaba, and the increasing activity of Asian technology giants in the financial services sector including insurance are bound to 'put the cat amongst the pigeons.'

14.1   THE BREADTH OF THE CHALLENGE

Analytics provide point solutions to many particular problems but beyond this, they provide a different and more insightful view in order to drive operational change, reduce risk and improve profitability.

Insurers who think in terms of a series of analytical point solutions which they hope to join up at some time in the distant future are perhaps no better than a railroad company building the stations and hoping that at some time in the future a railway line might join them together. The reality is that each element of the insurance 'value chain' is irrevocably linked to all other parts of the insurance business, for example:

- Customer retention is as much based on personal experience as on price.
- Underwriting is based on the cost experience of the insurer, which links to the effectiveness of the claims management process.
- Fraud is often linked to distrust of the insurer as a result of lack of transparency rather than just the behavior of isolated or even organized claimants.

Were an organization to place data and analytics at the heart of its proposition, then perhaps the insurance business would be organized differently:

- Functions would be built around the data and analytics, rather than practices being dependent on derived insights.
- Employees would have a different training and background, and be much more technologically savvy.
- The customer would be very close to, if not at the heart of, the insurance business.

Transparency will also be transformative both within and external to the organization. Insurers will always have an absolute duty to their stockholders to remain profitable, and to the regulator to remain solvent but in the future will this also look different in some way? Perhaps with better insight, insurers will turn out to be cleverer than the regulators. Maybe in some cases that is already happening.

Another big issue to be addressed is how established insurers will react to 'analytically orientated' new entrants to the market. These newcomers will have sufficient know-how to satisfy regulators and commissioners as well as greater customer insight and an ability to manage the analytical maze. Emerging new North American insurers such as 'Lemonade' and 'Guevara' threaten to disturb the status quo of insurance as much as Uber has done to the taxi industry. Perhaps the traditional market will fight back. Cities created 'Uber' equivalents using licensed taxi cabs and in doing so used modern ideas to transform their own operating model.

There will also be 'wild cards' such as Blockchain which will fracture the traditional insurance distribution model, perhaps in a way that no-one really yet understands. The whole Blockchain model of a 'distributed ledger' approach – the creation of a central but relatively unowned and unadministered database – seems at face value to have enormous potential to 'rock the boat' in terms of distribution. But, as was recently commented, is this akin to 'putting a rocket under a chariot'?

14.2   FINAL THOUGHTS

Even as this chapter is written, it is possible to see change to the insurance industry almost in 'real time.' Online commentary such as Insurance Entertainment[3] which describes itself as 'The Skinny' – which in street language refers to 'what's hot and cool' – spills the beans on changes on what seems to be a daily basis. To many observers it looks like there has been an increase in the speed of change. What has happened to an industry which almost prided itself on its conservatism and steadiness? Did it just reach the tipping point and then all of a sudden start to transform?

Whilst it is tempting to suggest that data and analytics are the sole causes of change, the insurance industry has always existed in a volatile external environment, be it due to weather conditions, economic conditions or increasingly the impact of new risks. The effect of new entrants, competition and regulation will also continue to force change, as well as the influence of 'bright young things' who enter the insurance industry recognizing that there is money to be made.

To what degree will the insurance industry change as it absorbs new thinking from other sectors or professionals? It's not difficult to increasingly recognize the impact of retailers on the insurance proposition but what will happen when completely new approaches are brought into the fold? How might the influence of behavioral experts supplemented by analytical insight affect the underwriting process?

To what degree (if at all) can the lack of trust of insurers by policyholders be restored as a result of greater transparency? Does one of the real problems of trust rest in the interpretation of the small print of policy wordings at the point of claim, as the customer strives for the lowest possible cost by accepting restrictive coverage and in the end doesn't get what they thought they had paid for? Data and analytics may prove to be many things to the insurance industry but are not a panacea for all industry challenges.

Analytics and the digital insurance customer will increasingly be closely intertwined but perhaps the hope of creating an entirely paperless insurance environment may prove to be one more fallacy of the technological age. People use computers to create and amend documents but at the end of the day still print them out on paper. According to some experts[4] this is because:

- There is a linkage between reading and annotating in that many who read tend to underline or annotate articles as they read them.
- People are better at organizing paper than organizing electronic files.
- People often read multiple documents at the same time – and lay them out side by side.

■ There is greater physical comfort in reading from paper rather than online, especially in the case of lengthy documents.

Even in a transformed analytics-fueled insurance future, the industry may still find it difficult to move away from the quaintness of using paper (even if the manner of distribution is changing from hard copy to soft copy which in many cases is still printed out).

There is no shortage of news and thought leadership, and the challenge for many is where to start. Even those who have started their analytical journey might privately confess to being overwhelmed with information. On any given day there are multiple white papers created and distributed, news feeds distributed and examples of innovation shared. Many of these are online and a list of suggested sites is included in Appendices D and E. Some of these sites can be accessed free of charge, others require subscription. This appended list is not comprehensive and is offered without recommendation but may provide some options to the reader. Attempting to record all these new ideas on paper is difficult but it is hoped that a publication such as this will at least provide a place to start.

Change can be unsettling, perhaps especially so for the insurance industry which is still in mid-stream as it grasps new ideas and technologies. This is not an insurance-specific issue, as US President Obama commented in 2015:[5]

Part of people's concern is just the sense that around the world the old order isn't holding and we're not quite yet to where we need to be in terms of a new order that's based on a different set of principles.

In a recent presentation at Lloyds of London,[6] Don Glaser, President of Marsh & McLennan who are international insurance brokers, emphasized that insurance is an industry which 'offers not only freedom from the financial and emotional burdens of loss, but also freedom for the pursuit of innovation, investment and the creation of value.'

The insurance industry as a whole remains set to have a glorious future, enabled and not threatened by data and analytics. Effective use of these capabilities based on firm and secure technology platforms, and with data-driven leadership, will allow the industry to continue with its core functions of 'enabling economic growth, the taking of risk and innovation.'

Despite such turbulent times, we can at least be certain of one thing: that the ghosts of the founding fathers of the industry sitting in their angelic coffee shops in the sky will continue to look down and ensure that the basic principles of insurance created over 300 years ago remain intact in this new transformative era. All this is no big deal, they might say. After all, hasn't data and analytics in one form or another been at the absolute heart of the Real Business of insurance since the insurance industry began?

NOTES

1. Peters, Tom. *Re-imagine!: Business Excellence in a Disruptive Age.* London: Dorling Kindersley Ltd, 2003.
2. Levine, Rick, Locke, Christopher, Searles, Doc and Weinberger, David. 'The Cluetrain Manifesto.' Published ft.com, 2000.
3. http://insuranceentertainment.com/ (accessed May 17, 2016).

4. Liu, Ziming. *Paper to Digital: Documents in the Modern Age.* Westport, CT: Libraries Unlimited, 2008, pp. 142–149.

5. Watson, Paul Joseph. 'Obama Calls for Collectivized New World Order.' Published by Infowars, 2014. http://www.infowars.com/obama-calls-for-collectivized-new-world-order/ (accessed January 5, 2016).

6. Glaser, Dan. Presentation to Insurance Institute of London by Dan Glaser, President and Chief Executive of Marsh and McLennan, November 9, 2015 at Lloyds Old Library. (Reported in the Chartered Insurance Institute Journal, December 2015, pp. 34, 35.)

Recommended Reading

Biddle, P.G. *Tree Root Damage to Buildings. Volume 1 Causes, Diagnosis and Remedy.* Wantage: Willowmead Publishing, 1998.

Blackstaff, Michael. *BCS Finance for IT Decision Makers.* British Computer Society. London: BCS, new edition, 2006.

Burdett, Arnold, Bowen, Dan, et al. *BCS Glossary of Computing and ICT.* British Computer Society. London: BCS, The Chartered Institute for IT, 13th edition, 2013.

Chartered Insurance Institute. *Centenary Future Risk Series.* London: Chartered Insurance Institute, 2015.

Davenport, Thomas H. and Harris, Jeanne G. *Competing on Analytics: The New Science of Winning.* Brighton MA: Harvard Business School Press, 2007.

Dearborn, Jenny. *Data Driven: How Performance Analytics Delivers Extraordinary Sales Results.* London: John Wiley & Sons, 2015.

Donkin, Richard. *Blood Sweat and Tears: The Evolution of Work.* Abingdon: Texere, 2001.

Flood Repair Forum. *Repairing Flooded Buildings. An insurance industry guide to investigation and repair.* London: BRE Press, 2006.

Hyde, Malcolm, McCarthy, Brendon, and Deacon, James. *Property Insurance Law and Claims.* London: Witherby Publishing Group, 2010.

Lamond, Jessica, Booth, Colin, Hammond, Felix, and Proverbs, David. *Flood Hazards. Impacts and Responses on the Built Environment.* London: CRC Press, 2011.

McGee, Prof Andrew. *The Modern Law of Insurance*, 3rd edition. London: LexisNexis Butterworths (Butterworths Law), 2011.

Merkin, Professor Robert. *Insurance Law – An Introduction.* London: Informa, 2007.

Stubbs, Evan. *Business Analytics.* London: John Wiley & Sons, 2014.

Thomas, Rob, and McSharry, Patrick. *Big Data Revolution.* London: John Wiley & Sons, 2015.

Data Summary of Expectancy of Reaching 100

TABLE B.1   Likelihood of reaching 100

Year of birth	Male, %	Female, %	Both sexes, %
1912	0.3	1.1	0.7
1913	0.3	1.1	0.7
1914	0.3	1.2	0.7
1915	0.3	1.2	0.8
1916	0.4	1.3	0.8
1917	0.4	1.4	0.9
1918	0.5	1.6	1.1
1919	0.7	1.9	1.3
1920	0.6	1.8	1.2
1921	0.7	2.1	1.4
1922	0.8	2.3	1.6
1923	1	2.5	1.7
1924	1.1	2.7	1.9
1925	1.2	3	2.1
1926	1.4	3.2	2.3
1927	1.6	3.5	2.5
1928	1.7	3.8	2.8
1929	2	4.2	3.1
1930	2.3	4.6	3.4
1931	2.5	5.1	3.8
1932	2.9	5.6	4.2

(Continued)

TABLE B.1   (*Continued*)

Year of birth	Male, %	Female, %	Both sexes, %
1933	3.2	6.2	4.7
1934	3.6	6.8	5.2
1935	4	7.3	5.6
1936	4.3	7.9	6.1
1937	4.6	8.4	6.5
1938	5	8.9	6.9
1939	5.2	9.3	7.2
1940	5.4	9.6	7.5
1941	5.7	9.9	7.8
1942	6	10.3	8.1
1943	6.2	10.6	8.4
1944	6.4	10.9	8.6
1945	6.6	11.1	8.9
1946	6.9	11.5	9.2
1947	7.1	11.8	9.5
1948	7.4	12.2	9.8
1949	7.7	12.5	10.1
1950	7.9	12.8	10.4
1951	8.2	13.1	10.6
1952	8.4	13.5	10.9
1953	8.6	13.7	11.2
1954	8.8	14	11.4
1955	9.1	14.4	11.7
1956	9.3	14.7	12
1957	9.5	14.9	12.2
1958	9.8	15.2	12.5
1959	10	15.6	12.8
1960	10.2	15.9	13.1
1961	10.5	16.2	13.3
1962	10.7	16.5	13.6
1963	11	16.8	13.9
1964	11.2	17.1	14.2
1965	11.5	17.4	14.5
1966	11.8	17.7	14.7
1967	12	18.1	15
1968	12.3	18.4	15.3

TABLE B.1 (*Continued*)

Year of birth	Male, %	Female, %	Both sexes, %
1969	12.5	18.7	15.6
1970	12.8	19	15.9
1971	13.1	19.4	16.2
1972	13.3	19.7	16.5
1973	13.6	20	16.8
1974	13.9	20.4	17.1
1975	14.2	20.7	17.4
1976	14.5	21.1	17.8
1977	14.8	21.4	18.1
1978	15.1	21.7	18.4
1979	15.4	22.1	18.7
1980	15.7	22.4	19.1
1981	16	22.8	19.4
1982	16.3	23.1	19.7
1983	16.6	23.5	20.1
1984	17	23.8	20.4
1985	17.3	24.2	20.7
1986	17.6	24.5	21.1
1987	17.9	24.9	21.4
1988	18.2	25.3	21.7
1989	18.5	25.6	22.1
1990	18.9	26	22.4
1991	19.2	26.4	22.8
1992	19.5	26.7	23.1
1993	19.9	27.1	23.5
1994	20.2	27.5	23.8
1995	20.5	27.8	24.2
1996	20.9	28.2	24.5
1997	21.2	28.5	24.9
1998	21.5	28.9	25.2
1999	21.9	29.3	25.6
2000	22.2	29.6	25.9
2001	22.6	30	26.3
2002	22.9	30.4	26.6
2003	23.2	30.7	27
2004	23.6	31.1	27.3

(*Continued*)

TABLE B.1 (*Continued*)

Year of birth	Male, %	Female, %	Both sexes, %
2005	23.9	31.5	27.7
2006	24.3	31.8	28.1
2007	24.6	32.2	28.4
2008	25	32.6	28.8
2009	25.3	32.9	29.1
2010	25.7	33.3	29.5
2011	26	33.7	29.9

Source: UK Department of Work and Pensions (2011)

Implementation Flowcharts

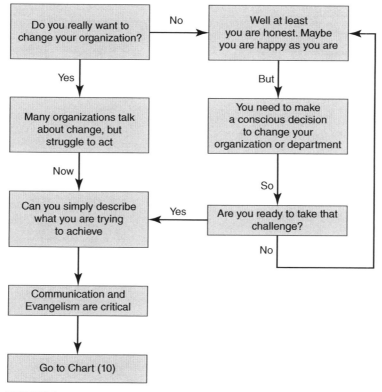

FIGURE C.1 Creating the Analytical Insurer

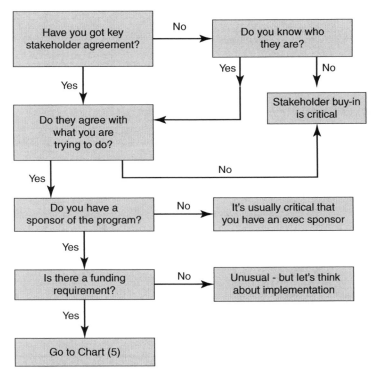

FIGURE C.2 Management of Key Stakeholders

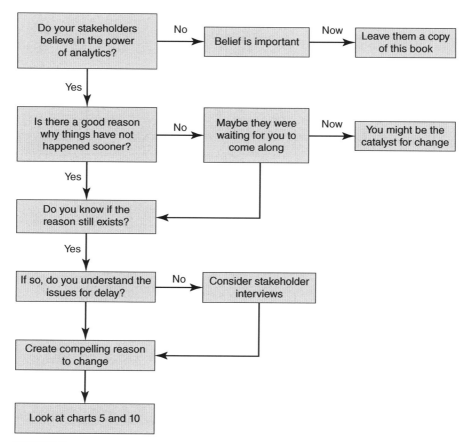

FIGURE C.3 Stakeholder Buy-In

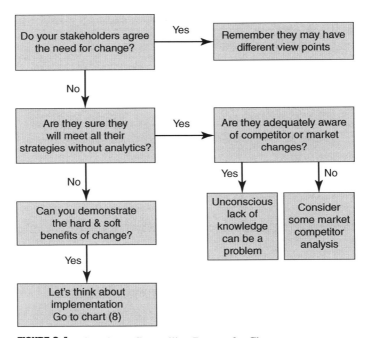

FIGURE C.4   Creating a Compelling Reason for Change

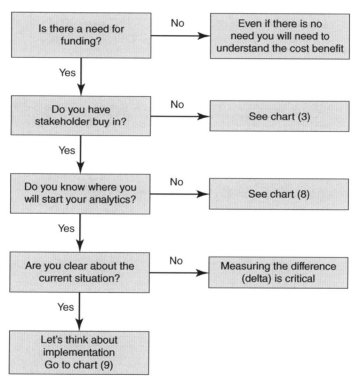

FIGURE C.5   Making a Case for Funding

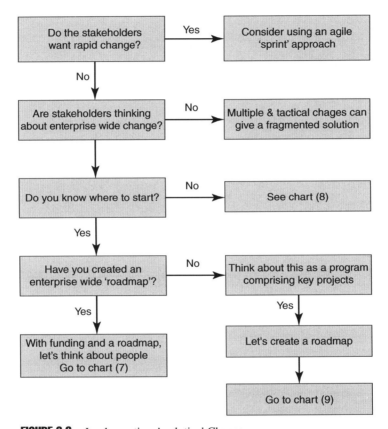

FIGURE C.6 Implementing Analytical Change

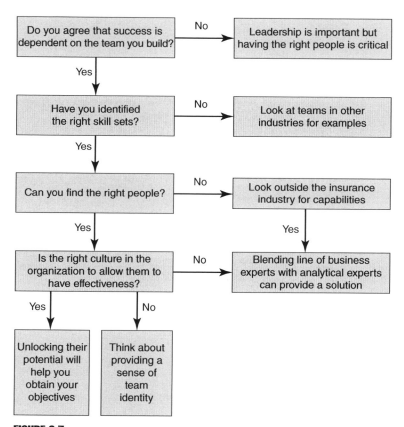

FIGURE C.7 Recruiting the Team

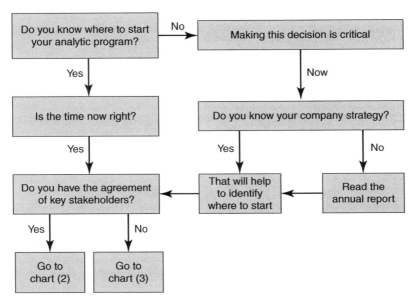

FIGURE C.8   Starting Point of Change

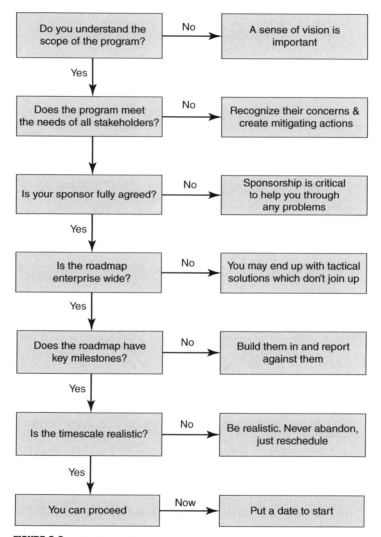

FIGURE C.9   Creating a Roadmap

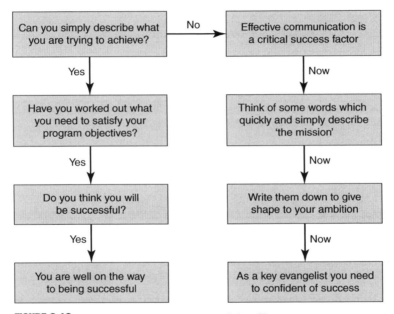

FIGURE C.10   Communications and Evangelizing Change

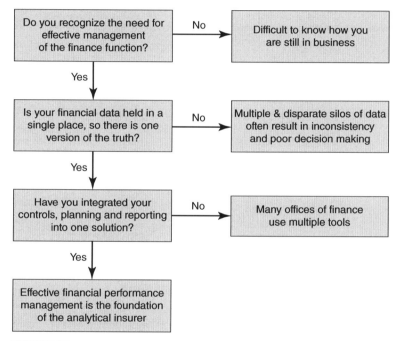

FIGURE C.11 Effective Financial Performance Management

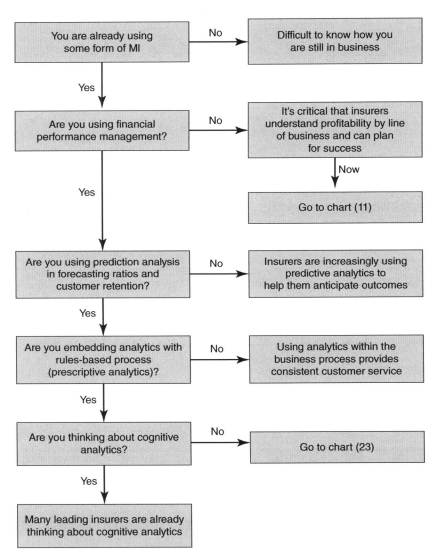

FIGURE C.12   Current Use of Analytics

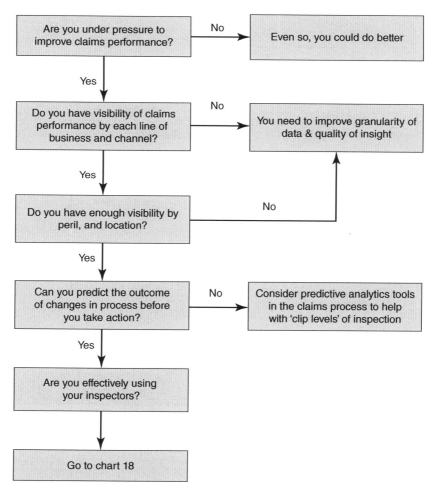

FIGURE C.13 Claims Management

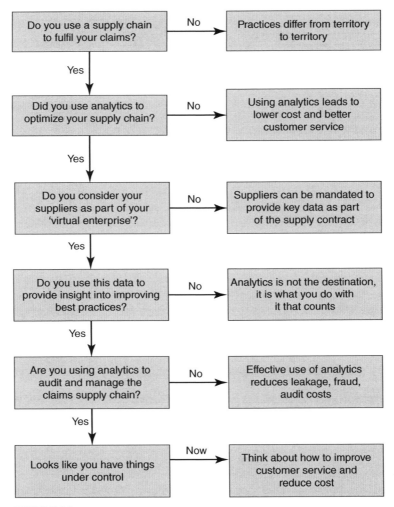

FIGURE C.14   Analytics in Claims Supply Chain

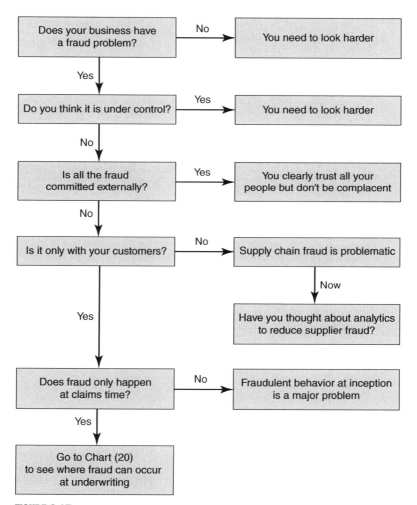

FIGURE C.15   Managing Fraud

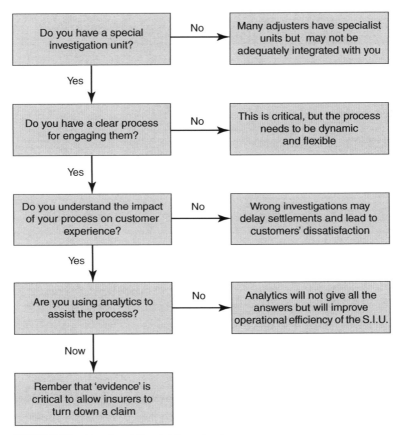

FIGURE C.16 Fraud and Special Investigations

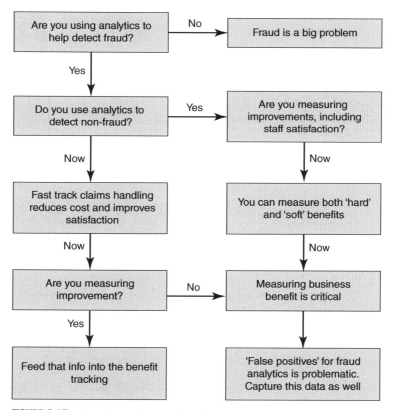

FIGURE C.17 Fast Track Claims Handling

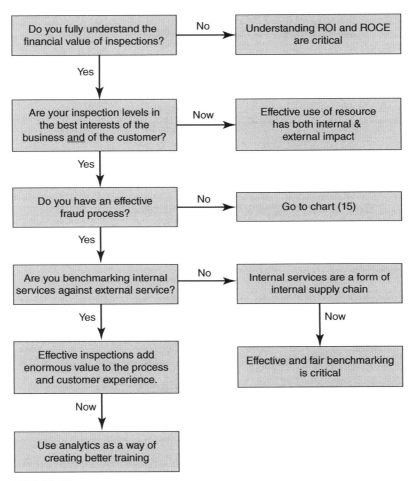

FIGURE C.18   Inspectors and Adjusters

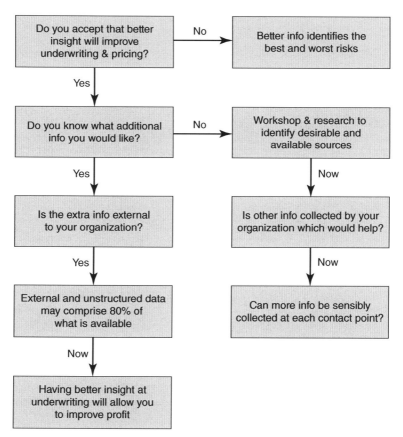

FIGURE C.19 Analytics for Underwriting

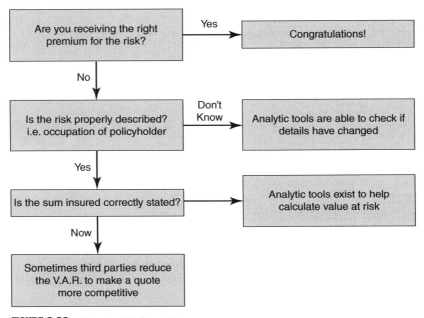

FIGURE C.20 Fraud at Underwriting

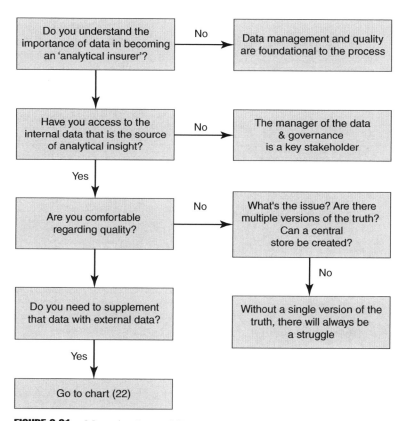

FIGURE C.21   Managing Internal Data

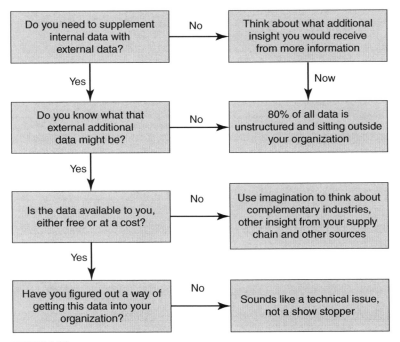

FIGURE C.22   Managing External Data

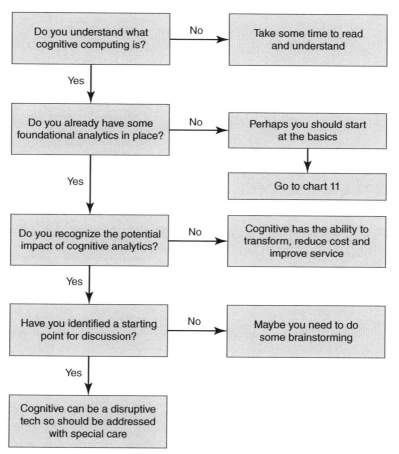

FIGURE C.23   Cognitive Analytics

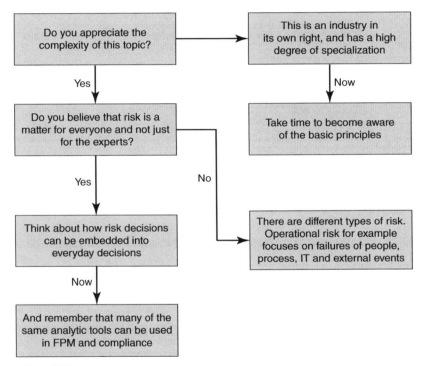

FIGURE C.24   Risk Analytics

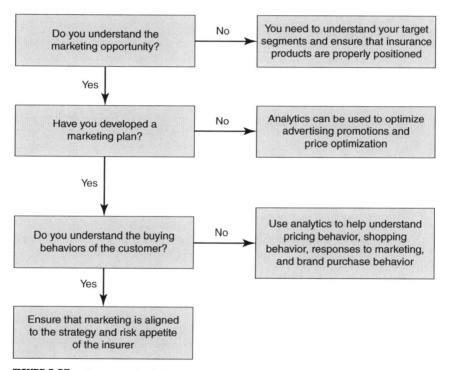

FIGURE C.25 Customer Analytics

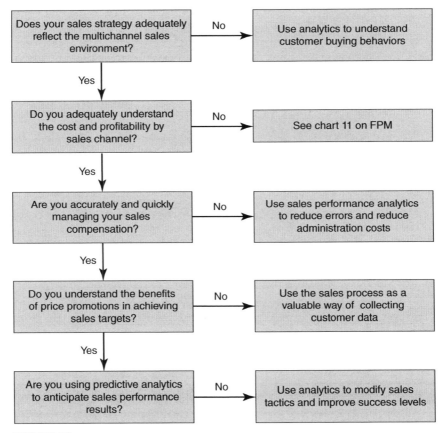

FIGURE C.26 Sales Performance Analytics

Suggested Insurance Websites

Asia Insurance Review	www.asiainsurancereview.com
Best's Asia-Pacific Weekly	www.ambest.com/bestweek
Clay Research Group	www.theclayresearchgroup.org
Cover	www.covermagazine.co.uk
Insurance Entertainment	www.insuranceentertainment.com
Insurance ERM	www.insuranceerm.com
Insurance Hound	www.insurancehound.co.uk
Insurance Law360	www.law360.com
Insurance Networking News	www.insurancenetworking.com
Insurance Newslink	www.insurance.onlystrategic.com/
Insurance Post	www.postonline.co.uk
Insurance Thought Leadership	www.insurancethoughtleadership.com
Insurance Times	www.insurancetimes.co.uk/
Intelligent Insurer	www.intelligentinsurer.com
Risk and Insurance	www.riskandinsurance.com
youTalk-insurance	www.youtalk-insurance.com

Professional Insurance Organizations

ACORD	www.acord.org
Airmic (UK Association for Risk and Insurance)	www.airmic.com
Asian American Insurance Professionals	www.aaifpa.org
British Insurance Brokers Association	www.biba.org.uk
Canadian Institute of Underwriters	www.ciu.ca/
Chartered Institute of Loss Adjusters	www.cila.co.uk/
Chartered Insurance Institute (UK)	www.cii.co.uk/
Insurance Institute of Canada	www.insuranceinstitute.ca/
Insurance Institute	www.insuranceinstitute.com/
Department of Insurance, Financial Institutions and Professional Regulations (US)	http://difp.mo.gov/licensing/
Institute of Automotive Engineer Assessors	www.theiaea.org
Insurance Accounting and Systems Association	www.iasa.org
Insurance Council of Australia	www.insurancecouncil.com.au
International Underwriting Association	www.iua.co.uk/
South African Insurance Association	www.sais.co.za
The Subsidence Forum	www.subsidenceforum.org.uk

4Ps of marketing 92

A/B testing 106
ACORD data management company 205
acquisitions 30–31
actuarial management 27–28
adapting 171, 208
admissible evidence 131–132
age issues 96, 99, 140–143
agents 13, 34
aggregator sites 214
'agility'
 challenge of 104–105
 implementing analytics 196
 new product development 103–104
 risk appetites 47
 risk management 105
analytics
 see also Big Data and Analytics; cognitive
  analytics
 descriptive 6, 207–208
 hierarchy of 6–7
 how they work 17–24
 important elements 24
 network 64–65
 next generation 7–9
 predictive 6, 20–22, 207–208
 prescriptive 6, 22–23, 207–208
 social media 96–97
 tools/tooling 191, 207–208
 voice 65–66
 'was/will be' table 227
APIs *see* Application Programming Interfaces
appliances, household 217–218
Application Programming Interfaces (APIs) 23
arson 113–115
asset and liability management 28
auto industry 13, 71–73, 155–161, 211–214
 see also car industry; motor...
automatic reserve 78
automation 173
aviation insurance 220

bancassurance 145–147
banks/banking 47–48, 145–147
behavior segmentation 99
Big Data 3–6, 81, 139–140
Big Data and Analytics 9–17
 between data and analytics 9–10
 digital homes 214–215
 employees, impact on 181–182
 geographical perspectives 14
 intermediaries 13–14
 Internet of Things 15
 key imperatives 10–13
 leadership influence 180, 181
 scale benefit/size disadvantage 15–17
 telematics 163–164
 underwriting 52–54, 188
BIM *see* Building Information Management
Blockchain 43, 171, 230
Blood, Sweat and Tears... (Donkin) 208
body shops 13, 71–73
brain friendly learning 174, 178
brands/branding 100–101, 103, 146–147
Bring Your Own Device (BYOD) 207
Building Information Management (BIM)
 57–58, 163
burial insurance 136
Burton, Anthony 182
business intelligence 18–20
business interruption 79–80, 219
BYOD *see* Bring Your Own Device

capital management 28
captive insurers 12–13
car body repair shops 13, 71–73
car industry 13, 71–73, 173
 see also auto industry
cargo theft 154
'cashing out' 71
casualty insurance 11–12
 see also general insurance
category managers/management 17, 67
CDOs *see* Chief Digital Officers

centennial life expectancy 144–145
CEOs *see* Chief Executive Officers
certification 208
CFOs *see* Chief Finance Officers
change management 191–192, 231
Chartered Insurance Institute (CII) 208
Chief Digital Officers (CDOs) 189
Chief Executive Officers (CEOs) 92
Chief Finance Officers (CFOs) 45, 47, 48
Chief Risk Officers (CROs) 42–45, 48
CII *see* Chartered Insurance Institute
claims 61–89
   see also loss adjustment
   auto repairs 71–73
   complex domestic 73–77
   contractual entitlement 61–62
   cyber security 87
   fraud 62–66
   future aspects 215, 217, 218–219, 224
   indemnity 61–62, 170
   inspection 74–75, 77–81
   insurer behavior 125
   marketing 106–107
   'moment of truth' 61, 69, 70, 97
   motor assessing 81–83
   property 66–71, 84–86, 124–125
   supply chain management 66–71
clean-up process, fire 125
cloud computing 9, 40, 206
cognitive analytics 6, 7
   future aspects 222, 225
   prescriptive analytics 22
   public liability 132
   tools/tooling 207–208
cognitive computing 23–24, 88
collaboration 172, 208
colleges 191
commercial insurance 162–164, 218–219
commission 146
communication
   competences 208
   organizational culture 192
   stakeholder management 198
   talent management 172
compensation 127–130
competences 168–169, 208–209
computer 'appliances' 206
computing
   cloud 9, 40, 206
   cognitive 23–24, 88
conduct risk 99
conferences 177, 186
'connected' homes 162, 215
consequential loss 79–80
construction quality 79
contextual analytics 8–9, 225

contracts, 'zero hours' 218, 222
contractual entitlement 61–62
costs 110–111, 213
cotton industry 182, 183
CROs *see* Chief Risk Officers
culture *see* organizational culture
customers
   see also marketing
   acquiring 93–96
   changing providers 93
   claims servicing 88
   CRO as advocate 45
   digital 105–106, 124–125
   emotional aspects 68, 96
   future aspects 228–229
   good service 94–95
   industry churn rates 93
   life vs general insurance 137
   loyalty 93–95, 189
   retaining 93–96
   segmentation 98–99
customization 99
cyber security
   claims 87
   D&O liability 134
   future aspects 221
   implementing analytics 190

D&O *see* Directors and Officers liability insurance
dashboard design 158
data
   see also Big Data...; data...
   finding value from 6–7
data management 202–207
   data quadrants 202–203
   governance of data 203
   implementing analytics 186–187, 202–207
   key criteria 203
   MDM 203
   quality of data 204
   security 207
   standardization of data 204–205
   storage of data 205–207
data matching 204
data ownership 221
data platforms 206
data reuse 141
data scientists 189
death/death rates 124, 138
decision-making 27, 46–49
defined benefit plans 135–136
defined contribution plans 136
dehumidifiers 111–112
demography 87–88, 97–98
descriptive analytics 6, 207–208
detection of fraud 64–65, 157

'Devil's Advocate' role 200
digital customers 105–106, 124–125
digital evidence 131–132
digital homes 214–218
digital investigators 73–75
digital process roadmaps 76
Directors and Officers (D&O) liability insurance
  133–134, 163, 190
disclosure, regulatory 29
disruptive technology 179
distribution channels 33–35
distribution management 35
divestments 30–31
domestic claims 73–77
  changes in process 75–76
  digital investigators 73–75
  early attention 75
Donkin, Richard 208–209
drought 115
drying process, flooding 111–112
duplicate data 204, 205

Ebola outbreak 136–137, 223
economic volatility 140–141
EIOPA *see* European Insurance and Occupational
  Pensions Authority
embedded value 28
emotional aspects
  claims 68, 96
  customer experiences 96
  implementing analytics 187, 201
  subsidence claims 115
Emotional Intelligence (Goleman) 187
employees 181–183, 198–199
employers' liability 127, 130–131
employment 173–174
empowerment 198–199
endowment insurance 135
ethical issues 53, 197
ETL *see* extract, transfer, load process
EU *see* European Union
Europe 38, 111, 120, 159
European Insurance and Occupational Pensions Authority (EIOPA) 38
European regulations *see* Solvency II
European Union (EU) 159
evangelism 192
evidence, digital 131–132
eXtensible Business Reporting Language (XBRL)
  30, 39
extract, transfer, load (ETL) process 205

fabrication 129
face-to-face training 176–177
FCA *see* Financial Conduct Authority
finance *see* Office of Finance

Financial Conduct Authority (FCA), UK 34
financial performance management
  (FPM) 218
financial services 146–147
Financial Technology (FinTech) 42–43
financial tools 80
FinTech *see* Financial Technology
fire 112–115
  claim example 124–125
  clean-up process 125
  deaths 124
  fraudulent claims 113–115
  location 113
first mover advantage 103, 185
First Notification of Loss (FNOL) 75, 84, 223
flooding 109–112
  causes 152
  costs of damage 110–111
  drying process 111–112
  factors to consider 110
  future aspects 215, 217
  Hurricane Katrina 110, 121
  likelihood 110–111
  location 152–154
FloodRe, UK 154
FNOL *see* First Notification of Loss
Forbes magazine 100–101
4Ps of marketing 92
FPM *see* financial performance management
fraud
  claims 62–66
  fire 113–115
  future aspects 213, 216
  location 151, 157
  opportunistic 63–64
  organized 64–66
  property repairs 67
  telematics 157
  underwriting 56–57
  workers' compensation 128–130
future aspects 211–225
  auto industry 211–214
  challenges 229–230
  commercial insurance 218–219
  digital homes 214–218
  employee resistance 183
  industry linkages 229
  life and pensions industry 221–223
  new entrants 229–230
  non-core activities 223–224
  outsourcing 223–224
  reflections 227–232
  specialist risks 220–221
  stakeholder vision 193
  super suppliers 223, 224–225
  talent management 173–174

GAAP *see* Generally Accepted Accounting Principles
general insurance 11–12, 136–137
Generally Accepted Accounting Principles (GAAP) 29–30
Generations X and Y 142–143
geo-location experts 149–150
geocoding 150–151
geography of insurance 14
'golden period', claims 75
Goleman, Daniel 187
governance of data 203
Group Life Insurance 135
growth, profitable 10–13

hail events 119–121
health insurance 144, 222
healthcare 11–12, 162
hedging 28
HEPS *see* Hydrological Ensemble Prediction Systems
high net worth insurance 220–221
homes, digital 214–218
household appliances 217–218
human resources (HR) 173–174
Hurricane Katrina 110, 121
hurricanes 110, 121–122
Hydrological Ensemble Prediction Systems (HEPS) 153

IASA *see* Insurance Accounting and Systems Association
IFRS *see* International Financial Reporting Standards
IKE *see* Integrated Kinetic Energy approach
implementing analytics 185–209
incremental improvement 196, 201
indemnity 61–62, 170
independent agents 13
industry data models 205
influence 179–181
information
  see also data
  MI 187
  sharing 150
information technology (IT) department
  business intelligence 19–20
  employee empowerment 198
  organizational culture 189–190
innovation 103
insight, technological 170–171
inspection
  business interruption 79–80
  claims 74–75, 77–81
  levels 77–81
  reserving 78–79
  subrogation 80–81
Insurance Accounting and Systems Association (IASA) 190, 208

Insurance Act 2016, UK 169
insurance companies
  basic elements 16
  functions 3
insurance industry
  key drivers 28–29
  structures 2–3
insurance institutes 190
insurance people *see* people in insurance
insurance premium indicators 158, 212–213
integrated decision-making 27
Integrated Kinetic Energy (IKE) approach 122
intermediaries 13–14, 17
International Financial Reporting Standards (IFRS) 29–30, 41–42
Internet of Things (IoT) 15, 83, 162, 211
interruption of business 79–80, 219
IoT *see* Internet of Things
IT *see* information technology department

K&R *see* kidnap and ransom insurance
key performance indicators (KPIs) 106–107
kidnap and ransom (K&R) insurance 123
knowledge 24, 170, 174–180
KPIs *see* key performance indicators

leadership 178–183
  employees 181–183
  evangelism 192
  influence 179–181
  key attributes 178
  knowledge and power 179
  understanding resistance 182–183
learning
  brain friendly 174, 178
  competences 208
  face-to-face training 176–177
  formal qualifications 175–176
  key methods 174
  reading materials 175
  social media 177–178
  structured 175–176
  talent management 171, 174–178
  technology 175–176, 177–178
legacy knowledge 24
legislation
  see also individual Acts; regulations
  ethical issues 53
lexicons of technology 206–207
liability insurance 127–134
  D&O 133–134, 163, 190
  employers' liability 127, 130–131
  product liability 132–133
  public liability 131–132
  workers' compensation 127–130
liability management 28

life expectancy 144–145
life insurance
    bancassurance 145–147
    basis of 137–138
    economic volatility 140–141
    engaging with the young 141–142
    general insurance 136–137
    key concerns 138
life and pensions insurance 135–148
    see also life insurance
    business drivers 11
    customer loyalty 95
    digital era 143–145
    future aspects 221–223
    mortality issues 138–140
    older people 142–143
local conditions 97–98
location 149–165
    analytics 149–154
    cargo theft 154
    fire damage 113
    flooding 152–154
    fraud 151, 157
    geo-location experts 149–150
    geocoding 150–151
    importance of 149–165
    information-sharing 150
    telematics 155–164
    terrorism 152
loss-adjustment 81, 83–84
    demographic time bomb 87–88
    domestic claims 75–76
    intermediaries 13
    property repairs 70–71
loyalty, customer 93–95, 189
Luddism 182–183

malingering 129
management information (MI) 187
marine insurance 220
marketing 91–108
    acquiring customers 93–96
    'agility' 103–105
    branding 100–101, 103
    claims service 106–107
    demography 97–98
    digital customers 105–106
    4Ps 92
    future aspects 229
    multi-channel approach 105–106
    new product development 103–104
    omni-channel approach 105–106
    price/pricing 92, 100–102
    promotion 92, 100
    retaining customers 93–96
    segmentation 98–99

service delivery 102–103
    social media 96–97, 100
master data management (MDM) 203
measurement of business intelligence 18
media 100
    see also social media
mentoring 176
mergers 30–31
MI *see* management information
Millennials 141–142
misrepresentation 31–32, 66
'moment of truth' 61, 69, 70, 97
monitoring
    RPM 162
    subsidence 118
mortality 138–140
motor assessing
    see also auto industry
    claims 81–83
    future needs 83
    role of assessor 82
motor insurers 157–158
multi-channel approach, marketing 105–106
multivariate testing 106

National Association of Insurance Commissioners
    (NAIC), US 34, 53, 159
net promoter score (NPS) 94–95, 96
network analytics 64–65
New Orleans, Hurricane Katrina 110, 121
new product development 103–104
new 'real business' 1–24
    Big Data and Analytics 10–17
    historical aspects 2
    how analytics work 17–24
    transformation 2–10
next generation analytics 7–9
non-core activities 223–224
NPS *see* net promoter score

OBD *see* On Board Diagnostics
Office of Finance 25–36
    acquisitions 30–31
    distribution management 35
    divestments 30–31
    finance challenges 26
    finance and insurance 27–29
    financial analytics 32–33
    GAAP and IFRS 29–30
    integrated decision-making 27
    mergers 30–31
    misrepresentation 31–32
    performance management 27
    regulatory disclosure 29
    reporting 29
    roadmap development 201–202

Office of Finance (*Continued*)
   sales management 33–35
   Securities Acts 31–32
   social media 32–33
   SOX Act 31–32
   transparency 31–32
OLAP (Online Analytical Processing) cube 19
older people 142–143
omni-channel approach, marketing 105–106
On Board Diagnostics (OBD) 161
Online Analytical Processing (OLAP) cube 19
open relationships 199–200
operational efficiency 10–13
operational risk 43–44
opportunistic fraud 63–64
optimization, pricing 101–102
organizational culture 188–193
   cognitive computing 24
   communication 192
   evangelism 192
   stakeholder future vision 193
organized fraud 64–66
outsourcing 223–224
own label branding 103
ownership of data 221

pandemics 222–223
paperless insurance 230–231
patent, Snapshot 155–156
patient monitoring, RPM 162
pensions
   see also life and pensions insurance
   EIOPA 38
people in insurance 167–184
   employment 173–174
   future of insurance 173–174
   knowledge 174–178
   leadership 178–183
   learning 171, 174–178
   talent management 167–174
Perez, Salvador Minguijon 156
performance
   KPIs 106–107
   management 27, 218
personal recording devices 161–162
personal risk management 138–139, 140
Peters, Tom 227
Pitt Report, UK 154
place, 4Ps of marketing 92
point-level geocoding 151
political risks 122
Ponzi schemes 222
population 87–88, 97–98
power 179, 180
predictive analytics 6, 20–22, 207–208
premium optimization gauges 158, 212–213

prescriptive analytics 6, 22–23, 207–208
price/pricing 92, 100–102
privacy laws, EU 159
private pensions 141
problem solving 171–172, 208
'producers' 34
products 92, 103–104, 132–133
profitable growth 10–13
Progressive insurance company 155–156
project programs 195–197
promotion 92, 100
property and casualty insurance 11–12
   see also general insurance
property insurance 109–126
   claims 66–71, 84–86, 124–125
   digital customers 124–125
   digital homes 214–218
   fire 112–115, 124–125
   flooding 109–112, 215, 217
   hail events 119–121
   hurricanes 110, 121–122
   subsidence 115–118
   terrorism 122–123
public liability 131–132

qualifications 175–176, 208
quality
   construction 79
   data 204

ransom insurance, K&R 122
Re-Imagine (Peters) 227
reading materials 175
real business *see* new 'real business'
recording devices, personal 161–162
recovery process *see* subrogation
reflections 227–232
regression analysis 21–22
regulations
   see also Solvency II
   disclosure 29
   technology 158
   telematics 158, 159–160
'regulator', terminology 199–200
reinstatement cover 62
reinsurance 12–13, 28, 46
relationships 199–200
Remote Patient Monitoring (RPM) 162
repairs
   auto 13, 71–73
   property 66–71, 84–86
   repairers 13, 84–86
   subsidence 118
reporting 29
representative worker groups 193
Request for Information/Pricing (RFI/P) 67

reserve creep 79
reserving 28, 78–79
resistance, employee 182–183
restoration contractors 13
retail brands 146–147
retaining customers 93–96
retirement benefits 144
Return on Investment (ROI) 180–181
RFI/P *see* Request for Information/Pricing
The Rise and Fall of King Cotton (Burton) 182, 183
risk-adjusted decision-making 46–49
risk appetite categorizations 47
risk aversion 139, 140
risk management 37–49
   'agility' 105
   Chief Risk Officer 42–45
   commercial insurance 219
   key imperatives 10–13
   personal 138–139, 140
   reinsurance 46
   risk-adjusted decision-making 46–49
   Solvency II 37–42
   unpredictability 45–46
Risk Management and Own Risk and Solvency
   Assessment (RMORSA) 39
river flooding 112
RMORSA *see* Risk Management and Own Risk and
   Solvency Assessment
roadmap development 200–202
ROI *see* Return on Investment
roles, changing/new 189–190, 197
round-table events 176–177
Rowntree, Joseph 52
RPM *see* Remote Patient Monitoring
'Rules of Evidence' approach 131

sales management 33–35
Sarbanes-Oxley (SOX) Act 2002, US 31–32
satellite navigation techniques 214
'scrum' technique 104
second-stage supply chain management 69–70
secrecy 193
Securities Acts 1933/1934, US 31–32
security 31–32, 207
   see also cyber security
segmentation 98–99
self-drive cars 214
'self-service' claims-handling 107
senior leadership 179–181
sensors 213
sequential improvement 196, 201
service
   analytics as a service 223–224
   bancassurance agreements 146
   customer loyalty 94–95
   delivery 102–103

   financial services 146–147
   future efficiencies 228
   'self-service' claims-handling 107
   shared services 40
shared services 40
sharing information 150
'single version of the truth' 19, 27
skillsets 207–209
Skipton Building Society research project 143
Snapshot patent 155–156
social justice 52–53
social media
   digital investigators 73–74
   learning 177–178
   marketing 96–97, 100
   Millennials 142
   Office of Finance 32–33
solvency 10–11, 16
Solvency II 37–42, 212
   BIM 57
   cloud computing 40
   criticisms 39
   European model 38–39
   IFRS 30, 41–42
   shared services 40
   'sweating the assets' 40–41
   three pillars 38–39
   US model 39
Solvency III 212
SOX *see* Sarbanes-Oxley Act
Special Investigations Units 216
specialist insurance 54, 220–221
sponsorship 194–195
spreadsheets 18
staff *see* employees
stakeholders 193, 197–198
standardization 201, 204–205
storage of data 205–207
strategic alliances 197, 212
strategy creation 193–202
   analytics as empowerment 198–199
   building project program 195–197
   implementation flowchart 202
   implementation program 194–197
   implementing analytics 193–202
   key steps 192–202
   program sponsorship 194–195
   relationships, open/trusting 199–200
   roadmap development 200–202
   sequential improvement 196, 201
   stakeholder management 197–198
   status quo measurement 195
streamed data 4–5
structured learning 175–176
subrogation
   inspection 80–81

subrogation (*Continued*)
  principle of 170
  product liability 133
subsidence 115–118
  main causes 116–117
  prediction of 116–118
  repair process 118
super suppliers 223, 224–225
supply chain management
  claims 66–71
  difficulties 68–70
  reinvention 76–77
  second-stage 69–70
'sweating the assets' 40–41

talent management 167–174
  collaboration 172
  communication 172
  employment 173–174
  foundational knowledge 170
  future aspects 173–174
  human resources 173–174
  new competences 168–169
  problem solving 171–172
  qualities/capabilities 169–172
  quick learning/adapting 171
  talent analytics 168, 173–174
  technology 168, 170–171
technology
  see also information technology department; Internet of Things; telematics
  Blockchain 43, 171, 230
  digital investigators 73–75
  disruptive 179
  FinTech 42–43
  insight 170–171
  learning 175–176, 177–178
  lexicon sites 206–207
  maturity of market 98
  new competences 168–169
  new 'real business' 1, 22–23
  prescriptive analytics 22–23
  public liability 132
  talent management 168, 170–171
telematics 155–164
  see also user-based insurance
  commercial insurances 162–164
  dashboard design 158
  digital homes 214–218
  fraud detection 157
  history of 155–157
  key components 155
  life insurance 137
  location 155–164
  marketing 92
  more than technology 160–161

motor assessing 82–83
  motor insurers 157–158
  product liability 133
  regulations 158, 159–160
  underwriting 55–56
telemedicine 162
terrorism 122–123, 152, 220
Test-Achats case 102
theft 154, 216
tied agents 13
TIKE *see* Total Integrated Kinetic Energy
tools/tooling, analytic 191, 207–208
Total Integrated Kinetic Energy (TIKE) 122
traditional skills/roles 168–169
training
  see also learning
  face-to-face 176–177
transformation 2–10
  Big Data 3–6
  finding value from data 6–7
  hierarchy of analytics 6–7
  insurance industry structures 2–3
  new 'real business' 2–10
  next generation analytics 7–9
transparency
  future aspects 218, 229, 230
  life insurance 141
  Office of Finance 31–32
trees, subsidence 116–118
trusted advisors 194–195
trusting relationships 146–147, 199–200

UBI *see* user-based insurance
UK *see* United Kingdom
underwriting 51–59
  areas of business 51
  Big Data and Analytics 52–54, 188
  BIM and analytics 57–58
  data available 54
  digital homes 214–215
  emerging insurance types 52
  fraud avoidance 56–57
  implementing strategy 188
  organized fraud 66
  specialist lines 54
  telematics 55–56
  user-based insurance 53, 55–56
United Kingdom (UK)
  CII 208
  digital evidence 132
  employers' liability 130
  fire 113
  flooding 153–154
  fraud and location 151
  Insurance Act 169
  telematics 159

United States (US)
  fire 113
  flooding 111
  hail events 119–120
  IASA 190, 208
  RMORSA 39
  Snapshot patent 155–156
  talent management 167
  telematics 155–156, 159–160
universities 191
unpredictability 45–46
US *see* United States
user-based insurance (UBI) 155–164
  see also telematics
  auto industry 212
  other than auto insurance 161–162
  underwriting 53, 55–56

V2X concept 160
Value Added Tax (VAT) 70
value from data 5–7

variety of Big Data 5
VAT *see* Value Added Tax
velocity of Big Data 4–5
veracity of Big Data 5, 149
virtual loss adjusters 88
voice analytics 65–66
volatility of economy 140–141
volume of Big Data 4

whiplash injuries 157
workers' compensation 127–130
  entitlement categories 128
  fraud 128–130
worst case scenarios 123

XBRL *see* eXtensible Business Reporting Language

young people 140–142

'zero hours' contracts 218, 222

Printed and bound by CPI Group (UK) Ltd, Croydon, CR0 4YY

11/01/2023

03179201-0001